SPIRITUAL WEAVING

GOD PERFECTLY UNITING PAST PRESENT AND FUTURE WITHIN A HOLY WEAVE.

THE WORD OF GOD TO A COMMON MAN

To: Heather
Grace & Peace

PETER F. SERRA

Order this book online at www.trafford.com
or email orders@trafford.com

Most Trafford titles are also available at major online book retailers.

Print information available on the last page.

ISBN: 978-1-4907-8405-2 (sc)
ISBN: 978-1-4907-8404-5 (e)

Trafford rev. 09/12/2017

www.trafford.com

North America & international
toll-free: 1 888 232 4444 (USA & Canada)
fax: 812 355 4082

Contents

Book 2

Beginning

In the beginning
God made man
Breathed into his
Nostrils and life began

Secular interests
Worldly affairs
Misguide the lost
Confuse and delay
All who are searching
Seeking the way

Truth of beginning
Christ Jesus King
Sent into the world
Life's message to bring
A rainfall in summer
A searchlight in dark
A gentle reminder of God's
Unfailing love

Amen.

Legacy

Who knows when the beat of life will cease?
What then should we say to those we, have, to leave?
"My children listen to your father as I pass along to you
The reality of life that was given in my youth
At the age of thirty-three God did come to me
And speaking words convincing my soul was then set free.
Belief became the anchor denying drift in waves
And calm within life's storms has followed all my days.
Truth was all around me cutting through life's fog
As a beacon shining with warning and with love
I focused on its light and danced within my heart
And ever since that day I knew where I belonged.
Pay attention to the truth that others will deny
God is always with us every moment of our life.
Unless a man seeks wisdom, his days find emptiness
Filled with uncertainty and laced with happenstance.
Absent a foundation that keeps an even keel
Sometimes he can capture the object of his prize
But mostly there's an emptiness caused by stubborn pride.
And when the final beat and darkness fills the eyes
The failure to embrace God's love comes as great surprise
Follow the example of knowledge right and wrong
It lives within your heart and sings a gentle song
Absent condemnation the peace of God is found.
When life finds-falter unsteady is our walk
The impact that then follows sings a nagging song
Harrowing in content leaving scars and tracks of wrong.
They never are forgotten but lay anchored in the deep
Returning without warning to break our restful sleep
As apparitions moaning lamentation for what's lost
They cry loudly accusation of a life lived in the dark.
Alas they are but echoes ringing in the mind
But still they carry impact of a former time
Opportunity came knocking and no one could it find.
Heed the voice of wisdom and sleep will then be sound

Without tossing frightful nightmares that echo days long gone
Denied the peace of God by the pull of wrong.
Limit the anguish bucket let it not be filled
And life will find true meaning even when uphill!"

Proverbs 19:20 Listen to advice and accept instruction, and in the end, you will be wise.

Preface

I'm always amazed by the intricately connected content of the bible; when I stumble upon a truth that is proclaimed in the Old Testament and finding it come into fruition in the New Testament there is a continued appreciation for God's word. We are led into the greatest treasure presented to mankind, simply because the content of the scriptures constantly-reveal and offer to us, not only our own personal truths, but the entire spectrum of creation is continually being made to be understood; no matter, if living in the long gone past, present or future, God's truth is everlasting. One would think that this ability to make creation understood, along with the enormity of the feat of prophesy, outlining in detail God's interactions with both humanity and the enemies of God, from the very first sin to the end of the current age is unfathomable, and, in truth it really is. And in truth we have no understanding of how God accomplishes and knows all. However, throughout creation and prophesy the uniting aspect of truth shines brightly and is the instrument that forms a perfect weave! It is this truth of God that inspires and guides us all.

I have never written a book with the intended content clearly defined, and the subject wrapped neatly, in need only to be unwrapped and typed into the book's content. However, the bible is such an intricate weave of interconnecting thought that brings inspiration throughout its content, making the writing of thoughts so much more motivating and inspirational, so much so that it's like having the road ahead arrayed with arrows pointing to the next connecting thought. What I'm really saying is, as long, as we are seeking guidance from above we will never be led astray.

The understanding of God's word is from a common man's perspective. For the most part, the content is slowly revealed by the inspiration given within the Holy Scriptures. Life experience is also presented as a shared personal experience, and in general terms the content addresses the commonality of human beings. This commonality speaks to us of our shared needs, failures, emotions and desires; everyone has experienced hard times, are possessors of a sin nature, and all of us have enjoyed happiness or found sorrow entering when we least expect it. In all unannounced situations, there is the constant awareness of God being with us. At least there is such awareness when we have been the recipient of the gift of faith. Without the awareness of God as reality there is no telling to what depth of turmoil we will be taken, absent the anchor of truth.

In many avenues of life's experience, it is God who enters our lives at the lowest point wherein we believe there is no hope for the reversal of the condition of our lives; this also is a shared experience, with perhaps, many of the children of God. Perhaps, a man needs to be convinced to the point of no longer being able to deceive himself, into thinking there is a way out of the darkness, that probably emerged from the actions of self-imposed affliction? Additionally, most of us who have been saved through divine intervention didn't have a clue as to the depth of captivity, until we heard the truth of our lives.

The overall intent of the writing is to bring into focus the inner workings of this poor man to the awareness of those I love. I recognize that at some point I will no longer have ability to convey to my children and grandchildren the love I have, not only for them but for all who call Jesus, "Lord." A candle is not hidden under a bowl and the truth is not meant to be proprietary, rather, it is meant to be heralded and applauded by all who have been given the ability to see through the eyes of love. A light is shone into the darkness to lead those who are seeking a way out.

Even if there are some who are not seeking the freedom of light's illumination, once truth (light) is brought into the dark the natural reaction is to move toward that which was heretofore unknown. It is this light that has been given to all of us who have found salvation and eternal life; having been the recipient of such a gift, it is my understanding that's its meant to be shared with all who will accept such reality. God has called his children to be communicators, in all aspects of interaction with others; mostly, it is through the manner in-which we conduct our lives. Honesty in our lives will attract others to the truth; hypocrisy, is present when the speech we present conflicts with the manner in-which we conduct our lives. Hypocrisy, will not attract, it will cause others to recognize the deception in the presentation, and fail to permit truth its moment to advance.

Additionally, if just one word written in this book encourages someone to seek to know the God of all creation, or answers a question that builds up their faith, then, the effort put forth has been more than worth it! Everything written within is for the glory of God, and in testimony to his wonderful gift to mankind.

The actual surrendering of one's life to a cruel evil dictatorial people is a colossal feat of courage and love! All who have been the recipient of such sacrifice made by our Lord, Jesus, have rejoiced in the freedom gained and have mourned at the foot of the cross as well. We have also rejoiced at the resurrection's dawning, announcing to the world, ***"He is risen!"***

All scriptural quotes are taken from the New International Version of the bible, except where otherwise noted. All quotes are made in bold italics.

Proverbs 3:5-6 Trust in the Lord with all your heart and lean not on your own understanding; in all your ways acknowledge him, and he will make your paths straight.

2 Corinthians 4:16-18 Therefore we do not lose heart. Though outwardly we are wasting away, yet inwardly we are being renewed day by day. For our light and momentary troubles are achieving for us an eternal glory that far out-weighs them all. So we fix our eyes not on what is seen, but what is unseen. What is seen is temporary, but what is unseen is eternal.

1

CHANGES

The apostle Paul tells us we are to fix our eyes on what is not seen. This does not mean we are to negate the reality we live in. We must recognize his words to us are an explosion of reality! We had Jesus with us on this earth, and at that time he was very visible. His time with us on earth was temporary, but he has moved on from the temporary to the eternal. Even though Jesus has gone back home to the Father his presence upon the earth is and has continually increased, through those of us who embrace truth. Jesus is Truth.

At times, the world is faced with an increase in evil, at these times there appears the most noticeable changes, simply because, as in the case of wars, everyone not only sees the change but feels the impact. Such increases of evil are changes that resemble a tug-of-war between opposing forces. It becomes self-evident even to those who will not admit to the reality of wrong. It is at these times of increased evil that the power of God is made increasingly more pronounced upon the world stage. The power of God is not shy and is found at times in apocalyptic (radical breakthrough) events. Such events are found in revivals within groups, or singularly, the purpose of which is to strengthen the church in times of trouble. Radical breakthroughs from the unseen into the natural world are perhaps more frequent than we may think. Those most prominent include the Annunciation to Mary, the Birth of Jesus, the warning to flee from Herod into Egypt, along with numerous others mentioned in scripture, but the myriad of heraldry concerning God making his presence known takes place within the spirit of man; within the unseen. We look at the external revelations with emotional awe that shocks and shakes our consciousness because we have been conditioned to deny truth. This was not always the case, as man was made to walk closely with God. The reality of the now unseen was a normal occurrence and did not startle our senses. With sin came a tremendous change in our understanding of the truth concerning God. Our awareness of God began to fade into the unseen, as each succeeding generation from Adam, increasingly lost such truth and was replaced by unknowing. When that which is, unknown, is made known there are several reactions that can and do take place within the person experiencing such revelation. Being renewed in spirit brings us back to the reality we lost. The world is still in denial of the unseen. In the last century, the advance of materialism has gripped the consciousness of the unbeliever. Even within the churches we find a lack of focus upon the unseen, regarding the promise of eternal life. It is rarely mentioned.

When we are changed into a soul set-free there is a period wherein the Holy Spirit places an impenetrable barrier around us, as would a newborn-wrapped in a receiving blanket, with parents constantly attentive to the newborn's needs. After which, when the child has grown into adulthood (he has ability to defend against the slings and arrows of the Evil One) the once very pronounced attentiveness of God no longer appears as before. God our Father is still with us, but we have learned to pray and be renewed daily, in the same way a soldier will keep his weaponry in readiness against the enemies of country. The war that we are faced with is twofold: internal and external. Both internal and external attacks by the enemy (sin and its originator) brings to us temptation and condemnation inherent in failure. When we focus upon our failure and become fixed upon the inner voice of condemnation, we can lose track of the power given to us through our faith in the one who loves us. Losing contact with reality brings about a withdrawing change that will eventually force us into a corner of darkness. Like a child given a timeout in a corner we are forced to withdraw from holiness by an authority of condemnation, absent the love and hope of commutation of sentence, until love tells us to come out from there. God makes his presence in our lives even more prominent when threatened by the advance of evil. It may appear that evil is unstoppable, but in the final analysis all sin will be judged and destroyed. This withdrawing change is an offshoot of the "Sin and Doubt" syndrome, originally written in a previous work, and will be discussed in a later chapter.

Focus on what is unseen

We may want to ask ourselves, "How can we focus our eyes on what is unseen?" Just because we have not seen a thing firsthand does not mean we cannot envision what has been related to us through scriptural declarations. We were not there at the baptism of Jesus, but the account in scripture paints a compelling picture. The baptism of Jesus is a unique radical breakthrough into the natural world. We see and hear through the heart and mind the occurrence depicting the presence of God the Father, the Holy Spirit and Jesus, that permits us to envision an explosion of truth, regarding the Holy Trinity, accepted and embraced by those of us with the gift of faith. The baptism of Jesus is a greatly different depiction from the day of Pentecost. The narrative of the Holy Spirit coming down from heaven in the form of a dove, does not speak to us of power and might being given to our Lord, rather, it is speaking to us of love. ***Matthew 3:16-17 As soon as Jesus was baptized, he went up out of the water. At that moment heaven was opened, and he saw the Spirit of God descending, like a dove and lighting on him. And a voice from heaven said, "This is my Son, whom I love; with him I am well pleased."*** *Within the depiction of the baptism we can envision and feel the love of God for his Son.*

When the Holy Spirit is given to the apostles on the day of Pentecost there is a strong blowing wind and what appeared as tongues of fire that came to rest on everyone in the house. They were given a pronounced and visible ability to speak in foreign languages, along with every other possibility that accompanies faith. This speaks of power to wage war against the evil in the world that had kept people ignorant to the unseen reality of God. Heretofore people expressed their belief in God, but perhaps only a select few knew such reality anchored deep within them. The majority were conditioned by the mechanics of the law and this aspect of religious life may have clouded their ability to focus upon what is unseen. When we are so concerned with appearing compliant with law, a legalistic mentality is the natural outgrowth, and in such an environment the need to find approval from the lawyers who determine compliance, becomes the defining aspect of a person's life. Lost is the desire to find approval from God. Lost is the focus of truth and in its place the seed of doubt blossoms. We were not with the prophet Isaiah when he was present in the throne room of God, but we can imagine the sounds of Seraphim singing of God's holiness. We can envision the transformation of Isaiah as he is touched with a burning coal from the altar of God, and we can imagine his joy (the same joy we felt when the reality of truth awakened us from darkness), as he's told his sins are forgiven and his guilt is removed! Focusing our hearts and minds on what is not seen does not mean we are blind to the reality present in the supernatural, or, the infinity of creation within the handiwork of God. We can look to the heavens and even though we cannot envision its content, our mind will never find a place that declares: ROAD CLOSED.

The same is true when we look deep into our self. We can see the lights of the heavens or else we may, at first, find darkness because we had not attempted to explore the depths of eternity within our own existence. No matter which direction we decide to travel, up into the heavens or down into the depths of our very soul, we can find the reality of eternity. Finding eternity to be not-only a concept but is in-fact reality, given to us by truth, we then have a basis for proving our convictions; God is eternal. Truth is the reality that everyone recognizes and accepts in the same way everyone can conclude that the lie is a proven-truth regarding its existence. There is a difference between the two: truth is eternal and has no need for change, it stands alone unaffected by the ever-changing environment within the whole of creation; deception is reliant upon change for it to persist. Persist: "To continue steadily or obstinately despite problems, difficulty or obstacles. To continue being widely believed or accepted despite evidence or proof to the contrary." Deception cannot stand-alone! It is continually attempting to present itself as truth for it to be able to continue within existence. It must continually change, adding additional lies to the initial presentation hoping to build a foundation, that may appear to some, at best probable, and at least, possible. TRUTH IS ETERNAL. GOD IS ETERNAL. WE ARE DESTINED FOR ETERNITY. JESUS IS TRUTH. JESUS IS ETERNAL. TRUTH STANDS-ALONE. THE HOLY SPIRIT CONVINCES US OF TRUTH AND HE OPENES OUR EYES. HE CONVICTS US OF NOT ONLY THE LIES IN OUR OWN LIVES BUT CONVINCES US OF THE REALITY WE COULD NOT SEE OTHERWISE. IN SO DOING WE ARE ENABLED TO ENVISION THE REALITY OF THE UNSEEN.

Nature

Everything in life is marked for renewal by the consistency of nature. Everything is temporary within this world that we inhabit. No matter where we look there is death and renewal. Everything has but a short period (of time) to exist in this present life that we have been given. All that we see within our view of time-allotted vanishes from our sight. It vanishes with regularity within the seasons of the year. This may sound depressing but in truth it is the excellent design of God that is continually changing us into an improved status. Improved above the status of the first of creation, simply because we have now experienced hardship and sacrifice, which did not exist for us in the beginning. Adding such knowledge of sacrifice improves our condition. Knowledge added will-always improve the existence of the one who gains understanding. As such we are an ongoing work of art, continually being perfected through the understanding of what cannot be seen with the eyes of man.

The world denies the unseen

Is there any doubt why the old saying urging people to enjoy life, within the illusion of hopelessness, afforded in the belief in the finality of man's existence, has gained acceptance down through the centuries? ***Isaiah 22:12-13 The Lord, the Lord Almighty, called you on that day to weep and to wail, to tear out your hair and put on sackcloth. But see, there is joy and revelry, slaughtering of cattle and killing of sheep, eating of meat and drinking of wine! "Let us eat and drink," you say, "for tomorrow we die."*** *For the most part the changes in nature are repetitive. I shave my face today and tomorrow the growth is back. The sun breaks through the horizon and sends its message for the night to depart. The seasons of the year are set into motion and continually find themselves on time, so much so that we have dated their arrival.*

Mindset

Again, there's this mindset within humanity, beginning, or at least the beginning of official exposure, during the time of Isaiah the prophet (approximately 750 BC) and persisting to this present day, within those who believe life to be a linear line that begins with birth and concludes with death, urging people to say, "Why not party and have a good time without any intrusion of conscience or question of morality? Death is the finality that mocks all of our efforts." Having a "good" time is fine so long as the activity is focused upon good. As such, the mindset of limitless unbridled existence, while we still breathe persists, and keeps hidden the truth given to us in Christ. The two things that persist within the understanding of all in nature are these: truth and deception. Truth remains unchanging and deception is always present in its many contrived appearances. Jesus said: ***Matthew 6:19-21 Do not store up for yourselves treasure on earth, where moth and rust destroy, and where thieves break in and steal. But store up for yourselves treasures in heaven, where moth and rust do not destroy, and where thieves do not break in and steal. For where your treasure is, there your heart will be also.*** *Clearly, we are hearing of the* *promise of life after death of the body, for the dead have no use for treasures. This promise of life is a constant truth that speaks against an unbridled existence.*

Here are some of the enemies of truth: ***Mark 7:20-23 He went on to say: "What comes out of a man is what makes him 'unclean.' For from within, out of men's hearts, come evil thoughts, sexual immorality, theft, murder, adultery, greed, malice, deceit, lewdness, envy, slander, arrogance and folly. All these evils come from inside and make a man unclean."*** *This entire list of wrongs clouds truth and encourages belief in the totality of death, being the total end of life. Of course, those apart from Christ will find total death when the body dies. This perhaps, adds to the confusion surrounding afterlife reality. Whenever the aforementioned-things that make a person unclean are called into the light the lie will always rise-up to its defense. Let's recognize that while we are all grouped into the unrighteous (sinful) general descriptive, there is a particular-significance associated with the specifics mentioned. Such specifics are pronounced as* ***"unclean."*** *The usage of the word unclean simply means sinful. Generally, speaking, an unclean act is one that involves a serious fault.*

Herein we can understand, human desires are ruling the individual in both thought and deed. It is from within a man that all manner of abomination is formulated. When the focus is upon sinful, the thoughts of man cannot see the unseen truth and the consequence attached to the infraction against God's laws. Where the unseen is denied therein all restriction is removed from the conscience of man and he then becomes, ***"unclean."*** *A mindset of impure behavioral focus, absent limitation, existing in extremes, will always be labeled as* ***"unclean,"*** *simply because of the distance one has created between truth and the failure to identify wrong.*

What's seen is temporary

Certainly, within the reality of what is seen there is truth. There is no doubt presented to us in the changes that surround us daily.

However, the apostle Paul is speaking to us regarding death's perception of finality, being prevalent within the mindset of the world. Such incorrect assumption is countered by the twenty-third psalm. ***Psalm 23:4 Even though I walk through the valley of the shadow of death, I will fear no evil, for you are with me."*** *Within this one verse the psalmist alerts us to the reality of afterlife; post bodily existence. He is pointing us to the reality of eternal life. He is also showing to us the trust in God that all of us must have. The psalmist uses the term,* ***"shadow of death"*** *and (in order) to fully understand the intent of the wording we must recognize the word* ***"shadow"*** *is closely associated within the translation to the word, "illusion." As such, when we recognize the full implication of the usage of the word,* ***"shadow"*** *this somewhat imperceptible cognition (the usage of* ***"shadow"*** *does not immediately speak to us as deception), is brought clearly into focus when we substitute shadow for its close relative, "illusion." We then find truth jumping off the page saying: "Life! Life is continuous when we are in Christ!" When we come to this understanding what we find is the desire to no longer live as men and women captured within such illusion that only offers to us hopelessness.*

The mindset of such hopelessness, (within the unseen reality of eternal life), has managed to perpetuate down through the centuries, because man has failed to embrace the truth of God's eternal reality, and because his very own desires have cast a shadow over his reasoning, to the point of enslavement. They reason, "What does it matter how we conduct our lives, there is no one to say this is wrong or right. Why waste the time we have trying to adhere to the perceptions of right and wrong when in the end, it matters not? Who is going to say, 'you are wrong' when it is obvious we see no visible guidepost to which we must focus upon?"

It is interesting to recognize the conscience to be unseen and a part of us that is undeniable. It is this rejection of eternal life, so prevalent in the world's makeup that gives artificial support to those whose desires lead them into the illusion of death's finality, wherein, they are never given the light necessary to see clearly, the truth that is obvious to all who will but recognize the renewal of all things in life. All things, mankind above all others, for it is mankind who is renewed to eternal life. The physical aspect of life is renewed in the time of its season, (healing of wounds or disease, and ultimately renewal in the resurrection to life), and the spiritual also finds daily renewal from the indwelling of the Holy Spirit.

Continual renewal

Continual renewal is this proof within nature that shouts-out to the inhabitants of the earth: "It is my desire for man to live forever, in peace, joy and love of family." All that is required for us to see this truth is to permit its light entry into our lives. It is time for all to recognize the time for forgiveness is now and the clock is running down not only for the individual, but also for the entire world. Failure to recognize God is also a sin needing to be forgiven! I find it somewhat intriguing that people will not move toward what is right. We will not naturally desire to do what is right when all things in nature having purpose are required (by the brilliant design incorporated by God) to move in the direction of said purpose. Of course, not all things in life have free will. While spiritually dead (enslaved by our sinful nature), the will of mankind is torn by nature's attraction to move in the direction of wrong, leaving us compelled to step on the landmine of compulsive deception placed continually in our path. There is no one righteous; as such, both criminals and law-abiding citizens, who disbelieve in God are captured by, ***"Eat drink and be merry, for tomorrow we die."*** *Without God that is a very true statement!*

Spiritual guidepost

Have we forgotten the words of the psalmist? ***"I will fear no evil for you are with me."*** *We have lost our way because we have not held-fast to the guidepost that is the Lord. He has been relegated to the status of non-existence in the hearts and minds of many, who have chosen to be self-directing vehicles traveling through the valley of the illusion of death. Can we imagine the look upon the* *faces of those who have chosen so badly, when at last the Day of Judgment arrives and they stand before God knowing that they have been tricked, by the illusion of self-gratification, and the darkness that was always present in those whose vision had been continually fixed upon their self? Self-gratification, or the never-ending quest to find peace through the offerings of the world is an illusion simply because it cannot be done.*

We cannot satisfy a spiritual need for God with a physical substitute. We can satisfy for the moment, hunger and thirst, but when the spirit cries-out to be united with God there is no substitute. God is Spirit and in the creation of man he gave to us himself. It is this separation caused by sin that denies to us the truth of our need. We then are led away as prisoners seeking peace that only accompanies freedom. The prisoner is denied not only the ability to find freedom, but he has been made forgetful of the loved-one left behind. He is kept in the darkness of ignorance, but he understands there is something missing besides freedom. He knows that once freedom is found then and only then can he seek to reacquaint himself with the reality he had been denied. He also knows that somewhere there is someone who will recognize him no matter how long he has been kept in the prison of darkness. This someone will then fill in the missing pieces of his life. This someone is God, the loved-one he had rejected, denied, and declared to be fantasy. Once the prisoner is freed to see truth, he then finds the foundation that was denied to him within the former existence of living in darkness. He finds not only a foundation of hope and joy but in this new revelation he finds the spiritual guidepost that is the Lord. A major change!

Illusion

Illusion is, "A false idea, conception, or belief concerning something." Although mostly by conditioning, we think of illusion as the mirage (we are told) that occurs within a desert setting prompted by the mind confronted by desperation to quench a real pronounced thirst. It is this desperation that is akin to the hopelessness of those who have given reality to the finality of our existence as soon as the body dies. It is interesting that within interpretative understanding, concerning death of the human being, one defining aspect of such death is determined by the conclusive results pronouncing, "brain death" as an indicator that closes the book on a person's life. And so, not only the bodily sign (non-breathing) being a telling aspect for concluding the arrival of death, but the accompanying absence of brain activity also presents to us the reality of a transference of life from one existence to another; the absence of life as we now know it within the corporeal dimension is conclusive as far as the body is concerned but the spirit has never been dependent upon the body. Corporeal life, is the physical aspect of creation, but the absence of our spiritual/thinking faculty from the body need not be a determination for life's conclusion; our inability to detect brain function does not mean life and/or the spirit has ceased to exist. More to the point, such absence of brain activity points to a transference from the body to a purely spiritual existence. When the body dies, the brain also dies. The thinking faculty, which is our spirit, had utilized the physical brain to make functional the body! In death, the body no longer has need for functionality and in this the spirit returns to God who gave it. Major change!

<u>*Out of the body home with the Lord*</u>

2 Corinthians 5:6-9 Therefore we are always confident and know that as long as we are at home in the body we are away from the Lord. We live by faith not by sight. We are confident, I say, and would prefer to be away from the body and at home with the Lord. So we make it our goal to please him whether we are at home in the body or away from it. *Going back to what Paul said to the Corinthian church in the beginning of this chapter regarding,* ***"What is seen is temporary and what is unseen is eternal"*** *therein we find conclusive reinforcement of truth that breaks down the illusion of this life being temporary, as no one can see our thoughts! That is (to say), we are confronted with the reality of bodily death and in this there is no doubt upon viewing the dead. Our spirit/ thinking faculty has always been unseen, no one could see it in life and should we be surprised that it is also hidden from view when* *the body dies? The apostle Paul is alerting us to the truth given to him by the words of Jesus,* ***"even if he dies; yet shall he live."***

Paul points-out the fact that we are being renewed daily. This is the internal renewal of our spirit. We received a new spirit at the time of being born again; this new spirit is the down payment that assures us of eternal life, continually being renewed through our association and connection to the very source of life. We have in-effect been permitted once again access to the ***"Tree of life."*** *We have been permitted to once again drink of the,* ***"Streams of living water." John 7:37-38 On the last and greatest day of the Feast, Jesus stood and said in a loud voice, "If a man is thirsty, let him come to me and drink. Whoever believes in me, as the Scripture has said, streams of living water will flow from within him." By this he meant the Spirit, whom those who believed in him were later to receive.*** *The tree of life and streams of living water represent to us the very ingredients necessary for us to sustain life. They speak to us in a language we can understand, (inasmuch) as we can relate very easily to the bodily needs within our present condition, namely, hunger and thirst. Jesus also speaks to us in a language that is plain and understandable once we know the truth concerning him.*

John 4:10 "Jesus answered her, "If you knew the gift of God and who it is that asks you for a drink, you would have asked him and he would have given you living water." *The Samaritan woman at the well confirms to us the spiritual principle of asking, seeking and knocking, and in doing so we receive, find, and gain entrance through an open door.*

Again, ***John 6:48-51 I am the bread of life. Your ancestors ate manna in the desert, but they died. But the bread that comes down from heaven is of such a kind that whoever eats it will not die. I am the living bread that came down from heaven. If anyone eats this bread he will live forever. The bread that I will give him is my flesh, which I give so that the world may live.*** *What we are hearing, is the declaration from Jesus, that has the same meaning, as when he said that,* ***Man does not live by bread alone but by***

every word that comes from the mouth of God." *And so, there is the physical and the spiritual that needs to be nourished in-order to continue living after the body has died. While the physical is limited within the inevitable aspect of death, the spiritual is nourished by the truth brought to mankind by the Word of God-Jesus. Those of us who have received the bread of life, offered to us through the sacrifice of Christ are assured of eternity; even when we pass away physically. Those of us who are alive (bodily) when Christ returns will never die!*

We have been attached to the Vine of Life (Jesus). He is the vine and we are the branches. It is the vine that provides for the branches so long as they are attached to the source of life. As such, we are renewed daily from the source of life himself. ***John 15:5-6 I am the vine; you are the branches. If a man remains in me and I in him, he will bear much fruit; apart from me he can do nothing. If anyone does not remain in me, he is like a branch that is thrown away and withers; such branches are picked up, thrown into the fire and burned.*** *Let's see what Jesus is (actually) saying. A branch not connected to the vine is representative of a person who has fallen away from the source of life, it withers and dies, is picked up and thrown into the fire and is burned. This is of course a reference to the fires of hell. All of those not destined for eternal life will find the judgment of God. This is the final negative change.*

Belief is eternity awarded

John 11:25-26 Jesus said to her, "Your brother will rise again." Martha answered, "I know he will rise again in the resurrection at the last day." Jesus said to her, "I am the resurrection and the life. He who believes in me will live, even if he dies; and whoever lives and believes in me shall never die." *Well there we have it folks, plain and simple. No illusions or deceptions just the plain truth spoken by our Lord. What can we make of this duality of life, that is, the combining of both corporeal and spiritual existence to comprise a complete person? This is God's design, if we were total spiritual beings, what need would* *we have for a garden of fruit trees? We don't know what we shall become, but we understand that we will be like the Lord; a very good change!*

This faith that awards life is a gift that enables us to see (recognize to the point of belief and ultimately knowing) that which cannot be seen with our eyes. If we believe in the promises of Jesus, (in this belief we accept his sacrifice) while we still live in these bodies, we will never die! We will never lose our ability to think, and in this retention of thought we retain not only who we are but also attain eternal life. Our days upon this earth are numbered, but our days are never exhausted.

There is a point in a man's life in which his spirit dies (his way of thinking and his beliefs) and he is born again/made alive by the truth that unveils the illusion that he had accepted as reality. Such illusions, veils and deceptions once removed, brings to us great joy in the knowledge that rushes into our lives with unending revelation. Being born again is receipt of truth that permits the spirit/mind of man to experience the reality of truthful thought (life) and in this experience the gravity of our past beliefs are erased and tossed into the trash-heap of lies; and out from the land of darkness we emerge into the light! Joyful change.

In this new-life there is no death except for the bodily aspect to look forward too, for the one who is born again he has satisfied the biblical pronouncement that declares, **"It is appointed unto man to die once."** *(Bodily death.) As such, the spiritual aspect of our life has been awarded the promised eternity and we await the bodily death that must follow, absent the fear we would normally assign it, because it is in truth the, valley of the illusion of death. Where our Lord is, there can only be life, for he is,* ***"The way and the truth and the life."*** *A change of spirit is a change in our existence. If we are born again the first stage of change takes place while we are still alive in our body.*

When the time comes for us to leave the body we are again changed into a new existence. This should not come to us as a surprise or seem to be outside the realm of understanding. In the same-way, a seed is planted into the ground and from it a plant is born, so it is for us; we begin life at conception. Conception occurs through the transfer of life, and is not our final aspect of change.

The soul/life is God given. ***"And the Lord God formed man out of the clay of the earth and breathed into his nostrils the breath of life, and man became a living being."*** *This very intimate scene depicting God bringing man to life (conception's origin) is exactly the relationship he wants to have with his children. United in love.*

This parental love shown to us at the beginning and shown to us again in the sacrifice of Jesus upon the cross, is also a new beginning for mankind to once again be embraced by our heavenly Father. And we also recognize through scripture's pronouncement that, ***"What is of the earth returns to the earth and the spirit returns to God who gave it."*** *The new spirit received at rebirth returns to God who gave it when the body dies. This aphorism (forceful biblical truth) is repeated many times within the words of Jesus and should bring to us tremendous joy! The exception to the requirement of needing to be born again to continue onto eternal life is found only in little children, for they are possessors of the kingdom of God. Once we have total trust in God, as would little children for their parents, we are then admitted into the kingdom of God. This admittance is taking place in the here and now, for God has made us into his temple and he is living within us.*

The resurrection to eternal life is the final change for those who have been saved. Jesus will never lose any of us who have been given to him by the Father. This should alert us to the fact that we are always within the sight of the, ***"Good Shepherd."*** *Forgetting this fact can turn churches into social clubs and worship into noise.*

Veils

We can intellectualize between illusion that deceives and veils that deny our sight to the truth God wants us to see, but in the final analysis we are denied reality. While we are lost in this world we are like men in need of strong eyeglasses for us to see clearly. Almost every presentation of truth is countered by a veil or illusion attempting to deny to us the reality of life. We are told in scripture that the ***"evil god of this world"*** *keeps blindfolded many people, denying to them the good news of Christ. Distractions form the veils that deny to us the truth. Illusions are presented when we attempt to form logical conclusions to the things we perceive, absent the truth of God. There are many distractions presented to us externally, and others come to us from our desires that have not been made to recognize they are no longer in control.*

When desires are given the opportunity (desires that do not please God should not be in control) to act upon their urging therein we find the illusion of peace, but the muffled cries of the spirit, bound and gagged in the deep recesses of the heart remains. The result of being distracted or blinded to truth is captivity! We can never be free until the chains of slavery are removed from the spirit that seeks to be reunited with God. Once the spirit is set free the desires of flesh are sent to the place that held the spirit captive. The desires are held captive by truth and there will not be a prison break! Truth can never be defeated!

Full Circle

O green fields
Great ears rising
Ever pleasing and seeking
In silence crowned.
Gathered processed stored and shipped
Consumed by hunger found.
Returned, from whence it came.
Earth.
Dust.
Ground.

Ecclesiastes 12:7 "And the dust returns to the ground it came from and the spirit returns to God who gave it."

Renewal

The seed
Nighttime into day
An ocean's change
Just a drop away
The leaf from tree to ground
Is lifted-up again
Through the roots of life
The same God does for man
Mountains crumble
A rock is moved
Water wears upon stone
A man is resurrected called to life and home
No longer to be changed
No longer to be formed!

Job 14:14 "If a man dies will he live again? All the days of my hard service I will wait for my renewal to come."

Intuition detectives

2 Corinthians 4:2-4 Rather, we have renounced secret and shameful ways; we do not use deception, nor do we distort the word of God. On the contrary, by setting forth the truth plainly we commend ourselves to every man's conscience in the sight of God. And even if our gospel is veiled, it is veiled to those who are perishing. The god of this age has blinded the minds of unbelievers, so that they cannot see the light of the gospel of the glory of Christ, who is the image of God. *When someone is blind the images constructed by the mind were made by attempting to bring order into a world of darkness. As such, a presentation of deception had no competition simply because truth had not been made available; this is especially true when there is a preconceived denial of said truth as it pertains to the reality of God. Truth is received through the conscience that is always in the sight of God. Conscience can be understood as the very presence of God;*

although we were dispossessed from paradise God did not leave us alone; he went with us through the knowledge of right and wrong. I say to myself, "I believe in God" and my conscience does not reply, "Are you kidding me?" Rather, my conscience confirms this truth. Conscience simply means: "with-knowledge." Con, meaning "with" and science meaning, "knowledge."

We do what's right and we live in peace, we do what's wrong and we find condemnation. Some do not have a conscience they have a ***"depraved mind"*** *and have been given over to their desires.* ***Romans 1:28 Furthermore, since they did not think it worthwhile to retain the knowledge of God, he gave them over to a depraved mind, to do what ought not to be done.*** *We are as detectives with a built-in-filter that has ability to recognize right from wrong as well as what is or may be safe or harmful.*

Example: We can view a robin in a tree and find pleasure in its call, and in the same viewing a hawk enters the scene; we know the atmosphere has changed from peace to threatening. This perception of impending potential danger that can threaten peace is also incorporated into conscience; our ability to know and understand what is right and wrong also allows us to perceive the potential consequence for peace or the lack thereof. Apart from the actual knowledge associated with the nature of the hawk and the actual sighting of such potential, we are blessed with intuition. Such intuition is given to us because of the indwelling of the Holy Spirit. God has made us his temple (he has taken up residency in us) and because of this nothing can catch him off guard. What is presented as peace, having no threatening hidden agenda, based upon what is known of the nature of the robin is clearly understood. Everything is defined within a presentation of truth, absent distortions. However, we do not know what, let's say, may be the intentions of someone we do not know, but we can get a feeling of trust or one of warning absent knowledge of a person's background; of such a person, this is the Holy Spirit speaking to us through an intuitive presentation. As Paul says, ***"On the contrary, by setting forth truth plainly we commend ourselves to every man's conscience in the sight of God."*** *Again,* ***1 Corinthians 2:10-11 The Spirit searches all things,***

even the deep things of God. For who among men knows the thoughts of a man, except man's spirit within him. In the same way, no one knows the thoughts of God except the Spirit of God.

The Spirit searches all things, must be understood to mean even the thoughts of man. As Paul says, every man's conscience (his thoughts) are in the sight of God. As such, nothing is hidden from God, and in this we have become the recipients of God's evaluation of those things hidden from our sight. We are detectives in this respect: we judge and make decisions that define what is right or wrong, and like real law enforcement detectives we also get tips from God, alerting us to the wrong intent of others.

We don't say that the nature of the hawk is wrong, but we do recognize the potential of the hawk's nature. As such, we are alerted to the advent of what may be troubling to our senses. Again, we do not say the hawk is wrong, should he make a meal out of the robin, but we understand at some point in time such preying upon one another will cease. ***Isaiah 11:6 "The wolf will live with the lamb, and the leopard will lie down with the goat, the calf and the lion and the yearling together; and a little child will lead them."*** *Such peace will once again reign throughout all of creation, for all creatures will be sustained by the very source of life. We recognize that with the advent of sin into the creation of God all things and creatures found change! Just as man was told that he had to toil (in order) to bring forth sustenance from the earth, so it was true for all creatures to provide through toil and struggles (in order) to sustain their selves.*

Desire for change

Psalm 51:10 Create in me a pure heart, O God, and renew a steadfast spirit within me. *As previously stated, all things in nature find renewal. I look out from my window and it is clear to me the changing of the seasons. The trees declare the designed input of God. The earth itself faithfully presents to us the plentiful and generous giving of God. The oceans decrease in volume through the* *process of evaporation and release once again, clean water from the heavens in the form of rain. In this instance, as in all providing-brilliance incorporated into nature, we understand the intent of God for his creation to be always good. All too often we are looking outward to observe the continuous renewal in nature, but the most important renewal must take place within the heart and mind of man. This renewal takes place when man accepts his need. It is as the Psalmist (David) laments his sins and understands his need for renewal that his outreach for forgiveness is answered. Renewal's need is the same for all of us; we must recognize our need for renewal and understand it comes from God alone. Just as the seawater is cleaned from an unacceptable state for man to consume, so, it is the cleansing of man from his sins must take place for us to become acceptable to God. As the earth receives a seed and growth comes forth, so too a man receives grace through faith and is permitted to grow in truth. Within renewal of a person there is the forgiveness that lifts the heavy burden of guilt away. Such removal permits the shadows of impending gloom and depression to drift off into the distant horizon never to be burdensome again. The psalmist desires a renewed heart of purity brought about by the cleansing of forgiveness. He asks for a* ***"steadfast"*** *spirit, one that is unwavering in purpose. His desire has become fixed upon renewal not only of himself but renewal of his relationship with God. This desire is prompted by the shadow of foreboding anticipation hanging over his existence. Such unknowing and foreboding anticipation engulfs, as would a dark cloud threatening to envelope and deny life.*

The unseen and the obvious

Some things in life are obvious (fall and spring) and others are hidden and unseen. It is the unseen that is made known to us by the obvious change that has occurred. For instance, we have medicine that will relieve pain and its presence within us is made known through its impact on both the pain and the mind. There are other medicines that apart from the obvious actively work within the intent of its prescription. Such medicines can reduce cholesterol levels, prevent plaque buildup within the arteries and a myriad of others that we do not recognize through their impact upon the mind; their positive results remain hidden from conscious awareness, but like the pain medicines have a positive impact upon our condition needing help. There is also a need for help when the pain of guilt and its cumulative buildup causes our spirit to cry out for renewal to find peace with God and peace within our very own heart. It is this unseen renewal that is lasting and filled with the hope of eternity.

The Psalmist continues: **Psalm 51:12-13 Restore to me the joy of your salvation, and grant me a willing spirit to sustain me. Then I will teach transgressors your ways, and sinners will turn back to you.** *I must ask: What is this perception of right and wrong? What is this teaching that the psalmist is asking for that could be apart from the conscience of man? What can challenge our understanding of good and bad? Is this what he is asking when he desires to know the ways of God? Perhaps he's saying that he can understand right and wrong, and what is acceptable, but also is asking for confirmation from God, because he realizes he is a poor judge of himself and seeks to become totally reliant upon God and his ways? He desires the removal of any doubt.*

obvious

I walk through the woods and see the obvious signs that a campsite was established, made use of, and with respect for the land it was left clean. I don't need to see the person that utilized the land to know that people were indeed responsible for the signs observed. The magnificence of creation says to me someone of tremendous unfathomable depth is responsible. I don't need to see this person to believe he exists and created all there is. The existence of creation with its complex intricacies demands of the intellect such acknowledgement of the one who created it all. Moreover, when we add the complexity of life into the equation he who is unseen becomes obvious.

Conscience

The conscience is unchallenged in majority of faiths, however, there are those within the so-called religion of scientology, who actively seek to condition the mind and erase the conscience. Of course, there are those who will believe this "irritation" between what is acceptable behavior and what is unacceptable is derived through conditioning within the formative years of life, but then, there must be a beginning of such conceptual separation defining right from wrong. We understand the biblical beginning as it pertains to the sin of Adam and Eve, and the consequence being knowledge of right and wrong. As such, because there is this recognition of guilt and the absence thereof when we live correctly we know of the consequence of sin and existence of God. I suspect even the scientologists will agree that kidnapping and murder will invoke not only wrong depiction within their conscience, but, will also prove to them the correctness of conscience and the folly embraced by efforts to erase it from the consciousness of man.

Conscience confirms the biblical account of the first of mankind's sin and points-out to us the reality of the one who decides what is and is not acceptable; and still, it is not the same for everyone. We understand the concept of perfection only when it is attributed to the one, who, alone is perfect. We know of perfection and imperfection, only God is perfect; everyone and everything else in creation is imperfect because of the entrance of sin. There may be some exceptions to the corrupting influence of sin: the natural law of gravity and the mathematically intricate design of the cosmos have perhaps not been changed by the entrance of sin into creation, but certainly the imperfection of life has felt its sting. All things will pass away except for the word of God. It is he who set forth the ways in which we are to conduct our lives while we still have breath in us.

WRONG WILL ALWAYS BE DENOUNCED THROUGH GUILT AND RIGHT WILL ALWAYS BRING PEACE. WHERE WRONG HAS BEEN COMMITTED, THE LIE WILL ALWAYS RISE TO ITS DEFENSE.

Hope for the hopeless

The condition of hopelessness is brought about by belief in the finite existence of man and is only defeated by truth, present in both the obvious renewal in nature and the transformation experienced within the spirit of man. The thought process that receives a complete change (being born again) removes the hopeless mist of illusion and brings into awareness the reality of the promised eternity provided by God. Such hope is also presented to us in the color green, as each succeeding spring shouts to the inhabitants of the earth its receipt of the provision of God.

All of creation speaks to us of great hope. If this were not true, why have any concept of hope at all? Why bother to inject hope where there is only hopelessness? Hope is present because it is a reality that strikes back at the lies presented in denial of all that is seen and unseen. Life is a gift that requires us to understand a gift given is never attached to a time limit, saying, "Okay, time is up, the gift of life has run its course and it's time to die." Of course, we must understand that the one who gave to us life has done-so hoping we should not abuse the gift. There is a set of rules, and when rules are broken the giver is insulted. A parent buys a car for his son, and the son is given instructions regarding how he should drive and care for the vehicle; the son then purposely drives to the edge of a cliff and permits the car to plummet into a ravine filled with destructive rocks. A mountain stream is offered to a man dying from thirst; he drinks and is revived; after which he spits some water into the face of the one who gave it to him. These examples clearly display ingratitude and disrespect toward those who have shown to us kindness and love. No different from the sacrifice and love shown to us in the crucifixion of Christ. We have been given a pardon for our disrespect and ingratitude, and are once again offered the life-giving water and a vehicle (born-again spirit) with which, we can continue our journey upon the road of life, once our body has fulfilled its purpose.

Green

It's the color of hope.
It's the sight of renewal throughout creation
Confirming truth and love embracing.
It's rain that falls intently
A soothing breeze in early morn
Shelter from a raging storm
A kiss assuring hearts to dream, forests of abundant green.
From heaven's throne, he came to earth secured in wisdom's tome.
Concerned for the lost, thirsting for water at the root.
Hardened clay and detoured dreams
Dusty roads that lead nowhere, hopeless daily grind
When all else fails our means, we cry to
God and sometimes scream
It's then we know, love keeps life green.

Evergreens in splendor display mercy throughout winter
Others decrease in green with sighs
Captured by the cares of life
Without love it withers-dies.

Luke 23:31 "For if they do these things when the tree is green, what will happen when it is dry?"

This question concerning a tree having the vibrancy of life visibly displayed, and the dryness that accompanies a lack of such green pronouncement, can be understood as a change from good to bad. In the context of the evil displayed in the act of crucifixion it is understood as going from bad to worse. In the crucifixion event about to take place, we find the injustice accompanied by a lack of condemnation within those committing the act. Apparently, there was not a condemnation within the conscience of those who desired to rid the world of truth. Jesus is saying, things will get worse when the reality of God is no longer visible in the flesh that is being displayed in the sacrifice of the cross! He is saying, the depth of evil knows-not limits and when the goodness that he displayed in his life is set-upon attacked and crucified, only more atrociously cruel acts of mind-blowing evil will follow. The evil that inhabits the soul of many is like a raging fire, like the world of the dead and the desires of men; it will never say, "enough!" Evil will never cease of its own volition it must be destroyed by the hand of God!

Today, within the turmoil of the Middle East we have seen beheadings and people set on fire. Children have been sent into slavery, the kind of slavery being the most-evil. All of this is done in the name of a religion, a god and a prophet. None of which represents the one true God who desires us to love one another. Jesus did not say, "I stand at the door and knock, and if you don't believe what I say, I'll break it down and force you to think like me or else I'll kill you!" Jesus never forced anyone to believe in him or the Father who sent him. There is such an unabashed evil in the world today, that is perhaps attempting to become equal to the Nazi murderers of the last world war, that I must ask, what then, is different today in the consciousness of humanity, that does not cause great movement by the population of the world to end such terroristic evil; as did the last World War? Obviously, something has changed. Could it be, the leadership of mankind has moved closer to such evil and in this (change) will not risk damaging its kingdom or positions of authority? ***"If Satan fights against Satan his kingdom cannot stand."***

<u>*The heart that denies God finds folly*</u>

Psalm 53:1-2 "The fool says in his heart, 'There is no God.' They are corrupt, and their ways are vile; there is no one who does good. God looks down from heaven on the sons of men to see if there are any who understand, any who seek God." *This depiction of a fool is the height of all foolishness! There are so many acts of folly and so many ways in which one can be judged as unknowing, but with respect to denying the existence of God, there is no equal in ignorance; the one who does not see the hope of renewal of life in the reality of God, suffers greatly from the veils shadows and illusions that (with stealth) deny to him the truth, of both his own existence, as well as the reality of God. The man who*

denies the obvious truth concerning the existence of God, cannot find the change that makes possible being born again. It is true that the seeker will find truth and in truth find freedom, and at times it is the mercy of God that acts to bring awareness of truth to those lost in the illusions, veils and deceptions clouding reality; God acts first; a direct intervention on his part, apart from an altar call or orchestrated evangelical event. It is truth that brings about salvation for those predestined before the foundations of the earth were formed. Some have found themselves held so-captivated by the world's deceptions and allurements, that it takes a divine intervention for truth to breakthrough and announce reality.

Reward

"For our light and momentary troubles are achieving for us an eternal glory that far out-weighs them all." *Paul is telling us the troubles of this life are only for the moment and when they are weighed against the promise of eternity they amount to nothing more than a passing headache; it may be a severe headache, but he is saying, "endure" for our troubles are momentary. He is saying: "This too shall change!" He speaks of the eternal glory we shall gain; it's the fame or admiration given to somebody who does something important, something that brings or confers admiration. Such glory is a reflection, of Christ's sacrifice for us. It is an aspect of our unwavering desire to remain in accord with the truth we have been given. Basically, the receipt of such glory, also understood as someone having an excellent reputation imparts to others the correct and proper manner, in which to live. How great will our joy be in knowing we have passed from pain and troubles to peace? Wonderful change!*

Biotic and antibiotic changes

"Though outwardly we are wasting away, yet inwardly we are being renewed day by day." *All life has a building up and tearing down process. When looking, into the mirror, the face that stares* *back at me is far from the image of my youth. The tearing down process called aging is most efficient within its intent. In addition to aging and the illusion of total-death, there is the emotional pain that comes to us when we believe we shall be eternally separated from those we love, when death arrives. Here again is the recognition of the eternal, but in this context, it is presented in the negative, wherein only hopelessness is seen. Also, when I look inside myself, I see a difference in the thoughts that were so prevalent in my youth. The thoughts of my youth were not clear. I could see the stars in the heavens but I could not understand their light. I could see the trees and not imagine the Gardener who planted the first seeds. Everything was superficial; there wasn't the deep exploration and desire-within that seeks truth, not only of God and creation but the truth as it pertains to our own existence and purpose. We acquire an almost automatic deep seeking posture once truth has been embedded within the spirit's thought process.*

This promise of Jesus, "I will be with you always" is one that lends great strength against the image of aging and death. ***Matthew 19-20 Therefore go and make disciples of all nations, baptizing them in the name of the Father and of the Son and of the Holy Spirit, and teaching them to obey everything I have commanded you. And surely, I will be with you always, to the very end of the age.*** *Clearly, what we are hearing in the words of Jesus is that we are living in the last age or the final chapter in the book called man. As such, what we may be failing to recognize, is even when the body dies Jesus is still with us, and his presence alone is enough for us to be made cognizant of continued life, when the body takes its last breath. We are renewed every day by the presence of God in our lives. We may at times think that we have left him but in truth even in our most ardent attempt to run from him within the shame of sin, we are never successful. No matter the gravity of the sin that pulls us away from Jesus, it is he who keeps us and does not permit us to stray from the truth we have been given. This ability to keep all of us safe from the deceitful illusions and shadows of depressing thought makes clear to us the reality of life, in the here and now, and in the hereafter! At the time, Jesus spoke those words* *to his disciples, giving assurance that he will never leave them, they are now long gone. They have left this earth but are still in the presence of Christ. They are very much alive, for once we are transformed into the temple of God we are never absent from his presence; the presence of God in our lives permits transforming power for the continuance of life after the body dies.* **Ephesians 2:1-2 *As for you, you were dead in your transgressions and sins, in which you used to live when you followed the ruler of the kingdom of the air, the spirit who is now at work in those who are disobedient.*** *We are hearing Paul say to those who were apart from Christ that they were dead. Walking dead, unaware of truth. Should this situation (dead in ignorance and sin) continue until the last breath of the body, the ability to exist in a pure spiritual state of existence (retaining our cognizant awareness of who we are), will not be found in those who are spiritually dead.*

The reason for this is simple: sin that has not been repented and forgiven cannot approach God. It makes no sense that unrepentant sin should approach God prior to the Judgment. Is it logical to assume sinful man could approach God absent the righteousness given to us in the sacrifice of Christ? If sin can approach God, why then is there a need for the sacrifice of Christ? The continuance of life after the body has died is only afforded to those clothed in the righteousness of Christ. Even the tree used to crucify Christ found purpose after its death. So too it will be for us who are embraced (as was the tree) by the love of God.

Changing

The mist laid low upon the earth
A wall to block the sky
Hidden within its borders
Dampness raises gloom
Lending added weight to days
As thoughts within a storm

Though torch and lantern ready
To battle with its form
A greater light is needed
To penetrate hearts
Illuminating darkness with
Beams of wisdom's dawn
Ending deception by
Lifting out of sight
The mist-chilling vapor
Dispersed by God's sunlight.

2 Corinthians 4:6 For God, who said, "Let light shine out of darkness," made his light shine in our hearts to give us the light of the knowledge of the glory of God in the face of Christ.

The Barrier

Human ability and natural laws place limits upon our thoughts
And form for us a finite view giving power to what's lost.
The greatest of these barrier stones present themselves in caskets
The seed must be transformed into something it was not
And cease to be a seed but not to be forgotten.
Loss of limbs will not reduce my mind
Will not diminish spirit now or over time
And when my losses mount and body meets the grave
I still will not diminish, no, not even for a day!

John 4:36 "Even now the reaper draws his wages, even now he harvests the crop for eternal life.

Even now, (prior to the resurrection, and before bodily death), the reaper draws his wages. Even now he harvests the crop for eternal life.

Who is this reaper? ***John 4:38 "I sent you to reap what you have not worked for. Others have done the hard work, and you have reaped the benefits of their labor."*** *In this time of man's travel through the ages what we understand is that it is we who are sent into the field (the world) to reap the harvest others have worked so hard to make ready. These others are all of those who have come before us, and many have paid the ultimate sacrifice. Today, just by living a life that presents to others the right manner-in which to conduct ourselves is also calling recognition to the righteousness of our Lord, and the manner in-which he not only lived, but in the way, he died for us; selflessness, humility and love!*

I don't know what else Jesus could to do to make an impact upon the present state-of-affairs in another person's life; to turn their attention to truth. He did the hard work, demonstrably presented to all with eyes to see and ears to hear. His was not just talk; through his sacrifice suffering and death, therein alone should be enough for many to take notice of his willingness to die for others to live. Can it be we are so preoccupied with demands from both the responsibilities to the world and those we love that we fail to recognize the responsibility to God? It is he who wants to relieve or lessen the impact of such worries upon us. Worries that distract us from the truth we need to live this present life with peace within.

Matthew 11:28-30 "Come to me, all you who are weary and burdened, and I will give you rest. Take my yoke upon you and learn from me, for I am gentle and humble in heart, and you will find rest for your souls. For my yoke is easy, and my burden is light." *Peace and life is offered now and is confidently marching into eternity. The promise of eternal life now, and its realization, will make our hills and valleys seem to be just another day in the park.*

Desire

Fire to flame death to graves desires underscore
Their stated position upon fruition
"There's always room for more!"
In man, they are moving intent upon proving
Power and riches of worth
Effort and plans within his hands
To demand satisfaction from earth
Deceit from the start
They bring troubles to hearts
Of impetuous thought
In truth, they are calling
To those who are falling:
"Make ready a place for your God!"

Matthew 3:2 In those days John the Baptist came preaching in the desert of Judea and saying, "Repent, for the kingdom of God is near."

The desires of man are mostly opposed to the desire of God for us. There is confusion in the desires wants and needs within the understanding of mankind. There is and are many natural needs necessary for us to survive. Along with these necessary needs there are those that are presented to us in the form of conveniences made to make life easier, and in truth many have become necessary for modern day life. Just the idea of having no electricity will present a torrent of thought fixed upon both comfort and survival. Still, there are those desires that are neither necessary or helpful within our everyday life. Example: Excessive wealth breeds a thirst for power and a desire for power begets a close relative with an equal desire to control not only the actions of man but his thoughts as well. This is evil and opposed to the intent of God for his creation. When the actions of man and his thoughts can be controlled it is then made easier for evil to deny to mankind the truth presented in the sacrifice of Christ. We used to call a singular point of view "brain washing" but now it is called education?

Why do we suppose within such closed societies there is a ban on religion? Why do we suppose there is a ban on all religions except for those sanctioned by the state? What could be the reasoning for disallowing freedom of expression in the form of openly speaking one's mind or composing books or newspapers recording daily happenings occurring outside of such closed societies? Clearly it is an effort to control and make dependent upon the state all who are trapped by the desires of a few. The chief enabler of such captivity is fear. It is fear of the state, known to inflict not only total loss of freedom through incarceration but also loss of life. Such loss of life rarely has a negative impact upon those who pass such sentence upon the populace.

So, with only this small entrance of our thoughts focused upon the evil desires of man, what we may come to understand is that the depths of evil go well beyond the surface and live deep into the blackest of dark within man's soul. This blackness is the evil or wickedness kept hidden in the most remote corner of a man's soul. Even under the guise of religion there is found such wickedness. They shall not prevail! Evil is always in denial of itself. The lie is evil and is constantly being exercised by those having a voice in the world.

Evil's denial of itself is self-preservation. The criminal caught (even on camera) will deny it is he committing the crime. The elected official continually hides his identity and motives. The saying, "We all know when a politician opens his mouth he is not telling the truth." His practiced smile and gestures (hand and affirmative head movement) along with varying tones and pitch of voice declares to us the whitewashed and sterilized exterior that cannot answer a question with a plain "yes" or "no." This is done and accepted by many, even when we know they are lying!

Denial of truth is wickedness. I guess when the devil offered all the kingdoms of the world to Jesus, if only he (Jesus) would worship him, he was (really) in possession of such kingdoms and/or governments? This must mean all of them were and still are corrupt! But then it is as the bible says: ***"There are none who are***

righteous, no not one." *What the devil was offering to Jesus was the restoration to mankind of the administration of the planet, the position that we held in the beginning.*

The position of being in-charge of our own destiny is one of the most sought-after stations in life, by those who desire to be above the fray, above the everyday struggles and hardships presented to the common man; the ability to be off-of the "playing field" and to send plays down onto the field! The offering of the kingdoms of the world to Jesus meant it would be to the devil that we would recognize as God (in order) to obtain the illusion of being in control, and to him we would look in place of God; if only we would worship him. Such evil-criminality is still present in many today, and the evil they commit in-order to achieve the illusion of a carefree existence, absent the morality and laws of the one true God is highly visible within those placed in-charge of the administration of our very own government.

Blacker

Black the widow's cloth like sack of old
Declaring undying love to a starving world.
Black the hole in space theory's thought accepted
Blacker still the place of love rejected.
Black the ancient plague, sin from its first day
Drumbeats of clarity a mounting mournful dirge
Souls in darkness held hear a calling bell
Sounding for the multitudes of residential hell.

Black the cry that fails to move a friend
Black the beggar's bowl left wanting in its day
Black the heart and soul leading man astray.
Black the high-hat novelty
A show for commonality below the stratosphere
Begins to know what's needed when air becomes so rare.
A web of strands, knit one, purl two
Denies the find of truth as shadows sometimes hide
Beneath a sword hung overhead, saying,

"Sever yourself from lies!"

A hole-piercing hull points direction to abyss
Into black unending where none are ever missed.
Black the sailor's sea and black the eye of war
Black the robes authority in rooms of hearing worn
Deaf to truth pronounced in God's clarifying voice
A failure of the heart is revealed as cause.
Black the core of man construct of willful wrong
Black the pitch of night when starlight's beam should fail
Far off suns and meteors, stars of shooting fame
Comet tails of ancient lore, with or without names
Shall find as did the "rich man" reduced to deal with flames
Within the darkness and props of movie scenes
All, are just illusions of vivid blacker dreams.

Hurtful moving steps diminished until ceased
Hide inside the darkness as a lamp whose fuel is spent
Finds a blackened spiral, no beginning and/or end.
Black the day shall come with herald's trumpet strong
Black the day unveiling righteousness to song
Black the pall so-cast in the field of poison's call
Along the outer edges the slippery slope of wrong.

Black the day shall come when mankind finds despair
Within his mournful cry that finally understands
The black that hid his actions takes on a brilliant glare
No longer lies-are hidden when the Son of God appears!
Black had scoffed at sacrifice in ridicule of mercy's grace
Has looked the gift eternal life and laughed into its face.

Black is Judgment Day
For those whose-hearts have looked away
Their voices call to rocks and say: "Hide our souls away!"
A great divide is formed appeals cannot be made
There is no higher court or place to buy delay.

In the black of darkness in webs of self-made weave
The tortured souls cry-out as a victim in a trap
Finds no escape by any means, cannot attempt advance
Forlorn, alas forlorn, the hope for them has passed
Beyond the time forgiveness
Beyond the time of reach
Into the time of nothingness
As black as God perceives!

Revelation 6:12-15 And I saw the Lamb break open the sixth seal. There was a violent earthquake, and the sun became black, and the moon turned completely red like blood. The stars fell-down to the earth, like unripe figs falling from the tree when a strong wind shakes it. The sky disappeared like a scroll being rolled up, and every mountain and island was moved from its place.

Blind Vision

The ocean crossing of merchant ships with cargo beyond hope.
Why doesn't slavery disturb the conscience of man?
Days becoming nights without notice
The sounds of the ocean remain uncaring.
What have they done to find darkness?
What have they done to be lost in the desires of men?
Insatiable greed motivates the captain's swagger
Gold and silver places strength into the paddle and the song
While in the hold of the ship only crying and moans.
How has this condition of man grown into wickedness?
O the condition of man!
How blind is the vision of man?
Brother and sister exploited
Into the service of wickedness
The pitch of night
Has more-light than the vision of man.
Some eat their young
Some hunt for others
Man, will find his prey
In everything he touches!

Revelation 18:17-19 In one hour this great wealth has been ruined. Every captain of a ship, every traveler at sea, sailors, and seafaring merchants stood at a distance and cried out when they saw the smoke of her pyre. "What city could compare with the great city?" They threw dust on their heads and cried out weeping and mourning: "Alas, alas, the great city, in which all who had ships at sea grew rich from her wealth."

Slavery today

Let us not be fooled by the smiles and greetings of those held aloft by the strength of chains they place upon others. Slavery today is just as bad as it was two hundred years ago, in America. Households are purposefully divided by the state, rendering the family impotent and dependent upon handouts! There is a cancer marching across the world in defiance of both God and conscience! And still we have those who will not defend the weak or recognize such evil for what it is. We thought death by beheading was a thing of the past? Did we think the sword of the devil had been placed into retirement? No! His sword has always been the lie and it is transforming itself into acceptance upon the custom couches of the elite and those believing they are immune to the wickedness plaguing the earth. Do we think slavery only exists outside of America? It is wise for us to be concerned, for America is being transformed into many divergent paths that lead away from both God and freedom. Dependency upon others, mountains of debt, desires of the flesh, and the mind that will not recognize God are all manifestations of slavery. We live a changing life and all things are like putty except for truth. All that we see is finite. Much of what we see we do not understand. Even though we don't witness the end of an existence we have assigned reality to its inevitability. There is more to the sight of man; we can see in more ways than with our eyesight. There is intuition insight and inspiration and there is the voice of God that speaks to us in terms we understand immediately. He speaks to us the truth that sets us free and in this acknowledgement, there is no doubt that we have been brought into a reality that heretofore had eluded our sight.

This additional understanding, shores up the truth we may have heard about, but could not see or embrace until we had been touched and changed, into someone who recognizes the faults in his life. We cannot bring closure to eternity but we will continue to race into the starlit heavens in the belief in the continuance of their beauty. We cannot see the Majesty of God, but we have the promises of Christ and the witness of the Holy Spirit. It is the Holy Spirit who has convinced us of our need and convicted us of our sin. It is this light of truth that God wants all to see and embrace.

Candles

Wax and wick fuel to aspire
Tiny beacons of light contained in the fire
Radiant beams assuring the soul
Bring clearly the message from times of old
Let there be light to make sure the way
Out of the darkness where obstacles lay
Let there be light brilliant and bold
For all to see majesty robed
Let there be starbursts within the spirit
Proclaiming God's glory to all who will hear it
Let there be knowledge of he who is light
The Savior of mankind
Jesus
The Christ.

1 John 1:5 This is the message we have heard from him and declare to you, that God is light and in him is no darkness at all.

Eternity

Who can envision its end?
Who knows its height depth or enormous breath?
Who can get in front of it or run completely around?
Who can think fast enough outpacing with leaps and bounds?
Who can make a dent in it to say a step was gained?
Who can find a place boasting captured ground?
Stars and comet tails cannot find
The end of eternity or end of the mind
A place where rest is found and time can then recline.
When does
Eternity find its end
Forever find a limit
Bottomless a foot
A note finally fall
Its face finally made known?
Within the plan of God
Movement heeds, "halt"
All things shall bend a knee
In the presence of the Lord!

Acts 13:47-48 For this is what the Lord has commanded us: "I have made you a light for the Gentiles, that you may bring salvation to the ends of the earth. When the Gentiles heard this, they were glad and honored the word of the Lord; and all who were appointed to eternal life believed.

Consistent changes

Ecclesiastes 11:9-10 Young people enjoy your youth. Be happy while you are still young. Do what you want to do, and follow your heart's desire. But remember that God is going to judge you for whatever you do. Don't let anything worry you or cause, you pain: You aren't going to be young very long.

The book of Ecclesiastes, the, "Philosopher" is at times depressing. It looks upon life as unfair and pretty much, "useless." It centers upon death as the change that no one escapes, no matter how hard or how little one works; or how much one achieves and acquires, or does not achieve or acquire. In the short time allotted in this life it matters-not what we may or may not achieve; only salvation leaves an indelible mark, death wipes the slate clean and no one except for God remembers what was done or not done. However, everywhere we look upon earth or into the heavens we see changes that are built into the creation of all things. The most consistent changes are life and death. Built into such changes are the awesome timetables inherent in all of life. One can say both sin and death are not a part of the original design as they pertain to mankind, but they also have a timetable for elimination. Regarding the individual, sin is rendered impotent by the sacrifice of Christ and its road leading to death no longer holds the finality as it did prior to the cross. Man, still sins daily, but the remedy for its tenacity is much more potent. The remedy for sin is the love of God. Much of what we do and/or takes place in nature is repetitive. God needs to only change us once!

You aren't going to be young very long

When we are children we are constantly active. We are sent to school where our day is planned for us. After school and homework, we are permitted to play games with other children, or as is so prevalent in today's technological overreach into the world of a child, there is this fascination that grips the attention of the child, and becomes a part of life that is not life at all. It is an interaction without human contact. While it is, true there are computer games that permit more than one person to play the same game at the same time, and even to compete against one another, it is still not the same interaction that was so much a part of the sharing of childhood experienced by children growing-up just a few decades-past. As such, the time for a child to give his or her thoughts a chance to piece together the thoughts necessary for a well-rounded foundation, that anchors the fabrics of faith and hope, with the mortar of right and God, find limited opportunity to become the fountain of strength necessary for adulthood.

A child can live a life without having to worry or to anticipate pain, because he has found the source of protection that permits him to enjoy life. This protection is his parents. In the same way, as we move into adulthood we must also live this life with the carefree joy of the child, having the understanding that we are not alone; God is with us. For those who do not have both parents there is a cloud of unknowing that invades the heart of the child, and in this the spirit also is troubled. Such troubling is not immediately understood or even recognized by the child, but there is the internal recognition that something is missing. This missing parent makes manifestation of inferior thoughts within the child. In many cases, there is self-incrimination that without knowing what it is, has placed a verdict of blame for the lack of a parent upon the child. It is this self-incrimination that produces the thought: "There must be something wrong with me."

This feeling of being unfit or unequal to other children who are blessed with having both parents is-not understood, but over time can produce full-blown feelings of inferiority or lowliness believing there is no escape, causing a need to always prove such feelings wrong. Because there are many negative things that are common to the growing up process, having impact upon children, what we understand is that throughout all the many roadblocks that inhibit full potential, there is always the hand of God seeking to remove such negative thoughts. One way that God works to correct our negative viewpoint is to place people into our lives that he knows will help in the corrective process. After which we find there are others, who, perhaps with just a word of encouragement, when we think all has failed and all is lost, we are made aware by another's outlook of the situation by pointing us to just how much blessing remains.

God places others in our lives

2 Timothy 20-21 In a large house there are articles not only of gold and silver, but also of wood and clay; some are for noble purposes and some for ignoble. If a man cleanses himself from the latter, he will be an instrument for noble purposes, made holy, useful to the Master and prepared to do any good work. *The efforts of the world are sometimes found to have a negative impact upon all of us. This is not to be a surprise, for everything in the world is not working for our good. It is God who is always working for our good, and one way that he does so is to place others in our path when he knows we need to be reminded to reconnect with him. Jesus had said:* ***"All things are possible for those who believe."***

When we lose track of this powerful promise associated with faith we leave ourselves powerless to overcome the troubles life can and will throw at us. Troubles have tendency to dominate our thoughts and in this we are disconnected, making ourselves unavailable to the God who wants to lift us out from the seemingly impossible situation; the situation that we have labeled impossible, but have forgotten that nothing is impossible for God! It is at these times that we need to be reminded of not only our blessings, but of the one who made such blessings a reality in our lives. God does the reminding in many ways, in one, he sends to us someone who will have the right words of encouragement that will refocus us back to reality, and his ability to lift the burden of our present condition. Whether it is we who are being redirected or it is we who are the ones used for special occasions, (as the apostle Paul instructs Timothy, to be ready to serve,) the timing of God is always impeccable.

Up on the down stroke

Sure, life can be hard.
We can feel like we just can't cope.
That's when we must lift our hearts to heaven
And get up on the down stroke.

There are some who live in mansions
While others live in shacks
But hard times can put everyone off-track.

You might be wearing clothes from Calvin or the Thrift Supreme
But hard times show no favorites for suits or jeans.

So, when the hits you've been taking
Got you hanging on the ropes
Don't waste time behaving like you have no hope.
Lift your heart to heaven and get up
Get up on the down stroke!

Psalm 118:6 The Lord is with me; I will not be afraid.

Friend

It has been said, "A man is not complete
Until someone understands him."
The search for understanding is shared between friends
Questions and answers united to blend
Truth peace and love between friends.

The darkest of times cause trembling inside
Alone one seeks to run and to hide.
In the heart like rays from the sun
The friend brings comfort for pain
Ears to listen to heartbeats of rain
A calming voice soothing thunder's refrain.

The friend is where God has stored abundant grace.
The hidden things allowed to be seen
Trust in the friend to share what's inside
Is solemn the binding erasing all pride.

The friend is given to one and many
His heart is love sharing truth.
Gladly given to all who will grasp
Without hesitation, an open hand
All thanks to the friend who heals and cares.
Jesus.

John 15:13-15 Greater love has no one than this: that one lay down his life for his friends. You are my friends if you do what I command. I no longer call you servants, because a servant does not know his master's business. Instead, I have called you friends, for everything I have learned from my Father I have made known to you.

Reinforce

All things need to be reinforced replenished or renewed
A positive change healing life's wounds
We need occasional shoring-up renewal and patching
Of the walls of faith

In this regard, O Lord, you are great!
All our praise ascends, confirming faith that lives within.
All emotion sealed with love, says, "You are here with us!"
Every breeze as a kiss
A rushing wind that lives within
Throughout marrow flesh and bone
Healing heat of faith unfolds
With knowledge wisdom confidence
We look above with loving gaze
Reinforced by love and grace.

Isaiah 41: 10 "So do not fear, for I am with you; do not be dismayed, for I am your God. I will strengthen you and help you; I will uphold you with my righteous right hand."

Graduation

Perhaps the most unnoticed change, takes place within the unseen? I'm reminded of the words of Jesus when he tells us to know who we should fear. He tells us that those who can kill the body can do nothing afterwards; they can do nothing else! However, we are told, in the same breath, that it is God who can, after the body has died place both body and soul into hell. The body being thrown into hell is alluding to the second resurrection to judgment. When we are born into this world, we are exposed to a myriad of information, as would a child attending-school. The majority, of children will graduate from school and move on to whatever they are presented within the choices afforded to them in life. When it comes to graduation of the soul it is the reverse that is found; a small percentage of graduates will move on to eternal life; the road to life is narrow. This world that we live in is a great classroom, and it is solely up to us, with respect to being left behind or being graduated to the next level of existence. Truth is like a seed that has been planted. If planted into fertile ground the result will be a harvest of whatever is designed into the seed. Some seeds may fall along the roadside and the birds of the air will take advantage of their find, and still, other seeds may find rocky ground and the root system will not be allowed to grow deep, in this the plant will wither and die. The plant will find the initiating aspect of life heralding much promise, but the heat of the day and the turmoil of vehicles upon the road will not permit lasting growth. I have used this parable's thoughts, spoken to us by Jesus, (paraphrased) in-order to present the truth concerning where our attentiveness must be for us to graduate from the confines of limited life and into the unlimited offering of eternal life; for all who will recognize the reality of the one who created everything, within the honesty of perfection. The offering of life is truthful love. Some of us will graduate to eternal life; others will not. Again, a truthful reality!

Creation's change is universal

The world's sciences have traveled great distances of understanding, regarding the composition of the earth, and the vastness of the universe, and still, within the science presented to us today, they cannot offer to us an answer for the beginning of life or the beginning to the universe with any degree of certainty, except to say there was a "Big Bang!" Really? In fact, the perfection of the universe is of such critically planned existence (big bangs don't leave perfection in their residue), that had the sun been situated a bit closer we would have suffered tremendous heat that probably would have denied life and if it was any further away, the cold derived would also have adverse impact upon life. Additionally, the rotation of the earth is perfectly timed for all living things upon the earth. These aspects of nature are highly doubtful to be caused by accidental chance! Moreover, when we look out into the heavens we are confronted with the understanding that the universe is constantly increasing, and if the speed of increase were slower or faster the resultant impact upon creation would be highly negative.

Looking out into our galaxy known to us as the "Milky Way" we see the stars contained within; it's an awe-inspiring sight to behold. Now, let us contemplate what scientific knowledge has amassed within the last century, regarding the size of our own galaxy. Our galaxy contains 400 billion stars, (400,000,000,000) and is 100 light-years long, and 10,000 light-years thick, and each galaxy contained in our universe has billions of stars like our sun. It is estimated there are 100 to 200 galaxies within our universe.

Only God knows where eternity ends, if at all? We do know that the universe is constantly being enlarged, expanding, increasing and swelling, and in this we find calculation that can only come from intelligent and purposeful design. Our solar system which is a part of our galaxy has one star, (our sun), and the planets revolve around it. Light travels one-hundred-eighty-six-thousand miles per second. It takes approximately eight minutes for light from the sun to arrive on the earth. Wow!

We have encapsulated our universe within two points of light, but when universe is spoken in terms of entirety (all of creation) we are speaking of infinity; there is no limit to the expanse. Now, within this giant known to us as infinity we can only attribute this brilliant construction to the handiwork of God.

The myriad of life existing on our own planet, shouts out to us, "O God, how great thou art!" ***Psalm 19:1-2 The heavens declare the handiwork of God; the skies proclaim the work of his hands. Day after day they pour forth speech; night after night they display knowledge.*** *Again,* ***Romans 1:20 For since the creation of the world God's invisible qualities-his eternal power and divine nature-have been clearly seen, being understood from what has been made, so that men are without excuse.*** *When we contemplate the existence of God through the evidence displayed in nature, we must also include, not only the myriad of life abundantly exhibited on our planet, but we must also include ourselves.*

We have no excuse for not recognizing the truth presented to us in nature and our own lives! We might have an excuse if we were living in a fishbowl and not having the ability to contemplate the existence of God, but we are not fish. As such, there is no excuse for failing to recognize God through his creation. Concluding all that exists in the glorious presentation of nature, to be nothing more than accidental, is foolish. When we add into the evidence for intelligent design, what we must conclude, is the reality of God.

Additionally, we are unique, there is not one person alive that has the same fingerprint or the same chemical structure exhibited in DNA (Deoxyribonucleic acid), try saying that three times! Evidently, God got it right in the unique design of human beings! What this uniqueness in human beings appears to be saying to us is that the existence of mankind has-nothing to do with chance! These physical aspects of creation point to a structured, planned, designed, intended and premeditated outcome; having nothing to do with a theory alluding to accidental chance within the present-day existence of mankind! Every person born into the world is different and unique. Wow! Now that is what I call, creative, Lord. "How great thou art!"

The most current estimates guess that there are 100 to 200 billion galaxies in our known universe, and each galaxy estimated as having hundreds of billions of stars. A recent German supercomputer simulation put that number even higher: 500 billion. In other words, there could be a solar system out there for every star in in the galaxy! Our solar system has one star that we call the "sun." Does anyone really think, when we are resurrected to eternal life we will be sitting around playing cards? So much for retirement! Now that's a, BIG CHANGE!

Matthew 21: 18-22 On his way back to the city early next morning, Jesus was hungry. He saw a fig tree by the side of the road and went to it, but found nothing on it except leaves. So, he said to the tree, "You will never again bear fruit!" At once the fig tree dried up. The disciples saw this and were astounded. "How did the fig tree dry up so fast?" they asked. Jesus answered, "I assure you if you believe and do not doubt, you will be able to do what I have done to this fig tree. And not only this, but you will even be able to say to this hill, 'Get up and throw yourself into the sea, and it will.' If you believe, you will receive whatever you ask for in prayer."

2

PURPOSE

All life emanates from God and within such life there is purpose. One purpose of man is to recognize truth and within this awareness we are led to Christ. So much is said about the impatience of Jesus regarding the demise of the fig tree. Much has been written concerning the significance of this act and I don't pretend to understand or recognize every aspect presented. If there is one thing we know it is that Jesus (at times) taught through parables, and within the above depiction of an unfruitful tree we find both parable and actual occurrence. Clearly, we find the representative patience of God toward his creation reaching its limit. Perhaps, it was more than the failure of a tree to act in accord with God's design that caused Jesus to remove it from a place within existence to the place without expectancy? After all is said, it is the tree that is dependent not only upon God but mankind entrusted to be, "good stewards of the land." It seems, "thy will be done" pertains to all of creation?

Some have written commentary concerning a, "surprised Jesus" fully expecting the tree to have figs. One has even written a reason for his surprise: "Jesus did not have his divinity working at all times." Everyone equated the incident of the fig tree to the failure of Israel to remain faithful in their focus and purpose, as set forth by God. No doubt this is a fair recognition. Now let us ask a question: Did Jesus act rashly and impulsively because he was hungry and denied figs, where he had thought there should be? We know he was hungry, but this is the same Jesus who at the beginning of his ministry spent forty-days in the wilderness occupied by fasting prayer and temptation. Yes, we can look at scripture and find Jesus asking, ***"Will the Son of Man find faith upon the earth when he returns?"*** *This of course is not to say that Jesus did not know the answer to this question, not at all, rather it is a rhetorical question designed to set-off little mini-explosions in the mind. In the same way, Jesus knew the tree was unfruitful and used the blatant hypocrisy of the tree to point to a greater fault in man. Did Jesus have his own special resource? Yes, but it was not of the perishable kind. This is the same Jesus who told his disciples,* ***"I have food you know nothing about."*** *And it is the same Jesus who taught the following parable concerning a tree's failure, to show to us that God will exercise much patience and effort in the hope that we will fulfill the purpose of our life. Of course, we see the end of God's patience displayed in the cursed fig tree's demise. Realistically, the fig tree was already dead, for what does not bear fruit is apart from God, and cannot exist. The corruption process is active even when it appears life is present.*

Luke 13:6-9 Then Jesus told them this parable: "There was once a man who had a fig tree growing in his vineyard. He went looking for figs on it but found none." So he said to his gardener, 'Look, for three years I have been coming here looking for figs on this fig tree, and I haven't found any. Cut it down! Why should it go on using up the soil?' But the gardener answered, 'Leave it alone sir, just one more year; I will dig around it and put in some fertilizer. Then if the tree bears figs that year so much the better; if not, then you can have it cut down.'"

Within the parable above we hear the gardener ask for, **"Just one more year"** *and it is recognized within the deeper implication, of the impact of time, as applied occasionally in the spiritual context of language that,* **"One day is as a thousand years to the Lord."** *Surely, this was plenty of time (it displays the magnificent patience of God) for the nation of Israel to have gotten its act together and in the broader context encompassing all of humanity.* ***2 Peter 3:8 "But do not forget this one thing, dear friends: With the Lord a day is like a thousand years, and a thousand years are like a day."*** *If we apply this time being meaningless to God declaration in the literal sense depicted within spiritual language, the owner of the fig tree (God) is being asked by the gardener to give the tree one last season to fulfill its purpose; just one last season. A season enclosed within the year of three hundred sixty-five days, or expressed in spiritual language: 365,000 years. Time has no impact upon God, and yet, everything he does has perfect timing! Surely this is immense patience! The disciples of Jesus asked him,* **"Lord, how many times should we forgive our brother, seven?"** *Jesus replies,* **"I tell you, seventy times seven."** *Again, we are shown the immeasurable patience and tolerant capacity of God's love. Now let us understand that within the context of God's patience being tremendously forgiving, he is also aware of the fact that there are some who will bear fruit by the extension of time and there are those that will never bear fruit or fulfill the purpose of creation.*

The cursed fig tree did meet its demise within the physical withering and apparent dying, but in truth the fig tree had presented itself as healthy on the outside but its root system was already dead. This deadness represented the hypocrisy of the nation's religious rule, concerned only with the appearance of righteousness that afforded to them accolades, from those striving to enter the false kingdom of God. They presented and projected righteousness, but underneath their facade they were as corrupt as dead men's bones, absent any intent to fulfill God's purpose. These religious had been given the ingredients necessary for bearing fruit but had not. Unfortunately for those religious the pretense of righteousness was unveiled and the grand play with its accomplished actors had been determined to see its last curtain call. God turned on the lights and made visible the scenery constructed of lies. The people engrossed and misled by the screenplay and eloquent speeches, scripted to capture a portrait of righteousness, will have an excuse before God. For those willfully engaged in denying God's purpose for us, they will find a most critical eye as Jesus pronounces the words, ***"I never knew you!"***

What difference can we expect to find insofar as the outcome of our lives, should we continue to deny God's purpose for us? By not fulfilling the purpose of God we are already dead. Dead men have no potential for living a rewarding life. Jesus cursed the fig tree to help the religious realize their existing state of hypocrisy, and in this profound example of death (quickly engulfing), they should have found a more pronounced awareness of need for truth; a life with purpose and meaning. Everything in this world shouts to us our obvious need for God. Perhaps because it is so obvious we do not recognize the simplicity of its call to heed the signs of the season?

The book of Job states, ***"The Lord gives and the Lord takes away."*** *Again,* ***"I came into the world with nothing and with nothing I shall leave."*** *This should not be looked upon as a negative. Rather, if we honestly look upon the condition of our life (before God gave us purpose) it is the negatives that had inhabited our being that have been removed. Our friend Job, within his lamentation spoke truly, however, as with all scriptural utterance there is always more than what can be considered obvious perception. If the truth is told there are some who will leave this world with more than what they had upon entering, namely salvation. Predestination is understood in recognition of a foundational prerequisite, (God claiming us as his own before our birth), but still, it may be argued that our new spirit was not received until after we were born again. As such, we leave this life with salvation awareness, something we did not have upon entering.*

Jesus cursed the fig tree because it failed to fulfill its purpose. Let us look for a moment at the significance of the fig tree representing to us our need for dependence upon God. We need to eat to continue life. On a deeper-level we find God removing a source of false nutrition (hypocrisy) and with removal a true source of sustenance can be found. Moreover, the demise of the tree is warning to all that failure to portray and provide creation's purpose will result in judgment. The outward display of foliage, or, as in the case of the religious, an outward presentation of righteousness, could not negate the inherent deficiencies of deep-rooted darkness. The purpose of the tree was not only to provide figs. It was useful for offering shade and refuge from the heat or difficulties that the environment of life may present. It offered to man and to all of God's creatures of the earth the awareness of God's love for his creation. The religious leaders failed to provide the fruit of truth to the populace; the truth concerning God. They failed to give assuring comfort from the heat produced by the troubles in life, or, shelter from the rains that bring chills, when one believes they are totally exposed and left to their own resources. The very act of man seeking to satisfy his needs through the creation of God is an admission of our need. Most trees, even in death could still find purpose within the context of building materials, and in the case of the first creation it offered its leaves as clothing in a time of naked awareness. However, Jesus found no redemptive qualities in the fig tree even after death, and in this we recognize the underlining failure of those religious whose only concern was for their selves.

Let's not forget the tree embracing Jesus at the time of crucifixion had not known its true purpose until after being cut down and fashioned into a cross. This says to us that our own total-purpose is still hidden from our sight. Moreover, by Jesus displaying the power of God focused upon the unfruitful fig tree, as an example of failure to fulfill purpose, he brings us to a point where we should recognize where things were in our lives, where they should be now, and how they will ultimately be for those who will or will not recognize their need for God. Non-recognition of our need for God is tantamount to ingrate status. The fig tree was like the first supermarket that carried both utilitarian as well as necessary components, blended within an ambience pleasing to man and offering to us an awareness of our need for continued existence. Unlike the fig tree having perhaps a limited role in the grand play of life, we are much more complex. In this complexity, we find the fragility of life ever more present and the need for God that much more apparent. And so, we find it is true that God gives to us the vision necessary for life and he takes away the things that obscure our need for him. The foliage of a tree in-bloom will not catch us unaware of its hidden deficiencies solely because it appears wholesome from a distance. We have learned to recognize what is good for us and affords to us the components necessary for continued life, through our knowledge that God provides for all our needs. We will find all that we need if we look to him instead of the attractions of a good play that portrays righteous living, or the shining allurement of this world that seeks to advocate permissiveness never intended for mankind, within the design criteria of God.

Sad Me

I looked up at him shining down on me and I felt sad.
I knew that he would be there long after I'm dead.
With bold warning, I withdrew a sisal sword from my mind.
Cutting away at the old man sending him adrift among the stars.
I realized nothing could cut away at the fabric of my mind.
It was not dependent upon things of this world.
Nothing could touch cut bend or see the spirit of me.
Nothing of substance power or force,
persuasion deception erosion or loss
Nothing except for the one who gave it
could ignore destroy or save it.
This made me feel glad, so in the blink of
an eye the old man was back.

Proverbs 16:22 Understanding is a fountain of life to those who have it, but folly brings punishment to fools.

Understanding is meaning explained, wisdom is knowledge necessary for prudence and all of this is grasped through the guidance of big brother truth. We just might want to let that last quotation from proverbs bounce around within the corridors normally filled with activity produced by external intrusion. What is immediate in recognition of the obvious is the quality of life derived through understanding. Understanding of consequence relative to decisions made, without thought to the aftereffects will usually bring forth bad fruit. The deficiency of the fruit can have a great or minimal impact upon the quality of our lives, based upon the number of times we fail to understand the inappropriate and otherwise debilitating nature of a malnourished state of being. Herein we see the necessity for us to not only bear fruit, but it is required of us to bear good fruit, for ourselves, as well as those who we make-contact with. Our avowed faith leads others expecting to find the richness of a tree planted by the river of life. Within the understanding awareness of God becoming a reality of life, we are then treated to a resurrection-moment illuminating purpose, with meaning, that incorporates and infuses goodness to everything impacted by the gentle voice of wisdom urging us to abundant life.

Isaiah 45:9-12 "Does a clay pot argue with its maker, a pot that is like all others? Does the clay ask the potter what he is doing? Does the pot complain that its maker has no skill? Do we dare say to our parents, 'Why did you make me like this?' The Lord, the holy God of Israel, the one who shapes the future, says: "You have no right to question me about my children or to tell me what I ought to do! I am the one who made the earth and created human beings to live there."

The highest mountain

The passage above is a reminder of the absolute, unquestionable, position of authority that rests solely within the Almighty. It is he who created everything for us to live, and the purpose for this is clearly defined in our conscience.

Just as a pot has a specific purpose so it is all things in existence have purpose. All things do not have the same physical purpose, or the same value (responsibility) given inherently through the instillation of God himself into his creation. A tree bears fruit, gives shelter and in some is used for construction of homes people dwell in. Ultimately for some of these trees they are either sent to the fire to heat such homes or lay upon the ground to rot and return to the origin of its existence. In the final analysis, we must conclude that the purpose of the tree had been fulfilled. Yes, even with those trees that have fallen and over time shall rot upon the ground therein is purpose fulfilled. It returns to the earth from which it came. This is not only a form of renewal for the earth but everything that dwells upon the earth will benefit from such additive contained within the decomposed tree. This process of decomposition designed into nature by God, brilliantly displays the good intention and continual offering of goodness, permanently established within the completed handiwork of our creator. Decomposition may very well be a default system brought about by sin's entrance into the natural world? We understand all that God's creates is perfect, as such, when God created everything, creation was perfect and perhaps such perfection meant nothing experienced the death attached to sin?

Whenever we look at nature apart from humanity we find a continuous ability for such creation to adhere to the intent of the one who created for a specific purpose. Even within the things we may not have realized (early on) in the creative and seeking faculty of man we find additional purpose and/or usages. Example: A few hundred years ago, we would not have thought of a baseball bat or a wood console for a car but incorporated within the design of the tree God knew such usage would come to be. He also knew of the tree being used to crucify the, ***"Lord of Glory."*** *And so, we can recognize that God permits many things to exist, even those that can be utilized to fulfill the evil intent of man. What this tells us is no matter what mankind may conceive as purpose for himself therein lives the absolute knowledge vested within the creator to make all things right. No matter how we may incorrectly utilize creation,* *let's say, the pot, God has ability to correct its existence even when it is used to strike someone in the head with unrighteous intent. Can we say that the purpose of the pot was to strike someone? Of course, not, but the potential for misuse is inherent within all things in nature. Well, there is the deeper philosophical question asking, "If the pot was used to defend one's life during an unjust assault, will it then become added to the righteous purpose of the pot?" Of course, we must answer, "Yes." And so, we have arrived at the understanding that purpose is built into creation via intent and that everyone can recognize proper usage when utilized in a righteous manner. The pot is then credited with fulfillment of purpose (because of righteous usage) and dependent upon the lifespan of the pot there is no number in which such proper usage in a righteous manner is assigned. The same is true regarding the yield of a fig tree, it is expected to provide its purpose so long as it lives. This is no less true of the existence of man. We are brought into existence to fulfill our purpose, in the acknowledgement of God and in service to him.*

As with the tree we are expected to bring forth goodness reflecting God's intent for man. The apple doesn't fall far from the tree; it is readily understood they are connected. God and man are connected and this connection should be readily recognized, immediately understood, within the goodness exhibited within the provision of God and the works of men. ***John 15:5 "I am the vine and you are the branches. If a man remains in me and I in him, he will bear much fruit; apart from me he can do nothing."*** *The purpose of man is clearly defined in this passage from John. Producing the fruit-of-purpose fulfills God's intent, and should be recognized by us that such fruitful endeavors are not exclusively for ourselves, but are primarily for those who are not connected to the truth of God; without the truth of God the potential for achieving anything good is made to be singular and confined, in the understanding that even bad people know how to give good things to those they love. Let us remember, it is we who represent a good fig tree, producing such intended good-fruit for others. It is we who are connected to the source of life and in this we can share* *with others the fruit of truth. We must be the same on the inside as perceived by others in the manner in-which we live our lives. What does Jesus mean by his saying those separated from him can do nothing? Apart from Christ bad fruit is produced. Bad fruit or deeds will only lead to sickness and ultimately death and judgment. At that point nothing in a person's life is recognized as an accomplishment.*

If we fail to bear good fruit what good is anything we may have achieved, or anything that we may have amassed? ***"What good is it for a man to gain the whole world, and forfeit his soul?"*** *Jesus is telling us we need to be connected to him, in-order to not only fulfill our purpose and complete our potential, but to know what our purpose in life is. When purpose is, unknown many roads appear as wide and diverse, but nowhere is to be found the narrow and straight road that leads to eternal life. The struggles in life are made much more difficult when we attempt to overcome and achieve alone.*

Such failure of purpose will only find us under the same curse as the fig tree. Hypocrisy will not bring to us a full life or offer to us a blessing in the life to come. It was the hypocrisy of the fig tree, with its outward presentation, saying to all, "I am healthy and am producing much good as is intended in my creation by God." Underneath the outward deception lived the false and intended rebellion against God's intent. This hypocrisy points us to the lives of many whose outward façade declares allegiance to God, adherence to his purpose for us, but is denied within the unseen rebellion that declares a denouncement of God's purpose, and installs the will and desires of man in its place. When a man denounces God in favor of his nature there is going to be trouble.

Man, has already rebelled and has been contaminated by the infusion of sin from the very first disobedient act. It is this act of sinful rebellion that places hindrance and obstacles in the way of our true purpose. We find the desires of our lives are not concerned with the needs of others when sin rules. It is only when we are set free from sin's rule that we begin to understand the wonderful qualities contained within virtues. The need of others pertains to their reception and acceptance of truth; the truth that had been rejected or kept hidden in favor of our own pronouncement regarding purpose. Such purpose, very often places us at the pinnacle of importance and in this we are unable to see our real reason for living and our true potential, apart from the self-gratification derived from producing an outward picture of ourselves. Like the religious rulers during the time of Jesus, they craved the accolades from the common man; outwardly they were perceived as producing much fruit, fulfilling their potential within the intention of God, but underneath they were corrupt and unable to bear fruit that would certainly have aided the populace. They knew the truth of God, would not adhere to it and neither would they permit others the knowledge of his love. This is the height of hypocrisy and when truth is withheld wickedness emerges.

Natural inclination

In the utilization of the pot used for self-protection what we find with respect to righteous and/or unrighteous use is determined by intent. The pot is made from the natural resource of clay. This pot (representing us) was initially produced without any foreign substances that are intended to hinder and deny purpose and potential. We must also recognize not all materials are of natural origin. As such, their composition may be a mix of both righteous and unrighteous origins. The born-again spirit and the body of man is such a mixture of both righteous and unrighteous substances.

Example: *Synthetics (substances produced by chemicals) also have purpose and expectation of fulfillment, either righteous or unrighteous usage, dependent upon intent. These chemically manufactured substances can be medicines used to heal or weaponry used to kill not only people but also the environment or creatures within such environment. And so, what we understand is that we do not know everything relating to substances within nature or those manmade. Their purpose will be ultimately understood within the intent of the one who employs such material. The origin of man is both, of the earth and of God. It is God who breathed life into the clay of the earth and only then did man become alive. As such God's intent for man was and is righteous. When man denies his purpose he ultimately denies God. The one who is born again is made spiritually acceptable to God but the body is still sinful. Such a blend finds a tug-of-war between knowledge of truth and the desire to live in accordance with God's ways, and opposing these are the desires of the flesh and the sin that is alive within us, continually urging us away from the ways God has made known to us.*

Multipurpose potential

The failure of a fig tree to fulfill its designed purpose finds condemnation. This curse can be looked upon as the declaration that took away life, which was initially granted within creation's purpose. Failure to fulfill purpose will always cost one's life. This one fig tree had displayed the external signs of fulfillment of purpose, but underneath such façade there was nothing but empty promise. There was no excuse for not producing the figs, not disease or any number of valid reasons was evident to Jesus. As such we witness the judgment of Jesus pronounced upon the hypocrisy (fault) within the existence of the tree. There is another lesson to be understood in this retelling of the cursed tree, and that is, within the existence of man there is built into his purpose great potential, so long as we are understanding/recognizing our creator's purpose for us. Acceptance of God is a vital aspect of our purpose and this can be clearly understood by acknowledging we have not come into existence without thought and work. Clearly all that is seen in nature is not accidental, as some would have us believe. Regarding the pot there was thought necessary to articulate its design, and work was necessary to bring such natural resources together in a meaningful manner. This purposeful creation is no less true in mankind. Lastly, there is consequence for not fulfilling purpose. The fig tree episode is both an accounting of an actual event and a parable combined. The underlining recognition of the fig tree's disappointing offering (its appearance of promise) finds the same disappointment in the exterior presentation of those who outwardly acknowledge the reality of God's truth, but underneath their presentation is the hypocrisy that brings forth the judgment of God. Just as in all of scripture we will find deeper meaning so long as we seek to find it, so it is with our purpose in life. We are not one dimensional with-regard to purpose.

Service

While it is true that all of humanity has the purpose to know, and to love, and to serve God, within this structure there is the ability to step forward and continue the intent of our creator, which is diverse. Not all of us have the same calling in life, apart from our needing to know love and serve God. There is tremendous diversity within the myriad of occupations presented for man and many purposefully serve the betterment of mankind. Example: Doctors and nurses as well as those who provide essential services are all recognized as perfectly well and good in the eyes of God. Those who will not work to provide a service for the betterment of mankind and creation have failed to bear fruit. The words of Jesus in response to the disciples regarding who would be the greatest in the kingdom of God makes us aware of our purpose: ***"He who would be greatest among you must serve the others."***

Jesus showed to us his purpose throughout his public life as one who continually served with intent to make better the present condition of man. It is only when man fails to recognize his basic purpose (know love and serve God) that he begins to fail in all other aspects of life. Let me say that again: failure in life comes to us through our denial of purpose incorporated within man, as a part of God's original intent for man. On a basic level, such service orientation directly articulates the desire of God for man to love one another. When man's love is focused upon self, when his knowledge is limited to his own intellect (the fool is now being born) and finally, when his purpose is prideful-self-centered and self-promoting therein lives the curse spoken to the fig tree, ***"You will never bear fruit!"***

Unlimited potential with faith

The potential of man is and never has been limited so long as we are connected to God in the knowledge of his righteous intent for us. This is realized in his love for us, and in this overall recognition that it is we who are both servant and sons. We were not created for God to serve us. ***Matthew 21:28-31 "What do you think? There was a man who had two sons. He went to the first and said, 'Son, go and work today in the vineyard.' 'I will not,' he answered, but later he changed his mind and went. Then the father went to the other son and said the same thing, he answered, 'I will, sir,' but he did not go. Which of the two did what his father wanted? "The first," they answered. Jesus said to them, "I tell you the truth, the tax collectors and the prostitutes are entering the kingdom of God ahead of you."*** *The willful failure of the one son, who said he would do as the father wanted, goes beyond the hypocrisy of pretense. It is a lie that had to be made with the intent to deceive the one who loves us the most. It is this degree of deception wherein total trust is placed in a son that is most hurtful in the eyes of our, Lord. Such was the condition of the religious during the time of Jesus. By Jesus saying that tax collectors and prostitutes are entering the kingdom of God ahead of you, he is speaking to those whose false, outward expression of righteousness does not go undetected by God. He is highlighting the fact that he (Jesus) did not come into the world to save the righteous but to save the sinner. As long, as a man will think himself to be righteous he will continually be placed at the back of the line. Both the Pharisee and the sinner have the capacity to be cleansed from the sins of their lives, but if one thinks he is not a sinner salvation becomes very improbable. There will come a time when the last chance to bear fruit will have passed and in this the tree is chopped down and tossed into the fire.*

There comes a time to grow up

It is true that while we were children our parents served us, and, we began to understand the true place for our parents. Just as the pot can never be lifted above the potter, so it is we can never rise above God. If in our minds and hearts, we place ourselves into a superior position, therein the flower of pride has bloomed. It is exceedingly immature for us not to recognize the sacrifices our parents have made for our welfare; the same is true when we fail to recognize the sacrifice made for us in the Cross of Christ.

Potential denied

All too often we are prompted by so-called church leaders to focus upon: "If you do this and this and this, God will do this," kind of theology. There appears to be one continuous campaign to raise funds, albeit through a pledge, or a partnership involving tithes and/or sermons seeking donations within the "do this and get that" theology of so-called prosperity churches. One example of this is the seemingly constant drone from church leaders (mostly the electronic church wherein they have been dubbed the, "Name it and claim it congregations"), seeking donations under what they present as truth in scriptural understanding. Simply because tithing is mentioned in the bible it is presented as a practice that should be carried-over into the present-day church; implying, God will enrich those who practice tithing.

Stoning people to death is also mentioned in scripture and should we continue such action today? The problem with modernizing tithing within Christianity is that it places limitation on what is acceptable to God; we all know there may come a time when everything we have may be asked for. Within the example of the life of Jesus, he demonstrated our need to understand that God will always provide for our needs. He will not only provide but he will permit miracles entrance into the believer's life. That is, God will make a way for us when we cannot see any way possible. ***"But if you believe, you will receive whatever you ask for in prayer."*** *This understanding permits us to become a part of the overall purpose of God's intent for man. Tithing sounds too much like a modern day financial portfolio management firm. The church of, "You give you get! God is now your financial manager!"*

Acts 4:36-37 Joseph, a Levite from Cyprus, whom the apostles called Barnabas (which means the son of encouragement) sold a field he owned and brought the money and put it at the apostles' feet. *This man named Joseph sold the field in support of the needs of the church and its members. He was not coerced badgered or constantly imposed upon to do so; moreover, he gave all the proceeds of the sale to the church. In the church's early-history the followers of Jesus had received the Holy Spirit and in this receipt God placed upon the heart of Joseph the need for him to support the church in this manner. It is possible that what takes place with Ananias and his wife in the following chapter of Acts was a desire by them to gain acknowledgement and favor from the apostles, in the same way Joseph brought honor to himself through obedience to God. Joseph was honest and truthful while both Ananias and his wife had lied to the Holy Spirit and it cost them their lives. There was no pressure on anyone to sell all they owned and give the proceeds to the church, as such, regarding today's constant outreach for tithing from church leaders, what we see is the (complete) opposite of what had taken place in the early church. Everyone knows there is a collection taken during the service and to constantly focus on the tithing issue is to indirectly say to the congregants, "Come on, you cheapskates, fork it over!" We here so much about "seed planting" and the expectation of many returns in our "investment" one might think we are sitting-in on a Wall Street meeting of bankers. The desire for self-acquisition will always find additional needs disallowing completion of purpose, and the incompleteness of a life lived totally concerned with self-promotion. When we serve others what we find is blessing, for in such service the tree bears fruit. Again, there is no set amount or limit to the blessings God will give to us, as such, our giving to others should always have the caveat: unlimited. There may come a time when we must give considerably, (not necessarily in a church setting), and when our heart is right we will recognize such a time. We can look at the time Jesus fed five-thousand people with just a couple of fish and five loaves of bread, in this we see that it is God who provides, fulfilling his intent for others. As the disciples aided to alleviate a need, so it is we also help to provide within the provision of God.*

Tithing has set a limit upon our giving that says, "requirement met!" The Old Testament witness concerning the ways in which people should conduct their lives, and how they should treat the giving of resources for the upkeep of temple operations, has had its place in time. The tithing aspect was fulfilled in its proper timeframe, and should not be made a requirement or continually suggested by church leaders as New Testament protocol. The apostles never asked Joseph to sell his land and then give to them the proceeds; he did this because he saw the need and was moved by the Holy Spirit to do so. Many others, who owned land or houses also gave willfully all they had for the needs of everyone. The believer in Christ's message and the knowledge of God providing for all should find its proper place of recognition. The utmost responsibility of man within the myriad of our needs is for us to be found to be good and faithful servants in this life. It is of utmost importance to fulfill our purpose, which is summed up in the Lord's Prayer. **"Thy will be done on earth as it is in heaven."** *This acceptance-qualifier within our purpose is basically for us to know God and the love he has sent to us in the person of his Son. From this foundation of knowing God all meaning and purpose in life is presented, in the same way a banquet table is set before a king; nothing is hidden. Notice, the church members gave everything they had from the proceeds of land and home sales. No comparison to tithing! Why aren't we following New Testament foundational behavior? The answer is simply that the leaders would have to relinquish their luxurious lifestyles!*

Dependence

It was from the failure of mankind that we became in need of a Savior. Everything in life has needs in-order to survive. When, was it determined that man has no need apart from his own ingenuity and self-reliant prideful attitude? When, was it determined that so long as there is shelter and food and of course the Internet that man is then perfectly provided for? When, was it forgotten that the grave is still looming largely upon the horizon of man's existence? Within the world's population both individually and collectively as a whole there seems to be a discounting or outright denial of God. Is God denied and discounted because man has found defeat in death? He laments, "There's nothing I can do about death!" Or else, "We have looked-into the purpose of God for us, and we have thumbed our nose at the prospect of having to follow a designed intent to love each other as God has loved us."

Reset

Now that is an interesting thought. We have been reset (by being born again) to follow creation's design. This should not come to us as something farfetched. After all God knew us before he created the foundations of the earth, and so it is not a great leap of understanding that he should know exactly who we are and to who and/or what we shall give our allegiance. We will follow the designed intent set forth by God, or we will choose to become a self-directing vehicle driving through life within the darkness of our hearts, absent true direction and unfulfilled purpose that ultimately will face the grave and the great Day of Judgment. We will face judgment because of our failure to concede to the reality of truth clearly seen in all of creation. As a light is lit to show to us the way, so it is also shining within us declaring the knowledge of what is acceptable to God. It is our responsibility to choose. How fair and just is God? Even with God knowing who he will save (believe him) he still permits those destined for judgment (judgment equals conviction) to live in-order to prove his prejudgment (predestination) to be correct. Just as Job with all his trials proved God to be correct in his assessment of him.

Idolatry is failed purpose

Isaiah 44:9-10 "All those who make idols are worthless, and the gods they prize so highly are useless. Those who worship these gods are blind and ignorant-and they will be disgraced. It does no good to make a metal image to worship as a god!"

In this statement by Isaiah what is found is truly remarkable. An unveiling of truth is taking place not only within man's failure to render to God what belongs to him, (indicative by his actions, contained within the manufacturing of gods), but, man is perhaps inadvertently, admitting to the existence of someone of higher status, thus there is no excuse for the rejection of God, only to be replaced by the unrighteous intent of man. Belief or knowing of life, understood to be higher than the existence of man is self-incriminating. Yes, it shows an awareness of another lifeform totally apart from humanity and unburdened by limitation and death, but in this, recognition, a man is confronted with a choice regarding which God and/or gods to recognize and ultimately follow. The preaching of Isaiah clears this up in the minds and hearts of those who did not know of the one true God. Still many chose not to listen to truth, just as mankind today, refuses to listen and affirm truth.

This refusal on the part of mankind to recognize truth is repugnant and insulting to God. How can man make an idol-image and expect to find some sort of reward or advantage from manmade objects, representing the imaginations of men? It is obvious mankind had found frustration within his own limitation; and in the desire to break free from limitation, relied upon intuitive knowledge that understood, not only, limitation but also his creation origin.

This advantage prospect is probably the most compelling argument for such creativeness in the heart of man's ambitions. You see, mostly all of man's ambitions are self-centered and hardly ever righteous in the eyes of God. As such, it may be a factoring thought and/or a contributing motive in the rebellion of man to search-out and to find a god who will permit all of man's ambitions and desires within the heart and soul that decides to live in darkness. Let us recognize that within the greater understanding of darkness, what we find is an intention to not divulge a hidden agenda. With bad intent therein lives deception and purposeful deception is wickedness. Where there is purposeful deception we will always find its creator, the devil. Idol worship is in-effect worship of evil spirits who have aspired to become gods. While it's true idols are labeled as, ***"nothings"*** *by God, what we can and will find within* *the worship of such* ***"nothings,"*** *is a clear invitation to the evil spirits positioned against God to fill the vacated position caused by man's rejection of God. Man, exercises faith (wrongly, apart from God) and when he gets a response he is duped into thinking he has found a reality of heavenly proportion; this adds confirmation to the initial intuitive knowledge pointing to creation. So-true are the words of the prophet:* ***"Those who worship these gods are blind and ignorant-and they will be disgraced."***

The reference to being blind is understood as living in the darkness of unknowing; clarity is never found in one's own inner-being. The declaration of being ignorant is one that is obvious: anyone who chooses to insult God, to replace him as the author of all that exists is not only ignorant, but is foolish, to think God can be circumvented, dethroned, made to be equal to the imaginations of man, is surely on the road to becoming, "disgraced." Worship of idols for profit or advantage is on par with selling one's soul to the devil. It is not as direct as the temptation of Jesus in the desert, but indirectly it is in the same category. Worship was given to not only receive advantage over limitations, but also, there is the attempt to satisfy the demanding for material acquisition.

Advertisement

When an opening for a vacant position is presented in an advertisement therein will be found the requirement(s) expected of such candidates applying for the position. The apostle Paul in his visit to Greece noticed they had a tremendous number of gods, (just as Isaiah had preached against idols, here again, we find idolatry running wild among the Gentiles). It can be safely-said, manmade idols were produced on-demand for the specific purpose of the buyer. One may very well have walked into an idol maker's shop and requested a god to protect against a malady or a potential crisis or to be blessed with prosperity, or any number of the imaginations of man. One thing is perfectly clear: when there is a vacancy in the heart because man has rejected or is unknowing God, there will be many candidates aspiring to fill the position.

In this situation, we will always find the chief of demonic activity seeking to fill the vacancy either directly or through a myriad of surrogates. As such the trap that was set by man's own desires, his denial and refusal to adhere to his true purpose, finds the deception of evil spirits to have some merit; inasmuch, as the demonic forces will not miss an opportunity to convince the idolater of their worth, through the appearance of fulfillment of such desires requested by man to the god. Therein we find many who have fallen for this deception within false religions. These religions are not unknown to us and are widespread within certain regions of the world. In other instances, are kept at a lower level of awareness for fear of retribution. Certainly, there would be outcry here in America should we continually find dead chickens representing sacrificial offerings to the gods of voodoo or witchcraft on our front lawns. In-truth all the activities associated with witchcraft and voodoo, directly or indirectly will ultimately find worship of the Evil One. There are many things that are idolized; we even have television shows titled "idols." The underlining purpose of idolatry is the love of fame and fortune and/or advantage over our mortal and limited condition.

There is no other

Isaiah 45:5-6 I am the Lord, there is no other god. I will give you the strength you need, although you do not know me. I do this so that everyone from one end of the world to the other may know that I am the Lord and that there is no other god. *The Lord is most direct in his declaration that there is no other Lord, God, Creator, Giver of Life. He makes this declaration because he loves us! If God did not love us (as his children lost in the darkness of unknowing him) why would he care if we fell into deception and ruin? Now, in saying that he will give to us the strength we need even though we do not know him, what we find in the presentation, is that God provides for our needs even when we do not know him. He makes it rain, the crops to grow and the oceans to bring forth their bounty for the betterment of man. He creates light and darkness, blessing and disaster. He creates light for us to understand and* *he brings forth disaster to capture our attention. When disaster strikes, man will always set his sights toward God, even if he had never recognized him before. Wherever there's darkness preventing-knowledge it is God who lifts the darkness with his light. This is abundantly true for those who were held in darkness, kept blind by the* ***"evil god of this world."*** *(I am always fascinated by the bible using the descriptive of,* ***"this world."*** *Perhaps there are other worlds wherein there is an evil attempting to keep from the inhabitants the reality of the one true God?)*

Purpose

What purpose they who think not of God?
Who will save this wanting lot?
A balance beam of right and wrong
Takes not a forward step
Toward he who for sinners kept
The book of life before man breathe his first breath.
No purpose but receive
The pardon from God's throne appear
In flesh and blood behold
The sacrifice of God's own Son
He lives to save our souls.

Ephesians 1:11 In him we were chosen, having been predestined according to the plan of him who works out everything in conformity with the purpose of his will.

Told what we must do

Acts 9:4-6 He fell to the ground and heard a voice saying to him, "Saul, Saul, why do you persecute me?" "Who are you, Lord?" "I am Jesus whom you are persecuting," he replied. "Now get up and go into the city, and you will be told what you must do." *Saul (Paul) is told what he must do. While he was walking along going about his normal business of persecuting the infant church of Christ, he is brought into the reality of what his true purpose for being consisted of. It had remained hidden during the* *time of service to the religious rulers; their purpose was to remove any vestige of the truth of Christ's sacrifice for humanity. Paul embarks upon the task of bringing the good news to the world with the fervor of a man driven by both truth and the knowledge that he had contributed greatly to the darkness that had also held him in captivity. He is a man seeking to make amends for the damage he had incurred upon others. Such damage went so far as to being a party to the stoning of Stephen to death. He understood the task given to him and probably was critically aware that the same people he had served, would now be concerned enough with his conversion to label him a traitor and threat to their positions as religious rulers. Within our own conversion, we are aware of what we must do to begin to fulfill our purpose as God had intended. The very first thing we do after being born again is to read God's word. We want to know everything possible about the one who saved us!*

When we look at the life of the apostle Paul we see a man driven by love and truth, and perhaps self-condemnation. This determination is never diminished even with the knowledge that he is causing uproars just about everywhere he unveils deception, coupled with religious narrow-mindedness present in the world; and in the very synagogues he so vehemently defended at the expense of Christ's truth. Let's ask a moving question, one that's particularly penetrating and effectively relevant. First: Who was it that called-out to Saul while he was traveling to Damascus, in-order to continue the persecution of Christians? Yes, it was Jesus who put the brakes on Saul's persecution of the church. Second: Now let us ask one more question: Did this appearance of Jesus come before or after his ascension back to his Father's house? Chronologically Jesus had already ascended into the heavens, but here we see him transforming Saul, the hit man for the establishment into Paul of Christ. We are nine chapters deep into the book of Acts before Paul is converted. Earlier the Holy Spirit had been given to the apostles in Jerusalem on the day of Pentecost, in the second chapter of the book. And so, we must ask how this was accomplished? One other time that comes to mind, where we see an apocalyptic entrance, (which simply means a radical breakthrough) by God into the affairs of man is during the baptism of Jesus. The Holy Spirit comes down from above in the form of a dove and the voice of God the Father is heard saying, **"This is my Son, whom I love; with him I am well pleased."**

And so, what must we conclude by these breakthroughs into the natural world from the supernatural, especially when we see the account of Jesus being taken up into the heavens to be reunited with the Father? Our concept of distance traveled must be put aside and placed into an understanding of mystery. The omnipresence ability of God to be everywhere is highlighted for us in these occurrences. God is always with us, but he does not always make a big entrance, save for the few times in scripture that have attached to it the specific purpose of God and for the enlightenment of man. Surely there is the concept of a dimensional separation between the natural and supernatural spheres of existence; it cannot be seen by us, but then, neither can we see our thoughts. The natural world is one where movement is physical and measured; the movement of thought is beyond our ability to measure in terms of speed.

Idols

***Acts 17:16 While Paul was waiting for them in Athens, he was greatly distressed to see that the city was full of idols**. Paul is distressed, extremely upset and unhappy over the rampant idol worship that he witnessed permeated throughout the city. In his distress, he formulates a plan to introduce to them the one true God they had labeled,* **"The unknown god."** *Paul sees that the people are already religious and he needs only to point-out a new morality and truth heretofore unheard of in Athens. The people were accustomed to the understanding of gods who are above the existence shared by mankind. They were so aware of the gods that they had an entire industry geared to making the objects of worship assigned to the oversight into the affairs of men. They were in tune with the latest of gods who happened upon the scene. The industry that produced the idols would always support a new god, because it added to the demand for a product that had nothing to offer.*

Unfortunately for the idol-maker craft the one true God, about to be introduced, had forbidden idol worship a long time ago.

Paul distressed everyone connected with the idol making and worship industry. The craftsmen, priests, priestesses and temple attendants along with all who had invested faith in what was now being denounced as fantasy! Paul was bringing truth to the people of Athens, and in one fell swoop he shook the foundations of deception's grip that made it impossible for them to know the one true God. The idol maker industry along with the backing of everyone connected to the idolatry-for-profit scheme was not about to sit idle and let the golden goose perish. The word is spreading throughout the countryside and when Paul gets to Ephesus a riot breaks out directed against his preaching against false gods. Paul had left Athens and is now in Ephesus. Ephesus was located in modern day Turkey and can be reached by way of the Mediterranean Sea; a sea journey of approximately one-hundred to one hundred and fifty miles east of Athens.

A silversmith named Demetrius had called a union meeting and stated: ***"Men you know we receive a good income from this business. And you see and hear this fellow Paul has convinced large numbers of people here in Ephesus and practically the whole province of Asia. He says that manmade gods are no gods at all."*** *It was probably then that the riot started. We should not be surprised that the message Paul preached was toppling an industry that made a good income from the product it produced. Demetrius may have recognized through his intimate awareness of idol-making, the truth preached to the people by Paul. As such he was attempting to forestall the inevitable downfall of the industry that had been so lucrative. Demetrius recognized that the secrets guarded closely by the idol-makers, were being revealed, and the fresh air of truth had blown away the clouds, sufficiently enough for the people to see clearly. The clear voice of truth was also revealing something the people had never heard. They were being told that this one true God was seeking them! This one true God had sent his Son as a sacrifice for their sins and this one true God loves them! A tremendous revelation. Throughout the world and* *here at home the idol-maker industry has not been vanquished, they still have customers. I would love to see the reaction of Paul if he could walk into some of today's modern churches and places of worship. No doubt he would make more enemies. Even more interesting would be the look on his face if he found a statue named, Paul.*

The most potent form of idolatry

There are many things and even persons that some people may come to idolize but the most potent of all offerings to mankind is the worship of one's self. Therein we find the enamoring prospect of man himself achieving the god status formerly thought to be only present in images formed in the imaginations of man. Now we find that anyone seeking to become a god need only accept the fact that he is indeed a god! Acceptance of this has deeper implications than are present upon the surface of the offering. Just as the topping of a cake hides what is inside the layers, so it is with the pronouncement of godlike status within the heart of man. This also was and is the desire of the Evil One. It is he (Satan) who sought to become not just a god, but he aspires to be God. When a man finds-himself enamored with himself, and believing there is no limitation placed upon his actions, and that guilt presented by conscience is something that should be stripped away from the mind, therein we find someone who has been led into a place that offers nothing but empty promises; he will never find the peace associated with truth, or his true purpose.

It is a disgrace to not fulfill one's responsibility and authority vested in the human condition by God. As children, our parents are responsible for us, and as adults the world and family places much responsibility upon our shoulders. Sadly, there are many who refuse to be responsible parents or honest law-abiding citizens within society. If we cannot be trusted to care for the immediate responsibilities to family and society, it is likely we will not be focused upon the purpose God had intended. One of the adverse repercussions of failure to fulfill purpose and potential, is the nagging consequence of deeper and deeper involvement in the problems attached. By placing our responsibilities upon someone else, what we find is a constant attempt to avoid such purpose and potential; in this we are denied the life intended by God, in the here and now and in the life to come!

Obvious

Right and wrong perfection and flawed
Points-out a concept that can't be ignored.
Absent this truth why have any laws?
Why label as criminal the ways of man?
Why are some things accepted and others condemned?
Reason assaulted by folly-deaf to the soft voice within
A trip to the outer fringes bends to all blowing winds.
What is apparent cannot be denied.
Truthful conditions are not in debate-
neither is man's inevitable fate.
Good is no doubt a much better state.
What then is a man who sees not the gate?
Who knows not the signs of errant 'til late?
Who denies the truth placed into his hand?
A moment in time-breath quickly exhaled
Unknowing denying the clear view ahead
Is a life that has failed eternity's test!

Proverbs 27:18 Take care of a fig tree and you will have figs to eat.

Matthew 7:15-20 "Be on your guard against false prophets; they come to you looking like sheep, but on the inside they are really like wolves. You will know them by what they do. Thorn bushes do not bear grapes, and briers don't bear figs. A healthy tree bears good fruit, but a poor tree bears bad fruit. A healthy tree cannot bear bad fruit, and a poor tree cannot bear good fruit. And any tree that does not bear good fruit is cut down and thrown into the fire. So then, you will know the false prophets by what they do."

You will know them by what they do

We will know the truth by the way it is presented. We will know truth by the manner-in which those speaking such truth, conduct their lives. Speech does not need to be of the spoken variety, actions often are telling. Everything in life that is presented to us within a public setting is scripted, pruned and orchestrated in such a manner so as, to not permit imperfection entrance. The smiles are plastic; hand gestures are contrived and deliberately made to be identifiable. Cupped-hand and semi-circled movement is clearly the action of one seeking to be non-telling. It is so timid and non-threatening, as well as not real, for there is no real emotion behind the gesture. It is a non-offensive movement with intent to recognize the masses but underlying it all is the reality of, "I couldn't care any less." Authoritative gestures are intended to forestall inquiry into wrongdoing. Finger pointing while denying an accusation (especially from one in a position of power) is meant as a threatening gesture. There is much to consider within the constant array of tactics designed to not make known the underlying guilt, motives, and actions of wrong. Still, we are warned to guard against false prophets, who will not serve God or his purpose; neither will we see the good fruit that must accompany the man or woman of God, in the pretentious hypocrisy many believe is hidden from view.

"A healthy tree cannot bear bad fruit." *Jesus is telling us to be on guard against those who may look like they belong to the flock but in-reality they don't. Their motives are like wolves seeking only to destroy. Their intent is much more devious, for once they gain a foothold in the congregational flock their primary purpose is to find a leadership role among the sheep in-order to deny to them the truth. A sense of permissiveness, is introduced into the fold and in this there is a broadened understanding of what is acceptable. This is not much different from the ongoing internal compromises we are confronted with throughout life. Heralded as the teachings of Jesus, these false doctrinal interpretations, presentation of falsehoods, presented to new converts (everyone was new to the faith then, and even now, there are always new converts), these so-called prophets were causing a directional change away from truth* *to the point it may be almost imperceptible to those weak in the faith. The attention of the flock is made to focus upon the so-called prophet and all attention and awareness of being in the presence of God during worship and/or church gathering is lost, lending a social club attitude to the atmosphere. When we're unmindful or are denied the understanding that during times of worship or church gathering, that we are in-truth presenting ourselves before the Lord, our worship is absent the reality of both awareness of the presence of God and the love we must show to him. Certainly, this misleading will force us to lose track of our true purpose in this life. Yes,* ***"Be on your guard against false prophets."***

Desire what will advance God's purpose for us

Psalm 90:12 Teach us to number our days aright, that we may gain wisdom of heart. *NAB*

The above scripture depicts the proper and correct manner-in which we should approach life. We do not properly number our days, simply because we don't have the proper guidance or understanding of when life shall come to an end. The ability to number our days properly will gain for us a heart of wisdom.

We can be wise in many areas of thought, that points to the way we should live; but to have a heart of wisdom is to compile intellect and reason with the attributes of love. In so doing we are freed from the burden of the specter of death; wisdom recognizes the reality of God and recognition of the total purpose of God for us; there is no longer the depressing foreboding sadness made manifest by the illusion of death's finality; the promises of Christ lend and fortify anticipating joy for the life to come! We begin to understand that many things clutter our lives and are unnecessary; they present a hindrance to that which is important and should properly find our attention. The more clutter present the less time there is to focus upon our true purpose.

The above verse from the prayer of Moses is one in which he has attributed total recognition of the power of God to accomplish anything. He is mindful of his as well as the sins of the nation being set before God, and in this alone he is terrified, because of the consequence such transgressions produce; there is always a consequence for sin; just ask the king of Egypt how his failure to heed the warnings of God ended. As such, he asks for a heart of wisdom in-order to accomplish the true purpose of life that extends beyond just the pure intellect of man. He wants the emotional center of his life to be made alive, by combining his intellect, reasoning and emotions, he will then gain a complete sense of wisdom, necessary to fulfill his true purpose. He ends the prayer by saying, ***"May the favor of the Lord rest upon us; establish the work of our hands for us-yes, establish the work of our hands."*** *He is asking the Lord to permit the work that God accomplishes to be seen by all; he wants the work of God to be reflected in the works of mankind. In addition, he is asking to permit the work of man to prosper with the approval of God. By showing us how to number our days properly we learn not only to prioritize our activities but also to ask for the things we need in-order to fulfill his intended purpose for us. The primary purpose of God's intent (for us) is and always has been our salvation; once that is accomplished every other gift-wrapped blessing is made known. We need only to open the gift. All other times of blessing (before salvation) have come to us as unknowing children at Christmas time; never knowing the real Santa Claus is our parents. We were taught to pray: "Our Father, who art in heaven." Even when we don't know him, he is there for us!*

Ask, seek, knock, speaks of dependence

Matthew 7:8 Ask and it will be given to you; seek and you will find; knock and the door will be opened to you. For everyone who asks receives; he who seeks finds; and to him who knocks, the door will be opened." *If today, we find ourselves in need we may lapse into a language that's related to code. There's a difficulty in our makeup that prevents us from asking for help. I suspect at some time in the past this was not the case. Neighbors and even* *strangers were more in-tune with the needs of others. With respect to strangers it is recognized that from the largest of charitable organizations to the panhandler on the street, the charity of others has been abused. As such, people have become distrustful when asked through advertisements, or directly, to give, and perhaps those in need did not want to be lumped-in with the scam artists; a consequence of such distrust caused reluctance on the part of the receiver and giver's positions.*

It had almost become laughable when beggars would enter a subway car in New York City with a request for donations; this asking soon became flavored with a small amount of intimidation, adding to the belief that there was not an existing need. Instead, what was presented as need became understood as scam! Ultimately, what was always immediately alleviated at times of need within communities, found withdrawal from the afflictions of others, and deception's intent impacted those truly in need. On a larger scale, charitable organizations today have also found sufficient scandal, that has placed a doubtful cloud over the asking for help. This doubtful barrier of disbelief also impacts our belief in the existence of God, because there are also scam-artists within established churches and some of these so-called preachers have been dragged off to prison in tears! Jesus is pointing us to, he, who alone is incorruptible; he who has never been associated with deception; in this (truth) we ask of God with confidence and in our realization and trust we will never be disgraced, disappointed or deceived!

By asking seeking and knocking we are displaying the wisdom that recognizes our dependence; understanding dependence tells our pride and wariness to "relax," permitting humility to take its rightful place in the presence of God. Once we recognize our dependence we must then acknowledge to what and to who it is we are dependent upon. There were many times Jesus spoke in parables, but in this-instance we are given direction in plain simple language. There are those who are still having trouble asking for help from God. They know how to demand from others what is believed to be "entitlements" but to ask of God finds no avenue of approach. The descriptive of entitlement has worked its way into vocabulary; no longer, is what was worked for exclusive in the understanding of what a person is entitled too. Because we understand a person in need should not be left to starve to death and is "entitled" to be rescued from his condition, the descriptive of entitlement has been expanded to mean all of man's needs being accommodated by government. We demand of government and they produce because we are made to believe in entitlement meaning "needy." Has God been usurped by worldly authority seeking to replace him? Even within the inner recesses of our heart we can find it difficult to internalize our needs; animosity has been established within an entitlement mindset; completely opposed to recognition of something being earned. It is only with God do we receive what has not been earned! We deserve judgment but have received mercy.

Pride of course is an inhibitor against "asking" but there is something else interwoven into the fabric of humanity, that prevents the realization as too just how fragile and dependent we really-are. It may have to do with the aspect of society that believes the inability to acquire, the most common of necessities is a weakness, and the inability to acquire the luxuries is a total failure. Finding one's self not acquiring the things of the world is equated with weakness and failure, and the opposite shouts of independence and success. Even when such failure to acquire is accepted by the individual because of cultural indoctrination or discrimination, one must not show the emotional sadness of defeat or else a slip in the community may follow. Of course, there is the chance that failure to acquire will bring about anger, and in this the laws of man are subject to be broken under the false narrative declaring, "All that matters and motivates is acquisition," because, 'I am entitled to this!' no matter what means are employed."

"A real man does not cry." Within some cultures this ability to keep the valid emotion of grief bottled-up is a mark of manhood. And so, we find counterfeit beliefs are slowly injected into the mindset of the young. By permitting such beliefs entrance into the mindset of a society an avenue of perpetuation is established,

wherein the inherent foundational weakness stands unopposed until the strong wind of truth appears and blows away the clouds of deception, that, precluded the knowledge of our need to understand our dependency upon God; the attainment of manhood is also not defined in the illusion of independence, as the world would have us embrace; such adulthood comes to each of us the day we acknowledge the reality of God and acquire the desire to seek the true purpose of our lives. There are many false descriptions applied to what the signs of manhood imply, but there will come a time for plain speech and situations that demand of us the acknowledgement that we are not as independent as we may have thought.

Faith

Faith is the vehicle through which we ask, seek and knock. There is no set ritual in which we are to conduct ourselves in the presence of God. We can humbly ask, or shout-out with trembling timbre as in sorrow, or we may knock insistently; all methods, along with every reverent posture are permitted within our Father's house. Once we recognize our need and ask for help, the problem begins the resolution stage of existence. Asking seeking and knocking is the true mark of manhood; it casts pride aside for the betterment of our lives and permits understanding to guide in our true purpose. In some cases, there is direct intervention on the part of God where the failure to acknowledge the help we need is present for the asking; but because we have failed to ask does not mean that God will not come to our aid. His purpose for us must be accomplished even when we have not recognized him. We don't need to knock to gain access to God; he is always present in the person of the Holy Spirit, who has transformed us into the temple of God. By telling us to ask, seek and knock he is making us aware of the respect that must be shown to our Father. "Honor thy father and thy mother" is a commandment that teaches us an acceptable mannerism in which love is presented. Jesus spoke plainly to us again when he advised us to have faith in God. Some have completely discarded his words and they attempt to deal with life-concerns ill equipped, without the presence of God in their lives.

Others are concerned with only their personal brand of faith, while some place faith only in themselves. The fact that they continually fail never enters-into the equation for living an abundant life. The first step upon the road to a life filled with success is to be cognizant that we are not traveling alone! Success for the one who follows Christ is the fulfillment of purpose. Again, this purpose may only be to live our lives with the understanding that we are not leading others astray, by projecting one lifestyle with our lips but displaying another in the actual manner-in which life is conducted. When we are continually aware of the presence of God in our lives there is no disconnect in the focus and purpose of our lives. We can only imagine where God is when we have not turned on the faith engine for a while. In fact, without exercise we may begin to doubt the engine's readiness, and in times of need we may panic away from the ability to focus. It is then that we hope the battery for the engine is not dead. Emergency engine-generator sets that provide electrical power during outages are regularly exercised within large office buildings and hospital settings, in-order to reassure the readiness of such equipment. In performing these tests confidence is raised and mishaps are avoided. We also must test ourselves to see if we are in the faith, as the scriptures instruct us to do.

One may say, "I have no faith." This is of course a failure to understand that we exercise contemporary faith every day. We trust that the airlines have performed the necessary maintenance. The weather will be good when we arrive at our destination and the street vendors have complied with the health regulations, that we trust are enforced. We place our trust in the things that we know can and do fail us, and still we find resistance in seeking God who will never fail to come to our aid. The psalmist writes, ***"God is seeking those who are seeking him."*** *Both acquired-contemporary and God-gifted faith must be exercised with prudence. Faith is the foundation that permits inherent talents to be utilized to the fullest-extent, in-order to fulfill the righteous purpose given to us as a child of God. Once faith is present we then have the instructional foundation of wisdom that only comes from God.*

All faith exiting the natural dimension of existence must be placed at the feet of God. To do otherwise is to set into motion the wheels of failure that can and will attempt to place us under their enormous weight. Exercising our gift of faith in God displays the proper attitude of humility, always accompanied by respectful truth, aimed at affecting changes within our lives, and on a greater scale changes in the world that are so desperately needed. Subconsciously it is the desire to see come to fruition the promise of Christ's return.

Faith announces us through prayer

When we are conscious of the desire to enter-into the presence of God it is such awareness that announces us. Even though we have the Spirit of God dwelling within us it is our awareness that calls us into his presence. Absent such awareness, we are like a boat absent a motor. Faith is the boat and the motor is the awareness that gives movement and force to our desire to enter-into the presence of God. It is true that God is omnipresent but unless we are consciously aware we will never be able to communicate on a meaningful level. We really-don't need to knock in-order to gain entrance to the presence of God and the kingdom; we are continually in his presence because it is he who has taken up residence within us. In the same-way the first of mankind was instilled with the very presence of God by his breathing into the man the ***"breath of life,"*** *so it is the receipt of a new spirit through being born again bestows upon us new life. This new life is the awareness of reality present in the mercy we have received. The one who receives mercy knows where such mercy has come from. God is not a God of confusion and in this straightforward transformation given in mercy we are made certain of the reality of the new life given to us in the appearance of truth!*

Jesus spoke many times through the expression of parables and-also plainly when he told us to, ***"have faith in God"*** *and again when he instructs us to* ***"ask seek and knock."*** *Some people have discarded his words and others refuse to listen. They attempt to* *deal with life's concerns ill equipped absent the presence of God in their lives. This notion that it is their lives is also a failure to acknowledge the one who has given life to mankind. Those who refuse to listen to the truth concerning dependence, not only in our present state of being, but by denying truth they have forfeited the promise of afterlife given to all who will but acknowledge God to be correct, and man to be in need and/or dependent in the here and now for continued existence.*

Faith

It's everywhere.
Darkest night
Sunshine bright
Deepest hole
Heaven's height
Mother's hand
Children's eyes
It's everywhere.

Food court vendor
Used car fellow
Airline tickets
Cool wine cellar
Smiling faces
Unknown land
Hidden thoughts
In outstretched hand
It's everywhere.

Judges, lawyers, doctors, kings
Movie Stars playground swings
Ancient ruins bones and sand
Stake a flag
In hearts of men
It's everywhere.

Yes, we are a faith-filled people
In a world of rising din
But sometimes fail
The whisper of the voice of God within!

Mark 11:22 Have faith in God, Jesus answered.

Dependence

We can't walk on water because we walk alone.
What we permit defines us and what we ignore blinds us.
Truth gives us wings and wrong denies the King.
The illusion of independence puts all in arms reach
Printed in self-help books and dangled in our face
Like fishing lures and baited hooks
Presented by the learned as all we need to pass
Alas, empty words find vacancy as sunshine goes through glass.
All there is and nothing more finds need to understand
The giver of all truth did not begin with man.

Plant a seed and watch it grow harvest it time.
As long, as, rainfall finds the land a grain of wheat will grow.
As long, as, sunshine's presence denies to us the cold
A tree invites with branches to all in nature's plan
"Come enjoy the offering the gifts from God to man."

Be mindful of the river's flow and seasons understand
For what we think is ours alone will pass from hand to hand.
Wisdom of God's design makes us aware of our dependence.
Absent understanding, the life we live finds end
As thought concludes a sentence
As ink is drained from pen
The breath of man releases flesh to dust again.
Reliance upon God is what we need to stand
Walking upon water needs his outstretched hand.

Luke 11:2-3 He said to them, "When you pray say," 'Father, hallowed be your name, your kingdom come, give us each day our daily bread.'

Instruction

The old man's vision
And the young man's dream
Are different from the start
The old man sees the road ahead
And knows the trouble parts

The young man dreams of future paths
In hurried steps to take
But rarely heeds the warning signs
Of old man's mistakes

Signposts roadblocks detours curves
Inclement weather and vision that's blurred
Upon every road, you travel my son
Remember, the Lord is your light
From daybreak 'til night
He'll always be with you
Pointing to right!

Laurels of rock crown mountain peaks
Truth is displayed in falling leaves
Hidden the snares downturns of life
Presented to man in packages bright.

Pay heed to the seasons.
Reject all lies.
Meadows valleys plains
Deserts beaches jungles caves
Rivers and hard terrain
Without God
All of life's journey is hardship and pain!

Proverbs 1:8 Listen, my son, to your father's instruction and do not forsake your mother's teaching.

What do you want to be when you grow up?

It seems we are confronted with that question throughout our youth. Parents and others are asking of us what we have planned or what we desire to become when we are old enough to enter-into the workforce. The actual question should be framed in this way: what is the true purpose of your life and what must you do to actually-find your true purpose and see it fulfilled? I'm sure not too many children will answer the question with any amount of understanding until they are-allowed to grow in knowledge.

While it is true, many of us imagined ourselves becoming any number of persons when we looked at the future, but in truth not many of us had any idea as to what we will eventually become. Our footprint will be most pronounced within our own inner circle of family and friends. It may also be true of the old-adage, "Like father like son." Having a father or mother who is a doctor may very-well plant the desire in the child to also seek to become like his parents. The same is true in almost all the avenues presented to the youth of the world. However, for the greater part of us there is very little awareness (if any at all) with respect to knowing what we want to be when we grow up. In fact, most of our seeking to fit into a societal niche may take a most circuitous route. The twists and turns of life can and do lead us along many lengthy and indirect paths. Life lived correctly with purpose validates existence. Jesus said, ***"Be holy, as your Father in heaven is holy."*** *When we tell a child to "be good" we are saying the same thing.*

Given the constant demands made of us by society and family, throughout our working years, we may not glimpse our true purpose as God intends until such retirement rest is granted. If truth is told retirement is not all the rest that we may have envisioned and longed for while still having to go to work. What is most important is that we ultimately find the true purpose of this life that we have been given. Living a life that is pleasing to God and to ourselves (a clear conscience) is a good part of our purpose. If we please God we will not find the condemnations of conscience that can make life abundantly miserable. We will not continually find ourselves *asking, "If I only knew then what I know now, life would be different today." That declaration is probably true, but, all the hard times we experienced in our past have formed the person that we are today! Yes, there may be some things that haunt us, but in truth the experience has made us more compassionate and apt to empathize with others who are experiencing the same circumstances. We might say that learning through experience is a valid route to understanding and in understanding we find wisdom, (not to repeat our missteps, but to warn others of the dangers that may be present) and with wisdom we recognize the presence of God in our lives. Wisdom originates in God alone. It is written: "**Wisdom sings her own praises: From the mouth of the Most High I came forth. In the assembly of the Most High I declare my worth.**" NAB*

At times in our life we have found trying circumstances (most of which I dare say have been of our own making) but because we can look back with God at our side, those times that seemed to be so devastating, no longer appear as the threatening specters of their first appearance. With the aid of God, we have been brought through the fire and can live in the peace that only comes with the knowledge of purpose, and reality of the God who loves us.

Calling

To be called to serve
Requires clarity of purpose.
Requires God's strength.
Such strength is derived from
Truth love and majesty.
Understanding comes from
Hurt hunger and poverty.
It's really, a call
To live in the Kingdom.

It's an offspring maker.
A birthright stamp.
A kiss for common man.

It's a blessing and kind of frightening.
You see, such a call comes from God alone.
It transforms flesh and bone
Into Kingdom priest and home.

Acts 9:4-6 He fell to the ground and heard a voice saying to him, "Saul, Saul, why do you persecute me?" "Who are you, Lord?" "I am Jesus whom you are persecuting," he replied. "Now get up and go into the city, and you will be told what you must do."

High Heat

The world is filled with troubles that come and go as thieves.
Unexpected as the rumbling earth and heart attacks of pain.
They appear as either loss of life or eternal gain.
The heart of man has trouble deep within
Caused by truth rejected conflicting with his sins.
The one who is selected and blessed with words to heal
Has not the option silence in compliance with the world.
Truth cannot be shuttered inside a vault.
As in volcanic action high heat bursting from the crest
Will burn away deception and always win the test.

Jeremiah 29:9 But if I say, "I will not speak anymore in his name," his word is in my heart like a burning fire, shut up in my bones. I am weary of holding it in; indeed, I cannot.

<u>*Unity promotes purpose*</u>

Joshua 24:14-15 "Now fear the Lord and serve him with all faithfulness. Throw away the gods your fathers worshipped beyond the River and in Egypt, and serve the Lord, but if serving the Lord seems unreasonable to you, then choose for yourselves this day whom you will serve, whether the gods your forefathers served beyond the River, or the gods of the Amorites, in whose land you are living. But as for me and my household, we will serve the Lord."

Joshua declares that his entire household will serve the Lord. Therein we see the unity that must accompany not only those who choose to serve the Lord, but for all to achieve peace and unity in the home. On a larger-scale it is now posited to the nation: "What will you do with respect to serving the Lord?" The people reply that they also will serve the Lord. Contained within the declaration of Joshua concerning his household, is the representation of his leadership position, beginning in his home and extending outward amongst the nation. A man must first get his own home in order before he can attempt to manage another's activities. It is written in the parable of the ***"Three servants"*** *also known as the parable of the* ***"Talents." Matthew 25:29 "For everyone who has will be given more, and he will have abundance. Whoever does not have even what he has will be taken from him."*** *Another way of stating this is to say, whoever is responsible in small matters greater responsibility will be given to him, but for the one who does not manage well in small matters, even the little he has will be taken away. This then falls into a spiritual-law designation, in the same way that faith exercised in the power of belief must elicit a response, and persistence in prayer must also produce, as emphasized in the parable of the,* ***"Widow and the corrupt judge."***

Now let's multiply these examples of faith present in unity of purpose, as they apply to our home, our church and our nation, and the response produced is immeasurable. We understand that God honors and blesses those who desire to live in accord with his purpose for us. God is the head of the household of mankind, and deeper still, all of creation. He has presented to us the same question Joshua presented to the nation of Israel.

Even those who do not serve God understand truth and the connection with him. Example: When Joshua sent out spies into the city of Jericho they were hidden in the home of a woman named, ***"Rahab."*** *She had revealed to the spies that the king of Jericho was aware they were in her home. But still she hides them and makes a stunning statement:* ***Joshua 2:8 "I know the Lord has given this land to you, and that a great fear has fallen on us, so that all who live in this country are melting in fear because of you."***

These people had their own gods and still they knew that the nation coming against them was not only completely united in purpose, but also united in service to the God who had forced the Egyptians to release them from slavery. The inhabitants of the city of Jericho knew that the God of the Hebrews had led them through the wilderness for forty-years, in which they not only survived but grew strong.

Once we are given the peace that comes with the knowledge that God is with us, we are united in purpose within our self. No longer is the tug-of-war between the desire to do what is right, and the desires of the flesh as potent, such unrighteous desire is no longer a hindrance to fulfill the righteous purposes of God. He gives to us the ability to achieve.

It appears to us today there is a great division in our nation. There are those who will serve the way of the world and seek to not mention the name of God, and there is the voice of others who will not serve the wishes of government gods and/or the politically powerful, striving to erase God from the thoughts and hearts of men. In place of an overall recognition of the nation being dependent upon God, they would insert their selves into the provider for the nation role. It is recognized that a great divide has captured the thoughts of many and such capture is insistently subjecting the populace to droning irritable emanations within the never-ending struggle for political dominance. This divide can never find sufficient common ground to cease from tearing apart the unity so arduously constructed from the foundation of trust in God. These opposite mindsets within political parties have gained converts throughout the nation. It is basically the parties of good and evil and neither one is motivated by the altruism they present.

In the beginning of the nation it was easy to unite under the banners of truth and freedom. It was a given for everyone to easily understand the blessings derived from the acknowledgement of God. This acknowledgement is service to God and in our united service we grew as a nation and continually found the blessings that have come to be expected from God. The word "indivisible" incorporated within the "Pledge of Allegiance" simply means to be incapable of being separated. If we look at the attacks from the antireligious, what we find is a constant bemoaning aimed at disunity. I have never heard of the politically correct crowd demonstrating against any other religion except Judeo-Christian adherents. Many of these antireligious give terrorists a pass! From the disunity brought about by the constant attempts to erase God from the lexicon of society, the consequences are most pronounced within the home. The household finds disrepair because of the absence of both father and God, such unbridled corrosiveness in the form of lies permits its poison to flow into the streets and ultimately infect the nation. This constant cry to remove God from the hearts and minds of the nation is being done, utilizing the spiritual principle of persistence in prayer! The greater the irritant produced by the news outlets, demonstrations and other forms of communication, the more people say, "What must we do to shut them up!" The hoped-for result of those causing such irritability is to find a point in time where their objectives are fulfilled. Such fulfillment is totally against the purpose of God for humanity. The problem with those making demands is that they will never be satisfied, no matter what concessions are made! The spiritual principle utilized by the ungodly is found in the parable of the **"Widow and the corrupt judge."** *And so, we see the enemies of truth and God will not hesitate to utilize the spiritual principles highlighted within the teachings of Christ in order to achieve their goals.*

Nimrod's folly today

Early in the history of mankind we find there is a unity of people but they lacked a unity with God. Man, had moved east and settled in a place called Babylonia. Everyone spoke the same language and they were unified under one great goal. They built a tower to make a name for themselves. This was a direct attempt to dishonor God. Perhaps it was an attempt to forestall and avert a possible judgment of the same magnitude of the earlier flood? So, we see that man can be united as a nation but if not united under God it will not survive. It's interesting that the same enemy that brought God's judgment upon the world is the same one who is still attempting to create man in his own image and likeness. This is evident in the turmoil present in many nations of our time. Evil is seemingly running unchecked. So much so that in some nations there are tremendous destructive forces at work. We must ask ourselves what is the reason for such tyrannically destructive acts of both, destruction of property and lives? The answer may simply be that evil desires to destroy what God has created, and in the destructive process recreate with the emphasis upon both tyrannical rule (forced unity and worship) and removing any remnant of freedom, given to mankind in the creative purpose and intent of God.

Such evil is killing people under the outward banner of fanatical theocracy and/or unabashed terroristic evil. The overall aim of the dictator is to remain in power and receive worshiping accolades from those they have come to dominate. The overall aim of tyrannical terroristic theocracy is to erase everyone who will not worship the god of the state.

This is a great difference from the choice God had given to the Hebrew people, when they are asked if they would choose to serve the Lord. Both dictator and tyrant- theocracy are serving the same evil purpose but from different perspectives. Ironically a house divided cannot stand, and so what we see are factions of evil fighting against each other, attempting to lead by taking authority, which is exactly what their father has done from the beginning of evil's desire to become a god, and this is exactly what the antichrist will do when he arrives on the world scene claiming to have authority existing in him alone.

With unity, there is power. Let's look at two separate occasions where unity is displayed: first, is the appearance of the Holy Spirit and the voice of God the Father at the baptism of Jesus. We see the Holy Spirit descending in the form of a dove. This represents both peace and unifying love between Father and Son. It is significant as the example of our need for unity within our relationship with God, extending to family and finally within our nation. When we look at the Day of Pentecost we see the Holy Spirit descending as if tongues of fire. Such fire is the power of God given to the church, for they were all of like-mind (united) and intent upon serving God.

It was at, this time, the word of God was preached and there wasn't a language barrier! However, it appears there is much-less power within the churches today, as was present in the foundational beginning of the good news being spread to the ends of the earth. Perhaps, while there is a passive disunity within different branches of Christianity regarding theology, there is also aggressive differences of understanding existing in the interpretative teachings of Christ; this aspect alone may be enough to divide what was meant to be indivisible and in-turn weaken the overall ability of the church?

United

In the beginning man was united.
As our numbers grew competition for leadership
Stirred a poisoned brew.
Families went off in different directions
For even within a family a poison can be made.
Even the strongest of poisons can be overcome
If the remedy is taken before its work is done.
Before the credits of the show are shown.
Before the curtain falls and the marquee lights go dark
We never are too old to choose to serve the Lord.
It's then we understand
Family is unity of love that never fails.
Even in the trials of life no matter what the weather
The family of God must always stay together.

There will always be wars trouble grief and strife.
The family of man needs to set a steady righteous course.
We cannot have a ship with sails set in all directions.
The ship will go nowhere and pull apart.

Recognize our need
To reach the hand of God
Grab hold of love from high above
Speak truthful words that unite
The purpose of this life
With compassion of the heart
Unity is brought
Back into a world
It has long since forgot!

Psalm 133:1 How wonderful it is, how pleasant, for God's people to live in harmony. *GNB*

3

SIN AND DOUBT

This chapter has been reprinted from a previous work, "Snapshots of Inspiration." In this chapter, a correlation between the sin-nature of man and the impact it has upon faith will be examined, in effort to overcome the negative aspects of doubt. Intent is to build awareness of the forces or tendencies drawing us away from God. Once recognized, we may then minimize the negative consequence hindering spiritual growth in both faith and understanding of our relationship with God. Spiritual growth should not in this instance, be looked upon as something that increases as one can imagine a plant sprouting, rather, it may be better understood by the absence or diminished frequency of sin. With the absence of sin, good fruit will come forth to inhabit the place formerly occupied by weeds.

Matthew 28:16-17 "Then the eleven disciples went to Galilee, to the mountain where Jesus had told them to go. When they saw him, they worshiped him; but some doubted."

The above scripture takes place after the resurrection of Jesus, and still some doubted what their eyes clearly saw. Apart from the expression of doubt exhibited by some of the disciples, also included is the worship of Jesus. I point this out to those who doubt the divinity of Christ. Jesus did not stop the disciples from worshiping him. As such, his acceptance is answer to those who would reduce his stature below equality with God. Apologetics (defense of Christian doctrine), in this area is not the aim of this chapter,

however, because within this depiction we find both acceptance and doubt it is important to understand that the disciples are depicted as worshiping Jesus, even though some clearly doubted what was self-evident.

When we find our self in doubt it is then we must resort to worship; within worship we are given the necessary spiritual structure that overcomes our natural inclinations to deny truth. Sin is more than a conscience headache. It continually attempts to make dull the Sword of the Spirit. It cradles the denial of God and inhibits truth. Our human nature is sinful. This should not be confused with the various kinds of sin. Rather, it is our very existence that has been corrupted. The redemption of man is a two-part process. First, we are born again and receive a new spirit, the bible calls this receipt a ***"down payment"*** *that assures us of our salvation. However, the body is awaiting renewal (the culmination or final aspect of salvation) that will come through being resurrected to life everlasting.*

Man, disobeyed the command of God and the consequence of disobedience was absorbed into our total existence. We were changed. Imperfection became the reality of our existence. When a substance is incorporated into another a different reality comes into being and the former will no longer exist. In the disobedience of man his totality was changed from a state of holiness to that which is denied the claim of belonging to God.

Man's days no longer equaled eternity. Like an untreated infection sin lives in us. From the moment of disobedience declivity was established and struggle began; sin seized opportunity, and we, like lightning falling were destined to return to the dust of the earth. We were denied access to the ***"Tree of Life"*** *and dispossessed from paradise, but God went with us in the knowledge gained through disobedience. We then began to understand the cost associated with sin. The condemnation of conscience mocked our failure to trust in God's prohibition, and all things were then subjected to doubt, brought about by the advent of deception's emergence from the shadow of evil's intent. Right and wrong is not just conceptual,* *it is fact. We recognize stealing is wrong and murder is wrong, even those who murder and steal do not want to be murdered or have their goods stolen. It will make even those who commit crimes angry to become a victim. Therein we see truth in its universally unshaken, undeniable strength, not only conceptual but actual-fact. One consequence of sin is called conscience. All of us, either victim or criminal find agreement within conscience. It brings to us the awareness of evil in the world. It established a questioning posture, asking if things presented to us are true. From the moment of deception's beginning the doorway of doubt was brought into existence and it has continually forced us to divert our focus in-order to weigh and consider consequences, of a failure to recognize its appearance. By opening the doorway through disobedience doubt took-up residence within our thinking faculty and it became a part of our reality. The word of God has been given to us as the antibiotic against this infectious condition; it is pure and complete truth. By doubting God's pronounced-prohibition we entered a downward spiral culminating in the actual act of disobedience. By accepting doubt, sin seized its opportunity for fruition and we made it a companion and component of our lives. We had never been exposed to the curveball of deception and like trusting children we listened to the voice of Sin without doubting. We doubted God's word simply because we heard the Corruptor's voice present to us the promise of things unknown. What horror must have invaded the hearts of those (so trusting), at the recognition of deception? Certainly, this Serpent, this great Deceiver, was not unknown to them, for he had access to the garden of God. Trusting children, listening to the voice of a corrupt adult.*

Conscience is a nice word that literally means, "With the knowledge or understanding of what is right and wrong." "Con" from the Latin meaning "With" and "Science" meaning "Knowledge." Some ask, "Why did God allow man to sin?" "Certainly, he could have shielded us from the Evil One's deception and protected us from ourselves." The answer may simply be, it was necessary for mankind to fall upon hard times, because God wanted instilled in us the character traits that can only be appreciated through experiencing adversity. Tough love? Was God complicit in our downfall? Not really. We were fully aware of the prohibition set-forth, and in this awareness, we rejected obedience for the allurement of the unknown. Prior to disobedience we were not burdened with the knowledge of right and wrong. It was not until we began to contemplate the actual act of disobedience did the slithering encroachment of sin find footing of possible surety. However, God knew beforehand how we would choose regarding his prohibition. As such, we lost temporarily our immortality and gained added awareness necessary for the finishing aspects of creation. Deception threw us a lemon and God made lemon juice out of our injury.

Without the first of mankind falling into sin what need would we have for courage? Who's threatening us? What need for mercy and forgiveness? Who did wrong? What need for compassion? Who's suffering? Appreciation of God's love for us, without adversity, entering-into our existence was an equation we could not understand. Those who receive mercy are grateful and only the recipient fathom's the gift. God loved us and still he allowed us to be separated from him for our good. Much later it was Jesus who suffered the ultimate separation as he took upon himself the sins of the world. By doing so, reclamation of what belonged to God began (in the formal sense of purchase price paid) and the learning of hard lessons set-forth by hard times and struggles was initiated. We understood the pronouncements of good and the denouncements of evil but it was not until the advent of Christ's victory over death, did we receive the ability to not only hear but to heed the inner voice of truth that cost so much for us to acquire.

Even with redemption the sin that lives in us has ability to erode our faith. Just as the first creation ran-off and hid after recognizing their sin of disobedience, we also have an instinctual or reflexive response (closely associated with self-preservation) to flee from holiness. Sin cannot approach God and so our nature is continually pulling us away. This fleeing is done on a conscious level, but is also taking place within the automatic mechanism incorporated within the body and not dependent upon conscious thought. When people are held within darkness, they are denied the light of truth, and remain unaware of light's freedom-giving qualities, that dispel imaginations produced within a world without light. Sounds may be heard in the dark but no one can be sure of the cause unless light reveals the surroundings. Our nature embraces the lie (strongly hides from the reality of consequence) rather than come into the light of truth. Sin repels us away from God and this causes us to doubt. The further we are pulled into darkness the more we are given to be unsure of truth; with insecurity of truth we fall victim to doubt.

Even we who have been allowed into the light are not immune to the instinctual reaction to flee from holiness when we sin. While we are consciously aware of being clothed with the righteousness of Christ and permitted into the presence of God, our nature makes it impossible to remain sinless in thought and/or deed, thus a tug-of-war is established between body and spirit. Our physical nature will produce the fruit of its existence and our new spirit, received at rebirth, will produce the good things of God. As such, we must recognize our need to run toward God and never to allow the condemnations associated with failure to place distance between us. Perhaps this is one reason why Paul writes, ***1 Thessalonians 5:16-17 "Be joyful always; pray continually; give thanks in all circumstances, for this is God's will for you in Christ Jesus."*** *The one who is joyful signals to all the knowledge of God, and the one who prays constantly, will never succumb to the eroding aspects of sin and doubt. We will hold fast to the surety that is God's truth. Most of us have experienced the reflexive response of shielding our eyes, when emerging from darkness into the brightness of the sun. Our response to the light is quick and determined after only a few hours of darkness, say, within a movie theater. A lifetime within the darkness of unknowing is dispelled by the joy of truth as its light enters through the doorway to our hearts. God's light does not repel us; it surrounds and protects.*

Recognition of need

Mark 9:19. "O unbelieving generation," Jesus replied, "how long shall I stay with you? How long shall I put up with you? Bring the boy to me." *Jesus had come upon some of his disciples and teachers of the law arguing. The disciples of Jesus could not drive-out an evil spirit from a boy. The father of the child wants Jesus to help. He asks for help and adds to the request,* ***"If you can?"*** *Jesus replies,* ***"If you can?"*** *and continues by saying,* ***"Everything is possible for him who believes."*** *Within that statement by Jesus we see the potential for our own faith. The man laments his condition by stating:* ***"I do believe; help me overcome my unbelief!"*** *In this statement by the man we see the conflict of belief and disbelief simultaneously present in all of us because of the sin-nature seeking to hide from truth. Is it a wonder, why, Jesus quantifies the strength of faith in terms we can understand? Faith the size of a mustard seed can accomplish the impossible, sadly, doubt the size of a mustard seed can prevent it. In- order to please God, we must believe he exists and in-order to exercise the power of faith we must also believe the truth presented to us in the words of Jesus:* ***"Everything is possible for him who believes."***

It is so true what the scripture says, ***Matthew 15:8 "These people honor me with their lips, but their hearts are far from me."*** *We can now begin to appreciate the meaning of a double-minded man. He is a man exhaling the truth of God with his intellect and simultaneously denying this truth within the darkness of his heart. The men arguing with the disciples were teachers of the law. They had seen or heard of the miracles performed by Jesus and still their sin-nature kept them blind to the truth before their eyes. There is always the exception, some know truth but consciously align themselves with evil to gratify their own desires. This is the case with the Evil One and all of those who made the decision to rebel against God fully knowledgeable of his supreme authority. How great then is the pull of sin that will knowingly rebel against God, fully aware of ultimate demise? Yes, in many there is a non-belief in God, and subsequently they fail to recognize the need to have their sin-nature arrested by grace. In many, anger is produced* *over the mere mention of the God they do not believe exists. This contradicts logic, highlights the lie they live, and heralds the truth living deep within their core but adamantly refuse to admit! I don't believe in Mickey Mouse and I don't get angry toward those who do, and so, why do the so-called atheists get angry when they hear of God? Truth will always rattle the cage holding mankind captive. Is it a wonder why, "bad news sells?" We have an attraction for sin; it's our nature. It's not counter to the grain of desire pulsing within our veins. Thus, there's a struggle within us to do what we know is good, but we cannot do it until the knowledge of God permeates our lives and sets us free to be what God intended. Conscience is an intricate part of our judgmental process. It's like a navigational compass pointing us in the direction God wants us to travel. It may be accepted as the very voice of God instilled within, from the inception of hard times and struggle.*

Understanding desire controls the fire

The spirit is supernatural in creation's origin, as such, was never intended to be dominated by the subordinate nature of the flesh. The spirit in man is God giving of himself, but the flesh was created from the earth. The flesh is subordinate because it is created and the spirit is of God himself. The potter can never be subordinate to the pot. I do not think with my foot, but the foot can communicate to me an ailment. The flesh is not the thinking faculty of man, rather, it is the aspect of man that makes us human and contains an alert mechanism installed by God, bringing to us awareness of hunger, thirst, pain and other aspects of life. If allowed to rule, excess will always be demanded by our human desires. Like a raging fire that will never say enough, so long as fuel, oxygen and temperature are present, desires and dictates of human nature cannot be removed from a leadership role until truth sets us free; until truth puts out the flames. With truth, there is understanding and in understanding there is God's light illuminating his grace. Sin is the monkey wrench that is thrown into God's creation, placing us into an out of order condition.

*Incorporated into the design of man is an automatic system that brings attention to our bodily needs. This is a good system and when working properly maintains bodily functions at optimum abilities. However, like a failure of a governor that controls and regulates the speed of a turbine the needs of man can be thrown into unwanted and dangerous operation when the thought process is overridden, that is, when the thought process is not in control. Want and desire can be mistaken for need and in this failure to discern, excess will never say, "enough!" It is written: "**Human desires are like the world of the dead, there's always room for more!"** When we know the warning or alert mechanism is not working properly, we may then repair the condition. Understanding our propensity toward wrong, when ruled and/or set free from the corrupt nature of the body is a great step toward achieving initial victory and positive outcomes in future struggles. In addition to recognition of sin's rule we must also realize we need help to defeat this body that has usurped the rightful place of our thinking faculty.*

The fire of God is greater than the fire of desire

Regaining control and lessening human desire is accomplished by realizing something is not working properly, and it's not our thinking faculty. It's not we making poor choices in our lives, it is the sinful nature that rules and dictates.

Jeremiah

Let's look for a moment at the prophet Jeremiah, he had become reluctant to do what God required and declared his intention to not mention him any longer. He is then compelled to do what is right because the very presence of God had become a permanent part of his being; it was like fire imprisoned within his bones. As such, he had no choice in the matter. The presence of God within his life shattered the rebellion emanating from a desire of flesh to rule. Jeremiah, had given admittance (his reasoning) to the natural reaction to retreat from God, under the excuse attributed to his personal troubles, associated with all who point-out the failures of others. In this case his thinking (intent) and physical desire found agreement. The fire of God is greater than the fire of intent and desire. God's fire (the knowledge of what is right and the ability to do it) destroys the duality of outward physical presentation and inner hidden agenda that attempts to deceive others as well as our self.

Rebellion is a veil designed to obscure and deny the reality of man's helplessness. It is the outward expression of sin that desires tenacious control through an alert system never intended to rule. Doubt, brought about by sin's deception, stokes the flame of desire, targets the core of our being, and attempts to destroy our freedom to choose what is right. This then, is the true intent and depth of darkness, but God's light emanating from within, radiates outward and restores a broken system, that has impulsively reacted to the constant signaling stimulants presented externally and from within. Until our hearts are focused upon God the lip service reality prevails.

The apostle Paul inquires, ***1 Corinthians 3:17 "Don't you know that you your-selves are God's temple and that God's Spirit lives in you?"*** *He is asking this question of us who have recognized God and have been born again, because some have found themselves slowly returning to a former way of life. These are those who have not permitted the word of God to grow deep roots as Jesus apprises us within the parable of the seeds. He (Paul) recognizes that while our conscience is making us aware of right and wrong, he could not, and neither could we adhere to the warnings of conscience, because we were ruled by our sin-nature. I want to repeat that again: Conscience warns of sin, and with sin there is always consequence in the here and now as well as in the hereafter. And so, we have within us the struggle to do what is right. Anytime we place ourselves at the pinnacle of importance we invite erosion of the character traits gained through sacrifice and adversity. When we dilute the character of virtue we invite sin and doubt to erode the fabric of freedom and faith. Through external means there is an abundance of struggles that continually attempt to distract us from* *the truth that God exists and he has not left us. Through all our struggles God has always remained with us.* ***Matthew 28:20 "And surely I will be with you always, to the very end of the age."***

The message of Christ that continues to reverberate is one in which he continually states the reality of God. The prophets proclaimed this message but they were not heeded. As such God sent his Son and still people refused to render to God that which belongs to him. The disciples and all who call upon the name of the Lord in good times and in times of struggle proclaimed the reality of God. So, must we, for even the smallest of voices can impact a life with the message of Christ.

Now, back to the failure on the part of the disciples to drive out an evil spirit from a boy. We find that Jesus is successful. He frees the child from the evil spirit's influence and the disciples ask, **"Why is it we could not?"** *Jesus tells them,* ***"This kind requires prayer."*** *What Jesus may be saying is that it takes more than words to drive out the bad influences in our lives; more than lip service.*

<u>*Doubt is persistent*</u>

Let's look at the story of the rich man and the beggar named Lazarus, as told to us by Jesus in the gospel of Luke (16:19-31). It is my guess that this account is a depiction of what is to come, in general terms, because Jesus places the rich man in the circumstance of eternal damnation, which is clearly post-judgment, and it centers on the consequence befalling those who fail to see the hardships of the poor. However, the example showing the persistence of doubt within the story is supportive of the attributes of doubt.

In death, the rich man has no identity, while Lazarus enjoys not only the surroundings of paradise but he has his identity intact. In life, the rich man had everything he wanted and obviously was not burdened with the struggles that accompanied Lazarus. Even in death the rich man still did not understand Lazarus was no longer his servant, or dependent upon the crumbs that fell from his table. He was asking Abraham to have Lazarus bring to him a drop of water to place on his tongue, but was told, a great divide separates them and no one can crossover. He then entreats Abraham to allow someone to, ***"return from the dead"*** *to warn his brothers of the place he now found himself. There's little doubt the rich man would have volunteered his services. Abraham responds by stating,* ***"Your brothers have Moses and the prophets and even if someone were to come back from the dead they still would not believe."***

Here again, is the doubt that persists, even if we should see truth raised from the dead! As in the subject verse of this chapter, Jesus had been resurrected from the dead and his disciples (brothers) still had doubts. Even if someone were permitted to return from the dead to tell of the hardship that befalls those denied the presence of God, people would still find doubt present, and injecting itself into the reality of what is clearly seen.

During Jesus' good works the disciples witnessed the resurrection concerning the friend of Jesus, also named Lazarus, and others. In this we can then begin to recognize the persistence of doubt associated with a preconceived determination in the heart and mind of man. Witness to the resurrection of Jesus was not the first time they had been exposed to the so-called impossible being accomplished! When we determine something to be impossible, denunciation and doubt will always be presented by the sin-nature of man.

The purpose of sin is to deny God his rightful place of leadership, and to deny the penalty attached to its stigma through doubt. Erosion of faith and truth through doubt, created by sin, can manifest itself within innumerable distractive ways, aimed at the continuance of captivity and its accompanying baggage. These erosive distractions, away from reality, (brought about by the incorrect and sinful reasoning of man) are sometimes called addictions or compulsive behavioral dictates. Our captivity prior to salvation was acutely terminal, so much so, we sought to find release from the condemnations of conscience within the shadow of doubt, made manifest by sinful lifestyles that offered to us the illusion of peace, through drugs and activities designed to deny truth and remove our thoughts away from the reality of our condition.

Shadow

Get behind me, O doubt!
Your time has ended.
Your shadow is transparent.
Your whisper wanes and fails.
Your attachment is severed.
Your song of mourning, sorrow, impending doom and death
Has sung its last at dawning, as truth appeared so blessed!
Your twisting mist of shadow obscures no longer sight.
You stand in abject narrows from which you cannot hide.
Now doubt-yourself, within your darkest glare
And hear the voice of laughter where once lived despair!

Psalm 23:1-4 "The Lord is my shepherd I shall lack nothing. He makes me lie down in green pastures, he leads me beside quiet waters, he restores my soul. He guides me in paths of righteousness for his name's sake. Even though I walk through the valley of the shadow of death, I will fear no evil, for you are with me; your rod and your staff they comfort me."

Recognition marks a turning point

Recognition of our condition comes about through the light of grace received. Freedom requires commitment to the way of God's intent, otherwise a foundational shift will occur causing erosion of faith, lending courage to an already defeated enemy, ever seeking to dominate and destroy. We cannot do both, a foot in heaven and another in the fire-fueled by human desire. This will eventually leave us exhausted from the revolving door activity that brings us into proximity of finding truth believed, but never permits exit to know it for sure. There are many things we do not understand and cannot comprehend. As slaves ruled by our sin-nature we cannot understand the ingrained and undeniable internal conflict completely, but we know something is not right. We cannot fathom the enormity of eternal life or God's everlasting love. We try to encapsulate eternity within the rearview mirror of our lives and continually find ourselves wanting. We sometimes do not understand why it is bad things happen to people who don't deserve the cards life has handed to them. We do not have ability to understand how God knew all his children before he created the foundations of the world, but we believe it to be true. We believe that God is always with us and in control, no matter how terrible the slings and arrows of this life may sting and hurt. Ultimately God will make all things right, in this there is no doubt! ***Galatians 6:9 "Let us not become weary of doing-good, for at the proper time we will reap a harvest if we do not give up."***

Gentle Malady

If this faith of mine is false, I must be nuts!
If truth trust and love is a sickness, I must be nuts!
What medication did I take to end up wanting good?
Going from aggressive insanity to passive peace
Everyone loved my lobotomy of the heart.
There's a divide called good and bad
Happy and sad night and day wrong or right
These are not concepts but actual-fact
But with a concept I am convinced
God is! God is! God is! Who he says he is.

Exodus 3:14 God said, "I am who I am. You must tell them: The one who is called I AM has sent me to you."

Lack of immediate consequence emboldens and encourages doubt

When we know, what it is that hinders our faith we then acquire ability to remove such obstacles and once again we become powerful witnesses for truth, as on the day we first believed. On the day, we first believed there was no doubt in our minds and hearts that God's presence in our life was made known, and in this knowledge God took his rightful place of reality within which freedom is gained. On the day, we first believed the flesh bowed to the appearance of God in our lives and was removed from the unlawful position of dictator. What has happened since then, is the slow erosion of faith caused by sin that continually injects doubt through the insistence of the flesh, to once again rule in our lives. So, true are the scriptures that say: ***Rev. 2:5 "See how far you have fallen."*** *Again,* ***Rev. 3:5 "Strengthen the things that remain."***

There is apparently a natural falling away from the truth we have received. Within the context of having one foot within the promise of eternal life and the other in the grave the struggle between true and false continues until we are made whole once again. On a fundamental level this is the conflict in man (the struggle between good and evil) and the remedial provision of God. Within this struggle lives the sister of sin, the cloud of doubt that attempts to reinstate the darkness of despair that formerly inhabited our lives. ***2 Corinthians 4:16 "Therefore we do not lose heart. Though outwardly we are wasting away, yet inwardly we are being renewed day by day."***

Doubt gains assurance within our reasoning because there is not always an apparent immediate consequence for sin. Lightning does not fall from the sky and render the offender into a charcoal-gray puff of smoke. Not at all, the consequence for sin seems far from justice. Lawbreakers seemingly escape the justice most would expect should occur. This then probably reinforces a belief in the, "Sin does not exist" doctrine within secular humanist declarations. It would also add doubtful impact to those wanting to do right and live in accord to both conscience and God's pronouncements. It may also seem at times to be folly to live a righteous life.

Jeremiah 12:1 "Lord, if I argue my case with you, you would prove to be right. Yet I must question you about matters of justice. Why are wicked men so prosperous? Why do dishonest men

***succeed?"** Jeremiah may very well be asking God for understanding within the confines of his struggles. He sees the wicked prosper and the dishonest succeed and he wonders why? He understands that a malady has infected the thoughts of the people who pay lip service to the established acceptance of God, but underlying their outward position, say to themselves, **"God does not see what we are doing."** It is apparent to us today that many have adopted the position of those in the time of Jeremiah. The sin-nature has cast sufficient doubt for us to deny the existence of God. Inward denial and outward expressions of disobedience are encouraged to increase in potency, where the illusion of justice-denied is present. It is indeed a downward spiral that leaves little room for handholds of escape once we allow doubt to gain a mustard seed of weight; it pulls us down and further from truth. The mental tug-of-war is only offset and won through the strength of prayer. Connection with God allows men to run with horses and not become weary.*

***Jeremiah 12:5 "If you have raced with men on foot and they have worn you out, how can you compete with horses?"** The erosion of faith through sin giving birth to doubt, may be so subtle that we need to be reminded of the depth of our fall and the weakened state it has left us in. Thus, the admonishment by Jesus to strengthen the things that remain and to recognize how far we have fallen. With admonishment, we gain strength through knowledge and recapture our true position of faith within the core of our being. What goes on within the core of our being is reflected in the outward expression of our lives.*

*God's question regarding Jeremiah's inability to race with men, may be encouragement for him and for us to understand our adversarial encounters are not exclusively rooted in human beings. The war between good and evil is ongoing and we are a big part of it! If we get tired of the struggles against men and wish to throw up our hands and deny God his voice in our lives, how then can we ever hope to find victory over far greater enemies within the spiritual realm? Paul the apostle tells us basically the same thing when he instructs us to put on, **"the armor of God."** The armor of God transforms us into the equivalent of the armor plating of* *tanks-it makes us bulletproof! We become resistant, not only from external deceptive attack but also from the internal denunciation and condemnations of conscience littering our present day. If we permit sin's internal condemnation opportunity, it will produce the negative response that causes us to seek the illusion of not being seen. Just as corrosion will eventually eat away at the most reinforced armor, the influence of doubt will erode the armor of God. We must maintain the suit of armor we have been given. This is done through connection with God. Maintaining our connection with God negates the effects of sin and doubt.*

We may convince ourselves that certain things are kept private within us, but we cannot deny the way in which we live to those with eyes to see. God does see and hear everything spoken in the heart and everything vocalized by the lips of man. Perhaps when the struggle to gain sufficient faith is achieved, we may then also be empowered by prayer to make a difference in the lives of others as well as ourselves.

A need to be vigilant

***Mark 14:37* "Then he returned and found the three disciples asleep. He said to Peter, "Simon are you asleep? Weren't you able to stay awake for even an hour?" And he said to them, "Keep watch and pray that you will not fall into temptation. The spirit is willing but the flesh is weak."**

Jesus returns (this takes place before the crucifixion) to the place he had left his disciples (Peter James and John) and he finds them asleep. He expresses his disappointment in their inability to stay awake and to pray. We can surmise Jesus had asked his disciples to keep watch and to pray in his absence, but they failed to follow his instructions; otherwise there would be no reason for being admonished for going to sleep. Jesus points us to our weakness. He is warning us not to relinquish our vigil to do the will of God. To do so gives confidence and strength to the flesh that desires a dictatorial position over our will as well as to denounce truth. Again, this is the withdrawal of our nature from the holiness of God and in turn dilutes our faith through disassociation. A relationship with others means involvement. We cannot go to sleep and claim to be involved in the activities of God or others. When we lull ourselves into thinking all is well and peace is within us, we may find suddenly there is an eruption that had been building beneath the surface of conscious awareness. We may find ourselves adrift in a place of confusion brought about by the slow advancement of a complacent heart. The soldier of Christ must remain vigilant and ready to serve with the weaponry given to him upon the day of enlistment into the Army of God. It may be sufficient to say that in most things involving human desire, wanting to do a thing, is probably a thing that should not be done. The desires of flesh are mostly in opposition to the will of God. Is it a mystery that we become weary and seek sleep? We know the struggle within us has the proclivity to rage contempt, as much as a prisoner's failure to reject memories of liberty lost. The prisoner may be in the cell but he is always thinking of a way out. Vigilance is paramount if we wish to keep wrong confined and the spirit of truth vibrant and actively running toward God.

Struggles

It seems when we master the walk along comes the struggle to talk.
There's a struggle outside of the gate and a struggle within
Companions of sin bringing welts filled with pain.
Like the wobble of a top at the end of its spin
We struggle to remain upright.
As a ship listing we look for a pier of support
As would a ghost, slanted and bent
Diminished by every breath.
Like the advent of troubling days
And water rushing the shore to lord over sand
We struggle with footing that's wet
And struggle sometimes to forget.
At times, we struggle to recall
A time when struggles were spent
And always we wonder just when
When the struggles will end?

Isaiah 65:16 "Anyone in the land who asks for a blessing will ask to be blessed by the faithful God. Whoever takes an oath will swear by the name of the faithful God. The troubles of the past will be gone and forgotten."

<u>You of little faith</u>

Matthew 14:28-33 "Lord, if it is you," Peter replied, "tell me to come to you on the water." "Come," he said. Then Peter got down out of the boat and walked on the water to Jesus. But when he saw the wind, he was afraid and beginning to sink, cried out, "Lord, save me!" Immediately Jesus reached out his hand and caught him. "You of little faith," he said, "why did you doubt?" And when they climbed into the boat, the wind died down. Then those who were in the boat worshiped him, saying, "Truly you are the Son of God."

It is not only frustrating for us to be confronted by this unwarranted doubt but it must also be frustrating to God. In that moment, immediately following the miracle of walking on water, and the wind bowing to the Savior's will, we find understanding recognizing Jesus as, Emmanuel, God with us. This same recognition of untarnished faith appeared to us the moment we received God's grace; the veil of deception clouding our lives was lifted. In the above scripture-quote there are many things that come to mind as we picture this portrayal but the thing that should be fixed into our higher level of perception is Peter crying out, ***"Lord, save me!"***

Peter did not need the empowerment of the Holy Spirit, who would come to them on the day of Pentecost, in-order for him to understand his need for Jesus, to save him from being captured by the uncaring water surrounding him. All too often we are confronted by the storms of life, we know we need help, and perhaps we also may be sinking into depressing and dangerous surroundings, so let us remember Jesus is always reaching out his hand for us to grab hold of, and in this there is the surety of deliverance from seemingly impossible conditions. When we are threatened on any level of life it is not a matter of how much faith we have, rather, it is understanding that Jesus at that point in time is not placing us on a faith scale to determine if our trust in him is sufficient for him to act in our behalf. No parent would act in this, are you deserving fashion? Jesus is called, ***"Eternal Father" (Isaiah 9:6)*** *and in this, we must never doubt his willingness to come to our aid.*

Fabric Testing 101

"Attention class, I am proud to introduce to you, Dispatcher Grey.
He is your deceiver for tonight."
"Goodnight students, pay close attention.
In the daylight, you'll need stealth.
A test a grab a grip
Pull apart, tear divide, snatch, injure and strip.
All these, will come in time
Patience is the hunter's bow that causes man to slip.
A peck a rip then shreds
Lift him up knock him down
Stay deep behind the set
Daze the man all you can
The rest cannot resist
The fabric of family enters the abyss.
Big fish eat
Big cat bites
Big dog barks at night
Sharks don't miss with their kiss
Little ones can't hide.
Study hard within the dark
Avoid light.
Class dismissed."

Mathew 12:29 "Or again, how can anyone enter a strong man's house and carry off his possessions unless he first ties up the strong man? Then he can rob his house."

The tourist

The negative aspect of sin and doubt can persist for a short time even within the throne room of God. The prophet Isaiah finds himself out of contact with reality. He is swept away by the sights and sounds of the throne room, but is not made aware of his role within the assembly. Like Isaiah we must overcome our halfhearted belief in-order to become the emissary of the message of truth. He is an observer of reality and not a part of it, until he's forced by holiness into the truth made manifest in the presence of God.

In the sixth chapter of the book of Isaiah the prophet is acting like a tourist as he takes in the sights and sounds of the throne room. He says, ***"I saw the Lord seated on a throne, high and exalted, and the train of his robe filled the temple."*** *Isaiah snaps out of his tourist mentality as soon as he hears the Seraphs announce the holiness of the Lord:* ***"Holy, holy, holy is the Lord Almighty; the whole earth is full of his glory."*** *He realizes he is a sinful man in the presence of God and laments his forthcoming destruction. It is then that one of the Seraphim takes a live coal from the altar and touches the coal to his lips, saying,* ***"See, this has touched your lips; your guilt is taken away and your sin is atoned for."***

Here's what happened: Contact with holiness transformed his unholy condition of disbelief into that which is acceptable to God. His failure to recognize the presence of holiness was set aside and forgiven through recognition. This sounds quite just. His guilt is removed and his sin is atoned for by the touch of holiness. Many of us have been touched by the hand of God, if this were not the case our worship would be in vain and we would be no better off than our previous focus (lost in darkness), residing in a land offering no hope. The universal reality of right and wrong (truth) would then be reduced to just a concept limited to only the individual, without substance, for no matter which side of the equation we may be attracted, the sum would always equal the captivity associated with obliviousness.

Within this deception of false understanding, insanity would then become our closest relative, from whom it would be impossible to flee. In this we would find hopelessness, desperation and despair, wars, greed for power, and the illusion of wealth would be enhanced through our belief in the finality of man's existence. Seems to me much of that still abounds. ***Isaiah 22:12-13 The Lord, the Lord Almighty, called you on that day to weep and to wail, to tear out your hair and put on sackcloth. But see, there is joy and revelry, slaughtering of cattle and killing of sheep, eating of meat and drinking of wine! "Let us eat and drink," you say, "for tomorrow we die!"*** *The failure to recognize the commands of God will always lead to the disillusionment associated with false beliefs, causing us to deny truth, and in the-process disobey God.*

Isaiah was awakened to recognizing truth and within his realization the baggage of guilt contained within his life was exposed for all to see, and therein the statement, ***"your guilt is removed"*** *is necessary for the prophet's well-being. His sin of not recognizing the presence of God and holiness is atoned for, but the baggage of guilt must be removed from the one who serves God. In the presence of holiness everything hidden is brought into the light of truth, and can no longer ambush us with guilt and remorse for past failures. It has been exposed by the holiness of God who accepts us the way we are, at this moment, we recognize our ignorance that kept us from knowing he is correct and we are not. Those of us who continually dwell upon the past are destined to relive the distasteful moments within the painful clarity of truth. This then is one reason we are to keep focused upon what lies ahead, for what is in the past cannot be changed. We cannot completely forget but to have something removed is to be able to view it from a distance.*

Memories are like a passing cloud that triggers thought through its portraits, then quickly dissipates from view. To remain focused upon its movement and projection prolongs the dissipation and brings more details to mind. Dwelling upon the past is to keep hurt within us and to attempt denial of the healing touch of holiness. Remaining focused upon the past distracts us from the present.

Isaiah was permitted into God's presence and shocked into reality by the awareness of everyone around him. Unless we are touched by holiness and made aware of our woefully imperfect condition we will never be permitted to attain the true potential God desires for us; peace from condemnation and abundant life. The recognition of holiness made amends for Isaiah's lack of understanding, removed his guilt and atoned for his sins. From the throne room and the altar that the Seraph took the burning coal is brought to us the need to recognize the sacrifice of Christ. Isaiah was about to embark upon a mission of God's intent. There would be no room for past baggage. ***Sin and guilt tend to chase after us, and keep us focused upon the past. Sin and doubt make a blur of reality and can turn our worship into meaningless repetitions, having lost the truth of the presence of God. These can lull us into a,*** ***"God does not see what we are doing"*** *mindset, which is a loss faith.*

<u>Truth</u>

Matthew 5:14-16 "You are the light of the world. A city on a hill cannot be hidden. Neither do people light a lamp and put it under a bowl. Instead they put it on its stand, and it gives light to everyone in the house. In the same way let your light shine before men that they may see your good deeds and praise your Father in heaven." *We may see the loss of light (truth) in many ways, brought about by the slow erosion made possible by sin and doubt. In addition, seemingly repetitive imperceptible aspects of our lives, denied sight to others (usually those aspects we do not want seen in the light of day), can lead us into increased degrees of doubt. These can become a seedbed watered by acceptable internal compromise that will add rapidity to the increase of existing doubt, to the point of believing,* ***"God does not see what we are doing!"*** *Clearly this kind of erosion marks for us a need to stay focused upon God, who is ever before us. Sin and doubt can be likened to a shroud blocking the emanation of light, but also is muting the sounds of joy that must naturally emanate from the living. Whole congregations can be silenced into mechanized worship, because sin and doubt have so clouded the reality of the presence of God. And so, not only must* *we be on guard against those slings and arrows shot at us from external sources, but we must also guard our heart against the denial of truth by the internal influence of our nature that seeks to run and hide from God.*

Sustaining Grace

O Lord,
Find my helmet dented
My shield bruised and worn
See the tatters in my clothes
And scars upon my bones
See the sharpness of my sword
And find me ever watchful
In the day of your return
I have watched in readiness
The hail of sling and dart
But you, O Master
God and King
Have preserved
My heart.

Luke 12:37-38 It will be good for those servants whose master finds them watching when he comes. I tell you the truth, he will dress himself to serve, will have them recline at the table and will come and wait on them. It will be good for those servants whose master finds them ready, even if he comes in the third watch of the night.

High Fire

There's power
In the day mercy enters in
Announcing to the spirit
"A new life now begins."
There's power in the day
Freedom's breath we take
To do the things we knew as right
But we could not break away.
There's power in the knowledge
Of he who sent his flame
To burn away deception
Allowing truth to reign.
Like sanctifying embers
Engulfing us with love
You sent to us high fire
Your presence from above
O burning flame of power
Containing torrents
Of God's grace
Saving rain from heaven
Wash upon this place
Strength within us dwell
And a fortress-make!

Acts 2:1-4 When the day of Pentecost came, they were all together in one place. Suddenly a sound like the blowing of a violent wind came from heaven and filled the whole house where they were sitting. They saw what seemed to be tongues of fire that separated and came to rest on each of them.

Renew

Renew the moment of your grace
That brought me to my knees
Renew the childlike faith
Of when I first believed
Joy was in my heart
Like finding a lost friend
See how far I've fallen
How I've failed to grow
See how weak and feeble
I stand before you, Lord.
Draw close to me.
Although I seek
My faith is weak
Like fire that's grown cold
As coal turns gray around its edge
And is forgotten at the core
Somewhere I lost my way
Somewhere I lost my cross.
In the knowledge of my loss
My voice cries out with pain
"I cannot live with halfway home
Or halfway in the grave!"
Send the fire lost
Into this waiting heart
Renew my faith with binding cord
Renew this man, O Lord.

Ephesians 6:18 "And pray in the Spirit on all occasions with all kinds of prayers and requests; with this in mind be alert and always keep on praying for all the saints."

I AM

Without the eyes of faith
Who can see?
Some never understand
Life is in he who is
"I AM."
Character must be built
To awaken from dreams
In some the dream continues
Deeper until death
Great is the blindness
That shrouds the soul
Veils of layered darkness
Denying life complete
Rejecting the mind of good
To end up in defeat
If you heed the Word of God
Know this:
Passing may envelop all the senses
And darkness can sweep vision from the eye
Stilling the heart when the final beat arrives.
But, we shall continue-on
As light from the beginning
As eternity's persistence
Knows not a final dawn
Of praising and exalting God
With thunderous applause!

Psalm 46:10 "Be still, and know that I am God; I will be exalted among the nations, I will be exalted in the earth."

Matthew 18:1-4 At that time the disciples came to Jesus, asking, "Who is the greatest in the Kingdom of heaven?" So, Jesus called a child, had him stand in front of them, and said, "I assure you that unless you change and become like little children, you will never enter the Kingdom of heaven. The greatest in the Kingdom of heaven is the one who humbles himself and becomes like this

child." *Unless you change and become like little children you will never enter the Kingdom of heaven. Now, that is a powerful statement by our Lord. This does not mean we are denied salvation, rather, it points us to the lost of this world who have denied and doubted both the existence of God and the penalty associated with disbelief. For those of us who have been born again, we have received a new spirit of faith and trust, found only in the innocence of a child. When the truth of God was revealed to us through God's grace, whatever pride present in our lives was removed, and the humility necessary for entrance into the Kingdom of heaven was added. There was no doubt in our hearts and minds that the presence of God was made manifest in our lives. We were born again, made new, just as little children and we believed and trusted in God implicitly. We were not affected by any doubt or uncertainty! We must always be on guard against the natural aspects of our existence that seeks to challenge the truth we have been given. It is not that we can never enter the Kingdom of heaven, rather, it is the understanding of foundational drift that seeks to remove us from the reality we have been blessed to recognize. Again, it is our sin nature that seeks to hide from truth and in this aspect of our present life we must be vigilant against this repelling force.*

One final thought, apart from the subtle erosion of faith brought about by our sin- nature, there may come a sudden shock to our existence (such as the loss of a loved one) that impulsively, through our emotions causes us to rebel or run from God, this is a failure on our part to recognize the reality of death within this corporeal existence we all share. This kind of emotional shock is understood. It sends us into places we hope will shield us from such reality. Unfortunately for us within this emotional upheaval and otherwise panicked state we often do not run toward God. It is also a failure to recognize that at the proper time God will restore to us the righteous desire of our hearts. Just as in most cases of salvation, the sudden appearance of truth rapidly changes the direction in which we were traveling, so too, a sudden onset of sorrow or other damaging occurrence can cause us to not only question our faith, but to discard or place it into a state of suspension that has lost its meaning. Fortunately for us, while we may think we have abandoned our faith in God, he has never abandoned us to our hurts or sorrows; he remains faithful. Just as a parent will allow his child to run off into his room to sulk, over what is important to him, so it is, God allows us to run off and hide but he never leaves us alone. Amen. ***Revelation 21:4 "He will wipe every tear from their eyes. There will be no more death or mourning or crying or pain, for the old order of things has passed away."*** *In addition to the doubt that occurs through our sin-nature's influence there is the accompanying doubt that continually masks the reality of death. We know death to be a reality but we will always place it into another timeframe; another foggy and hazy existence, that while it is taking place all around us we never apply such reality to ourselves. It is no different from the hazy persistence of doubt produced within the truth as it pertains to God; denial of truth that is known to be reality.*

Innocence

Sermon and Homily are my two best friends
When we go to sleep
Sermon guards the window
And Homily the door
Both love to bark
But Sermon loves to roar!
Mother says,
"Okay, they can sleep in your bed."
You see, my friends have button eyes and tails of fluff
They can never cause a fuss.
And so,
Jesus, on you I will depend
You are my, "real" best friend.

Luke 18:16-17 Jesus called the children to him and said, "Let the children come to me and do not stop them, because the Kingdom of God belongs to such as these. Remember this! Whoever does not receive the Kingdom of God like a little child will never enter it."

Advanced Training

The fishing hole mysterious and safe
For us to cast a line in search of the "big one"
We were sure to find.
The flattened rock and old tree stump
Were the favorite spots
for launching expeditions, when days were very hot.
The fishing hole wasn't very deep
Sometimes we would swim around or just wet our feet.

It's amazing how the legend of the "big one" could persist
When no one saw him throughout all our childhood bliss.
Such faith adds excitement to children's hearts at play
Perhaps it's all in training for faith in God one day?

2 Corinthians 13:5 "Examine yourselves to see whether you are in the faith; test yourselves."

2 Corinthians 5:6 Therefore, we are always confident and know that as long, as we are home in the body we are away from the Lord.

4

CONSCIOUSNESS

Consciousness is basically self-awareness. On a deeper level (especially when right or wrong is injected into thought) the interaction is not exclusively singular; our conscience is the installation of knowledge received from disobedience to God's instruction and the subsequent advent of sin; simply explained it can be accepted as the voice of God within us. Some have asked, "How does God speak to us?" They are continually seeking God's voice, as if, awaiting the clouds to part and the voice of God declaring his proclamation; they are awaiting an answer from the supernatural with the ears of the natural man. God's voice to us is the soft whisper that assures of our actions being good, and the somewhat louder voice that condemns those actions or thoughts that oppose his will.

Conscience is not the same for everyone; religious teaching or self-determination add to the conclusive findings within us. An example of this is the determination by Paul that his eating meat offered to idols was not sinful, because his faith allowed him to do it and his conscience did not condemn him. However, the brothers in Jerusalem thought the complete opposite; they determined that it would be a sinful act for them. This is the freedom given to us in Christ; we are not encapsulated in a religious system that determines a sinful act for everyone. Such interaction with self can be peaceful or condemning dependent-upon whether there is a conflict between reason and conscience. If we do the right thing we will find a clear conscience absent guilt. Doing the right thing all the time may not be possible for sinful man, but being consciously aware aids in the strengthening of the internal mechanism called willpower. Fortunately, we are not alone in the struggle to do good because God is always with us. Reasoning, for the most part is outranked by conscience whenever there is the question of right or wrong.

When we are unconscious there is no interaction with self and in this there is no awareness of anything. Having had the need for an operation that required general anesthesia, I can testify to not being aware of the proceedings that encompassed several hours. In this instance, we are made to be oblivious to what is taking place but we are still alive. We have not lost life, and still we have been made to be unaware. There is the belief by many that when the body dies there is also a complete unawareness that overtakes the one pronounced as dead. However, we cannot give definitive closure affirming this widely-accepted belief because of the negatively reported accounts relating to unawareness at the arrival of death, simply because there is a loss of awareness reported in such instances; from those declared dead and later have returned to the living. Offsetting the negative reports are the positive accounts of afterlife or post physical death reality. Such positive reports come to us from those who have been pronounced dead by medical professionals, and have been returned to life following-activity that restored life back to the physical. The apostle Paul is clearly stating that our consciousness is viable whether in or away from the body, when we are saved.

There is a distinct likeness within the states of unconsciousness; (death, medically induced, or head trauma) wherein, self-awareness is nonexistent. However, in the case of death there is the belief in self-awareness when the body dies in Christ. In the person recognized as being unconscious brought about through anesthesia or head trauma what we find is the ability to continue the interaction with one's self after the drug has worn off or the physical trauma has healed. In the other, recognized as death, what is found is inconclusive without biblical input; inasmuch, as a concrete answer to the self-awareness aspect being present or absent, at the-moment of bodily death, finds personal witness of both positive or negative experience; but, both reports confirm the promises of the bible. The positive report reflects the manner in-which a person lived-life with acceptance of the reality of God, and his offering of salvation. Such a person had been born again in the truth of Christ and received salvation. The negative report is also a litmus test reflecting a person's denial of the salvation offered through Christ's sacrifice.

We have been given tremendous witness from both, those who have been pronounced dead by medical science and after-which have returned to life's conscious state of awareness. The witness is both affirming the existence of a continuance of self-awareness, and, also declarations constituting a negative report. That is, to say, those who have died and later have been revived, these have nothing to report regarding afterlife consciousness. As such the conclusiveness to the question, asking if there is life after death of the body, remains for the greater majority unanswered. Much of the witness compiled from interviewing those who have had near death or actual death experiences reflects a positive report affirming a continuance of life; it is this witness that affirms afterlife reality. In the dual witness (positive or negative) given to us by those who have returned from a state of being pronounced as dead, there is a need to inject all other witness as is made available to us. Such witness comes to us from the Holy Scriptures.

Given the testimony of scripture what is found is consistent with the previously announced awareness and unawareness experiences. Where the individual has died in the knowledge of salvation through the sacrifice of Christ, the spirit, which is our thinking faculty remains uninterrupted. And in the case of the unsaved individual they have nothing to report; no continuance of thought. This is in complete agreement with scriptural pronouncements.

We must also recognize there needs to be a triggering within the individual that permits the transfer of the spirit to another state of existence. This transference does not take place simply because a state of unconsciousness exists. An awareness of death taking place must be triggered for transfer of consciousness, apart from the body.

A third witness speaks of a troubling, frightening and horrific experience, making such a deep impression that the persons involved in such experience completely turn their lives around; they make a complete positive change in their lives by being made aware of the afterlife reality. Perhaps such experience is their born-again moment wherein they are made aware of afterlife and the reality of such life absent God?

Matthew 4:4 "It is written: 'Man does not live on bread alone, but, on every word that comes from the mouth of God.'" *In the above scripture, we are alerted to both the physical and spiritual needs of man. It is the sacrifice of Jesus that brings to us the ability to continue our existence once the physical aspect of life has died. Just because the body has died it does not necessarily follow that the thinking aspect of life should also relent to the laws of nature. In fact, it is the supernatural that exists in the ability to think. This is made known to us from scripture:* ***"In the beginning the Lord God formed man out of the clay of the ground and breathed into his nostrils the breath of life."***

This breath of life is the giving of the Spirit of God to man and in this giving a living person is derived. As such it is of supernatural origin and not subjected to the laws of nature. It is only when we are separated from the source of life do we lose our ability to be self-aware when bodily death occurs. Being born again is the restoration of the spirit initially given to man, as such, the declaration by Jesus to Nicodemus that he (Nicodemus) must be born again to acquire ability to not only see, but, also to enter the kingdom of God, confirms reports of either positive or negative afterlife experience. Within the kingdom of God, whether, in or away from the body, there is no loss of consciousness because we are united to the very source of life. Apart from the kingdom death declares: "Nothing."

When separated from the source of life

Death at this point is total. It is written: ***"The dead know nothing."*** *If truth is to be told, all that exists in the natural world requires a reinstalling aspect to continue within the natural existence of reality. This reinstalling aspect in man is the* ***"born again"*** *experience. The born-again person has his corporeal body within the natural world and his born-again spirit awaiting transfer into the supernatural (pure spiritual existence).*

Here again it is written, ***"What is of the earth returns to the earth and the spirit returns to God who gave it."*** *This ability to exist outside of the natural aspect of creation comes to us through the sacrifice of Jesus. It is this sacrifice of his life that enables us to once again be united to the reality of eternity with meaning.*

Now, what could be the triggering mechanism that recognizes death of the body, and in so doing permits the spirit to be removed from the confinement of flesh and bone? In reality-the spirit is not confined totally within the body; we can certainly project our thoughts outside the confines of flesh; we do this every time we enter-into prayer and consciously present ourselves in the presence of God. Perhaps a final exit of the spirit is permitted at the arrival of death and is reliant upon the same determinations made by the medical profession when pronouncing the arrival of the death of an individual?

The thinking faculty that is our consciousness recognizes there is no longer a need to be present within the individual, simply because the individual's body has ceased to exist within the inevitable aspect of death. A watch may stop functioning but it does not mean the battery is dead. The same is true with the existence of our consciousness; the body may no longer have viability but it does not mean the spirit is no longer in existence. The spirit is the control mechanism for the body administered through the physical brain, and once the body dies there is no longer a reason for such controlling mechanism to remain.

Can we imagine a moment wherein the distinction between life and death of the body is so thin it produces the near-death-experience or an out of body experience? The person experiences the initial transfer only to be told to return to his body, or else, there is nothing to report other than being unaware that anything had taken place. I think this is a plausible conjecture. Again, a watch battery can be removed by the watchmaker when the watch no longer is operable from a mechanical perspective, and the spirit given to us at rebirth is returned to the Maker of Mankind. Just because we do not see the thinking process at the time of death, via medical devices indicating brain activity has ceased, does not mean the thinking process has ceased. The physical brain is dependent upon the spirit but the spirit is not dependent upon the brain. The battery of the watch will remain viable even when the mechanical function of the watch has failed. It is written: ***"What is of the earth returns to the earth and spirit returns to God who gave it."*** *Using the same watch maker analogy, the battery (spirit) receives recharging daily from God, and when the watch (body) dies there is no disconnect because we have been constantly connected to the source of life. This truth written in the book of Ecclesiastes, pertaining to the spirit of man returning to God is not an all-inclusive truth. Some will not immediately continue with self-awareness because the,* ***"dead know nothing."*** *Jesus spoke in parables on many occasions and other times he spoke plainly. I'm reminded of the disciple who wanted to leave Jesus so he could bury his father who had passed away. The disciple is told to let the dead bury the dead. Those not alive in Christ whether living or deceased are considered dead. If we are not made alive in Christ while we are in the natural realm of existence, we will have no vehicle in which to approach God; we are in-fact already dead and unable to understand the words spoken by our Lord. Sin that has not been forgiven through the sacrifice of Christ cannot approach God. As such the consciousness of those not in Christ awaits the second resurrection to judgment wherein they will once again be made aware of themselves.*

Romans 1:17 For in the gospel a righteousness from God is revealed, a righteousness that is by faith from first to last, just as it is written: "The righteous shall live by faith." *Simply expressed, faith is belief in the pronouncements of God. God called Abraham righteous because he believed God. Faith is not reliant upon our intellect. Although one can reason the reality of the existence of God and of the supernatural realm, proof that is given to us is the gift from God that we call faith. All of us were in the category of believing no proof is possible as it pertains to the existence of God, but once we received the gift of faith through grace, we understood, we believed and we knew of the reality we had previously denounced.*

In the third chapter of the gospel of John we are made aware of the conversation between Jesus and a Pharisee named Nicodemus. Jesus imparts to Nicodemus that he must be born-again to enter the kingdom of God, in addition he adds, absent being the recipient of a new spirit he (Nicodemus) could not even see the kingdom. The kingdom will remain hidden while in the body or when the body dies. This information is explosive! Jesus is telling all of us that we need to have our old way of thinking replaced with truth, and with the receipt and acceptance of truth we are then given the spirit capable of continued existence after the body has died. We have been given, once again, the spirit of truth that we had received at the beginning of creation, and discarded through the act of disobedience and disbelief. We did not believe God's pronouncement that we should not eat of the fruit from the tree in the center of the garden. And so, it was through disbelief and disobedience that we lost eternal life, and it is through belief and obedience that we have once again received it. We have received the ability to see clearly while at home in this earthly tent, and after the body has returned to the dust from which it came, we will still be aware of who we are. We have been given the spirit that is guaranteed for all eternity. We shall be restored to the initial prototype of mankind at the resurrection of the body to eternal life. In fact, we will be improved from the original design because we can now understand much more due to the hard times and struggles we have experienced in this present life. Courage compassion mercy and other virtues could not be understood by Adam and Eve simply because there was no need to understand. This sounds to all of us as one heck of a miracle! Of course, if we do not believe in the existence of the supernatural realm we will find it impossible to even acknowledge the reality of miracles. C.S. Lewis in his discourse on, "Miracles" breaks down humanity into two types of individuals. One being the "Naturalist" who has no belief in the supernatural and credits all there is to exist within the natural realm, thus, so-called miracles are naturally occurring events. The other individual is labeled by him as the "Supernaturalist," and in this, we find the miraculous gift of faith comes to us from outside of the natural realm. If faith in God and the supernatural dimension could be embraced through natural occurrences perceived by the senses, then there would be no one who doubts. However, because faith is a gift that occurs within the spiritual aspect of humanity, and is experienced on a personal level, the avenue for belief through testimonial witness is explained away by the doubters, as just a part of the complexity inherent in the human condition.

Mark 5:34 He said to her, "Daughter, your faith has healed you." *We can paraphrase the words of Jesus by saying,* ***"Your faith has made you whole."*** *In this instance, the woman received a healing because she had faith in God's mercy and his ability to heal her. She was made whole. The same is true when we recognize our need to be made whole as it applies to the spiritual aspect of our existence. All physical and spiritual infirmities (sin) find positive remedial cure at the feet of Christ. It was perhaps the testimony of others that brought her to Jesus. Others who had either received or witnessed a miraculous physical healing, wherein otherwise there may have been nothing but desperate hopeful desire for her to reach out beyond the confines of the natural abilities of man and tap into the unlimited ability of God. Certainly, faith was her last resort and she was not disappointed!*

I think therefore I am

Another interesting aspect of belief requiring proof is the obstacle of proving our very own existence. The French Philosopher Rene Descartes tackles this question with the most obvious of explanations, "I think therefore I am." Wow! It is with the spiritual aspect of humanity that we prove our existence. If the spiritual is proof of our existence why then is it not proof of the existence of God and the supernatural realm in which he inhabits? The spirit/mind is the connection to the physical brain and the spirit/ mind is the connection between mankind and God. Without the spirit present within the body there cannot be physical life, and without a new spirit received through being-born again there can be no continuance of life after the body dies; no continuance of consciousness. It's obvious to us that when viewing the dead, the spirit is no longer present. One must ask, "Where has this soul/spirit gone?" The answer to this question has been clearly annunciated in the bible.

Unfaithful

Deuteronomy 32:20 "I will hide my face from them," he said, "and see what their end will be; for they are a perverse generation, children who are unfaithful." *They were children who were unfaithful. They had failed belief in the reality of God. As such, God declares that he will aid their unfaithfulness by hiding his reality from them! He also says,* ***"and see what their end will be."*** *The beginning of their end starts with permitting permanent residency to the falsehoods pronounced by the world that seeks to also hide the existence of truth. It is perfectly okay for us to admit our lack of faith and in this admission, ask for the faith necessary to see such truth. It is written,* ***"The Lord looks down from heaven to see if there is anyone seeking him."*** *In this, we recognize that God will not hide himself from those who are seeking truth. One such truth is that we cannot completely become fully aware of who we are until we come to the reality of who God is. Our consciousness cannot be told to rest until we permit truth to stop the war of denial.*

Hebrews 11:6 "And without faith it is impossible to please God, because anyone who comes to him must believe that he exists and that he rewards those who earnestly seek him." *The ultimate reward for seeking God and finding him is eternal life. God is not hiding himself from those who earnestly desire to know truth. We cannot find peace within us until the truth of God is found and accepted. Even though we may be unaware of the truth, it is within us. We were made to disbelieve, (by worldly deception coupled with our sin-nature) to be unaware of the prison that keeps our spirit bound and gagged within the darkness of unknowing, manufactured by the world and our sin-nature that desires not to be exposed; we were held within the darkness of ignorance concerning God, but should we be inclined to explore reality, to seek truth, to release ourselves from the deceit that denies God, he will remove the blindfold, so that we can see clearly. Indeed,* ***"The truth will set you free."***

Deuteronomy 29:5 During the forty years that I led you through the desert, your clothes did not wear out, nor did the sandals on your feet. *Before we get to the point where God determines that he will, "hide his face from them" what we are finding is a tremendous inability to recognize God, even when he has not tried to hide his reality from them. These people lived a life (perhaps filled with a heavy burdensome amount of hardships) but throughout all forty years they were continually aware of the miracles provided by the one who not only freed them from a life of slavery but also provided for all their physical needs. Clothing not wearing out and sandals denied the natural wear caused by friction, is hinting at eternal life.*

Now, let us look at the parallel pathway taken by Jesus when he speaks to the crowds through the usage of parables. ***Matthew 13:34-35 Jesus spoke all these things to the crowd in parables; he did not say anything to them without using a parable. So was fulfilled what was spoken through the prophet: "I will open my mouth in parables, I will utter things hidden since the creation of the world."*** *Clearly, Jesus spoke in parables so they would not understand. Who are these who should not understand? All of those* *who God had decided should not understand, but, for all others God did not hide his face (truth) from them. Later, we see the disciples asking for understanding of the parables, and Jesus explains to them the wonderful metaphorical expressions that symbolized the truth, that many have found and many have not been permitted to understand.*

Sight

Feel the rushing wind
Descending flame embrace
Deep within me praise
And worship of your name

No sight from birth
Until the spirit heard your voice
Wisdom's light leads the heart
Truth to show the mind our God

Bound and gagged by deception's bite
Made blind inside
Truth appeared and life made clear
No longer can death issue fear

O the blessing that is sight
Even when our vision fails
Or is absent from the start
We can see the truth of God
When searching with the heart

There are many who say, "I can see"
But, really, have no sight
For they have denied the truth
Contained within God's light.

2 Corinthians 5:1 "Now we know that if the earthly tent we live in is destroyed, we have a building from God, an eternal house in heaven, not built by human hands."

Now we are aware, when the body dies we will continue-on for eternity, for we have received the down payment assuring us of this promise. We have received the Spirit of new life purchased for us in the shed blood of Christ. We have been made new, born again by the truth of God.

Consciousness absent understanding

Matthew 13:13 "This is, why I speak to them in parables: 'Though seeing they do not see; though hearing they do not hear or understand.'" *This statement by Jesus is the same as,* ***"I will hide my face from them."*** *There are some things we are aware of and others that present to us not even an inkling of suspicion. And then there are those things that one may think to be obvious, especially to those who know us best, and yet, such thoughts of obviousness may be foreign to those we think should be aware. This is most pronounced in the mind of Jesus when he goes missing and ultimately is found in the temple speaking with the elders. When Jesus is found his response to the concerned admonishment of his mother is such that he says,* ***"Why did you have to look for me? Didn't you know I had to be in my Father's house?"***

He is responding with the depth that goes beyond the physical recognition present within the here and now, rather, within the question is found the simplicity of truth; with pure-innocence he asks, "Where else would you look for me, didn't you know I had to be home?" Whether or-not Jesus knew of the far-reaching implication of his question is food for thought, but we understand that at this point Jesus reunites with his family, is obedient (honor thy father and thy mother), and grows in knowledge. Jesus growing in knowledge and wisdom may be a bit of a mystery to us, simply because he is incarnate God. As such, by sharing in humanity he subjects himself to all the challenges inherent within humanity; these to include growing in knowledge and every other aspect of the human condition except for sin.

Unlike dodgeball truth keeps us in the game

When we look at the life of Christ and the truth he presented to the world we can recognize the injection of resistance by others; the lies and counterfeit rebuttals designed to prevent our focusing upon his teachings. False actions and thoughts given support by a society or persons will find perpetuation until we become aware of the wrong derived by such thoughts or actions. These false thoughts or actions placed into existence highlight the counterfeits presented to mankind throughout all time; such occurrences are a part of the nature of man to deny and hide from truth. They are described as counterfeits because they do not represent truth. As such, with the revelations brought to us by Jesus we have a foundation in which we can remain focused upon truth, and not be led astray by sights sounds and demonstrable actions meant to capture our conscious thoughts within a vacuum, absent the fresh air of truth. The foundation for all truth is the life of Christ. When we get hit with truth it keeps us in the game!

Truth is like a radiant star meant for us to follow to our destination of eternal life, and the lie is the counterfeit leading the unsuspecting to the flame. The moth is attracted by light but it does not distinguish such light to be flame until it is too late! Truth is like a railroad track, having ties and spikes and rails leading us in the direction intended no matter what side of the track we may be on. The world is filled with attractions and distractions away from acceptable living and meant to be attractive to the sin nature of man; it's also filled with people adept at the manipulation of truth in such a way the counterfeit is easily digested by many; especially, when one has never been exposed to the truth of life. When we are aware of the straightforward unchanging direction of absolute truth there is very little chance of losing our way along the railway of life. Just as a railroad track is narrow and defined without ambiguity so it is with the presentation of truth given to us from the life of Christ.

A change in awareness

Years later Jesus would once again enter the temple but this time he would show his displeasure as to how the property was managed. What he found was corrupt management and a failure on the part of those entrusted to fulfill the purpose of the owner of the property. What he found was a failure on the part of those who had been given the responsibility to work the land and to bear fruit; they would not give to others the tools of truth necessary for them to enter the field and fulfill the purpose of the one who owns the property. We find the descriptive of, "tools of truth," highlighted by the apostle Peter, as he responds to a question by Jesus: **"Lord, where would we go? Only you have the words that lead to eternal life."** *Only you possess the tools of truth that can defeat the deceptions of the world making it possible for us to receive eternal life. It is during the ministry of Jesus that an entirely different perspective of God is presented to the people. No longer are the people to be bound by the religious rule of those who determine adherence to or transgression against such religiosity. They are being set free from such tyranny by being made aware that God loves them!*

Unity

There is a strikingly conscious sense of community during the time of Jesus, highlighted for us at the time he is found in the temple speaking with the elders. Family friends and neighbors got together and made the trip to Jerusalem (the distance between Jerusalem and Nazareth was ninety-three miles), to celebrate the feast of Passover. Surely, safety in numbers was among the top reason for traveling in groups, as there was an awareness of wrong-doers not only present in the consciousness of those living in the region, but this mindset was prevalent throughout the entire world. The recognition of those who do wrong and harm to others had become an embedded conscious fact, and in this knowledge people united in-order to thwart the plans of those whose hearts have been derailed from the road of acceptability. As the group is returning from the celebration of the Passover and renewal of appreciation for the wonderful miracle of freedom they have enjoyed, someone asks, "Hey! Where is Jesus?" An entire day had passed before they realized Jesus was not among them. They probably walked back to Jerusalem in record pace and after three days of frantic searching they find him in the temple and the rest is history. I believe the entire group had searched for Jesus. The sense of community and problem solving impacted everyone in the group. This community search is what was expected and thought to be the normal reaction when a member or members of a group are in need. Jesus is lost. His whereabouts is unknown. His family is frantic. When he is found, peace is once again restored to the hearts of those who love him. At the death of Christ, he is once again lost for three days and when he is resurrected joy is restored and "life" is pronounced to humanity! Mankind was meant to be united to God. We should ask, why is it some people have great difficulty in asking for help? If we cannot ask of others how can we find the need great enough to ask of God? There is a problem with the existence of pride; perhaps, it is the inherent belief of being independent and powerful?

Some of us have set-out upon the journey of life surrounded by family, friends and neighbors thinking that Jesus is among us, only to find that it is we who have left him behind, we had focused on life's distractions and lost sight of what is most valuable. Slowly we come to the realization that leads us to search frantically, throughout the myriad of activities sights and sounds in life, and we lament our inattentiveness to the people and things we hold most precious. Large communities and activities can sometimes cause us to lose sight of what we take for granted. We can become so involved in all that is taking place around us, we can fail to notice the obvious. A continuity of thought is one that remains focused upon what is most precious; along with all the blessing derived by the presence of such goodness in our lives. Celebrations and attractions are fine, but let us remember, without Jesus there is no party!

The presentation of Jesus in the temple

According, to the law of Moses on the ***eighth day*** *it was time to circumcise Jesus and it was also the day he is named. Also in accord with the law of Moses all firstborn males are to be dedicated to the Lord, and it is in this venue that Jesus is presented to God within the temple setting. In Jerusalem at that time was a man named Simeon, and it was his desire to see the salvation of the Lord before he died. He believed God would grant his request and in this he was attentive and filled with expectation.* ***Luke 2:29 "Sovereign Lord, as you have promised you now dismiss your servant in peace. For my eyes, have seen your salvation, which you have promised in the sight of all people, a light for revelation to the Gentiles and for glory for your people Israel."*** *There was also an eighty-four-year old prophetess named Anna, who never left the temple, but worshipped night and day fasting and praying.* ***"Coming up to them at that very moment, she gave thanks to God and spoke about the child to all who were looking forward to the redemption of Israel."***

This initial entrance of Jesus into the temple is met with small recognition except for the two who were waiting in anticipation. Had anyone heard the declarations of Simeon and Anna? It appears that not too many people were awaiting the salvation of Israel. They were perhaps cognizant of the prophetic utterances promising a Messiah who would bring to the world a light of understanding never-before imagined. They were aware of the promised salvation from God, but were they fully aware of its meaning and the manner in-which such salvation would be brought to fruition? It is hard to imagine an empty temple with no one available to hear the good news of the Christ Child's arrival, but for those who were anticipating his arrival they were not disappointed. They had been given the realization of all they had hoped for. In the same-way there are many today, who are aware of the promise of the return of Jesus to the world he had left. The world he had departed from, but a world now covered in the residual truth of God and the monolithic universal power for salvation present for all who will but reach out and receive. Are we anticipating the second coming of Jesus?

Ancient Vision

The world ancient and vast
Presented a challenge for early man
United in language and common speech
The progression of man moved further east
Settling down in a place that was known
They decided to call Babylonia home.

Plans were developed for city and tower
To reach the heavenly power
Not rocks or stone but bricks born of fire
Met the condition of what was required.

God disapproved of their pride-filled plans
He scattered them all into distant lands
And confusion was then the language of man.

He scattered them in all directions of travel
Ending their efforts in the place known as Babel.

Genesis 11:3-4 They said to each other, "Come let's make bricks and bake them thoroughly." They used bricks instead of stone, and tar instead of mortar. Then they said. "Come let us build ourselves a city, with a tower that reaches to the heavens, so that we may make a name for ourselves and not be scattered over the face of the whole earth.

A NATION UNITED WITHOUT GOD CANNOT LAST
WE MUST KNOW OF THE EXISTENCE OF GOD
FOR COMPLETE UNITY WITH SELF
DIVISION IN THE NATION WILL CAUSE A FALL
DISCONNECTION FROM GOD IN A
MAN WILL BRING HIS RUIN

Knowing

EZEKIAL 1:4 "There in Babylonia beside the Chebar River, I heard the Lord speak to me, and I felt his power." *There is a difference between knowing and believing. The person who has been transformed by the receipt of God's grace, he, just as the priest and prophet EZEKIAL, has felt the power of God. It is in this acknowledgement of God's power, present in our lives we not only believe but we know the truth of his existence. The recipient of mercy knows where such mercy has come from. The one who receives not only feels the power but experiences the resulting freedom produced by being set free from the captivity of the world's entrapment techniques, deeply invested in keeping people in the darkness of unknowing. Knowing is a conscious aspect of our existence! While it's true there are many things we are not aware of, but the truth of the existence of God is never in doubt in the one who has heard and felt his power.*

In addition to feeling the power of God actively working in our lives, we also have the witness of others who have testified to the change in their lives. We can see for ourselves the change in a person who has completely been removed from former negatively wrong lifestyles. This witness is clearly seen as an external proof of the presence of God actively working in a person's life.

Acts 12:11 Then Peter realized what had happened to him, and said, "Now I know that it is really true! The Lord sent his angel to rescue me from Herod's power and from everything the Jewish people expected to happen." *Even those who had been very close to our Lord find revelation and in such-revelation we find the exclamation,* ***"Now I know!"*** *Throughout scripture we are given presentations wherein we are made to understand, not only because it is written in God's word, but because what is written is also experienced within our own lives.*

Hebrews 10:34 You shared the sufferings of prisoners, and when all of your belongings were seized, you endured your loss gladly, because you knew that you still possessed something much

better, which would last forever." *Throughout scripture we are told of the knowledge of* ***knowing****, present within those who have accepted the truth of Christ's sacrifice and in such-acceptance there is the truth of God's reality exploding into the consciousness with joy. The hope for freedom no longer exists for no one hopes for what he sees. We know we possess eternal life; we are conscious of this reality! Coming to the fact of God's existence expressed as "****knowing"*** *as opposed to belief is at times for many a two-step process. For some of us the knowing aspect is immediate, given the depths from which one has been rescued. The deeper our captivity the more we believed there was no hope for freedom; however, once set free the impact of such a change shouts with definitive clarity throughout every fiber of our being: "My God! My God! My God!" When the freedom experienced is not so dramatically brought about, the knowing aspect of our faith may take a bit more time. Additionally, what we find is the witness from others and scripture, pointing us to the knowing aspect of God's existence. Those who have received mercy know where it came from.*

1 John 5:13-15 I am writing to you so that you may know that you have eternal life-you that believe in the Son of God. We have courage in God's presence, because we are sure that he hears us if we ask him for anything that is according-to his will. He hears us whenever we ask him; and since we know this is true, we know also that he gives us what we ask for. *In just these few verses we hear the declaration of witness speaking words intending to bring a knowing aspect into the life of the believer. Additionally, we hear the declarations written to the readers of the letter affirming their present state of faith. That is, they know God hears them and they know that what they ask of God they will receive, so long as it is in accordance with his will. In accordance with his will simply means that we do not know all the plans of God for either ourselves or others as well as the world, as such, what we receive from God will always be a part of his overall plans, for not only ourselves but for those that may be impacted.*

Disunity

In addition to consciously accepting and understanding the reality of the promises of Christ and the renewal of all who call upon him, we must understand the attempts aimed at disbelief and disunity (both within the church and externally) by worldly personalities consciously promoting an atmosphere of division, not only within like-groups of people but throughout the diversity of humanity itself. ***Jude 14-19 The Lord will come with many thousands of his angels to bring judgment on all for the godless deeds they have performed and for all the terrible words that godless sinners have spoken against him. These people are always grumbling and blaming others; they follow their own evil desires; they brag about themselves and flatter others to get their own way. But remember, my friends, what you were told in the past by the apostles of our Lord Jesus Christ. They said to you, "When the last days come, people will appear who will make fun of you, people who follow their own godless desires." These are the people who cause divisions, who are controlled by their natural desires, who do not have the Spirit.*** *So much for those politicians who presented themselves as persons who will unite the country. So much for those people who would silence the truth of God by denying him and by doing everything possible to remove him from the classrooms of our youth and everywhere else that pronounces his existence. At least we have been given the means through which they can be identified as antichrists in this present day! These are the people that cause divisions within the church the community and the country. There are politicians today whose only mission in life appears to be to cause deep chasms of division based upon ideological beliefs, race, and of course to solidify a mindset in groups of people by attempting to think for them: "All people of color must vote this way and let us not alienate this or that group of people for fear they will vote as a unified block against us." Whatever happened to individual thought? Whatever happened to the ability to think for one's self and to determine, what is a correct way to speak think and act?*

Good against evil, rich against poor, the learned looking-down upon the unlettered and of course the divide within the diversity of cultures: black, white, red, brown and yellow, all are presented to us as blocks of people having one perception when pertaining to voting in a particular-election. All people are grouped together by voices promoting a herding atmosphere when attempting to elicit a certain response at the voting booth. At the root of all the attempts at disunity is the lie! At the entrance of the lie there is the continuous onslaught of condemnation against all who do not think like them, purposely geared to keep unity from approaching a level of peaceful existence. The title of "community organizer" should rightfully be called "troublemaker." ***"These people are always grumbling and blaming others."*** *There is already the very pronounced disunity produced by the good and evil aspects existing within governments of the world. Those that subdue the occupants of a given country, and those that lend the appearance of a level playing field, to the inhabitants within democracies declaring a myriad of opportunity; while underlying such declarations a class of perpetuation is maintained by affordability; granting to those having voice the sometimes-overbearing presence of forcefulness regarding the direction in which a society will travel. With all the disunity in the world it is amazing that there is (in some-instances) a sense of unity within the churches of God. I say this because apart from some church communities there is a constant droning from the electronic television-church for tithes and partnerships that one must ask, "Is there anything more important in the ministry of the Word that could possibly overshadow the constant pleading for contributions?" A man must ask himself, "Is the request for fifty million dollars from a television preacher to purchase a personal Lear Jet really necessary for the continuance of ministry?" Many local pastors, priests and ministers of the gospel are doing God's work without a Lear Jet; what then makes this television personality in such need?*

It becomes difficult to trust such personalities when they appear surrounded in opulence. Some have been dragged off to prison in tears and another had given his congregation a deadline to raise money, or else, "God will take him home," which also can be understood as God threatening to kill him. Given all these shortcomings exposing the darker side of questionable ministries shouldn't we ask the question as to why many have found their selves separating from such noise-making churches that have failed to recognize they are continually in God's presence? This failure to recognize the presence of God leaves a church or ministry as an empty shell; useless. It is troubling when mankind finds himself continually attempting to give to the world the appearance of godliness and in the often unseen, behind backdoor operations, there is the ugliness that God frowns upon, and his children avoid. There are many reasons for the empty pews. People have, in all good consciousness left the churches, but they have not left the truth of Christ's sacrifice or the salvation it has brought to them.

Scam Shame

Beware of those fancy suits
And their hard sell of worldly pursuits
They'll invite you to purchase
A prayer cloth that's worthless
Or shares in an earthly campaign
It bolsters their image theatrical visage
Rewarding with mansions and things
They are not serving the King!

2 Corinthians 2:17 "Unlike so many, we do not peddle the word of God for profit. On the contrary, in Christ we speak before God with sincerity, like men sent from God.

In all aspects of life there is much diversity, but people are basically defined within two groups, those who find the conscious awareness of God to be a known fact of life and those who do not. For many, such awareness will not find fruition in this life; will only be made recognizable on the great Day of Judgment which will be too late. Why do we adopt the belief that God does not exist? I suspect there is more than one reason for this happening in-spite of all the evidence that shouts to us of the creative genius of God. At the top of such reasoning, I suspect is the pride that originated all sin. The rebellion against God continues in both spectrums of either conscious awareness or unconscious defiance. One other recognizable aspect of rebellion is the conscious act of defying God which is so prevalent in today's groups of people united in the effort to erase him from the speech of mankind. These groups of people hide under the umbrella of atheism that says to the world, "We don't believe in God." I don't place my faith in cartoon characters, but just because I don't believe they exist does not mean they should cause me to become angry against the children who fantasize in such a world created by the imaginations of man. And so, we, are given a view into the hearts of those who attack believers on all levels, such attackers recognize God's truth and in such recognition- denial, they seek to minimize the threat to their rebellious lifestyles that are being exposed in the light of day! If they do not believe in the existence of God, why then should it anger them when others say that they do? Deep within these masqueraders lives the truth of God but they are pained every time they are brought into the declarations of believers; in this they strike-out at the very truth that they attempt to continually keep buried in their subconscious. We have looked at the believer, the unknowing disbeliever, and the people who say they do not believe but are consciously aligned with evil, dead-set against all that is good and holy. This is the prideful position adopted by the Evil One and finds continuance in his children.

Definitive biblical declaration

John 11:25-28 Jesus said to her, "I am the resurrection and the life. The one who believes in me will live, even though he dies, and whoever lives and believes in me will never die. Do you believe this?" "Yes, Lord," she told him, I believe that you are the Christ, the Son of God, who was to come into the world."

Declaration

Believe it or not the choice is yours
A handful of dirt a man in his plot
"Ashes to ashes and dust to dust"
A must in this world of natural stuff
Nothing can touch the thoughts of a man
Not age or rust corruption or dust
Not torrents of rain or downfalls of cold
Time's constant ticking gains-not a moment of old.

Romans 13:11 And do this, understanding the present time: The hour has already come for you to wake up from your slumber, because our salvation is nearer now than when we first believed.

Memory

The older I get the less speed in memory-recall I seem to possess. I can remember many things, but also, many things have fallen to the bottom and are denied access to my consciousness, as quickly as when I was younger; because of the wearing aspect of aging upon the physical brain. While I don't recall something as quickly as before, the command to recall a specific name or event-memory, from the spirit has not been removed, the attempt to find the memory continues even when I am no longer concentrating on the thought. Because of the lack of immediate retrieval, I move on to the next thought occupying my life. It doesn't mean the initiating, seeking of information from the spirit has ceased; the spirit has the information, and has attempted to download the sought-after inquiry back through the physical brain, but, has found a problem in communication through the normal pathway; the spirit continues seeking for a route in which such information can be transmitted and once found appears in my consciousness once again. It could take hours for the spiritual process to complete the delivery of the sought-after memory through a pathway in the brain, and may even wake us from sleep; upon finding an avenue into conscious awareness, the spirit rests from the endeavor. It may be the recalled thought also, does not have the staying power of my youth, but everything else in my nature has been slowed by the aging process; should I not expect a decline within the physical brain as well? We find this continuing effort to recall, not a singular function of the spiritual process of administration; the spirit, when finding an untruth that we had unknowingly digested, (but should have recognized) because the truth in such instance has already been catalogued within the spirit, the spirit then endeavors to correct our misplaced and erroneous filing, by making us aware of the improper digestion of untruth. Again, we may be awakened in the middle of the night once the avenue within the physical brain has been found and permits entry into our consciousness. As Paul tells us concerning the spirit searching the deep things of God, and so too our spirit also searches all that is us and the house cleaning of untruth is ongoing, even when we are unaware of the process taking place.

Some memories are like annoying pop-ups on our computers (they never seem to be able to sink to the bottom). Although this may be annoying what it may tell us is that the spirit is not making decisions as to what we can remember or what should be depressed totally within the subconscious. However, in the case of the conscience there is perhaps never a moment wherein there is denied an avenue for us to not become aware of the warnings within the contemplation of wrong doing. This is reassuring in that no matter the degree of aging process deterioration and difficulty derived by such wearing of the cranial pathways (apart from disease) the conscience will always be viable. This is a reasonable assumption because if it were otherwise, without the advance-warning one might raise a "I did not know defense" when standing before the ultimate transparency, which is God's throne. While the normal pathway for a particular-thought may be worn-down by the aging process, the spirit seeks a new physical avenue through which the answer to the inquiry may be brought to my conscious awareness. It is the spirit that sends the sought-after answer to the brain, and once found, it is reported to my conscious attention and no longer remains dormant and suppressed within the subconscious. It is the primary function of the brain to collect information from the physical (natural world) and uplift it to the spiritual, where it is stored in memory forever, without any chance of loss. Therefore, our thoughts are always presented to God. I now begin to understand the meaning of the Apostle Paul's determination that once we are no longer bound by this earthly tent (body) we will find an explosion of not only understanding, but, all will be clearly defined, upfront and personal; no longer hindered by the unclear vision of our present understanding, as if viewed through a reflection of reality. The physical will no longer hinder thought, when we are existing in a pure spiritual state.

1 Corinthians 13:12 What we see now is like a dim image in a mirror; then we shall see face-to-face; what I know now is only partial; then it will be complete-as complete as God's knowledge of me. *GNB*

Just as all things related to bodily functions have found an inability to no longer perform as when youth had prevailed, so too, it is with the deterioration of the physical brain. The memories are not lost, because, like the permanence of a tattoo, memories are permanently imprinted upon our spirit. And so, as the deterioration of the body continues until completely inoperable, (physical death), the indelible memories have not been lost. Just as we can no longer do or accomplish many of the things that were relatively easy in our youth, so it is the physical brain is not immune to aging. Whatever is subjected to the aging process (all in nature) finds an equal opportunity detrimental reduction aspect, in every area of the body; no part of the physical aspect of life is immune from incremental loss of functionality.

Everyone experiencing the aging process will find a certain amount of memory loss that should not be included in the formal descriptive of "disease." It is a part of the normal process of aging, but like every other aspect of reduction, it is done within increments that do not deny continued interaction with others; and has no effect upon the spirit, no matter how much brain function loss is experienced. Loss of memory is centered in two main areas; our own inquires that attempt to remember, and, also externally, when we are asked if we remember a certain person place incident or thing. The Book of Revelation speaks of books being opened on the great day of judgment; we are these opened books, unaffected by any aspect of nature.

Revelation 20:12 And I saw the dead great and small alike, standing before the throne. Books were opened, and then another book was opened, the book of the living. The dead were judged according-to what they had done, as recorded in the books.

Warning

COLLOSSIANS 1:28 So we preach Christ to everyone. With all possible wisdom, we warn and teach them in-order to bring each one into God's presence as a mature individual in union with Christ. *There is a subtleness within the word "warning." The "war" consonant divulges the potential for problems should we not heed the wisdom spoken in the presentation. Not heeding warning, to cease from activities or remaining unmindful of the truth and reality of God will always find consequence in life. Discord will be found within our consciousness. It is our conscience that alerts and guards our integrity, principles, morality, and ethics; giving warning to avoid deviation from what we understand is acceptable to both conscience and God. When Paul speaks to the church within all possible wisdom, he is saying the words he's using to impact the church in a positive fashion are the very words/wisdom of God. The origin of all wisdom issues forth from the mouth of God.*

Sirach 24:1-4&8 Wisdom sings her own praises, before her own people she proclaims her glory; in the assembly of the Most High she declares her worth: "From the mouth of the Most High I came forth and mist like covered the earth. In the highest heavens, did I dwell, my throne on a pillar of cloud. Then the Creator of all gave me his command, and he who formed me gave me the spot for my tent, saying, 'In Jacob make thy dwelling, in Israel thy inheritance.' *NAB*

Note: The book of Sirach is listed among the books known as, apocryphal, and while accepted by Catholic, and orthodox branches of Christianity as divinely inspired, the protestant church as well as others do not. Instead, Sirach is recognized as the largest book of wisdom and acceptable for study. I have included this passage from Sirach because what is spoken by the author is clearly truthful. And since all wisdom originates from God the book in this instance is without doubt (in my humble opinion) divinely inspired.

It was Solomon who asked the Lord for the gift of wisdom. He didn't ask for riches or long life or any of the imaginations of man; he asked for wisdom so he could lead God's people correctly. Only the very foolish and prideful will find difficulty in understanding there is a wealth of wisdom that does not originate in them. And so, it is, we find the Apostle Paul declaring his words presented to us (the church) to be the most possible revelation of wisdom. Where there is wisdom there is truth and where there is truth there is the Lord.

Where there's anything pointing to wisdom and truth there is always a counterfeit competing for the attention and adherence to its presentation. **COLLOSSIANS 2:8-10 See to it, then, that no one enslaves you by means of worthless deceit of human wisdom, which comes from the teaching handed down by men and the ruling spirits of the universe, and not from Christ. For the full content of divine nature lives in Christ, in his humanity, and you have been given full life in union with him. He is supreme over every spiritual ruler and authority.** *We are being alerted to the falsehoods in the wisdom of the world and of the so-called wisdom presented everywhere else. We can find this kind of deception to be always present in the words of evil. Being conscious of untruth and the myriad of ways it may be presented should not be thought of as being paranoid; it is simply the exercising of prudence, carefulness forethought and farsightedness, that always will keep us steps ahead of the potholes, traps and circumstances that will not offer anything but disappointment, aggravation and lamentation bringing-to-mind the old saying, "If I only knew then what I know now things would be different."*

Memory

Memories are like
The movement of passing clouds
Quickly dissipating from view.
Remaining focused prolongs dissipation
Inviting thoughts old and new
Happiness tenderness joy
Caustic tragic painful too
Awaits the moment that renews.
Dwelling upon the past keeps
Certain things available, even-hurt.
Some things are sent to the bottom
Compressed depressed and weighted
They are not missed and no longer are invited.
But still, they appear unexpectedly
Like a snake and his hiss
Like a lion in the mist
Like the sounding of alert at night
But still, they are but memories
Awaiting God to make things right.

Proverbs 10:7 Good people will be remembered as a blessing, but the wicked will soon be forgotten.

What's up

Sometimes
We ask ourselves,
"Did I see that?
Was that real?"
Just by asking
We find something
Had taken place
Imagination or reality
Captured time and space
It may have been a dream
Of unknown things
Or a sound of crackling fire
With a deepened roar
Or release of truth
From the prison of bone
Singing, "Hallelujah!
What was lost is found!"

Attention has been given
To reality of thought
And inquisitively the question
And affirmation is sought.
Faith looks to the heavens
Seeking God,
Asking,
"Lord, what's up with that?"

James 1:5 But if any of you lacks wisdom, he should pray to God, who will give to him; because God gives generously to all.

Application of wisdom

The application of wisdom is always accompanied by recognition of where it has come from, and-also, how application of such wisdom is placed into practical life. Early in the life of the church there was a controversy (I'm sure more than just one), concerning some who wanted new converts to Christ to be circumcised, in compliance with the law of Moses. The position of those who had come from Judea to the newborn church in Antioch had caused some consternation, dismay, alarm and anxiety over what was being preached. Both Paul and Barnabas had entered-into a fierce argument with those who had caused such unrest. ***Acts 15:2 Paul and Barnabas got into a fierce argument with them about this, so it was decided that Paul and Barnabas and some of the others in Antioch should go to Jerusalem and see the apostles and elders about this matter.*** *It was ultimately decided by those attending the meeting in Jerusalem that no other burdens should be placed upon the Gentile converts to Christ; they did however, advise the people in Antioch they should not eat meat offered to idols or eat blood. What's interesting about this advice is the fact that there is acceptability on the part of Paul, when he is admonished, reproved and reprimanded because he had eaten food offered to idols with Gentiles. Does this sound like modern day politics? Paul explains that his faith, permits him to do so, and he finds no condemnation from conscience. He does however, say, just because he has faith that does not condemn him he will not eat meat offered to idols, if there are those who will judge him and in judging they will sin. After the meeting in Jerusalem it was decided that circumcision was not necessary for salvation; they did however, advise not to eat meat offered to idols and not to eat blood.*

Revelation 2:14 But there are a few things I have against you: there are some among you who follow the teaching of Balaam, who taught Balak how to lead the people of Israel into sin by persuading them to eat food offered to idols and to practice sexual immorality. *When we see this admonishment of the church in Pergamum there is the added sin of immorality attached to the offering of animal sacrifice to idols, and the subsequent eating of such meat. Clearly there is a connection to the meat offered to idols and the sexual immorality that followed within the perceived party atmosphere. And so, there is condemnation in the established methodology of leading people into sin through the deception* *present in the sacrificial environment. What we are hearing in the admonishment against both idol worship and the deceptive elements (immorality) surrounding such activity, leading others into sin is the warning to recognize the worldly wisdom of deception always present in the hearts of those who delight in causing others to fall into their traps. There is much to be said concerning those who set traps for people to enter-into, and then make of those so caught to be their slaves. The most common of traps present in today's world are the traps laced with drugs. The youth enter-into the traps, set by those who have no regard for the damage they will cause; their only concern is the amount of money they will amass from those compelled to keep retuning for more of the drugs that have taken over their lives.*

While this sounds very depressing there are those who have been trapped and in the receipt of the grace of God found freedom. A declaration of freedom cannot be silenced. The production of joy makes a wonderful sound. Hope realized is like lightning striking confidence into the heart of despair. Wisdom gained is the weaponry against the slings, arrows, traps and plans, derived in the dead of night, by those always seeking to rise above their perception of poverty. They seek to become wealthy in both riches and power, and they never realize how poor they (actually) are. These evil people have not known the wisdom of God, saying, ***"What does it profit a man to gain the whole world but lose his soul."*** *When we are conscious of the wisdom of God, we are made complete, and through our recognition of truth that's always shielding us against worldly wisdom's deception, there is the strength to stand tall in the daylight, unafraid of the presentation of dishonesty within evil's intent, present in both the knowing and unknowing of the world. Yes, some people do not fully realize the impact they have made upon the lives of others and then there are those whose main purpose in life is to create as much hurt and harm as possible.*

<u>*Deep in the grave asleep*</u>

Luke 8:53-55 They laughed at him knowing that she was dead. But he took her by the hand and said, "My child, get up!" Her spirit returned, and at once she stood up. Then Jesus told them to give her something to eat.

Matthew 9"23-25 When Jesus entered the ruler's house and saw the flute players and the noisy crowd, he said, "Go away. The girl is not dead but asleep." But they laughed at him. After the crowd, had been put outside, he went in and took the girl by the hand, and she got up.

Both depictions of the resurrection of the little girl are almost identical, except for the words in the gospel of Luke, who tells us her, **"spirit returned."** *The logical question to ask is from where had the little girl's spirit returned from? In one answer, we recognize that* **"little children are possessors of the kingdom of heaven."** *And so, it is easy for us to conclude the little girl had gone home to her Father's house. After all little children are born with the badge of born again acceptance. However, we must remember that everything Jesus did was for the glory of God. Remember, it was Jesus who said that the little girl was asleep, and elsewhere we find him saying the same thing about his friend Lazarus.* ***John 11:11 After he had said this he went on to tell them, "Our friend Lazarus has fallen asleep; but I am going there to wake him up."*** *A few moments later Jesus speaks plainly to his disciples telling them Lazarus is dead. Again, everything Jesus did was for the glory of God, and all of those who were beneficiaries of the miracles, ranging from healing the sick, casting out of demons and raising the dead had already been selected for God's glory to be revealed. Those also who died had been selected to enter the land of the dead, wherein the consciousness of the individual no longer exists. Jesus not only calls out to the spirit of the little girl to return but he also completely heals the ailment that had caused the death in the first place!*

Because God's glory (his excellent reputation for being merciful) is intentionally being displayed in-order to bring to the consciousness of others the reality of God's love and presence in their lives, what we find is the realization that both the little girl and Lazarus, upon the arrival of death had entered a deep sleep. This deep sleep is the place wherein everyone apart from salvation had to enter, until such-time as the death of Christ. It is at the death of Christ that we are made aware of what takes place. **1 Peter 3:11 He was put to death in the body but made alive by the Spirit, through whom also he went and preached to the spirits in prison.** *Once we understand the meaning of the words of the book of Ecclesiastes that states,* ***"What is of the earth returns to the earth and the spirit returns to God who gave it."*** *and,* ***"The dead know nothing."*** *We begin to understand that without salvation the dead cannot approach God (sin cannot enter into-paradise), as such, both the little girl and Lazarus were made to be exceptions (surely, they were both on the "you are saved listing") and they could very well have entered paradise. Remember, little children possess the kingdom of heaven and the friend of Jesus would not be denied entrance into our Father's house. In the same way, Jesus had declared to the thief on the cross that he would be with him in paradise, so it is we find Jesus upon his death preaching to those who had nowhere to go but to sleep (await) until Christ's sacrifice was made a reality.*

The apostle Peter says that Jesus went to preach to those in prison. What he is most likely meaning is the prison of eternal darkness. It is to these spirits that the good news of salvation is preached and those predestined for salvation were awakened to eternal life. Thus, Jesus says to his disciples that Lazarus is asleep and to the mourners in attendance at the little girl's home he also says to them that the girl is asleep. He does not immediately include them in the category of being dead, because he holds the keys to the living and the dead!

This sleep that had imprisoned humanity, is not the same condition that Jude speaks of, concerning those rebellious spirits being kept in chains and darkness until the great day of Judgment. ***Jude 6 And the angels who did not keep their positions of***

authority but abandoned their own home-these he has kept in darkness, bound with everlasting chains for judgment on the great Day. *These rebellious spirits have already been judged, they only await the final curtain call. It is perhaps the same place of darkness (the abyss) that Satan and others will be tossed into for a thousand years and afterwards once again be set loose to deceive the people of the earth; ultimately to be thrown into the fires of hell for eternity!*

Mark 15:21 A certain man from Cyrene, Simon, the father of Alexander and Rufus, was passing by on his way in from the country, and they forced him to carry the cross.

5

CARRY THE CROSS

Jesus is carrying his cross but he is not moving fast enough for those assigned the task of crucifixion. After receiving a scourging (great trouble or punishment) he is bleeding and the loss of blood has left him in a greatly weakened state. After the shameful trial that condemned him he was turned over to the whole cohort for punishment. A cohort was equaled to one tenth of a legion, and a legion could range from three to six thousand men. Jesus is handed over to at least three-hundred men for severe punishment that was usually reserved for the most hardened criminals and those who posed a great threat to Roman rule. After the warmup-punishment the main event was crucifixion.

The Roman soldiers were not interested in the innocence or guilt of those sent to them; they accepted that here was another of Rome's enemies and they were skilled in the art of torture. Setting an example for those who might think of opposing dictatorial rule was perhaps an everyday occurrence. We know there were those who deserved such punishment under Roman laws because Jesus was not crucified alone. The great difference in the crucifixion of Jesus was not only the fact that he was unjustly murdered but everyone knew of his innocence! The soldiers force a man by the name of Simon to carry the cross and he does.

Simon is from a place called Cyrene which was established as a Greek colony in the year 631 BC, and located in Libya. It is perhaps safe to say that Simon may have been a black man who stood out in the crowd that was following the walking tree. Certainly, none of those who condemned him (Jesus) before the Roman authority was going to volunteer to carry the cross even though they had cried out, ***"Let his blood be upon our hands!"*** *They weren't going to commit their selves to becoming ritually unclean. After all they were the righteous-ones! They were so righteous that they shouted,* ***"Crucify him!"*** *Even though they knew he was an innocent man; even though they were calling for evil to come forth and destroy innocence. The ugly task of aiding the executioners was beneath their self-righteous hearts. They could demand a death sentence but they would not otherwise assist in the execution. This is almost like the powerful leaders of today who declare war and rarely do they enter the battlefield or give up their lives in the endeavor. Yes, some wars are indeed righteous, but if we look at the turmoil in the Middle East today, we find a war has been declared on Christians and the elite leadership of such atrocity rarely suffers a loss of sleep! Here in America our leadership appears to be tone deaf to the cries for help.*

It is possible Simon knew Jesus or at least had heard of him. Certainly, the gospel writer knew who he was and knew of his sons Alexander and Rufus. So-true are the prophetic words of Jesus when he said, **Mark 8:34 Then Jesus called the crowd and his disciples to him. *"If anyone wants to come with me," he told them, "he must forget himself, carry his cross, and follow me."*** *We are being told that this life is not easy for those who want to do the right thing and for those who are identified as followers of Christ. In some countries of the world liberty to openly follow the Lord of Glory is not permitted and will come under the penalty of death! Persecution of Christians will always be with us in some form, so long as truth threatens to unmask lies. There has always been very little tolerance for those who profess the truth contained in the life of Christ. We should be on our guard in this our very own land of the free and the home of the brave, for the times are changing* *and the hatred for those who follow Christ is becoming much more evident. Just fifty-years-ago such attacks upon Christian belief in America were unheard of, but today it has become a clear divide as government attempts to compete for the hearts of the populace by pushing Christ aside. In many, it is government that appears to want to assume the role of gods. The unrelenting efforts of a few have silenced the majority and gained ground in their efforts to remove God within all public aspects of society. They will not attack other beliefs; it is only the Judeo- Christian faith that fails their tolerance; and they express considerable tolerance for those lost in the deceptions of false religions, simply because falsehoods do not threaten their deceptive exposure. Truth is always a threat to deception. We will carry our cross but it is Jesus who has placed himself upon it, and has made our lives so much easier in knowing he is with us and has given to us not just a history lesson about his life, but good news about all our lives having been born into eternity. Hallelujah!*

The walk of shame

As a child, I loved to watch parades and when we knew ahead of time one was going to pass we would situate ourselves somewhere along the route, guaranteeing a good view of the proceedings that entailed marching bands and various performers attached to the event. I suppose it was common knowledge among the populace of Jerusalem that a crucifixion was going to take place. Certainly, one in which the condemned was recognized as the Messiah of Israel would out of curiosity alone bring massive crowds to witness the event. Expectation among the spectators was no doubt varied, those who were waiting to see if Jesus would save himself and come down from the cross of corruption; the corruption being twofold in nature; the condemning of an innocent man by the evil hearts of those in power, is corruption steeped in the desires of men, and the corrupting sinful nature of man himself finding redemption within such a spectacle. On one side of the parade route were those who knew the truth of Christ. They had witnessed his good deeds and power to release all who were captured within the grip of the devil. Personified sadness on one side and delusional gladness on the other, formed along the parade route. Weepers for our Lord and the mockers against goodness formed a fixated, confused and expectant atmosphere that must have had the ruling religious somewhat apprehensive, given their knowledge of the murder about to be committed.

Within the mocking taunts was heard, ***Matthew 27:39-42 Those who passed by hurled insults at him, shaking their heads, and saying, "You who are going to destroy the temple and rebuild it in three days, save yourself! Come down from the cross, if you are the Son of God!" In the same way, the chief priests, the teachers of the law and the elders mocked him.***

Simon's thoughts

"I know this man.
He's barely recognizable.
He's not a criminal!
It's injustice!
Never have I seen
Such a crowd
Gather for death.
I'm stunned.
Crowds in the streets
Soldiers uncaring
Words thrown like daggers
Piercing and wounding
They cause him to stagger
Off to the left
Off to the right
Forward and back
Ever forward
Headlong in flight
Cobblestones greet him
As a betrayer's kiss
Cold and deadpanned
As if saying,"
"Greetings brother."

Matthew 27:42 "He saved others," they said, "but he can't save himself! He's the king of Israel! Let him come down now from the cross, and we will believe in him"

It is widely believed by many that Jesus had fallen along his route to **Golgotha** *but nowhere in the gospels is it recorded that he had in fact fallen. However, given the fact that Simon was forced to carry the cross we can understand there was probably some difficulty for Jesus to do so. After being tortured by the Roman soldiers it is an amazing fact that he is still alive at this point, and ability to carry the cross must have been a monumental task. It is safe to say that those wanting him crucified and tortured had probably given specific instructions to the soldiers, emphasizing to them not to have any thoughts of compassion for this man. Jesus had been labeled an enemy of Rome and a threat to the peace that Roman domination had brought. Whether Jesus had fallen isn't important, but the account of Simon being forced to carry the cross is something we should recognize as the hardships that can occur and are sometimes forced upon people. Life is filled with uphill battles no matter how rich or poor one may be. When Jesus speaks to us of carrying our own cross he is telling us to acquire the will to face hardship and injustice along with the consequences of life that may befall us as unintentional and/or intentional negatives. Jesus also is asking us to allow him to carry our troubles (our cross) because he states that his ability to do so is* ***"easy."***

Matthew 11:28-30" Come to me, all of you who are weary and burdened, and I will give you rest. Take my yoke upon you and learn from me, for I am gentle and humble in heart, and you will find rest for your souls. For my burden is easy and my yoke is light." *In such poetic-fashion Jesus is telling us he has ability to do the heavy lifting! He is telling us that by permitting him to help we will find rest for our souls. We will find rest for our lives in this present life and in the life to come we will not find it troubling! There will not be condemnation, only peace and eternal life with him.*

Different hearts

Mockers watched the Temple desecration
With victory expectations supporting worldly thought.
With evil generations, they looked upon the Lord.
His eyes closed shut earth rumbled forth its ire
Tombs gave up their dead and sky became a pyre!
Earthquakes parted ground tremors rushed the source
And laid awaiting movement at the foot of the cross.

In resurrection triumph the call of God remains:
"Come to me all of you, eternal life to gain."

Victory of the cross silent now the voice
That mocked the King of Kings
"O death, where now is your sting?"

Matthew 27:54 When the centurion and those with him who were guarding Jesus saw the earthquake and all that had happened, they were terrified and exclaimed, "Surely he was the Son of God!"

Truly an amazing exclamation by the centurion. It is amazing for us to hear such a revelation come from the mouth of one who took part in the crucifixion of Jesus. We understand that no one can say, "Jesus is the Son of God" without this knowledge being imparted to him by the Holy Spirit. Surely among the first acts of forgiveness after the death of Christ, is found in the exclamation by the Roman centurion. ***Mark 8:27-30 Jesus and his disciples went on to the villages around Caesarea Philippi. On the way, he asked them, "Who do people say I am?" They replied, "Some say John the Baptist; others say Elijah; and still others say one of the prophets." "But what about you?" he asked, "Who do you say I am?" Peter answered, "You are the Messiah." Jesus warned them not to tell anyone about him.***

Again, ***Matthew 16:15-17 "But what about you?" he asked, "Who do you say I am?" Simon Peter answered, "You are the***

Messiah, the Son of the living God." Jesus replied, "Blessed are you Simon son of Jonah, for this was not revealed to you by flesh and blood, but by my Father in heaven." *It appears the words of Jesus asking the Father to forgive them because they do not know what they are doing did not fall upon deaf ears. Yes, the centurion found forgiveness through the recognition of the wrong committed in that place of the skull.*

Thorns

Evil deception and doubt
Confusion darkness clouds
Noise laughter insanity-proud
Crying and mourning
Injustice unbowed.
Evil persists
Where God's not allowed.
Righteousness shunned.
Truth silenced by fear
Stills the heart
Barbaric power
Does what it will
At this ungodly hour.
A crown of thorns
Woven around his head
As if saying,
"Here is pain for a want-to-be-king
And here are the spikes to hold up your hands
Here is the wood that was given for you
Sturdy its trunk like the fig tree you slew.
A special place to grandstand
Holding your body erect
Spikes for you to caress
Terrible pain I would guess?"
"I don't want to do this."
To himself, the centurion exclaimed.
"The good deeds you've done
Families united where death broke apart
In the love of God, no longer divided!
I don't want to do this! Many a man I've crucified
But none were so innocent, have mercy on me
I who've brought you to this place.
Jesus, Son of the Living God!"

Mark 15:39 And when the centurion, who stood there in front of Jesus, heard his cry and saw how he died, he said, "Surely this man was the Son of God."

Matthew 10:28 "Do not be afraid of those who kill the body but cannot kill the soul. Rather, be afraid of the one who can destroy both soul and body in hell.

6

THE PERMANENCE OF HELL OR NONEXISTENCE

Within the words of Jesus there is implied a degree of punishment to be determined by the judgment of God. To be placed into the fire of hell should not automatically be considered a permanent state of torture; it should also be recognized as the means by-which God can totally-destroy both body and soul. The pronouncement of the existence of hell comes to us through the word of God, as such there should be no doubt among believers concerning this truth. However, most of the world's population has placed this truth into the category of fantasy, along with the understanding of eventual judgment for evildoers. Because many in this life escape the punishment of man there is this belief that death is final and all evil done in this life, upon death, is without consequence. This also is deception, seeking to deny truth to those lost within worldly pursuits that offer nothing of God. We know that God can do whatever he wants with the element of fire. The burning bush was not consumed; the burning coal from the altar of God did not render Isaiah into a torturous state of being and the fire within the cruel furnace of king Nebuchadnezzar's pride did not harm Daniel's friends, because God would not permit the fire to destroy them. It appears the fire of hell will become an eternal sentence no matter which extreme is so judged appropriate by God; eternal torture or nonexistence.

The permanence of hell is not in question; rather, it is the option of God that should be considered for us, to understand the place called hell as either eternal torment or a second death from which there is no return. It would appear God has the option to send to hell those he deems worthy of eternal torment, or else, for some, there is total- destruction. In the above passage, Jesus is basically saying, this life of ours will come to an end in its corporeal existence. As such, fear of those who can kill the body and then do nothing else is misplaced. We must recognize the one who has power over us, whether in or out of the body. By Jesus saying God "can" *destroy both soul and body he leaves open a sentencing to eternal torment or destruction in the lake of fire, which may very well be the place called hell.*

Certainly, there are those who deserve to be tortured forever, and then, there are those whose existence is worthy of a quick burn, or even varying temperatures and degrees of torment proportional to the deeds in life. God will dispense the perfect punishment to fit the sin. It does not take a great imagination to recognize some serious candidates for eternal torment. One would think those demonic forces arrayed against God would be on the list, and all of those who knowingly worshiped the Evil One. As for those destined for the lake of fire, in specific terms we know all liars, murderers, perverts, and everyone whose name is not written in the Book of Life are destined for the aforementioned-lake. This sounds like a large-number of candidates but it has been said, the road to heaven is narrow. Because scripture implies that some of the unsaved will be better off than others on the Day of Judgment the question begs to be asked, how so? I don't know if there is an answer but let's look closer at the words of our Lord.

Murderous thoughts and adulterous hearts
Are always married to lies.

Matthew 5:21-22 "You have heard that it was said to the people long ago, 'Do not murder and anyone who murders will be subject to judgment.' But I tell you that anyone who is angry

with his brother will be subject to the judgment. Again, anyone who says to his brother 'Raca' is answerable to the Sanhedrin, but anyone who says, 'You fool!' will be in danger of the fire of hell." *To kill someone is murder, but Jesus places murder anger and contempt, into the category of being worthy of judgment and in danger of hell's fire. The only issue remaining is whether the fire offers death or eternity on the grill? We should not fast forward the implication of eternal torture administered by the hand of God. It is an awesome thought for us to contemplate, the God of Love bringing about eternal pain in perfect proportion to the gravity of one's sins, or nonexistence. By contrasting actual murder with a desire to see its fruition, Jesus is placing thoughts and acts into the same vein of seriousness. Jesus is treating the physical and the spiritual with equal weight. Of course, this must be so. If we look at the words of Jesus as he accords intent, equal in culpability to the actual act, he leaves no room for sin to slither free. Jesus is bringing all aspects of sin into recognition and is not permitting a loophole for those within the pure spiritual realm. If all the unsaved are going to hell and they are to endure eternal torment, what then is the meaning of Jesus when he states,* ***"It will be better"*** *for some on the Judgment Day than for others? Man's penalties end with death of the body, but God's judgment is eternal no matter eternal flame or darkness. That is, as if to say, an offense committed in the here and now may very well face the penalty for breaking the laws of man, in addition, to facing the final penalty for failing to have such offenses forgiven by the ultimate Judge.*

Self-indulgence, violence, maliciousness and damaging others bodily, or through character assassination are highlighted by our Lord to be worthy of severe punishment. Reasoning suggests if there is severe punishment there may very well be punishment to a lesser degree. Having a choice in the matter, I suppose, everyone subjected to the judgment would choose to be totally nonexistent rather than to be tormented throughout eternity. Nonexistence is pronounced without ambiguity in the Book of Revelation because it refers to the lake of fire as the ***"second death."*** *In the same breath, the lake of fire is where the devil and others will be tossed into for* *eternal torment. We can understand why the devil will be tormented (in fact we applaud and praise God for this), but what about others? Are there some instances where people will be judged as harshly as those demonic beings? I can imagine one conversation: "Adolph this is your cell and Satan is your new cellmate."*

Will there be a lesser-degree of punishment? I do think the lesser punishment is total-destruction. The lake of fire, announced as the "second death" *may imply destruction to the point of nonexistence, and since the devil is tossed into it (for eternal torment) there is a duality of purpose suggested, as presented by Jesus in the subject scripture quote. All sin is related to the lie and has no constraints, by which it is inhibited, because, with the advent of the lie all manner of sinful manifestation was and is brought into being. Because of this, liars have been placed into the category of murderers and perverts, worthy of the lake of fire. The lie is made manifest in every imaginable form. Seemingly innocuous lack of truth in advertising, or, spin doctors attempting to whitewash the lie, or, the tyrant taking away freedoms in the name of religion; all are nourished in the same garden of plausible deniability, rooted in the constantly shifting positional change associated within the uneasy presentation of the lie. The world we live in is filled with the illusion of truth, but the true darkness is pervasive. The light of Christ is the only illumination given to us that is totally pure and can never disappoint us who follow.*

They wanted to be gods

Genesis 6:4-5 "The Nephilim were on the earth in those days–and afterward-when the sons of God went to the daughters of men and had children by them. These were the heroes of old, men of renown. The Lord saw how great man's wickedness on the earth had become and that every inclination of the thoughts of his heart was only evil all the time." *Nephilim is the Hebrew name given to the offspring produced by the union of fallen angels and the daughters of men. (The sons of God, is translated from the Hebrew text to mean angels.) They not only had contempt for*

God but they lusted after his creation. In this lusting, we can see why Jesus finds adultery of the flesh equal to adultery of the mind (spirit). This was a corrupting of the children of God by rebellious beings, whose pride would not submit to the reality of God calling his creation sons and daughters. This is truly contemptuous and I suspect worthy of eternal punishment in hell.

Moreover, this corruption and subsequent proliferation of Nephilim led to the flood with devastating results for mankind. It was as if the sin of man was not enough for those corrupting influences, they had to hurry the death sentence along the path to the grave. Mankind was in his infancy, so one may conclude the first demonic possessions inflicted by fallen angels, was child abuse in its worst form. This may have been a desire by demonic beings to destroy what God had created and an attempt to recreate within the image of all that is unholy. Thus, God began again after the devastation of the flood. This desire by fallen angelic host, to become gods has not drifted away into history. Today there are many who believe they are gods, all nice and comfy within the non-consequential world of, "God and sin does not exist." This new-age concept is at least equal to the stupidity first displayed by those who thought they could rebel against God without consequence.

Jude 1:6-7 And the angels who did not keep their positions of authority but abandoned their own home, these he has kept in darkness, bound with everlasting chains for judgment on the great Day. In a similar way, Sodom and Gomorrah and the surrounding towns gave themselves up to immorality and sexual perversion. They serve as an example of those who suffer the punishment of eternal fire. *The angels who did not keep their positions of authority and the immorality and perversion of Sodom and Gomorrah,* ***"serve as an example of those who suffer the punishment of eternal fire."*** *Within this expression by Jude we can see the most extreme forms of worthiness for eternal fire. This is the permanence of eternal damnation and not the quick burn implied by being tossed into the lake of fire, referred to as the* "second death." *Although, for now these are being* ***"kept in darkness, bound with everlasting chains for judgment on the great Day."*** *By Jude* *giving to us these two examples (demonic possession and the total depravity of Sodom and Gomorrah) we are alerted to the depths to which both the supernatural and natural world had defiled both God's sensibilities as well as the design and intent for mankind. One may conclude that all sin will be judged, but not all will be pronounced as worthy of eternal fire. Let's try to understand the lusting of those angels who had left their positions of authority. We can understand demonic possession, there are sufficient accounts within the New Testament, but it is difficult for us to understand angelic beings lusting over the daughters of men and producing offspring that the bible identifies as Nephilim. This leaves open for conjecture the idea that those identified as "angelic" may very well not be of the purely spiritual kind.*

If we fast forward to the time of Jesus we find many representations of demonic possession and in the one called, ***"Legion or Mob"*** *there is the pronouncement from them that their,* ***"time had not come to be tortured."*** *The admission by those called* ***"Mob"*** *leads us to the understanding that they were indeed cognizant of their impending doom, and somehow knew it to be not their time. They knew Jesus and they knew it was not their time for judgment, and so, they were aware of their guilt and they knew they had no excuse! We cannot conceive of torture infinitely accurate and proportionately fair, but God knows everything. They knew they would be tortured! Perhaps now we can get a clearer picture of one aspect of the brilliance of our Lord, as he teaches the disciples how they should pray,* ***"Thy will be done on earth as it is in heaven."*** *In this one sentence is summed up the complete purpose of creation. When we place our will and purpose ahead of God's intent we fail to follow design criteria. Jesus reiterates throughout his ministry for us to follow him. In so doing we will follow the will of God.*

It will be better for some

Luke 17:1-3 Jesus said to his disciples: "Things that cause people to sin are bound to come, but woe to that person through whom they come. It would be better for him to be thrown into the

sea with a millstone tied around his neck than for him to cause one of these little ones to sin. So, watch yourselves." *Once again Jesus displays to us the severity of sin of our own volition, and that of being caused or encouraged by those who intentionally set out to bring about the downfall of others. Jesus says, it is better to be drowned in the depths of the sea than for some to face the eternal torment God has in store. He is making a distinction with respect to those responsible for the downfall of others; nonexistence is too good for them. For those who would deliberately corrupt for personal gain or satisfaction, Jesus highlights their disregard and he holds them to a greater-degree of responsibility for their contempt and uncaring attitude. It is one thing to find yourself trapped by any number of worldly designs but to be responsible for designing and building such traps, knowing they will bring about the fall of others, is to invite eternal confinement and torment; God holds them in contempt. In some, whose desire promotes and otherwise demands the proliferation of evil, God finds them to be abominations equal to the first demonic possessions and the total abandonment of morality displayed in Sodom and Gomorrah. Only God knows for sure what happened in those places and only God can judge accurately the punishment deserved.*

Individual judgment

Revelation 20:13-14 "The Sea gave up the dead that were in it, and death and Hades gave up the dead that were in them and each person was judged, according, to what he had done. Then death and Hades were thrown into the lake of fire. The lake of fire is the second death. If anyone's name was not found written in the book of life, he was thrown into the lake of fire." *Here we see the conquering of death and the land of the dead (under the earth and under the sea), death and the place that held the dead captive is no longer in existence. Hades or the land of the dead (the underworld) is banished from existence.* ***"Each person was judged, according, to what he had done."*** *Well it looks to be one coin with two sides. Perhaps the second death is a total termination from existence, while for others a total death would be too lenient* *a sentence. The Book of Life is singular and contained within it are the recordings of God himself; he made the entries before he began to create this world. However, the judgment books are many. Whether life or judgment, we are these open books. The spirit of man records everything we have ever done in our lives. As we grow old we may mercifully forget certain aspects of our lives, but what has been imprinted on our spirit is like indelible ink, very long lasting. Just as those pure spiritual beings cannot keep hidden their thoughts and actions, so it is with the spirit of man. The individual is to be judged for the deeds of his own life, there will be no such thing as, "The devil made me do it defense." Actually- I believe that while there will be much gnashing of teeth, I don't think that anyone will venture into any kind of defense, since our lives will be like a crime being captured on a video recording; undeniable. I am at times just dumbstruck over the sheer power of God to reach into the grave, resurrect, judge and punish. Wow! There is no hiding place that will elude the justice of God.*

More or Less

Matthew 11:20-24 "Then Jesus began to denounce the cities in which most of his miracles had been performed, because they did not repent. "Woe to you Korazin! Woe to you, Bethsaida! If the miracles that were performed in you were performed in Tyre and Sidon, they would have repented long ago in sackcloth and ashes. But I tell you, it will be more bearable for Tyre and Sidon on the Day of Judgment than for you. And you, Capernaum, will you be lifted-up to the skies? No, you will go down to the depths. If the miracles that had been performed in you had been performed in Sodom, it would have remained to this day. But I tell you that it will be more bearable for Sodom on the Day of Judgment than for you."

Here again, we find Jesus making comparison with the most extreme sins of immorality and disregard for God, and those who knew truth based upon their own eyewitness to the miracles performed, and he judges those who knew with greater severity, than those whose depravity was disgusting and reprehensible in the sight of God. The words of Jesus do not imply that all will be punished equally. No, quite the contrary. Jesus states, it will be better for some than for others and he does not keep secret that which will cause severe treatment. ***"But I tell you it will be more bearable for Sodom on the Day of Judgment than for you."*** *Unwillingness to submit to the will of God is right at the top of the list of those worthy of eternal torment. Jesus went about his work on this earth performing many miracles, healing many, and freeing all who were held in the grip of evil, so, what Jesus is saying regarding those towns where many of these miracles were performed (but did not change their disregard for God) is that those who were living in total depravity within the cities of Sodom and Gomorrah would have more readily received the good news of salvation, because, at least within Sodom and Gomorrah there was no pretense of righteousness. Certainly, those fallen angels (like the unrepentant towns) had access, to not only witnessing God's miracles but they had access to God as well, which should have cured even the most severe case of rebellion.* ***"Fear of the Lord is the beginning of wisdom."***

These former angels had fallen into a realm of stupidity that has no equal! As such, their punishment will be most severe. Disbelief and unwillingness to come into compliance with God's will is something that has (I suppose) mystified the saved and blessed among us for all time. There is the belief by some that God does not exist and there is no judgment. Others know that God will do everything he says in his own time, but they still rebel, because they discount the punishment as being so far off that when the time comes they will have at least lived a life that was in accord with their own desires. This is seduction by illusion. Big mistake. Many are the lamentations at the appearance of a hangover. God is more than a hangover for the defiant, he is their worst nightmare personified. No one can imagine what God has in store for those who love him, and no one can imagine the torment God has in store for those who do not. For those who knew God and knew his existence to be the eternal giving of love, for these, who harbored a traitorous rebellious and hateful agenda against him and his creation, there is no way we could ever imagine his wrath.

Woe

Matthew 23:15 "Woe to you, teachers of the law and Pharisees, you hypocrites! You travel over land and sea to win a single convert, and when he becomes one, you make him twice as much a son of hell as you are." *Wow! Jesus really-unloads both barrels at those who cause others to sin. Again, we see the severity of judgment for those who cause others to sin. It is so true that to those much is given much is expected. These teachers of the law and Pharisees were treated to a snapshot of what they can expect at the judgment. They were hit with seven woes pronounced from the mouth of Jesus and there was nothing they could do about it, except to listen and inwardly foment at the truth burning into their façade of outward piety. Jesus called them,* ***"Whitewashed tombs, which look beautiful on the outside but on the inside, are full of dead men's bones and everything unclean."***

Most men faced with this tidal wave of truth would wither and fall to their knees in repentance at the sheer exposure of their hypocrisy, but not these self-righteous, they refused to bend to the will of God. What is amazing is the fact that those worthy of eternal fire are the ones who had professed being the closest to God. Breaking a sacred trust, whether vows of ministry or allegiance, always will find the woes of the Lord waiting to pronounce their judgment. Indeed, there will be much gnashing of teeth. The Pharisees and teachers of the law had won converts through deception. They knowingly misled new converts, and prevented others entry into the Kingdom of God, by denying the truth of God. Omission of truth is no less a lie. When truth is denied the lie is presented.

The Pharisees and teachers of law were likened to the children of their father, the devil. Jesus called him a liar and murderer from the beginning, having no truth in him at all. It was the lie that enticed the first creation to doubt and disobey God's command. We can now begin to understand why it is all liars along with murderers, perverts and others are slated for the lake of fire. The devil attacked mankind in his infancy with lies, and those demonic beings also preyed upon man in his infancy. Woe to them! To lie is an instant death sentence to be carried out at the appointed time the Judge so sets. Deceiving others is looked upon as a prime candidate for eternal flame, but to deceive one's self into thinking that a chance in hell exists, or a chance to dethrone God exists, is pure foolishness. The lie is so strongly abhorrent to God that even for someone saying, ***"Thus says the Lord"*** *(and the Lord did not say it) a death sentence is attached for misrepresenting God.*

With respect to the Pharisees and teachers of the law they not only misrepresented truth but they knowingly misrepresented God. They did what they did in-order to maintain their positions of authority and status over the common man. I guess one could say they loved to lord-it over others. When people covet their positions of authority over others, and attempt to control even the knowledge of right and wrong within the individual, it is equivalent to a vicarious or substitute misrepresentation of God.

Insomuch as the conscience can be looked upon as the voice of God within us, directing us to right and wrong, others have no right of denunciation, for with the mind of Christ there are no gray areas for needed light. Attempts aimed at subjugating conscience (to impose your will upon another) are disguises designed to remove the freedom given by truth. It's also a veil designed to obscure and denounce the will of God. To deny truth is to deny freedom on an individual basis. Whosoever the Son sets free is truly free and able to determine what is right and wrong, in general understanding, as in the commandments as well as on an individual basis.

There are situations and activities that for some are not considered sinful, while to others their conscience or religious teaching declares it to be a sin. One example of this is Paul eating meat offered to idols, his faith permitted him to do so, but others saw it as a sinful act. If we are to be judged on an individual basis we must never relinquish our ability to discern right and wrong as it applies to our own life. Thus, we are told to not judge others. As for those denied the truth to recognize what God requires of us, by those who wish to keep themselves in controlling positions as spiritual guides dwelling in a land of darkness, they are destined for the lake of fire. No matter how a lie is presented it will always have a faulty disguise. Fancy suits and robes or ornamentations of gold cannot distract away or hide the dirt and grime of the lie. It may not immediately be recognized, but will always be unveiled by the light of truth. It will always be clearly seen with the unveiling of time.

Regarding food that had been offered to idols there is a distinct difference between the church of Pergamum and the account of Paul's conscious participation in such idol food. ***Revelation 2:14 Nevertheless, I have a few things against you: You have people there who hold to the teachings of Balaam, who taught Balak to entice the Israelites to sin by eating food sacrificed to idols and by committing sexual immorality.*** *We must recognize the condemnation from Jesus concerning the church in Pergamum, for their practice of eating food that had been sacrificed (offered) to idols differs entirely from the account of Paul eating such food. In Paul's action, he is not trying to condemn those who had acquired such food, rather, he is quite at ease with his conscience because his faith in God permits him to do so. Paul was in the company of Gentiles and attempting to witness to them the good news of Christ; he was not there to condemn them. The truth had set him free from the blanket of condemnation that covered all of Judaism as far as infractions to the Law of Moses was concerned. However, pertaining to the church in Pergamum there were people attempting to deceive the church (in fact they had succeeded) into taking part in the practice of demonic worship; offering food to idols is ultimately recognized as worshiping false gods. Paul had not participated in idol worship but he did eat the food that was a part of such sacrificial ritual. In this he declares his faith permitted him to do so; there was no condemnation of conscience.*

<u>The loser</u>

Revelation 20:1-2 "And I saw an angel coming down out of heaven, having the key to the Abyss and holding in his hand a great chain. He seized the dragon, that ancient serpent, who is the devil or Satan, and bound him for a thousand years." *So much for tough guys whose bark is much bigger than their bite. Can we imagine the servants of the Lord waiting such a long time to be given the green light to chain up this devil? The angel is carrying the key to the Abyss and a great chain. This is the authority and power of God on display. I can almost see the hands being raised and the cries for attention, to be the one who snatches the devil by the neck and tosses him into the abyss. Finally, no more diplomacy as was the case with the conversation between Michael and Satan as they* ***"quarreled"*** *over the body of Moses. At that time, Michael ended the debate and deferred to the Lord by saying,* ***"The Lord, rebuke you!"***

No more debating with God or questioning his judgment as was the case of God declaring Job to be, ***"blameless and upright, a man who fears God and shuns evil."*** *Satan had replied to God's comment concerning Job in a manner that suggested Job's motives for being a good servant were not at all, of the goody-two-shoes variety.* ***"Does Job fear God for nothing?"*** *Satan wanted to be God. He places himself into the Seeker of Truth role of the Holy Spirit. It is the Holy Spirit who searches even the deep things of God, (motives and truth), and Satan was certainly probing and searching for any misstep he could possibly find, in-order to claim imperfection in God himself. Our own spirit searches our inner motives and through conscience alerts us to either good or bad decisions; the Holy Spirit is the conscience of God. Remember, when Adam sinned God said,* ***"Now the man has become like us."*** *"Like us," to mean, having acquired the knowledge of right and wrong. In addition, the Hebrew word for "us" is "Elohim" denoting or meaning a singular plurality. It is in this recognition the appearance of the Trinity is humbly presented. We should not let the reference to a singular plurality confuse us; we also are a singular plurality, that is comprised of body, soul, and spirit; and of* *course we understand that God is also speaking to those within his company, who also have the knowledge of right and wrong.*

His backhanded slight against the Holy Spirit was an unpardonable sin. To search is to seek, into a matter, to examine or to discover truth. We may search with honest intent to discover truth or probe with maliciousness. The devil had assumed the role of malicious prosecutor in his case against Job and by doing so he cast doubt upon the pronouncements of God himself, which reflects upon the role of the Holy Spirit. The Holy Spirit is known as the ***"Counselor"*** *(as is Jesus).*

Isaiah 9:6 "And he will be called Wonderful Counselor, Mighty God, Eternal Father, Prince of Peace." Again, John 14:25-26 "All this I have spoken while still with you. But the Counselor, the Holy Spirit, whom the Father will send in my name, will teach you all things and remind you of everything I have said to you." *Jesus had warned the Pharisees that to sin against the Holy Spirit was unpardonable. By attempting to sift through the motives of God in the Assembly of God, he (Satan) was presenting his case to be God. The accuser of man is not about to limit his accusations to just mankind. He is looking for fault in everyone in-order to claim the status of God for himself. He had set himself up as judge and is attempting to prove that his verdict is correct, and God is not. The devil did not care about Job and he tormented him to elicit anything that would prove God to be wrong in his declaration concerning the character of Job. The devil had used cunning and lies against the first of mankind, but now he is going to use brute force to make his point. He fails, as Job is everything God had credited him to be.*

In another place in scripture we see Jesus making a similar pronouncement about Nathaniel. He says of him, ***"He is a real Jew, there is nothing about him that is false."*** *This kind of evaluation is one we all would love to hear the Lord pronounce concerning ourselves, and in a way, the grace of God has said the same thing. The account of the seizure and imprisonment of the devil with* *relative ease by an angel of the Lord, begs for an answer as to why it is God had tolerated this arrogance in his presence for so long?*

It may be for the benefit of the onlookers who had gathered to, **"present themselves before the Lord." Job 1:6-7 One day the angels came to present themselves before the Lord, and Satan also came with them. The Lord said to Satan, "Where have you come from?" Satan answered the Lord, "From roaming through the earth and going back and forth in it."** *If there was ever a non-answer this is it!*

Satan injects doubt in the pronounced judgment of the Lord (concerning Job being blameless) and if, at that time God were to just deep fry the devil out of existence the question would have remained unanswered leaving everyone with a different impression of just who God is and what he is all about. It was an attempt to malign and it needed to be set right. God's policy has always been for us to reason with him. Transforming the devil into a crispy critter at that time may have left the impression that God is a dictator and unwilling to have his judgment questioned. But God allows this negative in-order to prove his position. It may be true that the closer we are to the Lord the greater are the attacks of the enemy. Certainly, it was that way for Job. This would certainly make sense, because Jesus is the Good Shepherd who leads his flock from the front, and not concerned at all with the war before him, he will care for all who will follow no matter what adversity is placed in our way.

Matthew 13:14 "The reason I use parables in talking to them, is that they look but do not see, and they listen but do not hear or understand. So, the prophesy of Isaiah applies to them." *It can be safely said, based upon scriptural analysis, that God can destroy body and soul in hell or he can torment for eternity those he deems worthy of such torment. Either way, we know the decision made is correct and just. We don't know how God can both destroy and/or torment in the one place called hell, but it's only one mystery we cannot fathom. I suspect it is not so difficult for God to accomplish either a living hell or total demise in one place. Mankind and* *supernatural beings have limitation and prohibitions placed upon their existence. Jesus is saying, in some people their hearts are fixed as stone, they will listen but not understand not only to the truth being spoken within such parables, but also within the deeper context of salvation they will never recognize the inference to the concept of predestination.*

We are given responsibility and are expected to fulfill our purpose. Life is not "duty free." Life is both taxing and rewarding. How we conduct ourselves determines the quality of life here and now but more importantly after the body dies. We were created for God's purpose, and to deny or deliberately refuse our purpose is to risk his judgment. Remember the fig tree that did not bear fruit (fulfill its purpose), Jesus cursed it and it withered and died. So, it is with us who do not complete the purpose for which we have been brought into existence. We can be destroyed at the root like the fig tree (cursed by Jesus) and tossed into the fire for consumption, or else, we may feel the pain of hell's fire and its torment knowing there is no reprieve. We have no concept of what God can conceive as punishment. It need not be the physical pain we envision; it could be mental (spiritual). Just as the wife of Pilate said she suffered greatly in a dream because of Jesus, does anyone doubt God can be a nightmare of unimaginable magnitude, throughout eternity for those he has judged to be worthy?

Let it go

Guilt of the mind
Sighs of the heart
Thoughts of intent
Acts without love
Let it go and make a new start
Now is the time for repentance and grace
Think not of tomorrow it will not save
There's no hiding deep in the grave
It will not forestall destiny's rage
Let it go and make a new start
God is forgiving up to a point
Reach for his pardon or spend life in the joint.

Daniel 6:26 I issue a decree that in every part of the kingdom people must fear and reverence the God of Daniel. For he is the living God, and he endures forever, his kingdom will not be destroyed his dominion will never end. He rescues and he saves; he performs signs and wonders in the heavens and on the earth.

Having taken a superficial peek into the options God has, with respect to destruction in the lake of fire or eternal torment, let us now take a closer but deeper look at one who is the recipient of eternal torment.

The Rich Man and Lazarus

Luke 16:19-24 "There was a rich man who was dressed in purple and fine linen and lived in luxury every day. At his gate was laid a beggar named Lazarus, covered with sores and longing to eat what fell from the rich man's table. Even the dogs came and licked his sores. The time came when the beggar died and the angels carried him to Abraham's side. The rich man also dies and was buried. In hell, where he was in torment, he looked up and saw Abraham far away, with Lazarus by his side. So he called to him, 'Father Abraham, have pity on me and send Lazarus to

dip the tip of his finger in water and cool my tongue, because I am in agony in this fire.' But Abraham replied, 'Son, remember that in your lifetime you received your good things, but now he is comforted here, and you are in agony. And besides all this, between us and you a great chasm has been fixed, so that those who want to go from here to you cannot, nor can anyone cross over from there to us.'"

The discourse between Abraham and the rich man is one that brings our attention to the dismal finality awaiting those who have failed to recognize the chasm of separation existing in this lifetime. While Abraham rightly makes known to the rich man the barrier existing between them and the connotation of great separation existing within the context of distance, there is also the subjective recognition implying substance between good and evil. This separation begins within the heart and becomes clearly defined as one moves through this allotted portion of life. While the discourse centers on Abraham and the rich man, we should not assume that all the departed-poor find an open door leading into paradise. Not at all, but what we may infer is it will be much easier for the rich to become distracted by all the so called, "good things" life has-to offer, and in the distraction, miss the ultimate good that is God. Abraham was a very rich man.

Genesis 13:2 Abram had become very wealthy in livestock and in silver and gold. *But he did not permit himself to become distracted by his wealth, which has the tendency to build into a man an independent attitude that forms a great divide of pride. Abraham is thought to be a symbolic representation in this parable presented to us by Jesus, but it may also represent the organizational chain of command within the kingdom structure. Sadly, for the rich man, it represents a total disconnect from God. God does not get involved with conversations with the condemned. He is concerned with the living; they are enjoying his presence and eternal life, as well as all the good things God offers. Abraham imparts a bit of dignity to the rich man by addressing him as* ***"son"*** *but within the designation there is the stark truth that clearly defines the category within the title of son as either good or bad. In life, all children are born into* *family and the title of son or daughter is given. Nothing can ever change that birthright. As such, the designation of son, accorded the rich man, is accurate and akin to a father speaking to a condemned criminal through the fixed barrier erected by ruling authority. We should also recognize for us to be viewed by God as his children we must also be born into his family; we must be born again as Jesus explains to Nicodemus in the third chapter of the gospel of John.*

The place called hell is widely recognized as the place denied the presence of God. This is a profound statement inasmuch, as we openly admit to the omnipresent ability of God throughout all of creation. Clearly the place called hell must be a new creation, wherein God has decided he will not be found. What does this place offer absent God's presence? Agony and nothing good are the two main ingredients that come to mind. With respect to the, "nothing good" aspect we should understand that from God's perspective justice is a definite good. However, from Abraham's viewpoint he rightly describes the condition of the damned. Agony is something we cannot imagine, because no one can imagine the torment God can and will impose on those who have chosen to align themselves with a self-centered existence in this lifetime.

The rich man was not asking for much, just a drop of water to ease his pain. Of course, water represents to us life and in this condemned condition there can be no life offered. No reprieve, no parole, no commutation of sentence, God's judgment is final. In life, the rich enjoy a certain amount of fame. They are accorded the best of life's offerings. Materialism and the coveting nature money engenders attracts many to those possessing such wealth. It is the blind leading the blind syndrome. Who is this rich man? He could be anyone, perhaps an ancient king. Perhaps modern man whose thirst for acquisition of the world's offerings no longer finds his self-captured by wealth exclusively. Instead, power and position is sought-after, in-order to impose upon others, the godlike attitude within the individual whose self-reliant demeanor has demanded a bolder and brighter spotlight. Such demands can and do carryover into all kinds of acquisition designs, the range of which finds residency within business to dictatorial evil.

All pride finds a common thread to pronounce itself. The identity of the rich man doesn't matter. He represents multitudes that have found damnation. They may be likened to a mountain of bones that share only death-death on display in the heat of naked exposure. We may also envision the, ***"valley of dry bones****" as seen by the prophet EZEKIAL. The impression is monumental and lasting. Throughout all of mankind's shared existence of mortality we find two complete end results. Both are derived from either the adherence to do good or the capturing allurement of man's nature, which rejects even the notion of an authority beyond self.* ***Psalm 42:2 "My soul thirsts for God, for the living God."*** *From the depths of desperation, we may now see the true agony of one who is separated from God. It is one thing to not know God while we are living this life of ours, but it is a completely different situation when one finally comes into direct proximity with God only to find it will be the last time to ever lay eyes upon he who is completely holy and good.*

This separation, complete with the lasting image of the one true God burned into the memory of the condemned, can cause one to cry out for just a drop of the previous reality; too no avail. While we are still alive in these bodies, our focus upon the things that last and bring to us good, throughout eternity, must not be distracted or lost in the activities that capture and make demands upon our time, to the extent we no longer have time to associate with God. Let us, like the psalmist, seek, ***"streams of living water"*** *while we can still be nourished by its life-giving qualities within the here and now of our lives. To do so is to guarantee we will not become beggars, lost in a place offering nothing but the failure and regrets of a life wasted in the vain pursuits of sin and death.*

"Even the dogs came and licked his sores." *This statement is basically an indictment of guilt looming heavily above the head of the rich man. To say even the dogs recognized the agony of Lazarus, and attempted to alleviate some of his suffering through the licking of his wounds, is to pronounce the most damning of evidence against the cold and callous heart of the man finding himself within the same inescapable predicament experienced by Lazarus during* *his life of misery.* ***"What we sow we shall reap"*** *is most evident in this depiction of God's justice.*

"The time came when Lazarus died and angels carried him to Abraham's side." *This added ingredient within the story highlights truth of the existence of angels. During the time of Jesus, a portion of the ruling religious rejected the existence of angels, while still, another party had held to the belief in such heavenly beings. It is difficult for us to understand how such a separation could occur since angelic appearances within Old Testament writings are clearly documented. As such, this addition to the teaching of Jesus also makes clear the truth concerning the angelic host. Lazarus went in style to the bosom of Abraham. He was carried, given a personal escort into paradise. One must think, this Lazarus person was one who knew God and still he had not blamed God for his sufferings. Just as Job did not blame God for all his trouble. An interesting thought connected with near-death and those declared dead, experiences, is the report from those returning from such experience; they bring back an account of being in the company of others (some known to them) who could very well have been an escort into paradise had they not been told to return to their lives on earth. Additionally, we hear the Apostle Paul reinforce the belief in other lifeforms when he declares:* ***Philippians 2:10-11 And so, in honor of the name of Jesus all beings in heaven, on the earth and in the world-below will fall on their knees, and all will openly proclaim that Jesus Christ is Lord, to the glory of God the Father.*** *GNB*

"At his gate was laid a beggar named Lazarus." *Within this statement, we find a twofold meaning. Lazarus was physically placed outside of the home of the rich man and in some instances within scripture we find the meaning of the word "gate" to infer the opening of one's mind to something that is happening.* ***Psalm 24:7-9 Lift-up your heads, O you, gates be lifted-up, you, ancient doors, that the King of glory may come in. Who is this King of glory? The Lord strong and mighty, the Lord, mighty in battle.*** *As such, we can safely assume that the rich man was fully aware of the presence of Lazarus; perhaps Lazarus could see the rich man's* *table filled with the best of culinary delights. But all he hoped for was the crumbs that fell to the ground; reduced to the level of a dog.*

"There was a rich man who was dressed in purple and fine linen and lived in luxury every day." *Purple is not only the color of royalty but it is symbolic of those who could afford clothing of color. This made the rich more pronounced and afforded to them the spotlight of recognition they craved from those who were of lesser value in their assessment of the human condition. One might conclude that he was damned if he did and damned if he did not wear such expensive attire. To dress in royal display would accord to him acceptance among his peers, while to dress down like a common man might very well have been received negatively by this same peer group. Either way it is what is inside the man that determines worth and not the color or value of the clothing.*

There is no doubt that during the time of Jesus there were those of means who had not fallen to the depth of uncaring ascribed to the rich man within the setting of hell. But these may very well have been few. This rich attire, display of excess while surrounded by such suffering and deprivation, as was the experience of Lazarus, only added to the mental agony of a beggar's condition. Virtually nothing was granted to the man who begged outside the gate of this earthly paradise-the rich man's home. It is fitting that this rich man finds himself outside the gates of heaven where not even the dogs can lick his wounds or relieve his agony. No not even the company of dogs is permitted to him.

"Father Abraham, have pity on me." *Poor Lazarus had to beg a short time in life, compared to the eternity facing the rich man's eternal punishment. His reward for greed and uncaring appears to be one of the poorest of investment returns, that will shake the godless to their core from everlasting to everlasting.*

What was the cause of Lazarus's death? Was it malnutrition? Did he just desire release from his torment so badly that his survival-instinct failed? Along with his hunger for food did his desire to live fail to compensate for the severe nature of his sufferings? Perhaps it was a combination of all the above? Still, we must wonder why it is he was brought to the rich man's home, and who are these Good Samaritans who transported him? For the answer to these questions we must look to the surroundings of the time. Certainly, there was no social security system that provided for the indigent. A man's social security system was his sons and daughters. To be without family was looked upon as falling under the curse of God, (God had not provided for this man's old age). The truth is we do not know how old Lazarus was when he died. Obviously, we can assume he was an older person but that would be to negate the reality of his declining physical health. Moreover, what we find is the underlining reality of one being totally dependent upon the good graces of the rich. It is apparent to us that the rich man in this town was not one endowed with kindness and compassion. As for the identity of the people who brought Lazarus to the attention of the rich man, seeking his favor toward Lazarus, we can only surmise that they were unable to care for him out of their own resources. Great was the responsibility of the rich. The rich were looked upon as favored by God's blessings. As such, they were thought to be pious and elevated above the common man.

Let us remember that the mindset at the time of Jesus, was such, that as, long as one adheres to the law, salvation with respect to acceptability by God was then guaranteed. Unfortunately for many their thoughts in this matter were shattered against the cold hard wall of reality and left to agonize in the hopelessness of despair; just as Lazarus had come to realize in his lifetime, and as the rich man discovered in the afterlife. Jesus points to the way of redemption, but is rejected by those whose self-righteous corruption of truth, regarding one's true condition (sinful) falls upon ears that understand his message but refuse to acknowledge his truth. To these whose priority finds acceptability within their reasoning that elevates self above truth, the reality of God's supremacy presented to them at the final judgment is tantamount to the light of truth that penetrates and saves those who believe the message of Christ. Unfortunately for them this revelation comes at the recognition of the undeniable truth of God, as they stand in awe of the justice administered with perfect precision.

Poor Rich Man

Life is reflected in the end.
Find a resting place of peace
Or agony that lasts.
Find a judgment no defense can beat
Or find the Tree of Life whose fruit is fresh and sweet.
Find the darkness absent light
A blend of screams regret's bite
A taste of just the smallest thing
Cannot be brought to land forlorn
When souls awaken to past wrongs.

All the while it's made known
What remains is bone
Spirit tied into a knot
Finds great the space
Across above it matters not
Rich men poor men without names
Are bound together by a flame
Burns forever without end
How great the chasm deep divide?
As deep as thought and twice as wide
What good is it to gain and find all had been in vain?

Proverbs 16:5 The Lord detests the proud of heart. Be sure of this: They will not go unpunished.

The Rich Ruler

Luke 18:18-25 A certain ruler asked him, "Good teacher, what must I do to inherit eternal life?" "Why do you call me good?" Jesus answered. "No one is good-except God alone. You know the commandments: 'Do not commit adultery, do not commit murder,

do not steal, do not give false testimony, honor your father and mother." "All these I have kept since I was a boy," he said. When Jesus heard this, he said to him. "You still lack one thing. Sell everything you have and give to the poor, and you will have treasure in heaven. Then come, follow me." When he heard this, he became very sad, because he was a man of great wealth. Jesus looked at him and said, "How hard it is for the rich to enter the kingdom of God! Indeed, it is easier for a camel to go through the eye of a needle than for a rich man to enter the kingdom of God."

I have read this account of the rich young ruler many times, and in some way, I find a degree of self-righteous pride emanating from this rich young man. He has already been apprised of his non-good status; Jesus revealing to him, none are good except for God. Still, the young man makes the declaration pointing to his adherence to the commandments and within this statement he seeks additional hurdles to overcome that would assure him of eternal life. **"Sell everything you have, give the proceeds to the poor"** *and then do what your initial instinct had led you to do. Seek out the truth of your life by following the example of Christ. Become dependent upon the mercy of God and not confined to the false dependency of riches; riches will not gain for you the kingdom of God and the prize of life. This young man did not hear what he was expecting. He may have been so blinded by his own appraisal of himself, expecting to gain accolades from Jesus that lauded the good life he had led. Instead, he is told he needs to make a sacrifice of all he held most precious; of what he had judged most needed to maintain not only his status within society but also the appearance of one willing to do what God requires.*

His attention is heightened only to be dashed upon the rocks of reality clearly making it understood, what he sought cannot be bought! He wants this challenge, to do more, because his riches are such that it is unimaginable to him that he could not accomplish whatever it was Jesus had found lacking in him. He is saddened to learn, is greatly disappointed by hearing it is not something he can accomplish with his wealth, except to get rid of it! When Jesus tells him he still lacks one thing, he never imagined how poor he really-was; his wildest dream could not have taken him to the depths of poverty presently surrounding his life. This reality was too much for him to understand, for in the mindset of those who have always found and expected deference from others, not only respectful of their opinions but their wealth, it was impossible for him to hear the truth spoken deep into the darkness of his unwillingness to change from ruler to servant. In many ways within today's reality we find a servant-master's mindset, especially within those elected to represent others, affording to them a voice that's so often denied the individual without wealth in both riches and/or celebrity status. Even the foolish among the wealthy and celebrated find avenues to project their thoughts into the minds and hearts of others. How sad it will be for them who do not hear the voice of Jesus saying, ***"Come follow me."***

We have now looked-into two conditions suffered by the rich. One of which is inherent in the class of the wealthy, which forms a malignancy of thought that produces a callous barrier around the heart of one so afflicted. We see this clearly in the story of the ***"Rich man and Lazarus."*** *The other is exemplified within the discourse between the rich young ruler and Jesus. His need to divest himself of the idolatry associated with his wealth and the power to make changes within his environment is all too much of a sacrifice for him to even begin to fathom. As such, his callous attitude is displayed in the unwillingness to find dependency upon God for his daily bread. His reliance upon worldly wealth to maintain an appearance of division between himself and the masses, to the exclusion of himself from the sinner category, based upon his determination regarding worthiness of the kingdom of God. Interesting is the fact that neither the rich young ruler, nor the rich man who finds himself in hell are afforded an identity. Even the little they had was taken away from them. In the one he has found the eternal surroundings of hell. In the other he only imagines hell to be upon this earth, absent the security of his wealth. Neither one is found to be acceptable to God.*

There is another form of idolatrous behavior associated with displacing the provision of God with worldly wealth. This is found in the desire to acquire. So alluring is this desire that the results one would usually associate with wealth-acquired, are also found in individuals whose attention is fixed upon achieving satisfaction in the offerings of the world. For an example from scripture let us look at a man called Gehazi, the servant of Elisha the prophet.

2 Kings 5:19-21 "Go in peace," Elisha said. After Naaman had traveled some distance, Gehazi, the servant of Elisha the man of God, said to himself, "My master was too easy on Naaman, this Aramean, by not accepting from him what he brought. As surely as the Lord lives, I will run after him and get something from him."

GEHAZI' PRICE

GEHAZI is a servant of the prophet Elisha. As the story is told, a man named NAAMAN (one who is wealthy and a commander in the army of the king of Aram) is seeking a cure for his leprosy in the land of Israel. He is referred to the prophet Elisha by the king of Israel and his (NAAMAN'S) expectations are that Elisha will come out to meet him and call upon the name of the Lord his God and in this he would be healed. Instead, Elisha sends his servant to him with instruction for NAAMAN to go and bathe seven times in the Jordan River and he will be healed. Sounds all too simple to NAAMAN whose expectations are such that given the letter of introduction he had carried to the king of Israel, along with those who accompanied him and the gifts of treasure at his disposal, he had thought the prophet would put on a display of great power in honor of his arrival with credentialed request in hand. NAAMAN finally follows these simple instructions and is healed. He attempts to bestow payment to the prophet with many gifts, but is told it is not necessary to do so.

It is then that the avaricious juices within the character of GEHAZI begin to spin the lie he understands will gain for him the wealth and position he had inwardly always craved. Ultimately GEHAZI is reduced to the fate one should expect from God. He had placed a price tag upon the free-gift of God and in so doing had reduced God to the level of one whose motivation for doing-good is profit. And so we see that the desire for wealth can also make it impossible for the poor man to enter into the kingdom of God. Not only did GEHAZI find a living hell on earth by acquiring the disease of NAAMAN, but he also had caused a cloud of despair within himself continually forecasting his future on the great Day of Judgment.

And speaking of future, not only did GEHAZI doom himself to a life of misery from that day forward, but he also caused all his descendants to live under the curse of God. One could say this form of greed displayed by Elisha's servant attaches with it hereditary impact of lasting proportion, from which there was no cleansing available. However, it is safe to assume such a judgment upon GEHAZI and all his descendants, can mean all of those directly descended from him, and in a broader sense all those whose greed equals or surpasses Elisha's servant. Such descendants will follow him into the grave to the ultimate judgment of either an eternal sentence in hell or else total-destruction of both body and soul, in the lake of fire also known as the second death. There is a time in a person's life that he finds it necessary to gather together the things of this world, and this is not usually a bad thing. It becomes bad when the desire to acquire trespasses across the barriers of legally acceptable and morally correct activity. Greed is bad and uncontrolled greed is even worse. For the one who remains fixed in this state of mind there is no redemption. However, many a rich man has found the error of his ways and repented. There was a chief tax collector whose name was Zacchaeus that Jesus honored by spending time in his home, the man was so grateful he made restitution to everyone he had cheated and salvation had come to this man. And so, for God all things are possible, even bringing salvation to a rich tax collector, which is as difficult as placing a camel through the eye of a needle.

Rare Find

Diamonds pearls emeralds jade
Joyous sighs rippling with praise
Visions of promises made
There's beauty and brilliance
In nature's parade.

The rare find plays music sublime
Inside the seeker's domain
The music passing through hands that are grasping
In vanity's clutches truth is obstructed
Rainfalls passing lightning flashing
Clouds hang knowing their reign.

Unknowing is man a rare find at his feet
Eternally blessed is the heart that seeks after peace.

Matthew 5:9 Blessed are the peacemakers, for they will be called the sons of God.

Mark 8: 34-35 Then Jesus called the crowd and the disciples to him. "If any of you want to come with me," he told them, "you must forget yourself, carry your cross, and follow me. For if you want to save your own life, you will lose it; but if you lose your life for me or the gospel, you will save it.

7

GAMBLER

It seems we have everything to gain and nothing to lose. If we are correct in placing our trust in God's promise of eternal life, we gain. But if what we failed to believe turns out to be true eternal life is forfeited. If what we believed to be true turns out to be false, then what have we lost? Nothing! It then makes no difference what we believed; eternal life was never a prospect.

If the believer and the unbeliever both find eternal darkness with no shred of existence after the body dies, then neither one has lost anything. So, what have we to lose by believing in the truth? Nothing. Only the one who discounts truth is placed into the potential loser category. The one who has not taken a believing position in the offering of eternal life, only he finds a loss. Again, only the non-believer has anything to lose.

If the believer's acceptance proves to be untrue, he has not lost a thing. He is no better off no matter what he believed. In fact, the believer will have most likely lived a life less troubling due to the lesser impact of condemnations emanating from conscience. Because there is the truth of right and wrong embedded within us, we must conclude that right and wrong will be evident in all decisions we make. If the unbeliever is wrong, he has lost eternity.

Let's understand that for those who gamble on the thought that life is no longer viable after the body dies they are making a great wager; their very lives. However, even then their handicapping logic (reasoning) is flawed, inasmuch, as the concept of eternity is accepted by man; the concept alone points us to the possibility of eternal life. Add to that the evidence of biblical testimony and the testimony of those blessed with faith and the longshot bet appears to be unbelief. The gambler believes there is no God or afterlife and when proven to be wrong he has then lost eternal life.

This analysis of both the believer and the non-believer, when placed into a gambling concept presents to us the logic behind belief. It can be likened to a man at a racetrack, refusing to accept a free winning ticket; he has no chance of collecting the reward because, "Nothing ventured is nothing gained." However, should the ticket offered prove to be valid then the one who accepts the free ticket finds gain. When the believer accepts the free ticket and truth wins the race, hallelujah! But if the free ticket proves to be a losing endeavor, it was still a free ticket and so nothing is lost! The same cannot be said for the one who refuses the free ticket, when and if it is proven to be a winner. All that is exclaimed at that point is, "Nobody knows the trouble I see, nobody knows my sorrow."

Of course, we understand nothing is entirely free, not even the free ticket for entrance into salvation's eternity; it too comes with conditions. We must first believe that there is indeed a difference in the two positions of belief and disbelief, otherwise no one would accept the conditions associated with the free ticket. Secondly, we must recognize that there is someone offering to us the free ticket, in-order to share with us a winning experience. Just as within a racetrack setting even the free ticket offered must have been purchased by someone; a price had to be paid.

<u>All actions have a reaction of good or bad</u>

What is important for us to recognize is the clear separation between good and bad, right and wrong, simply because such definition reflects upon the originator of what is acceptable and what is not. It is he who brought into existence his determinations of right and wrong. It is mankind, for the most part, that utilizes the concept of right and wrong in a manner that is not always in accord with the acceptability set-forth by God. And so, what we find once again is that by concept alone (as with the acceptance of infinity) a truth is presented that is undeniable. Everyone living in a society, no matter what the acceptable norms may be will find certain aspects to be universal. No one wants to be murdered, and the thief does not want his goods stolen.

The idea of perfection is a concept that is acceptable to the logic of man simply because we have the knowledge of right and wrong. The same understanding is true for infinity; we cannot imagine a roadblock somewhere out in the starlit heavens. We understand the infinite and eternal in the same manner when applied to God. We find acceptance in many aspects of life and we admit entrance to the concept of eternity and perfection because it is true; it is only when man finds the attachment of requirements that call for us to live in accord with the laws of God does he find the convenience of disbelief.

The laws of man and the laws of God are reflected in the conscience of man's condition, that while many-attempt to silence the inner voice of approval or disapproval, such attempts prove to be futile. There is perhaps a point in which man crosses over the line separating-good from evil wherein there is no return from the insanity inflicted by such evil acts. These people as we have seen earlier have been given over to their totally corrupt-debased minds. The reality of belief and disbelief (which is an offshoot of right and wrong) is a part of life whereby we make determination as to the information being placed before us. The concepts of good and evil, holy and sinful, total death or eternal life, each presents to us a decision to be made, requiring us to either accept or reject the facts as they are presented. All our decisions are lasting and will have an impact on someone or something; even if we attempt to correct a poor decision, the initial impact will have made its mark. The belief in certain things and the disbelief in others is diverse within the human condition. False religious positions separate people into the same category as does the believer in the truth of God and non-believer. In this instance, there is belief in a "god" but people are intentionally misled with respect to the truth of who God (really) is. False religions are perhaps a worse condition than having no belief at all. False religion has ability to capture through deceptions that install a belief that does not permit freedom outside of the entanglements constructed, perhaps from the time of birth until death.

Belief in certain things and declarations of the reality of God have been placed into the thoughts of man, but there is a difference between the two. The beliefs in the practical applications of life requiring our decisions are made solely with the intellect of man, but belief in the reality of God is made with both the intellect and faith given to all who will but ask to receive it. Faith is receiving proof of the existence of God, in the same way we understand that our thinking is not a physical thing. We are given proof to our spiritual/thinking faculty that enables us to understand beyond the physical senses of sight, hearing, taste, smell and touch. All our senses impact thought producing a decision of acceptance or rejection. Therein the concept of right and wrong is not only conceptually true but because we can see the impact of right and wrong it is indeed an actual-fact!

Notice given

Matthew 24:23-24 "Then, if anyone says to you, 'Look, he is out in the desert!' or 'There he is!'-do not believe it. For false Messiah's and false prophets will appear; they will perform great miracles and wonders in-order to deceive even God's chosen people, if possible. Listen! I have told you this ahead of time." *GNB God will always give us a peak into the future, to align our thoughts with the reality we are living in. What this means is that we have already been given the true Messiah, in this there is no need to continue to seek him, we know who he is! And we have also* *been given prophesy necessary for us to see the signs pointing us to revelations of truth.*

In the same way, we have been confirmed in our faith and convicted in our disobedience, for us to not miss the offering of the reality contained in the promise of eternal life. There is no one asking anyone to step forward into the reality of eternal life, absent the proof that confirms such belief. God gives to us the faith not only to believe but to know the reality of everything about himself along with the precepts of right and wrong as a universal reality. The experience of faith transcends our physical reality. Faith speaks to what is going on inside of the human condition and it uplifts every type of individual; the spiritual man attempting to reject temptations toward wrong, inherent in his sin nature; the carnal man who is ruled by his sin nature, wondering how it is that he is not in control of his life, and the natural man who is lost in the darkness of unknowing the word of God, but has been included in the offering of a free ticket to eternal life nonetheless. All of us must come to the realization that it is impossible for us to find freedom in this life, until we are brought to the truth that sets us free, and until such freedom brings to us the peace derived only from forgiveness.

Promised Vision

To know we are poor in spirit
Brings understanding to the soul
To acknowledge our sinful nature
Allows righteousness to grow
To be humble causes change
Within this earthly tent
Producing inner longing
That brings us to repentance

Repentance sheds the tears
That water seeds of faith
Producing the trees
Where the fruit
Of truth prevails
Bringing into focus
All of life's details

At the center of the truth
There is Love with outstretched hands
Bidding us, "Do enter" into the promised land.

Proverbs 2:9-11 If you listen to me you will know what is right, just, and fair. You will know what you should do. You will become wise and your knowledge will give you pleasure. Your insight and understanding will protect you and prevent you from doing the wrong thing. *GNB*

Eternity

In the beginning, God spoke:
"Let there be light."
So, began the journey into night.
Perhaps it was then eternity seized its moment?
Reality and concept intertwined
Bringing the reality of God's intent
And a concept for man who'll not understand.

Deep is eternity's day
Deeper still, is the concept arrayed
Vast is eternity's day
Brought into existence
And sent out to play
Grabbing hold of the mind
That can't understand:
A universe without limits
Time unending
A heart that loves not
A man absent breath
A world without meaning
A life lived for what?

Eternity's day is shining intent
Awaiting the words:
"Let man understand."
Eternity's day brings light
To the eyes, to the heart
And the minds of the lost.

The present is forefront proof for the will
But eternity's concept troubles us still.
Like light constantly shining
Existing to fill and always reminding,
God spoke:
"Let there be light."
Bringing joy into darkness
Strength into clay
Eternity's day is with us to stay.

Genesis 1:3-5 Then God commanded, "Let there be light"-and light appeared. God was pleased with what he saw. Then he separated the light from the darkness, and he named the light, "Day" and the darkness "Night." Evening passed and morning came-that was the first day. *GNB*

The full impact of not accepting the free-gift of life is not visible to us at this, point in time, and neither are the emotional upheavals fathomed, absent the actual impact of being rejected by God at the resurrection to judgment. Indeed, many will say, ***"Lord, Lord!"*** *and Jesus will respond to their protests with,* ***"I never knew you."*** *The impact of a later rejection is not understood fully today, because we have enough difficulty sorting out our lives that are filled with constant demands. It is also a fact that man does not want to admit to his wrongs, it is perhaps a part of the sin nature that is unwilling to be exposed. In some, even a crime caught on camera does not move the criminal to admit to his wrong. It is within this rejection of truth that we at some point find ourselves caught in a downward spiral (slipping deeper into the darkness of unknowing) that cannot be reversed until we understand our failure to accept the truth of our lives and of Christ. Once we have rejected the purpose of our lives, we then become married to sensory-slavery (insatiable demands from human desires) that rules through the impulsiveness of projected wants desiring instant gratification. This state-of-affairs leaves little room for patience and wisdom, that gives both time to judge and understanding to know what is right. Without truth life becomes akin to living in a land filled with fools, fear, disobedience and wrong.*

Wars

Apart from the internal war that takes place in all of us there is the all too familiar external wars that seem to be continually present in the world. The internal war ceases when the individual finds peace that is only available to him through the intervention of God. The external wars only find peace when an enemy is vanquished through devastation and death.

In both instances of war, internal or external, wherein a decision is possible, therein such decision is made for and/or against an action based upon the knowledge of right or wrong. Interestingly, both parties in the external war believe it is they who are justified in such war. The aggressor has decided that it is in his best interest to invade and capture the lands, people and treasures of others and the defender recognizes defense is a must for survival.

Then there is the present religious war enacted in the tactics of terrorism that says, "Everyone who does not believe in the god and the mandates associated with his laws must die." Herein a decision is to be made by those who would confront the atrocities of such evil and those who will just hope the movement to establish a dictatorial theocracy will stop of its own accord. These last alternatives of choosing to intervene or not, finds one decision correct and the other wrong; cowardice is present but hidden in the false belief that deep within the heart of all human beings is ample goodness to be able to reason with and ultimately to reconcile with the evil that never has sought peace.

"Cowardice" is used as a descriptive because it is hiding behind the category of passiveness; so long as the destruction and death associated with terrorism does not directly invade their own personal lives! But let those who present a mindset that purports a belief in the deep goodness in all of humanity be subjected to such atrocities, and they will completely reject former pronouncements and revert to offensive aggression, which should have been the posture initially!

And so, we must determine whether-or-not a failure to defend the rights of others who are subjected to terrorism is based upon the false belief that underneath all of us lives goodness, or the failure to defend the innocence of children is due to a closeness to the evil that precludes intervention. Even evil understands that a house divided cannot stand, and if evil fights against itself it will not last! So, it may be the leadership of the world's countries have, perhaps, moved closer to accepting such despicable wrongs as are committed by the terrorism throughout the world. This should not come to us as a shocking surprise, inasmuch, as we have been given a peek into the future condition of the world through biblical-prophesy relating to us that at some point the entire world will be united under the banner of wrong; united in the personage of the antichrist! What else can we say? Can we say that we have been kept in the dark concerning the horrific acts of barbarism? Can we imply that the constant awareness of the trials and persecutions of others have numbed our capacity to empathize with the suffering? Have we been encapsulated by a sense of contentment and in this are unwilling to face the evil reality present in the world? Or just maybe the poison of corruption has spread so vast and quickly that capitulation on the part of world leadership has invaded their very hearts and souls! Our leaders applaud an army traitor who deserted his company in a theater of war; we set free those whose only purpose in life is to kill us and we think that the evil in the world has not invaded the hearts of our own leadership? Indeed, it is insanity to think that we can convince the devil to repent! Furthermore, it is confusing to me why it is that those who profess an intolerance for anyone's infractions against political correctness wherein an emotional slight to the individual and/or a group's sensibilities is looked upon as an abomination to society (and great legal hurdles will be jumped to punish the offender), but beheadings of Christians and sexual slavery involving children is not a problem? If that's not hypocrisy what is?

The evil intent present in the world today is like air pollution that continually is placed into the atmosphere, eventually everyone will feel its impact unless the source of the pollution is stopped and/or reduced to negligible levels. Every time we choose and/or are forced to do wrong there is a consequence, and every time we fail to counteract a wrong there is also a degree of consequence for someone. Life is filled with consequence and it is up to all of us to minimize its negative impact.

No matter where we look in the world or inside of us we will find decisions that need to be made. So-long as we have ability to make an informed decision based upon what is correct we will find the peace that God wants all of us to enjoy. But when there is unwillingness to make decision to defend innocence against evil, peace then cannot be found, in either theater of life; within us or external to our thoughts and inner being.

Fool

A fool is one who is easily duped
He shakes his head with an affirmative nod
But never understands the words wisdom imparts
He's very critical of all save himself
He refuses to improve his state
Will not acknowledge he's at a loss
He tries to take the lead in life
As if it's he who's boss
He has a problem living deep within
It is the prideful mind of man
That causes him to grin
Causes him to laugh out loud
When nothing has been said
Life for him is taking place
All within his head
He knows-not the truth
Of life explained
Within the Holy Scriptures
That puzzles-not the brain
The word of God paints-not
A complex picture
Or offers confusion by design
It's the light of understanding given to all who'll ask
Or seek the way uplifting to the cornerstone of hearts
Alas, he sees the light but will not comprehend
In the darkness of his heart he cannot understand.

Titus 3:3 For we ourselves were once foolish, disobedient, and wrong.

Adam

The beginning made plain
Earth to the man is given to reign
No restrictions save one:
"Eat not from the central tree
Heed not the call of its promised song
Touch not or taste what is right and/or wrong."

One act of rebellion and man did gain
Days that are numbered lived in regret
Filled with troubles and ending in death.

First stroke of the whip hammer-full swing
Weaving of thorns and crowning to bring
Suffering and death for the Savior King!
In resurrection, there's singing of songs
Hands opened in praise
Beginning again eternal days!

John 11:23-27 Jesus said to her, "Your brother will rise again." Martha answered, "I know he will rise again in the resurrection at the last day." Jesus said to her, "I am the resurrection and the life. He who believes in me will live even though he dies; and whoever lives and believes in me will never die. Do you believe this?" "Yes Lord," she told him. "I believe that you are the Christ, the Son of God, who was to come into the world."

It is within the words of our Lord, that we are told directly and truthfully of eternal life available for all who will embrace the truth. Jesus is Truth. It's a simple decision for a good number of people who are inclined to understand the reality of the truth contained in the world, and, also this same truth existing outside of the natural confines of this life. There's a difference between the natural aspect of flesh and bones existing in the body of man, cohabitating with the spiritual dimension that is the thinking aspect of the truth, that's not made available to the physical senses. That is, to say, with our ability to think our physical senses bring to the thinking faculty the reality of the physical, but our spiritual/thinking is not meant to make the physical aware of the spiritual dimension. Thinking is the controlling aspect of creation that imparts directives to the physical body. As such the spiritual exists in both dimensions while the physical can only be impacted by the spiritual. It is this same unseen reality of faith that convicts and convinces us of our life lived in opposition to the declarations of right and wrong, as well as the reality of the God who loves us. It is the spiritual that communicates the directives in which we want the body to react, but when the opposite is in control (impulsive desires) therein we are ruled by the sin nature and the thinking faculty has then been reduced in its intended role in life.

Extended losers

We may not believe in the reality of God and his promises to all who will embrace his truth, and we can reconcile ourselves that if we are wrong in our determination then so be it! But what may be forgotten are the others, that we love may have been awarded eternity without us! They may very well choose to accept the free ticket into eternity only to find that we are not there.

The Search

Can there be an original thought in man?
Are we not fishermen in God's ocean of thought?
Are we not beggars along the shore?
Don't we hope to find a precious pearl or a part of ourselves?

Can we find what God wants to remain hidden?
Who are we kidding?
But God has revealed himself completely through his Son
For us to recognize our need.

Only in Christ does the darkness depart
And all his thoughts fill spirit and heart.

Jeremiah 31:33 I will put my law in their minds and write it on their hearts.

Ephesians 6:10-13 "Finally build up your strength in union with the Lord and by means of his mighty power. Put on all the armor that God gives you, so that you will be able to stand up against the Devil's evil tricks. For we are not fighting against human beings but against the wicked spiritual forces in the heavenly world, the rulers, authorities, and cosmic powers of this dark-age. So, put on God's armor now!" *GNB*

8

THE ARMOR OF GOD

It is understood by everyone in the Army of God concerning the war that breaks out in heaven, ends with the demise of the devil, and all who chose to revolt against God. The war against God and mankind is ongoing, and incorporates the evil inhabitants of the heavenly realms. Heaven as a specific place should not be confused with the still existing spiritual forces in the heavenly realms. Not only is there the evil that at times is so pronounced in the human condition, actively pursuing worldly aspirations, but we must also be prepared to stand against the, **"Devil's evil tricks."** *We didn't need to be reminded of the war presented to us by fellow human beings, or the internal war of human desires at odds with the understanding of what is right, presented to us in the knowledge inherent in conscience and the word of God, but we certainly needed to be reminded of the spiritual forces arrayed against the church (us) in this evil age. We may also need to be reminded that it is we who are the church, because of the indwelling of the Holy Spirit.*

In addition, we are told to, **"build up your strength in union with the Lord."** *This is accomplished by putting on the armor of God and remaining united in him. When we are prepared* *defensively by wearing all the tactical gear that God has provided for us, we then are given the confidence to face all the evil (tricks) schemes and attacks meant to return us to the former captivity, we experienced before we were freed by the truth of God. This confidence is the very same confidence a soldier will have when he is wearing his protective clothing; the bulletproof vest and weaponry assigned to him, along with all the other abilities attached with communication, having ability to call into the battle advanced weaponry as needed. Let's now look at the gear God has given to us and has instructed us to carry into this earthly battlefield, also involving spiritual forces not native to the earth.*

STAND READY WITH TRUTH AS A BELT TIGHT AROUND YOUR WAIST

The reference to wearing truth as a belt around the waist is recognized as the means of holding up our pants. Truth loosely held is not the monolithic structure that can withstand attack. The implication is that there may be a presentation of hypocrisy if what is presented on the outside is not the same on the inside. A loosely fitting garment has the potential to let inside the corruption of the world's dirt and grime. To be found exposed as one who is not adhering to professed truth, the impact upon others exposed to such hypocrisy is negatively compounded and the damage is greater. Wearing a loosely attached belt is to invite the possibility of having such truth torn away in battle; leaving us once again exposed to enemy attack that is never intended for our good. Not having truth in its most powerful presentation is tantamount to bringing a knife to a gunfight!

WEAR RIGHTEOUSNESS AS A BREASTPLATE

The soldier who enters battle without his Kevlar vest (breastplate) is leaving himself open to the slings and arrows constantly being fired by the enemy, in attempts to injure and remove us from the battlefield altogether. One aspect of righteousness is humility that not only protects from the external aspects of spiritual warfare, but also keeps the fire of pride from erupting; if given the opportunity to rage will weaken the entire structure. The other aspect of pride is displaying to the enemy and others the lack of understanding and training of the soldier, who foolishly entered the battlefield, indicating to the enemy that he does not believe is taking place! Again, a false presentation of truth is no different from those religious, who, during the time of Jesus' ministry and mission upon the earth, wore righteousness on the outer garment of their clothing, but internally, they were filled with unclean things. There is no difference today in those we see preaching material rewards that will be gained through adherence to their so-called interpretative understanding attached to the doctrine of tithing; when it is plainly recognized that they are in pursuit of worldly riches and not presenting the good news of Christ properly. By not proclaiming the good news truthfully, they are unable to see the torn and tattered breastplate they present. They are preaching the gospel of and for profit, and in their pretense, the true righteousness of God, along with his word are mocked by the rest of the world who are also using lies and pretense in-order to gain.

WEAR THE SHOES OF READINESS

If the soldier enters the battlefield absent the proper footwear, and instead he wears a pair of loafers in snow-filled mountains there will no-doubt be presented to the enemy the thought of, "Don't bother with this fool, he will not be on the battlefield for any appreciable length of time. He will (if he is lucky) be evacuated from the frontlines." The frontline is where Jesus is leading the troops, and in the broadest sense the soldier suffering from frostbite may be looked upon as a deserter. This dereliction of duty will have left his fellow-soldiers at a disadvantage because of his lack of readiness to aid in the fight. Indirectly, he has given aid and comfort to the enemy! If his feet can be frozen into a state of unpreparedness, so then, can the heart be unresponsive to the knock upon the door. Complacency is one of the greatest problems that we as the church are confronted with. Jesus had asked of his disciples, ***"Couldn't you stay awake for just an hour."*** *Let's remain ready to do good quickly, all the time.*

CARRY FAITH AS A SHIELD

If the soldier fails to take into battle his shield, he is probably oblivious of the battles taking place all around him. This unawareness can be likened to someone who has lost the ability to communicate, and, in this deficiency there is no ability to see, hear, or feel the impact of war. The soldier who is without his ***shield of faith*** *also loses the ability to communicate with his superiors; in the same way, we lose our ability to communicate with the Lord when a lack of faith is present. Without faith, "**we cannot please God."** The one who would please God must believe he exists! Faith, for it to have meaning must be connected to belief; if we do not believe in God there is no force present for faith to move, to become active. We might as well have buried the* ***shield of faith*** *into the ground that we will one day inhabit absent any hope of afterlife! The shield is meant to protect against poisoned arrows of the enemy, which have been dipped into the caldron of doubt.*

WEAR THE HELMET OF SALVATION WITH ACCEPTANCE OF ITS VALUE

The soldier who wears his helmet into battle absent the proper manner, in which it should be worn, may find his head exposed to the potential damage associated with loss of life; not just this life on earth but eternal life. Eternal life is the reward of salvation. If we do not hold dear salvation's value given to us in the sacrifice of Christ it is indicative of a loss of faith, and in this there is a loss of truth and in the loss of truth how can we then present ourselves to God in a condition of disbelief? We must learn to know what it is that pleases God. Let's not lose the restored innocence we received through being born again; let's remain cognizant of the added knowledge of truth, and in this we must hold-truth close and tight!

We must protect our thoughts from the corruption of deception; the helmet of salvation is worn for this purpose.

THE SWORD OF THE SPIRIT WHICH IS THE WORD OF GOD

During the time of Jesus, the sword was the ultimate portable weapon. It would be very difficult to defend one's self against an experienced swordsman. I suppose because of the strict sword-control-laws (I'm guessing such laws were present) the need for a method to defend was perhaps the motivation that initiated the martial arts in the Far East. I guess the sword was looked upon by those in power, in the same way many view guns in the hands of the populace today; both criminal and law abiding are grouped together; only the controlling aspect of society, were allowed, to protect themselves then and it appears that many within the seat of government today hold to the same ideology. There was no equivalent to the NRA or the constitution of the United States, to advocate for the legal possession of weaponry, especially, when we understand Rome was not a democracy. No matter what the restrictions were, that prevented the common man from defending himself, there was no weaponry that could prevail against the truth. With the advent of Jesus and the realization that God's truth is the ultimate defender, a sense of relief was installed into the minds and hearts of many. The world and the evil in it was being made to understand that not even a Goliath can withstand the presence of God's sword in the affairs of man. Even the world recognizes truth as the supreme defense, and it is for us to understand that we have been given the Armor of God in-order to resist the evil tricks and schemes of the devil. Awareness of such tricks and schemes are clearly defined in the word of God, and because we have the truth within us, we can sift through the worldly presentations, and on an individual basis determine what is trick or truth. We are not being made to understand that we should draw our sword and attack; we are given all the Armor of God as a defense against the slings and arrows, the poisons of deception, the corruption infecting, all who are not blessed to have God's truth. In the same way, a soldier must care for his rifle and all his equipment, so too we must keep our armor polished and ready to detect all the negative circumstances present in the world. The sword of truth can never be dulled; it remains sharp throughout all time.

Artful vision

All in nature
Is depicted through art
Comparing perception
Not commonly thought
The masters inspired
By nature's pose
Present on the canvass
Her excellent form
Of that which is hidden
And that which is known

Understanding brings
Knowledge of the complex
And of the simplest of things
Of right and wrong
Birds on the wing
The weak and the strong
The meek and the proud
The truth of God
And the liar unbowed

He colored the heavens
With infinity's brush
Showers of light
With just the right touch
Eternally wrought
With the embrace of love

By his command all can see
The work of his hands
The work of his Word
His marvelous plan
Intended for man
Amen!

Psalm 19:1 The heavens declare the glory of God; the skies declare the work of his hands. *GNB*

Matthew 28:1-6 After the Sabbath, at dawn on the first day of the week, Mary Magdalene and the other Mary went to look at the tomb. There was a violent earthquake, for an angel of the Lord came down from heaven and going to the tomb, rolled back the stone and sat on it. His appearance was like lightning, and his clothes were white as snow. The guards were so afraid of him that they shook and became like dead men. The angel said to the women, "Do not be afraid, for I know that you are looking for Jesus, who was crucified. He is not here; he has risen just as he said."

9

HE'S NOT HERE

In this account of the empty tomb we hear that an angel of the Lord comes down from heaven, an earthquake occurs and the guards positioned at the tomb are rendered like dead men from fear. The appearance of the angel was like, ***"lightning."*** *Both Mary's are present when the stone is rolled away and Jesus is not in the tomb.*

There is similarity in the description of lightning, lending itself to a bright-like- lightning presence. Elsewhere in the Bible, we hear Jesus use a similar descriptive when the ***seventy-two*** *had returned from their mission of spreading the good news. Jesus said,* ***"I saw Satan fall from heaven like lightning."*** *In the account by Jesus we can infer that Satan had fallen very quickly, not necessarily implying he shone brightly. In the appearance of the angel at the tomb, what we can infer is that his appearance was bright like-lightning and meant to attract attention. Only Jesus saw the fall of Satan from heaven and it was extremely fast! The angel at the tomb has a message to deliver and in this he is very much made to* *be seen by the women and the guards stationed at the tomb; in this there is no doubt everyone present saw and heard the messenger say that Jesus had been raised from the dead!*

Also in this account of the resurrection what we find is an earthquake has occurred, and a resurrection had taken place. This earthquake (I like to think) is the earth itself shocked over the release of Christ. Just as when Jesus had given up the Ghost, there was an earthquake at the very moment that he entered the world of the dead! Again, it was the earth itself shocked at the very presence of holiness entering the land of the dead. It is not as if the earth had never saw the release of one who had entered the darkness of death, but those who had formerly died and/or had been resurrected, did not have an earthquake at the entrance or the exit from such occurrences. These earthquakes were specific-announcements meant to bring to the attention of the living the importance of what had occurred. In addition to the earthquake at the death of Christ, we are told that, ***"many holy people who had died were raised from the dead."*** *Not only did Jesus raise some from the dead while he was alive but now with his death we see the power of God announcing to the world,* ***"Where death is your sting?"***

We are also hearing the time of the resurrection had taken place on the first day of the week shortly after dawn. The angel rolls away the stone and sits on it, while the guards are placed into a state of fear that renders them paralyzed, like dead men. I suppose with belief in resurrection to be fantasy, and belief in the supernatural being reserved for those who are touched in the head, the appearance of reality brings a paralysis that freezes the mind, and in this the whole being is shocked into a state of fear so great that movement is no longer possible. In fact, the fear may have been so great that even their thoughts were frozen in place. But as for those who were searching for the body of our Lord, they were relieved of their fears by the angel, who told them of the resurrection in the words, ***"He is not here; he is risen just like he said."*** *While it might be that the guards may have had a look of fright and confusion on their faces, the women may very well have had the sadness in their countenance restored to the joy God wants all of us to know.*

It is not unusual for those brought into the reality of the supernatural to fall-down like dead men, **Revelation 1:17-18 When I saw him, I fell at his feet as though dead. Then he placed his hand on me and said: "Do not be afraid. I am the first and the last. I am the living One; I was dead, and behold I am alive for ever and ever! And I hold the keys of death and Hades."** *I'm chuckling to myself at this point because there is no account of the guards being relieved of their fear. Still they may have been more afraid of the religious backlash, if they did not lie about the resurrection and say, "his disciples came in the night and stole his body."*

A great occurrence in the resurrection of Christ has taken place and all the religious can think of is a cover up? It is perhaps critical for us to note that it was Pilate who gave the permission to guard the tomb, based upon the report from the religious that Jesus had predicted he would rise from the dead. I'm convinced that Pilate was no doubt chuckling to himself, thinking that every one of these corrupt religious were out of their minds, to think that the dead can return to the living. Apparently, he (Pilate) may not have heard of the friend of Jesus, Lazarus, who the authorities were trying to kill because he was proclaiming his own resurrection by the hand of the Lord! He was perhaps also kept in the dark concerning the resurrection of many holy people when Jesus took his last breath. The resurrection of the widow's son and the leader of the synagogue's daughter finding the resurrection through the power of Jesus, also escaped him? The presence of doubt in the minds of those who clearly have placed miracles into the category of nonexistent reminds me of the words of Jesus, **"They will hear but not understand."** *Apparently, there is a blockage in the hearts and minds of those who have decided they will not believe in certain things no matter if the reality of such truth taps them on the shoulder and introduces itself. And there are those who have been prevented from understanding truth. Lastly, there are those who know the truth but will do all that they can to deny such truth to others. We are so blessed to have been given the faith to believe, and the word of God to instruct us.*

Final Vision

"A commotion of silence I see
Not very clear
People following a walking tree.
Noise surrounding a tiny hill
Foreboding and tense.
Is that a soldier walking toward me?
What is he saying?"
"You, take his arms!
You, take the tree!"
Life, moist upon his face
Dripping from his fingertips
Raining from his feet
Evidence displayed
Of sacrifice, complete.
A well was formed
Producing tears of love
Mixing with the streams
Of his precious blood.
Eyes searching vacant skies
In loneliness, he cried:
"My God, My God
Why have you forsaken me?"
Words that brought surprise
To those who hammered the nails
And gambled for his clothes.
One last cry to heaven's host
He bowed his head and released the Ghost.
Determined efficiency
Dishonor guard impersonal at best.
Few mourners, except the cloud overhead.
Fog caressing the earth
Gentle covering for the interred.
"Guard the tomb!
They shall not enter to steal him away!"
Third day grip broken.
"Look not for the living among the dead."
Sunrise conducting the chorus
Nature's witness in awe,
Resounding echoes in thunderous applause!
Death lamenting, "He lives!"

Isaiah 53:5 But he was pierced for our transgressions, he was crushed for our iniquities, the punishment that brought us peace was upon him, and by his wounds we are healed.

John 20:1-2 Early on the first day of the week, while it was still dark, Mary Magdalene went to the tomb and saw that the stone had been removed from the entrance. So she came running to Simon Peter and the other disciple, the one Jesus loved, and said, "They have taken the Lord out of the tomb, and we don't know where they have put him."

THE ACCOUNT FROM JOHN

John is the only disciple along with Peter who had witnessed the empty tomb. They did not see the angel, but they saw the evidence of the resurrection; the empty tomb and the former burial clothes, along with the strips of linen that had been wrapped around Jesus' head. John saw what was there and he believed. Both, of them did not understand, the pronouncement from Scripture that Jesus had to be resurrected, but as reported, John believed.

John is giving his firsthand account of what he saw, and he is reporting what Mary Magdalene had said. What is omitted and/ or different from the report contained in the gospel of Matthew, finds what should be expected when two people relate the same occurrence. They are not identical. It is not a purposeful difference, rather, it is a different report that concludes with the same outcome; Jesus has been resurrected. We don't hear the testimony of the other Mary (the mother of James), and we are not alerted to the angel whose appearance was bright like lightning, because John was not there when this occurred. He is reporting what he witnessed. We are not privileged to know of the fear present in the guards; all that is reported by Mary is that someone had taken the body of Jesus and it is unknown where he is. Additionally, John states that the resurrection had taken place early in the morning, ***"while it was still dark."*** *From John's perspective, it was early in the morning when Mary brought the news and in this he makes the determination* *that it was before dawn. I'm sure Mary and John did not get together and compare notes. Both Mary (Magdalene) and the other Mary (the mother of James) were reported as present when the stone was rolled away revealing the empty tomb.*

The report from the gospel of John concerning the resurrection of our Lord, says, ***"Then the disciples went back to where they were staying."*** *We are led to understand that Mary remained at the tomb crying.* ***John 20:11-14 Now Mary stood outside the tomb crying. As she wept she bent over to look, into the tomb and saw two angels in white, seated where Jesus' body had been, one at the head and the other at the foot. They asked her, "Woman why are you crying?" "They have taken my Lord away," she said, "and I don't know where they have put him." At this she turned around and saw Jesus standing there, but she did not realize it was Jesus.*** *At some point after the disciples had left, perhaps Mary relates to John the meeting with the angels and the risen Lord. It is this that John records in the gospel, everything prior had taken a secondary position simply because now it is Jesus who is witnessed and reported as alive! Mary is brought to this realization by our Lord himself.* ***John 20:15-16 Thinking he was a gardener, she said, "Sir, if you have carried him away, tell me where you have put him, and I will get him." Jesus said to her, "Mary." She turned toward him and cried out in Aramaic, "Rabboni!" (Which means "Teacher").***

Luke 24:1-6 On the first day of the week, very early in the morning, the women took the spices they had prepared and went to the tomb. They found the stone rolled away from the tomb, but when they entered they did not find the body of the Lord Jesus. While they were wondering about this, suddenly two men in clothes that gleamed like lightning stood beside them. In their freight, the women bowed down with their faces to the ground, but the men said to them, "Why do you look for the living among the dead?" He is not here, he is risen!"

THE ACCOUNT FROM LUKE

*There's that "**lightning"** appearance again! Once again, the gospel writer adds to our knowledge of what took place. We are getting an incrementally accurate picture of the entire occurrence from different viewpoints that will conclude the obvious truth that Jesus has been resurrected. The stone is reported as rolled away, as it is in every gospel. The stone would have been too heavy for the women to roll away; it was situated where it had to be rolled uphill which would make it increasingly more difficult to have been accomplished by either Mary, or together. They brought spices, and internally were imagining how they were going to be able to move the stone blocking the entrance to the tomb. No doubt they thought they could elicit help from a gardener of someone else. What they find is the entrance to the tomb is not blocked and they look inside to see two men in clothing that gleamed like lightning. I have to give those angels credit for the manner they introduce the resurrection; it could be expressed like this, "Duh, why are you looking for the living in a place for the dead? He's not here, he left a little while ago, you, just missed him." It was a definitely-subtle way to announce a miraculous event! The implication is that this event called resurrection happens all the time, why do you appear to be shocked? In any event, they get the message and report what took place to the disciples.*

Luke 24:9-12 When they came back from the tomb, they told all these things to the Eleven and to all the others. It was Mary Magdalene, Joanna, Mary the mother of James, and the others with them who told this to the apostles. But they did not believe the women, because their words seemed to them like nonsense. Peter, however, got up and ran to the tomb. Bending over, he saw the strips of linen lying by themselves, and he went away, wondering to himself what had happened.** In this rendering of the resurrection event we start with the women telling the apostles of what they witnessed. The report contains the same ingredients as previously mentioned. They brought spices to the tomb, the stone was rolled away, they did not find Jesus' body, and they are startled by two men whose appearance incorporated clothing that gleamed like lightning. The two men then relate to the women (in this account* *there is a group of the women who had gone to the tomb),* ***"Why do you look for the living among the dead? He is not here; he is risen!" *The narrative in all four of the gospels clearly reports the resurrection of Jesus!*

Work

They brought spices to the tomb
To alleviate the smell of death.
They found the empty tomb and wondered,
"What's the meaning of this?"
The work was blessed.
In their assigned task
Of service to the dead
They found what they did not expect
Their hearts were given rest.

They were first to know
The miracle of life
They did not doubt
The words spoken as in jest
"Try to understand
Looking for the living among the dead
Will never end the search
The one you seek has risen!
From the confines of the earth!"

Zechariah 12:10 I will pour out on the house of David and on the inhabitants of Jerusalem a spirit of grace and petition; and they shall look on him whom they have thrust through, and they shall mourn for him as one mourns for an only son, and they shall grieve over him as one grieves for a first-born. *NAB*

THE ACCOUNT FROM MARK

Mark 16:1-6 When the Sabbath was over, Mary Magdalene, Mary the mother of James, and Salome bought spices so that they might

go and anoint Jesus' body. Very early on the first day of the week, just after sunrise, they were on their way to the tomb and they asked each other, "Who will roll the stone away from the entrance of the tomb?" But when they looked up they saw that the stone, which was very large, had been rolled away. As they entered the tomb they saw a young man dressed in a white robe, sitting on the right side, and they were alarmed. "Don't be alarmed," he said. "You are looking for the Nazarene, who was crucified. He has risen! He is not here. See the place where they laid him.

It is no doubt an alarming situation to arrive at the burial place of Jesus and then find that the tomb has been opened and even more-strange is the fact that there is inside of the tomb a messenger declaring that the one you seek has been raised from the dead! The account goes on to say that the women were trembling and bewildered; this is a most-expected condition when the truth is spoken to the very core of our being. It was not the appearance of a, ***"young man"*** *that caused the fear; it was truth.*

Post resurrection appearances

I suspect for most of us had we been tortured, crucified murdered and buried, and in a short span of time resurrected, we might pay a visit to those responsible for such unjust sadistic treatment that we suffered. But Jesus is not interested in exacting retribution or appearing to those who committed the evil, no, he is focused on the very purpose of his mission, which was to suffer and die, and, in resurrection firmly establish his church on earth. Jesus was and is all about forgiveness, and had he turned the religious and Roman authorities into human candles what then would be the purpose? He is fully aware of the justice that will come to all evil doers at the proper time established by his Father; he's in no hurry to punish; the post resurrection time has been established for the forgiveness of man, and in this he makes his church aware of his visible presence in-order to confirm in their hearts the truth.

THE WALK TO EMMAUS

John 24:13-14 On that same day two of Jesus' followers were going to a village named Emmaus, about seven miles from Jerusalem. And they were talking to each other about all the things that happened. As they talked and discussed, Jesus himself drew near and walked along with them; they saw him but somehow did not recognize him.

Once again, we see the undercover Jesus, who in just a little time will permit his disciples to recognize him. Jesus inquires as to what they are talking about and upon their faces is clearly seen the reflected-sadness of broken hearts. The disciples, one of them named Cleopas asked of Jesus, **"Are you the only visitor in Jerusalem who does not know the things that have been happening these past few days?"** *Jesus inquires as to what things, and after being apprised he begins to educate his disciples. It is only when they had stopped and were having a shared meal do they recognize Jesus as he is saying the blessing. Their eyes are opened to the reality that Jesus has indeed risen and in their joy they return to Jerusalem and report to the eleven disciples that,* **"The Lord is risen!"**

Group-meeting

The gospel continues: While the two disciples were telling of their encounter with the risen Lord, Jesus is suddenly among them, saying, **"Peace be with you."** *Even after the greeting of peace the disciples are terrified; this is the result of not believing the reports, not only from the two disciples, but the testimony of the women who had seen the angels at the tomb, and, also the report from Mary herself, that she had seen Jesus. Jesus goes on to say to them,* **"Why are you alarmed? Why are these doubts coming up in your minds?"** *These same disciples had witnessed the resurrection of others by the power of God in the Lord, but still they had doubts, that even manifested in the actual appearance of Jesus! I recognize the words spoken to the rich man by Abraham in the parable of the rich man and Lazarus are true;* **"Even if someone were to return**

from the dead people would still not believe." *It is the purpose of Jesus to remove such doubt and replace it with the reality of the resurrection. In doing so he brings to all of us the great hope for eternal life!*

The depth of evil

It's very difficult for us to imagine the depths evil can and does sink into, but I suppose to begin to fathom what this existence may feel like and exist as, we probably must begin with arrogance, anger, vanity and pride; all of which when combined within the heart of man needs-not a reason to commit evil; it becomes a natural aspect of a person's life. It begins as covert opposition and as anger and frustration builds over being exposed, the covert attempts to destroy goodness are no longer hidden. Self-preservation of present status aimed at increasing dominance over others is always the major contributor to the prideful vanity present in arrogant evil. Such people act from motivations that are never concerned with the welfare of others, or, what is right. Having said this, the descriptive fits well with the evil that existed within the established religious rulers during the time of Christ's ministry. Their continued resistance, of overt and/or covert attempts to disparage, deny, and otherwise rebuke the good deeds and miracles performed by our Lord, makes plain to all the evil that had taken-up residence in the hearts and minds of those in opposition to the good and truth presented by our Lord.

Arrogance

Unwillingness to acknowledge truth is
A fool dressed in ignorance
Defiance at large
Passing through
Testing's temperament
With violence as a guide
The day and the hour
Will come as great surprise
When at last he sees
The well of arrogance is (really) dry
Wisdom's scalpel cuts to see inside
God pruning his garden
Discarding what he will
He keeps the wheat
Weeds are fed to flames

Eternal is the fire
It never kneels or wanes
The grave is found unyielding
Where arrogance remains
Lost, forever in the darkness
Absent even names
Constant now the anger
That brought to them the pain

Matthew 23:31-33 "So you testify that you are the descendants of those who murdered the prophets. Fill up, then, the measure of the sin of your forefathers! You Snakes! You brood of vipers! How will you escape being condemned to hell?"

Memories

Some memories
Speak gentle in the ear
Others mock with laughter
Remembrance of fear
That kept us moving deeper
Into the night of gloom.

God gave to us his mercy
He rolled the stone away
That kept us in the dark
Where none can hope, or pray.

Weak and captive we were held
With bindings, self-adorned
Until resurrection's morning
Brought peace to all newborns.

To the helpless and the hopeless
The crippled and the blind
The impoverished of spirit
The tortured of the mind

Resounding tidings cry:
"Sound the mercy bell!
To the living and the dead
The King of Kings has risen
Our Lord, has conquered death!"

Isaiah 9:1 "The people who walked in darkness have seen a great light; upon those who dwelt in the land of gloom a light has shone." *NAB*

The sidebar

John 21:15 After they had eaten, Jesus said to Simon Peter, "Simon son of John, do you love me more than these others do?" *Jesus may have taken Peter off to the side and out of earshot before asking him the question. Jesus is addressing Peter with the name,* ***"Simon son of John."*** *It was very common to formally address someone by indicating family lineage back then. In, this instance, it is akin to a boss saying, "Simon son of John, come into my office." Jesus does not say to him, Pete, old pal, do you love me more than these others? By doing this, Jesus is conveying the message that he knows the answer to his question, but is now slowly bringing awareness to Peter that all is forgiven for having denied him three times. When Jesus finally asks the question the third time, Peter breaks down and becomes very sad, and says to Jesus, I know you know everything,* ***"You know that I love you."***

The declaration of love by Peter for Jesus is necessary to reestablish what Peter may have thought was forever lost. There is no doubt that once the resurrection of Jesus is made known to them without a doubt, Peter mostly, but also the others faced the reality of their prior actions, and self-condemnations of conscience were greatly realized. All of them needed to be reaffirmed and reconnected to the reality of who they are, and what their purpose in the plan of God actually-constitutes. Perhaps the meaning of the words of Jesus, now, became highlighted? ***"Peace be with you."*** *Jesus gave to them the peace that would resonate above the crescendo of guilt, for deserting him; his peace would now enter deeply into the fortress of the heart, along with the love that now, is made so much more pronounced by the recognition of their faults and the forgiveness from Christ. They are just one step away-from becoming complete for the mission of declaring the good news to the world. They would await the day of Pentecost for the Holy Spirit in-order to be equipped to do every good work.*

Agape Vision

My God I love you.
You know it's true.
I love you, because you are Truth.
I love you, and for you alone I live.
I love you, for the blessings that you give.
I love you, for your guidance in the night
Yes, I love you, for your unequaled might.
My God, I love you, if I could, I'd kiss your feet.
My God, I love you, for making me complete.
I love you, for allowing me to share
A little bit of heaven
In knowing you are really-here.
My God, I love you, Lord, I love you I confess!
Yes, My God, I love you, for you are the very best!

Mark 12:30 Love the Lord your God with all your heart and with all your soul and with all your mind and with all your strength.

EZEKIAL 14:12-14 The word of the Lord came to me, "Son of man, if a country sins against me by being unfaithful and I stretch out my hand against it to cut off its food supply and send famine upon it and kill its men and their animals, even if these three men-Noah, Daniel and Job-were in it, they could save only themselves by their righteousness, declares the Sovereign Lord.

10

THERE'S NO ESCAPING LIGHT

The priest and prophet of the Lord is speaking to the nation of Israel attempting to make them aware of their blatant idolatry. He is telling the people they cannot hide what is present in their hearts; God sees all their idolatrous desire and is not pleased. Not even if Noah, Daniel and Job resided in the nation would he spare the judgment about to beset the land. However, to the people who have set up idols in their hearts and made of their faces stumbling blocks (EZEKIAL 14:3), God is speaking to them in effort to recapture their focus upon what is pleasing to him. Faces as stumbling blocks may refer to hypocrisy; what is idolatrous in the heart is shown in the countenance. This is of course a declaration of the awareness of guilt, attempting to keep hidden the desires of the sinful nature.

Unfortunately for those attempting to keep hidden the coveting and idolatrous thoughts, hidden in the heart, they are not understanding that they are always in the presence of God. Our thoughts are kept hidden (for the most part) from others but are always made to be loud and clear in the eyes of God. There are times we can tell when we are being subjected to a lie; facial characteristics and body movement sometimes give us a clue to the advance of untruth. Again, where God is concerned there is nothing hidden.

What was true of God back then in the time of the prophet is also true today, everything is completely exposed to the watchful eye of God, and nothing will go unpunished, or unrewarded. Yes, there is reward for doing what is right and pleasing, in the eyes of God. Not only do we feel better about what we have done, let's say, for the good of someone, but in the overall category of reward God has set aside for us treasures in heaven. This is perhaps what Jesus meant by telling us to store up treasures in heaven where thieves cannot steal and moths cannot destroy. There is always the opportunity for us to turn from things hidden in the heart, in-order to find once again the peace that was present before we decided to discount the ability of God to view our inner thoughts and desires. This is exactly what the Sovereign Lord is impressing upon the nation that has lost its way from the path of righteousness. When the desire to no longer, do what is right is lost, therein what is found, is a need to continually seek the places of darkness. Mankind will always think it is the heart that can conceal.

Changing

The mist laid low upon the earth
A wall to block the sky
Lending added weight to days
As thoughts within a storm
Though torch and lantern ready
To battle with its form
A greater light is needed
To penetrate hearts
Illuminating darkness
With beams from wisdom's dawn
Ending deception by lifting out of sight
The mist of chilling vapor
Dispersed by God's sunlight.

2 Corinthians 4:6 For God, who said, "Let light shine out of darkness," made his light shine in our hearts to give us the light of the knowledge of the glory of God in the face of Christ."

It is essential for our well-being to live life absent deception. It is bad enough that throughout the world there is a constant attempt by deception to gain a foothold in our minds and hearts; to make us believe something that is not true. A bad seed planted in fertile ground will produce a bad outcome, so it is with us who allow untruth to find the fertile ground that has been established in the foundation of truth given to us by the life of Christ. When we consciously harbor hidden aspects of our lives, deep within the very fertile and sensitive place of the heart, we are inviting a bad outcome. Such an outcome ultimately finds judgment and consequence based upon the idolatrous level we have allowed ourselves to reach. Idolatry can be found in everything that replaces God from the pinnacle of honor and desire within the heart and mind of man.

We rightfully place our family children and grandchildren in the most loved category, and this is a correct place for them to be kept; deep in the heart where love is found to produce all the good things of God. Somehow, we learn to love someone more than someone else, and this is not a fault in our nature. It is human to place priorities even within the category of love. Love's status is continually changing priorities; we marry, we have children and then come grandchildren; it is not that we no longer love wife or children but when grandchildren enter upon the scene it is they who demand our focus intently. We have not lessened our love for wife or children, we have refocused it upon the new member of the family, perhaps, because he is most vulnerable, coupled with an inherent protective instinct; in the same way God, voluntarily with love protects us.

While all of this is taking place within us, there must be the overall understanding that it is God who made all of us and in the understanding of creation, we recognize it is God who gave to us all the persons and things we love. He does not permit us to place into our hearts anything that is inappropriate; there is no place for idolatry in the heart of man. When God is set aside then all other *rightful inhabitants of the heart can also be placed into a secondary position in favor of the idolatrous and coveting nature of man. Let us always guard our heart, "**for it is the wellspring of life.**"*

Displacement

Displacement: "to put out of position; to oust from situation or office." Within the physical world that we inhabit, two objects cannot occupy the same space. It is either one or the other; both cannot claim sovereignty over such space. However, the heart of man has no such limit to the occupancy rule exhibited in the natural world. That is, to say, there is unlimited space for all lawful emotions to occupy. It is only when that which is not permitted by God, finds entrance into the heart, is there a conflict challenging love and loyalty. Additionally, there is no such allowance for displacement of a rightful position established by the acceptable behavior presented to mankind by God, who alone is the singular authority in all matters of the heart. Therein idolatry is unlawfully admitted and in such lawlessness God finds himself thinking of the destruction of the nation that has displaced him and truth in favor of the illusion of not being seen.

The prophet is bringing to our attention the great consequence of being disloyal to God, who has always been loyal to us. God has always placed his creation (especially mankind) within the deepest recesses of his heart and showered us with unfathomable love. Such displacement strikes-out at God, who is Love! If we can displace Love then everything else is an illusion, a mask, a copy, absent the depth and commitment found only in the originator of love itself! We should take a moment to think about how we would feel should those we love, prove to be untruthful concerning their professed love for us. We would be left in a state of emotional distress, but underlying it all would be our desire for them to understand their loss of love, and in such-recognition return us to the place in their heart that was meant to be. This is the very same desire of God; he wants us to see how far we have fallen away from the love we had for him. He desires of us to once again recognize all the love he has shown to us in the form of blessings, in both family and sacrifice made in our behalf. The sacrifice of Jesus hanging upon a cross is the absolute love of God for his children. Who among us who are parents would not willingly give up our lives for the sake of our children? Who among us would not sacrifice for the sake of someone else's children? Who wouldn't rush to the aid of a child in need, being set upon by evil? I think the majority will gladly rush to the aid of the child. This is the same love that is shown to us by the sacrifice of Christ, the love of God that we are now blessed to address as, Abba! Father!

Wisdom

"Wisdom sings her own praises."
Where joy pronounced, "unending,"
Wondrous truth descending
Into the heart is speaking
The whispered voice of God,
"Come to me."

Ecclesiastes 9:16-17 So I said, "Wisdom is better than strength." But the poor man's wisdom is despised, and his words are no longer heeded. The quiet words of the wise are more to be heeded, than the shouts of a ruler of fools.

Replacement

The trouble with the replacement of God for someone or something else, is the understanding in the one who is doing the replacement; he is aware that he is attempting to substitute God with a counterfeit representation of truth. When we find that God can be replaced therein the possibility to lose all else is made so much easier. The replacement of truth and love with a counterfeit is usually found to be the beginning of the road to ruin. Love replaced, is never replaced with love, it is mostly found to be substituted by a physical addiction and/or compulsive activity that never finds satisfaction, and in such a never-ending quest for fruition all else is cast aside. The unity of family, for instance, is found only in the cohesiveness of love. If one member of the family is lured away from both love and obligation to loyalty, the remaining members of the family are made to be lesser in strength, and their focus upon the importance of unity is diminished. Since we recognize God to be ***Our Father****, if we decide to abandon him to the counterfeit gods of this world, it is idolatry personified.*

Reaction

The reaction of God and the statements made to the prophet regarding a nation that has abandoned him for the myriad of counterfeits contained in idolatry, is the reaction of hurt! Yes, when we replace and/or attempt to substitute God for what is the equivalent of nothing, we find him to be angry, not only for his being shunned, but because he understands that we are on the road to ruin! He doesn't want to see us ruined, left at the mercy of the world and found to be trampled upon by the world's design to destroy all that God loves. A man can always find redemption when he places his hope in the Lord. Even when we have attempted to replace, substitute or denounce God and his love for us in favor of our own desires, we can and will find a contrite heart always accepted by a forgiving and loving God. Like the ***Prodigal Son*** *who had denounced his family, in-order to enter the world of substitutes, illusions, and deception, he had come to his senses and realized he would find total ruin within his current state-of-affairs that were not getting any better; his return home was met with a father's love and he was renewed and restored to his former station within the family. So, it is with all of us who have strayed away from the love of God and allowed the world's attractions entrance into our hearts only to be made captive by the things we had thought to be life's offerings. We need to understand, God is Life.*

Honesty

Honesty bonds people together
Like adversity and hard times
Mind to mind and heart to heart
Fabric sewn as marrow and bone
Heavy and taut the fisherman's knot
Honesty.

Proverbs 12:17 A truthful witness gives honest testimony, but a false witness tells lies.

Providence

How wonderful your providence
A waterfall unending, no measure of its depth.
Colorful gift giving of thought filled intent.
Everything a match a blend of taste and style.
Brilliant is your tapestry and genuine your smile.

Luke 6:38 Give, and it will be given to you. A good measure, pressed down, shaken together and running over, will be poured into your lap. For with the measure you use, it will be measured to you.

"Son of man, if a country sins against me by being unfaithful..." *Faithful: "reliable, honorable, and loyal." The opposite of faithful is the condition that has brought both anger and sadness to the Sovereign Lord, over the careless-manner such dedication to trust is tossed about, as just so much nonsense. The heart of a man is the place from which is derived either peace or trouble, hard times or restful nights. When it is troubled because of a failure on the part of someone to remain faithful, and committed to the love that was made manifest by God himself, what will be gained is the troubling condemnation that is presented when thoughts of disloyalty are compounded with their fruition.*

Spirit and conscience

In addition to the heart of man there is the spirit, the part of us that is our thinking ability; our ability to think, reason, and make judgments concerning what is right and wrong. Embarking upon a road that either finds acceptance or rejection in the thoughts of man will always find a consequence of either rewarding peace or condemning unrest. How this acceptance and/or condemning posture had come about in the thought process of man is clearly delineated within the creation narrative of the Holy Bible. Society may set the norms but no matter what the parameters may be there is always the clear distinction of right and wrong. As such, the creation narrative pointing to sin, as the cause for the conscience to stand guard over the thoughts of man, is proven to be the most supporting witness heralding the account of creation. Additionally, because there is an awareness of acceptable and unacceptable behavior the concept of perfection is made clear to all, the reality of God's existence.

Where did the understanding of God and right and wrong come from, if not from creation and the subsequent emergence of sin? (From which is derived the consequence of the knowledge of right and wrong.) Can there be any other explanation, for the knowledge of right and wrong? In addition, contained within good or bad action is found approval or disapproval pointing directly to a code of behavior set-forth from outside of the existence of mankind. And so, not only does our thinking prove our very own existence, but thoughts of good and/or bad must be concluded to have originated in the laws set forth as a guiding light within a newfound world of consequence, containing unknown myriads of variables. We needed to be aware of the pitfalls of life and in this we were given (not burdened) the knowledge of right and wrong, in-order to lessen our troubles and consequences. We were dispossessed from paradise (eternal life) but we were not abandoned; God went with us in the form of conscience.

Hard Times

It's a fact of life
When "self" is center stage
Love grows cold.
The fireplace absent fire
Permits anything approach
If only we would understand
Pushing to the edge
Invites a need to fly
If only we would think
Of the consequence of wrong
Troubles would lessen
Indeed, they would say, "Goodbye."
Dishonor ruins reputation
Shatters the peaceful heart
Brings separation
Between a man and God.
Dishonor is deception.
What does it mean?
Wake up!
Without the love of God
Your direction is pointing down
It's a fact of life
It's a hard time when a man hits ground!

Matthew 9:4 Knowing, their thoughts, Jesus said, "Why do you entertain evil thoughts in your hearts?"

Shipwrecked

Today we don't call it a shipwreck.
It's more like a bad credit rating
A bad reputation sinks us to the bottom.
It's true, God forgives.
The rules of the world are clear,
"We'll let you into the game
But there's a price to pay."
I suppose that's because we gravitate
Toward self-destruction?
The behaviorist thinkers
Don't need to devise intricate plans
Concerning the demise of man
We do it on our own.
We don't need a rudder shaft to fall from its bearing post.
Or a turbine reduction gear to screech us to a halt.
In the final analysis, it is "we."
We have done the damage of self-made wounds.
Without the outside help of unseen jagged rocks
Absent siren's call to lead us, fast astray
"Mirror, mirror on the wall" is all we need to say.
Conscience will tell us where it all went wrong
When sitting at the bottom of a life filled with storms.

Proverbs 13:6 Virtue guards one who walks honestly, but the downfall of the wicked is sin.

Guilt

Along with the knowledge of wrong there is attached to it the condemnation of conscience known as guilt. We admit to ourselves the wrong committed, but when it comes to acknowledging such wrong to others we will duck and weave in-order to keep wrong hidden. Because of the immediacy attached to consequence we will do all we can to avoid admitting fault. Even if it is not a specific law written upon the legal paper of society, but an infraction concerning loyalty and/or behavior that's unacceptable to others, we do not wish to have our hidden-self revealed.

The creation narrative informing us of the guilt and awareness of Adam and Eve, running off so they would not be found in a disobedient state, clearly bears witness to the truth that it is God who created us, and it is God who has set the limitations upon our thoughts and deeds. It is God who has permitted us the understanding of guilt and the consequence of sin, even though we were not fully aware of the consequence in its total impact. Today we are aware of the total impact to mean death, and unless we take the remedial action to ward off the sentence of total death, we will suffer the consequence that God declared to be just, but also has provided the means to avoid, through the sacrifice of Jesus.

Hebrews: 3:7-8 So, as the Holy Spirit says, "Today if you hear his voice, do not harden your hearts as you did in the rebellion, during the time of testing in the desert, where your fathers tested and tried me and for forty years saw what I did." *An entire nation failed to heed the inner voice of wrong! Not only did they see the physical signs of the reality of God but they went against the conscience, clearly recognizable as the inner voice of God attempting to guide us in the paths we should travel. By permitting the voice of God to go unheeded is to* ***"test"*** *God. What can we be thinking? We are fearful of the immediate consequence of earthly authority but when it comes to God, we may find annoyance in the nagging voice of regret, but why are we reluctant to acknowledge the ability of God to be just as immediate in his judgment as the worldly powers? Even the unbeliever finds the voice of conscience to be prevalent and pronounced when wrong is committed; why then is he not aware of the cause of the awareness and the one who whispers in his ear? There is perhaps more to just the physical malady of deafness; the heart also has ability to not hear the overtures laced within the condemnations of guilt!* ***Genesis 3:8-10 Then the man and his wife, heard, the sound of the Lord God as he was walking in the garden in the cool of the day, and they hid from the Lord God among the trees of the garden. But the Lord God called to the man, "Where are you?" He answered, "I heard***

you in the garden, and I was afraid because I was naked; so I hid." *Somewhere along to way we have learned to not be afraid of the consequences of wrong as it pertains to God.*

Conscience is a law unto itself

Romans 2:14-15 (Indeed, when the gentiles, who do not have the law, do by nature the things required by the law, they are a law for themselves, even though they do not have the law, since they show that the requirements of the law are written on their hearts, their consciences also bearing witness, and their thoughts now accusing, now even defending them.) *This piece of understanding speaks to us of freedom to know what is right and pleasing to God and the ability to do it based upon the faith contained in the individual; having nothing to do with the religious laws of men, but supersedes laws, dictates and acts regulating one's permitted activities. A man may reason an action to be permitted but his conscience is not moved in agreement. As such, the conscience overrules the reasoning aspect of thought; faith in Christ permits- one the ability to act without conscience condemnation, where the same action is condemned by the conscience of another, because his reasoning alone does not permit it. It (really) is an act of acceptance of understanding that we have been set-free to live life without the oversite of a listing of must-not-do directives contained within a religious system that may mean well, but in truth is placing limitation upon the power of faith.*

Example: Some people find drinking a glass of wine to be sinful. They are not wrong in their determination as it applies to themselves. It is only when they apply their determination of what is a sinful act to someone else that they find themselves judging others and in judging they may very well be sinning. Jesus came in-part for us to be set free from the religious system that applies all things to all people. Certainly, Jesus had no problem, not only having a glass of wine but he provided for others, gallons of the best wine at the, ***"Wedding feast of Cana."*** *Drinking wine during the time of Jesus was prolific. In fact, the name* **"Cana"** *means "Place of reeds" and* *so we may imply that the water in Cana was not of the best quality; which may have made drinking wine more palatable. It is true that the bible speaks to us about not becoming drunk by the consumption of wine, but this is completely different from someone determining (absent conscience condemnation) a glass of wine with his evening meal is appropriate. In fact, the apostle Paul had advised Timothy to drink some wine in an-effort to aid his health.*

1 Timothy 5:23 "Do not drink water only, but take a little wine to help your digestion, since you are sick so often." *GNB Within the advice given to Timothy we find Paul not only determining that a little wine is not sinful for himself, but he acknowledges to Timothy that it is okay for him to do so as well.* ***Jeremiah 31:33-34 "This is the covenant I will make with the house of Israel after that time," declares the Lord. "I will put my law in their minds and write it on their hearts. I will be their God and they will be my people. No longer will a man teach his neighbor, or his brother, saying, 'Know the Lord,' because they will all know me, from the least of them to the greatest."*** *This new covenant that speaks of God placing in our minds and hearts his law, speaks of freedom to know what is acceptable to him, not the laws of men and/or religiosity. Certainly, we will continue to speak of the Lord, but not in the terms that was so prevalent during the time of Jeremiah and the time of Jesus, wherein the complexity of the law had become a constant seeking of approval from the established religious.*

This is not the context that God wants, for his people; we were not meant to follow religious shepherds; we were meant to follow the Lord. By following the Lord Jesus, we can always find/ understand what is right and pleasing to him, because he is always within our hearts and minds. We are united in the Spirit of God.

Conscience is greater than reason

What we are able, to infer from the determinations presented to us in the examples from both Jesus and Paul, is that conscience is a greater function of the thinking ability called reasoning, simply because it is the very voice of God instilled within us that guides, permits and/or condemns actions on an individual basis. If we are to be called to answer for our actions on an individual basis, it makes no sense for everyone to be grouped into the same system of religious determination, (concerning what should not be done) when, in fact, such determination by the religious may limit freedom, in one, and in another, cause him to sin, by judging someone else. The laws of man continually find change, but the laws of God are eternal and perfect.

Isaiah 10:1-2 "You are doomed! You make unjust laws and oppress my people. This is how you keep the poor from having their rights and from having justice. That is how you take the property from widows and orphans. *It is amazing to me how in some cultures having the religious at the top of the leadership pyramid there is not an outcry from the common man, simply because of the constant assaults upon conscience. I recognize that in such closed societies, conditioning coupled with fear of the rulers will mute any objections to the outright injustices against the populace. Still, it is the laws of men that in these instances enter-into the extreme category, and ultimately will find the words of the prophet resonating in their ears:* **"You are doomed!"** *Apart from such closed societies there is the understanding that corruption exists within legal systems. Bribes are paid by the powerful and injustice miraculously appears. Can it be that there is no conscience and/or awareness that in the end all acts of wickedness will be answerable to the Supreme Judge?*

Prophesy

Sin deception injustice run wild
Wickedness mocking
Reason conscience and God
Deep darkness unbowed
All this and more
In the hearts of the proud.
The prophet's words
Of strength filled truth:
"You are doomed!"
From the moment of evil's embrace
The bricks for your tomb
Were forged in disgrace!

Isaiah 10:21-22 A few of the people of Israel will come back to their mighty God. Even though now there are as many people of Israel as there are grains of sand by the sea, only a few will come back. Destruction is in store for the people and it is fully deserved.

A new age

Isaiah 11:1 "The royal line of David is like a tree that has been cut down, but just as new branches sprout from the stump, so a new king will arise from among David's descendants." *Within the ninth and eleventh chapters of the book of Isaiah we are promised a new order of* ***judgment and justice*** *that will reside within the new king, who is a descendant from David's throne. We are so blessed to have witnessed the advent of this promise; it is only the actual crowning ceremony that we presently await. Jesus has made manifest the promise contained in the book of Isaiah, and in this the promised redemption of the people of God has been ongoing ever since the resurrection of our Lord. It is the new and final age wherein forgiveness is available for all who will admit that God is correct and we are not.*

Light

John 1:4-5 The Word was the source of life, and this life brought light to people. The light shines in the darkness, and the darkness has never put it out. *GNB When we speak of light we understand that it is this illumination that permits us to see. Light, even up to this very day is a mystery to science; it is described as either a ray or a particle. No matter, this duality of opinion, what is for certain is that without light we could not see. There is also a duality of understanding in the person of Jesus who is the light for the world. Without him there is also no sight (no correct understanding), as such, we need to embrace the light given to us in both aspects of life; physical and spiritual. Within the spiritual much of our sight is given to us in the form of faith. Without faith, the sun and the moon could shine on us constantly and we would not be able to see or understand the world in which we live or the life that we have been given. Therein many find themselves excluded from the knowledge of truth, God, and the purpose of life itself.*

Jesus brought into the world all the answers to the questions that have plagued humanity up until that time. He also brought the road map for us to escape the total death that awaits all of us who will not accept the very visible sacrifice of himself, in-order for us to be reunited to the life God wants, for us; restoration to eternal life. If only we can embrace the truth contained in the offering of eternity. We have been given witness of the resurrection of our Lord, and more than that we have received the new life through being born again, and in this we share in the truth, so obvious to us but remaining so hidden from those who will not or cannot see.

Testimony

Where can I begin?
How to speak the way of forgiveness and grace?
Enemies on every side, demons of this life
Alcohol gambling false thoughts debt and strife
Attacking unrelenting no freedom from regrets
Vicious undertakings sealed in every breath.
The things that remained: children wife and life
Were held as hostage through evil's ruling bite.
At the time of very last a voice is heard that said:
"You're lost, this your chance, receive
Truth will set you free, if only you'll believe."
I knew nothing but his presence then
So, in my heart I called and said:
"Lord, destroy my enemies and lay them to the ground!"
But then that voice said, "No, that's not how love is found."
To my knees crying soft once again my heart invoked:
"Lord, I know nothing, let your will be
done, forgive my outburst rude."
In silence peace secured within the inner halls
As my wife sung praises in words the angels knew.
Amazing transformation escaping spirit's tomb
As a newborn wakening from the confines of the womb
Stability like a seed transformed sprouting forth its shell
Former ways denied as I was freed from hell!
Three days of mourning for the past where I was blind
For all the things, I now see rushed shudders to my mind.
At last upon my feet in scripture found a feast
And from the ashes of that life walked out a brand new me!

Matthew 6:9-13 "Our Father in heaven, hallowed be your name, your kingdom come, your will be done on earth as it is in heaven. Give us today our daily bread. Forgive us our debts, as we also have forgiven our debtors. And lead us not into temptation, but deliver us from the evil one."

1 Corinthians 15:40-41 There are also heavenly bodies and there are earthly bodies; but the splendor of the heavenly bodies is one kind, and the splendor of the earthly bodies is another. The sun has one kind of splendor, the moon another and the stars another; and star differs from star in splendor.

11

SEARCHERS

It is very easy to get lost in the infinite universe that amazes and challenges our minds. Dedicating one's life to search the heavens for answers to the origins of life, or else, to search from pure curiosity is a good thing. However, when the answer to the origin of life has already been given to us, it can appear to some (believers) to be a waste of time. The searchers of today have an abundance of modern technological equipment at their disposal, and it seems the more technical the advances become, and the more revelation is achieved, the greater the questions become. Mankind is seeking to find the answer to the question of whether-or-not there is life elsewhere in the universe. Sometimes it seems as if we don't want to find the answers. Certainly, there are numerous accounts of angelic visitation (what can only be described as life) to the earth catalogued and gift wrapped for us within the bible, and modern-day reports of unexplained sightings, and still, we fail to recognize such immeasurably vast and infinite testimony.

*There are reports of sightings of UFO's all over the planet but it seems that such reports gain very little credibility no matter who is doing the reporting. We should ask ourselves this question, given the statement made by our Lord: "**My Father is always working and I must do the same.**" Is God still creating life and if so is it limited* *to the earth? In addition, at least one answer has been given to us and it is up to us to either accept or reject it; in the rejection, we are forced to once again gaze out into the heavens seeking to find life that may answer the core question as to our own beginnings. It seems to me that when mankind is given an answer that appears to be too simplistic, it is discounted out of hand and sent away in favor of complex theories asserting the origins of life. When man fails to accept creation's narrative as presented to us within straightforward truth, he then searches for a complex multifaceted intricate explanation (evolution or accidental), that finds the quest for answers as infinitely unending, as the heavens into which he is searching. The origin of mankind and our purpose has been clearly spoken to us; we don't withhold from our children our identity; why then would we expect God to keep us in existence without his revealing to us our status as his children? There are many who cannot or will not accept the truth even if they were hit on the head with a falling star! They are seeking a great and logical explanation to all that exists, except the understanding of God. As such, they search the heavens of infinite beauty, and in reward for their efforts they become a part of the mystery they so desperately wish to solve.*

Seekers

When our hearts are right
What we seek will find us
If we continually discount
And denigrate truth
We'll erect a wall
Of disbelief made of illusion
And grief.
We'll construct a battle plan
With man on top
And never will we understand
That God made us all.
The heavens above us
Like a lighthouse that guides our way
Speaks to everyone:
"This is the day the Lord has made."

Psalm 9: 10 "Those who know your name will trust in you, for you, Lord, have never forsaken those who seek you."

The Way

Thank God for our global positioning system. How in the world did we ever manage to find our way around the block? We have become so dependent upon modern technology that at times I don't want to leave the house without my global positioning system, for fear I might be detoured from my normal route to the grocery store! We are being made to be more and increasingly more dependent upon technology in-order to perform tasks that presented no problem to us just a few years-ago. Given all the thinking is being done for us by machines and computers it's a wonder why man is still traveling into the heavens seeking to unravel the mysteries of the universe?

The world is going to hell and there are those who are obsessed with star gazing. Aren't there enough mysteries right here on planet earth for us to be entertained? I suppose the last frontier offers to us much more than the hum-drum of planet earth. I'm wondering when these star searchers will come to the realization that not only on our planet is there turmoil and wars but should the truth be revealed (allowed to sink into the consciousness of man) we just might find such wars a part of the entirety of creation. ***Ephesians 6:10-12 "Finally, be strong in the Lord and his mighty power. Put on the full armor of God so that you can take your stand against the devil's schemes. For our struggle is not against flesh and blood, but against the rulers, against the authorities, against the powers of this dark world and against the spiritual forces of evil in the heavenly realms."***

Now that was a mouthful! ***"Spiritual forces of evil in the heavenly realms."*** *Sounds to me like the war that broke out in heaven is still ongoing. The spiritual war taking place upon the earth is a snapshot of the universal panoramic taking place throughout the heavenly realms. Yes, the heavenly realms; plural.*

We are not aware of this spiritual warfare in the heavens simply because it is apart from the natural realm that we exist within. We are not immune to the spiritual war; we are a part of it. If this were not true, why then are we told to put on the mighty Armor of God? There was a time in the lives of many of the saved where we were captured by the enemy's advances that appealed to the desires of the flesh. As such we were blinded to the war taking place and oblivious to the fact that we were indeed prisoners of said war! It was not until we were given access to the light of truth that we then were given ability to break free from the camp of the enemy and aid in the escape of others who are even now held unknowingly.

<u>The plague</u>

In the last fifty-years the influx of poison into the world's societies have so impacted the lives of those who are captured by the demon of drugs and alcohol, along with the fear that is brought to the loved ones of those so captured. How many times have we said to ourselves, "If the government (really) wanted to stop the influx of drugs into the country, they could do it; or at least they could do a better job of curtailing the amounts of drugs being smuggled into the hearts and minds of the young people afflicted by the allure of, "getting high." This thought of permissiveness on the part of government resonates in us to the point that we (actually) believe it to be true! We believe it to be true because it is! However, the act of drug usage has become so lucrative and even acceptable to many politicians, that the efforts to deny entrance to the country is but an illusionary cosmetic that says to us, "We are against such damaging behavior and destructive usage," but all the while there is the wink and the nod of approval. Should we be surprised that there are forces in the world attempting to capture and ultimately destroy, the creation of God, in-order to recreate everything in the image and likeness of evil? This is the objective of such spiritual war, not only on planet earth but throughout the universe as the apostle Paul informs us. Deception is not always blatant, more-often than not it is designed to be incrementally invisible. For instance, the idea of legalizing heroin, for personal use is not one that will receive immediate approval from the populace. As such, we see introduced and legalized a lesser intoxicant into the mindset of society; the formerly condemned drug called Marijuana that was and still is smuggled into the country has become just another way to placate the masses. Not only has Marijuana gained in acceptance by much of the youth of today, but it has gained legality. Incremental destruction of humanity in the eyes of evil is no less destructive in the final analysis; man, is kept oblivious to the truth of God, and ultimately is doomed! There is no rush to destroy immediately; evil is very patient and thinks, plans and schemes, in a long-term objective. Perhaps it is the idea of torturing slowly, as opposed to a quick death that encourages the incrementally designed demise of man?

The cure

The cure for deception is truth. The powerful who walk upon the earth are made subordinate to truth; the lie living within encapsulated environments, thought to be immune to the truth, have found exposure to the light is too great a force to confront. This is one reason why we are told to put on all the armor of God; such armor protects against the schemes of evil. Schemes: "plan; design; system; plot; to plan; to contrive; to frame; to intrigue." Sounds to me like evil is giving a lot of thought as to how it can contrive and/or frame our downfall within the world of today. It also seems to me that it would suit evil's designs if mankind were divided under many banners having to do with ideology as opposed to truth. Nothing is better suited to combat deception than the truth of God. The imprisoned by darkness have been set free by the power of God's light shining into the darkness, that held them not only captive but ignorant to the reality of creation; not only in the natural creation most visible in the heavens, but ignorant also to the spiritual battles that constantly rage all around us. We have been given truth in-order to keep us free; this is the reason we are told to wear it like a suit of armor.

Divisiveness

Everywhere we look there is a divide, a chasm, a line of separation that defines us and them. **.** *The "us and them" mentality for the most part is clearly defined in both permissiveness and restriction; the reality of conscience approval or disapproval. Divisiveness is the enemy of compromise and in compromise therein can be found agreement. Unfortunately for the country there are many dividers whose only purpose in life is to create distance between clearly defined ideologies.*

The road one takes to reach an agreement is always a doable task when the roads have all the signs clearly displayed. When distrust is present in the hearts and minds of a people the chasm widens and disunity becomes a way of life. Everyone believes it is their way that is correct and because they do not recognize the way of God they find constant strife that eventually must tear apart the entire structure. **"A house divided can't stand."** *In many instances, there is the pretense of unity that is somehow presented to the common man and seemingly is embraced. It is superficially embraced because there is a real unity in the neighborhoods, churches and communities of the common man but underlying all of this are the schemes of the enemy constantly attempting to divide. Unknown to many is the fact that it is the schemes of evil, the spiritual forces that are constantly pitting one element of society against the other. Opposing the schemes of evil is the force of truth and good, that has been introduced into the minds and hearts of mankind, not only by the laws of God ingrained in the hearts and conscience, but because good is self-evident as it is displayed in the actions of man. This presentation of truth has built a barrier against the lies and deceptions present in the schemes of evil.*

War

Suffering and loss are the fruits of war.
Happiness and joy are the victor's spoils.
Truth is the weapon that penetrates to the heart.
Deception is placed into the light of God.
Doomed in God's judgment
By the evil, it wrought.

Psalm 27:3-4 "Though an army besiege me, my heart will not fear; though war break out against me, even then will I be confident."

The idea of war does not necessarily have to be conducted in the purely physical state of activity; it can be a psychological and in most cases of awareness it is both. Once we recognize the enemy and his design to destroy as much of creation as is possible we are encompassed in a war that is evident in all fronts of confrontation. Fortunately for us this awareness is not leading us to a paranoid state of mind. In fact, being aware brings to us a sense of security. As the psalmist proclaims, even if he is confronted by an army of the enemy he will not be afraid, he will remain confident in the ability of God to vanquish his enemies!

2 Kings 6:15-17 When the servant of the man of God got up and went out early the next morning, an army of horses and chariots had surrounded the city. "O my lord, what shall we do?" the servant asked. "Don't be afraid" the prophet answered. "Those who are with us are more than those who are with them." And Elisha prayed, "O Lord, open his eyes so he may see. Then the Lord opened the servant's eyes, and he looked and he saw the hills full of horses and chariots of fire all around Elisha. *Our awareness of the protection God provides is not limited to the force he can generate against the evil plotting against good. He has provided for us eternal life, and in this we are not a people who live in fear of those who can kill the body, but after which can do nothing else. A soldier is aware of the dangers of war but if he is fixed upon such dangers he will lose some of his effectiveness* *to the presence of fear. We know the world crucified the Lord of Glory, and failed to extinguish his light; the same is true of us. The world can be and is at times a terrible place for those who identify with Christ, but as the apostle Paul tells us, our troubles existing now will be of little consequence when we finally are brought to the place God wants us to reach. Amen.*

Home

A place of shelter from storms
Where rain and cold can't harm
A place of constant warm
It's the heart where love is born.

Proverbs 10:25 When a storm has swept by, the wicked are gone, but the righteous stand firm forever.

Matthew 28:12-14 When the chief priests had met with the elders and devised a plan, they gave the soldiers a large sum of money, telling them, "You are to say, 'His disciples came during the night and stole him away while we were asleep.' If this report gets to the governor, we will satisfy him and keep you out of trouble." So the soldiers took the money and did what they were instructed. And this story has been widely circulated among the Jews to this very day.

12

INSTRUCTED CORRUPTION

Money may not be able to buy happiness but it sure can buy a lie. The chief priests and the elders huddled together and devised a plan to discredit the reality of the resurrection. They were accustomed to agreeing upon bribery; making the problem go away with the infusion of cash. In this case, it was a ***"large sum"*** *of money. Apparently, they had gotten a discount for the betrayal of Jesus by Judas. It certainly must have been a very large sum of money because the penalty for a Roman soldier found sleeping on watch was death! It also seems the ruling religious had a hook into the governor; maybe the governor had previously compromised his position (accepted bribery) and the failure on his part to remain faithful to both his position and to the Emperor could have possibly caused him not only embarrassment but his head as well? It seems there was a confidence in the ability to extinguish any blowback from the governor over the sleeping soldier infraction. This confident tone on the part of the chief priests was instantly recognized and understood to be a real solution for the soldiers guarding the tomb. "Yes, we understand that you have the governor in your pocket, so we agree with the lie you want to bring to the* *hearts and minds of those who have been convinced of his prophesy to rise from death." Bribing and buying witnesses to deny truth is nothing new in the world of politics. From the tongues of the chief priests and the soldiers came the lie that has not abated in over two thousand years! Let's remember, the soldiers guarding the tomb of Jesus, were eyewitnesses to the accounts in the gospels!*

Ecclesiastes 7:7 "You may be wise, but if you cheat someone, you are acting like a fool. If you take a bribe you ruin your character. *Again,* ***1Corinthians 15:33 Do not be misled: "Bad company corrupts good character."*** *Let's look at the definition of the word character: "All things that a person does, feels and thinks by which this person is judged, as being good or bad, strong or weak." Clearly what we are finding within the definition are the traits within a person define who he is and what he stands for. Within these presentations, we see a person's actions, feelings and thoughts comprise a person's physical, emotional and intellectual composition, and in this we can see the underlying motives for such corrupt acceptance. The Jewish religious rulers had the power to corrupt others through their positions of privilege and they enjoyed the unfettered ability to decide how the temple tax was best to be used. In this case of resurrection, they could not permit the truth entrance into the hearts and minds of those they held in religious bondage; to do so would be an admission to the corruption and in turn they would be recognized as untruthful and unrighteous. They had been in continuance deception of the populace and nothing was about to stop their charade centering on their example of righteousness; not even the resurrection of the Lord of Glory would deter them from the desire to maintain their positions of power privilege and greed that was so capturing to all who would fall to the allure of such wickedness and self-centered evil. They were so enamored in the power and position that permitted control of the truth and lives of those they were supposed to bring to the truth of God, that not even the most abhorrent of crimes, beginning with murder would affect their worldly pursuits. They were completely debased, devoid of both conscience and fear of the Lord; they were fools all dressed up for their ultimate demise.*

Harvest

Growth of blackened core leafing silent corridors
Pride from lofty branches spreads latent rain poisoned breath
Darkness creeping within keeping works of malice wrought
For naught its flood caustic touch Viper's cunning plan ensnared
Deceptive his of ignorance silenced by the Judge.

Tonic sweet a gallant feat of blood upon a tree
Weeds to wheat blissful passing
Life restored to everlasting!
A river passing desert ways, rejoice filled transformation
Holiness the healing kiss awakens hidden life
A forceful voice now commands:
"Keep the wheat, take the weeds to fire's strife!"

Matthew 13:40 As the weeds are pulled up and burned in the fire, so it will be at the end of the age.

Truth is the best defense

Daniel 6:4 At this, the administrators and the Satraps, tried to find grounds for charges against Daniel, in his conduct of government affairs. But they were unable to do so. They could find no corruption in him, because he was trustworthy and neither corrupt or negligent. *The politics of today engages in the very same tactics of corruption that attempts to remove or nullify the opposition to wrongdoing. I do think that those who were concerned with the incorruptible aspect of Daniel's life, had indeed taken the initial steps aimed at corrupting Daniel, by attempting to bribe or enrich him in some way in- order to bring Daniel down to the level of management. The present condition of incorruptibility portrayed in the character of Daniel, was a threat to their hidden agendas; truthfulness will always cause deceit to resort to any means possible in-order to survive. This failure to corrupt meant that there was now the threat of being exposed by Daniel to the king.*

So much of today's trouble emanates from a desire for power, riches, position and privilege, that for the most part is kept hidden in the hearts of those whose focus is to remain in their positions of privilege, no matter how negatively it impacts others. Nothing is held in a state of permanence; politicians can and are removed from office through the loss of election or by being exposed as lawbreakers. There is a state of existence that defines character in a man; it is the recognition of wrong and the desire to not find one's self in the position of being found weakened and controlled by the corrupting aspects of life's temptations. Being a corrupt, dishonest or shady person in some instances does not have anything to do with a person's need to survive, and almost always has everything do with wants and desires. Can we say that a person who steals some food in-order to survive is a criminal? I would think not. And so, corruption is linked to all of man's wants and desires and in this state-of-affairs or condition of corruption there are perhaps very few, if any, moral or conscience inhibitors that prohibit dishonest actions.

Titus 1:15-16 Everything is pure to those who are themselves pure; but nothing is pure to those who are defiled and unbelieving, for their minds and consciences have been defiled. They claim that they know God but their actions deny it. They are hateful detestable and disobedient, not fit to do anything good. *Paul is making Titus aware that there are those whose conscience and mind have found corruption because they have denied the truth of God. We can understand readily how a person's mind can become corrupted but to have the conscience corrupted to the point that all things are permissible points to pure evil! The people who have found the depths of corruption in all aspects of thought and deed, (to the point that all things are permissible, in-order to maintain their positions of wealth, power and privilege), absent the restraint of both conscience and reason have been let go by God, in-order for them to face destruction.* ***Romans 1:28 Furthermore, since they did not think it worthwhile to retain the knowledge of God, he gave them over to a depraved mind, to do what ought not to be done.*** *God is not going to waste his time on the totally corrupt; he basically removed them from any possibility of ever being able to* *find salvation. He knew from the beginning of creation how these people would disregard even the most heinous of evil acts, so much so that he pronounces judgment on them in the here and now; they have basically fallen under God's curse due to the uncaring and arrogant attitudes kept at the ready to defend their condition of evil, that has left them without any redeeming qualities.*

Arrogance

Unwillingness to yield to a righteous truth suggests
A fool dressed in ignorance defiance at large
He's passing through testing's temperament
With violence as guide
Soon he will find
The well of arrogance
Is really, dry.

Matthew 23:31:33 "So you testify against yourselves that you are the descendants of those who murdered the prophets. Fill up, then, the measure of the sin of your forefathers! You brood of vipers! How will you escape being condemned to hell?"

Luke 18:2-8 "In a certain town there was a judge who neither feared God nor cared about men. And there was a widow in that town who kept coming to him with the plea, 'Grant me justice against my adversary.' For some time, he refused. But finally, he said to himself, 'Even though I don't fear God or care about men, yet because this widow keeps bothering me, I will see that she gets justice, so that she doesn't eventually wear me out with her coming!'"

It looks like corruption was not only alive and well in the hearts of the religious rulers but also within the secular world of civil disputes. Since the judge in the parable is depicted as corrupt, we can assume he was one who would gladly receive contributions to weigh in heavily on the side of those who bought his favor. He had no fear of God or men. Sounds like someone totally devoid of fear of reprisal, having no need to ensconce himself within the charade so remarkably portrayed by the chief priests of the time. The only thing that caused him to change his judicial position was the insistence of the woman. What could have been the reason for not giving her justice from the start of her complaint? Perhaps he had already been paid to fix the trial in favor of one of his rich clients, sounds to be the most plausible explanation. Jesus told this parable to his disciples to impress upon them the need to be persistent in prayer. Persistence in prayer being a spiritual principle that even when applied in the secular world will bring about a righteous result even from the unrighteous! There is no segment of society that is immune from the corrupting influences made to be permanent fixtures in the daily operations of the world. Like the lie that has staying power so too it is the corrupt practices of men whose only focus is to exploit for profit the positions of power entrusted to them. Jesus could have used any number of personages seeking justice from the corrupt judge but he chose a widow.

In choosing to portray a widow, he is showing to us that even someone who has little influence and someone who is poor in the eyes of the rich and powerful, he is saying not only that persistence in prayer will overcome even the most embedded corruption, but in having wickedness bow to the cries of the weak, how much more will God come to the aid of us who are unable to satisfy the corrupt nature of those in power? We cannot wear God out to the point that he will acquiesce to our plea simply because we are annoying. No, he does so because he loves us and wants to come to our aid. Our persistence shows him that we understand that all things will be answered by him in his time and for his purpose; we do not know everything God has planned for us and so what we do receive in prayer is a part of his plan; not only for us but for those who may be impacted by the answered prayer that we sought after. All things in nature find corruption, all things find corruption because the totality of creation has been reduced from the place of perfection to the place that can no longer withstand the advance of time. We are being told to limit the advance of corruption into our lives by not falling prey to the temptations offered by position, wealth and power.

Genesis 6:11 Now the earth was corrupt-in God's sight and was full of violence. God saw how corrupt the earth had become for all the people on the earth had corrupted their ways. So, God said to Noah, "I am going to put an end to all people, for the earth is filled with violence because of them." *Here, we are only six chapters into the creation narrative and God has decided to destroy the people of the earth because of the corruption and violence that has spread all over the world. This should be a hint to us the next time God decides to end the existence of mankind because of such corruption and associated violence, always attached to the inability of some to understand that they are not the pinnacle of authority. The great flood and the efforts of Noah and his family to preserve all that God had decided to save should also bring to our attention the need for us to be on the "saved" listing that is continually being updated daily. Perhaps there will come a time when the listing will be full and then God will bring down upon the earth the devastation that has so executed his judgment in the time of Noah. Given all this history and prophesy shouldn't we pay a bit more attention to the times we are presently living in? The old saying reminding us that history repeats itself has been proven; as such, shouldn't we understand that time is moving in the direction of the judgment and there is nothing that can prevent the pouring out of God's righteous anger upon the earth and its inhabitants?*

We have already been apprised that all governments of the world are corrupt and belong to the devil. It is the system of corruption and not necessarily casting judgment upon all people involved in its administration. Certainly, there are some in government that not only know God, but they also live in accord with what is pleasing to him. The same is true for all persons in the world; the world is really-split down the middle into two distinct differences; the good and the bad!

Corruption

We don't need to mine for it or search the earth for signs of it
It makes a sound of brokenness, has held
its grip with off-pitch song
Since man first heard a serpent's tongue
revealing what is right and wrong.
A process born of prideful man 'til breath
has failed then called to rise
Within the flame of utter shame reduced by truth to withered rags
As if placed inside a vat of caustic and corrupting acts
Speaking laughter's hurtful smack,
"Got cha!"

Lies with hooks that lure in fancy suits and overtures
In this the laughter sounds as screams
absent of the worldly dreams.
Judgment sounds its mournful bell
pronouncing clear, "eternal hell!"
As honest as a mirror's face the life we lived cannot be hid
Not in the heart or in the grave, truth will
speak each thought in waves.
On the last and final day, the straight and narrow path appears
Reminding of the broken ways in defiance truth and grace.
Bearing witness loud and clear, "The Word
did come you would not hear
Your clothing now as rotted rags instead
of robes of righteous acts."

Jeremiah 13:6-9 Sometime later the Lord told me to go back to the Euphrates and get the shorts. So, I went back and when I found the place where I had hidden them, I saw that they were ruined and no longer any good. Then the Lord spoke to me again. "This is how I will destroy the pride of Judah and the great pride of Jerusalem. These evil people have refused to obey me.

Signs

So many signs and voices and still the world is blind.
It's an amazing thing even in today's light.
We have leaders speaking lies and scandals day and night
And still some people think their voices will not lie?
Woe to you for bowing to gods of gold and cash
Of idols made of stone and statues made of brass
For worship at the altar of murder, magic, lust
Indeed, your bones shall rot and no longer will you strut!

A cannon blast of truth will not turn a head
It will not make a path away from wrong or wickedness
If it's cold and dark and the mind and heart are dead!
Even when the heavens bleed and thick smoke fills the air
When the sun and moon are darkened when fire spreads like flares
When the moon's blood-soaked eye has a vacant stare
Still they will not listen to the signs and wonders clear.
"Turn away from wicked ways judgment day has come
In this the end of days there's no place to hide or run.

Revelation 13:1 Then I saw a beast coming out of the sea. It had ten horns and seven heads; on each of his horns there was a crown, and on each of its heads was a name that was insulting to God.

God will always give to mankind warning, sometimes with signs and wonders, to capture our attention, or mainly through the prophets, so that we may not become a part of the judgment that will beset the earth. With respect to the beast (the antichrist) mentioned in the above scripture what we find is the ability of the beast to amaze the entire earth. In this (amazement) everyone on the earth worshipped the dragon (Satan) because he had given his authority to the beast. It is the signs and wonders displayed in the power of the beast that has captured the attention of the entire population of the earth.

Jesus had come to the people with the authority of his Father, and he also displayed signs and wonders that captured the hearts and attention of many people. Because he did not present himself as the ultimate authority he was rejected by the world's rulers. But when the Antichrist presents himself upon the world scene he will project power that does not threaten the existing corruption that has been so much a part of man's accepted way of life. The idea that there has come to man a permanence wrapped in ultimate authority, capable of ensuring and maintaining the positions of those who will only bow down and worship the very incarnation of the evil they had for so long embraced, will be too much of a temptation for the elite political structure of corruption and deceit to reject.

As we look upon the world and the state of current affairs what we see is a continuous advance of evil that is always seeking to infiltrate and destroy all that is not openly embracing its precepts of hateful destructive intent. As we look inwardly within our own country what we find is an ignorance to the actual events that threaten the very lives of those who have been marked as targets for destruction, simply because they are without a position for or against the threats to civilization. Because they are not aligned with the god and so-called prophet that motivates hatred, they become the focus of evil's designs. The more a people can be kept in the darkness of ignorance to the forces of evil aligned against them the easier it will be for evil to fulfill its intent. American leadership (at least in the past several years) has shown little concern for the threats waged against us, and this is probably reinforced in their minds because they live in a world of sheltered and protected existence. It is also a possibility that they have given so much tacit acceptance to the evil in the world that said evil has made of them a lesser valued target? The message of hate spewed by those who believe they are serving a god and a prophet will ultimately be revealed for what it is when the evil is unmasked in the person of the Antichrist. No longer will they be led by their imaginations, they will have the object of their adoration set clearly before them, and in this they will be increasingly emboldened to acts of evil cruelty to their fellow-man.

Designed hatred

A touch of anger and pinch of night
A bit of tasty fright-filled fear
Sprinkled with the lies from below
A panicked flight toward the ways of wrong
A shot of poison from the tongue
Steers the weak to ways of wrong.

Leviticus 19:17 Do not hate your brother in your heart. Rebuke your neighbor frankly so you will not share in his guilt. *What we are hearing from those who kill, all who do not accept their prophet or god is that they have been instructed to kill us! They have been instructed to rid the world of the infidel! This must be the height of "instructed corruption." Are we being asked to believe that those terrorists do not have any idea of the wrong they have inflicted upon innocence? There's no doubt they are following the instruction of something or someone, but at what level of evil does someone have to be in-order to blindly follow without condemnation of conscience? The answer must be at the level of total evil? A totally depraved mind! Total evil must be understood to be fully aware of the acts committed and in the commission of such acts there is inner approval. How stupidly insane, and corrupt, must a person be to accept both the promise of eternal bliss, (when you kill yourself and a lot of people also), to receive the promised reward of debauchery in paradise, with seventy-two virgins, and still, they cannot understand that the god they are serving is the evil god of this world? It is one thing to corrupt a system of government, but it is a totally strange manifestation when evil is not denounced by world leaders in a pronounced and forceful way.*

Warning

I admit, I don't hold all the pieces to the puzzle.
Some things are kept hidden.
The sun the moon and spheres all appear so bright
But why is there no life?
Could it be, a long time back, footprints dotted Mars?
Did Saturn spin a different way and roads were built for cars?
Could Jupiter be found with excavation lines?
Measured and surprised did ships speed across its sky?
All within creation will find upward and then down
Some will find eternity and others wear a frown.
Disconnection from the one who made us all
Finds incremental judgment knocking on our door.
I see it plain and clear in solar system's
light the planets hang as globes
But absent is the laughter that comes from joyful life.
A giant jigsaw puzzle moving dot to dot
What was and is to come has definition not.
Conjecture is a trying thing like intended sport
It takes us up and down the field and sometimes truth is scored.
The mind of man was made for playful thoughts
Imagine this or that and see where it leads and ends
A rabbit's hole mysterious filled with twists and bends.
It would be nice to understand why the planets seem to stare
As does a statue, saying, "There's nothing living here."

Matthew 24:15-16 "When you see the desolating abomination spoken of through Daniel the prophet standing in the holy place (let the reader understand) then those in Judea must flee to the mountains, a person on a rooftop must not go down to get things out of his house, a person in a field must not return to get his cloak. *NAB*

The warnings contained within the word of God are meant to alert us to the beginning of the end of evil's reign upon the earth. As early as the great flood and the plagues sent down to the ancient Egyptian people there has always been a sufficient warning for man to turn from his evil ways. Those who heeded the signs wonders and miracles were spared the judgment of God. Anytime we find the truth being denied and attempts to keep it hidden we will find a limitation to the patience of God and the sometimes-catastrophic resulting impact for failure to heed and obey the truth of what is acceptable to the one who alone decides the limitations placed upon the thoughts and deeds of man. The character of those placed into leadership positions whether secular or religious, has ability to make harmful impact upon those who would follow their example. The religious rulers during the time of Christ were such that everything they touched or set forth into the community had the ability to contaminate the truth of God. They couldn't permit the truth entrance into the consciousness of the populace; to do so would be to expose themselves as the frauds they really-were. They had the choice of admitting to the reality of the resurrection of Jesus or to deny what was evident to those they contaminated with the influx of the bribe. The desire to continually feed a corrupt character by reinforcing a self-righteous belief, stems from the inherent inability to recognize the value of truth. Nowhere in the external display of righteousness is the internal darkness revealed. The costume of a clown does not guarantee a joyful heart and the smile of a ruler may not originate with acceptance of the gift set before him, but truth will always find the means to expose the inner workings of the heart.

Corruption is a refusal to live by the rules of God. We hear politicians speaking of "leveling the playing field" and we must wonder just what it is they are preaching? Are they speaking of equal opportunities, for those who have in the past been denied the ability to escape from the poverty and depression associated with a life, apart from the mainstream of existence? If so they have not heard the declaration of Jesus when he said, ***"We will always have wars and poor people."*** *Given this revelation regarding the world always going to contain the poor of society, what we find in the corruption laced political pronouncements is the presentation of illusion that speaks of achieving perfection in an imperfect world. Restoration to perfection can only be accomplished by God* *and when man presents his plan to afford everyone equality in both rights and riches he is presenting the very same façade of righteousness that the religious rulers made a mockery of during the time of Christ. With every election-cycle there is a catch phrase to capture the uninformed and the ignorant, that offers to them the hope and change from and to something better, but is never defined within the language of charlatans! Their speech, usage of language, appearance and plastic smiles are all an illusion offered in the vein of altruistic benevolence contrived in the backrooms of deceptive planning. There is very little thought given to the justice that awaits those who have abused truth by injecting corruption into the mainstream of society. No different from the chief priests bribing the soldiers to lie and repeat a fabricated deception, that was not difficult to convince the populace, simply because resurrection was not then and is not now a normal occurrence. As Abraham said to the rich man situated in hell, "**Even if someone were to come back from the dead they still would not believe."** Nothing is impossible for God; this is something the chief priests failed to recognize, along with the ultimate judgment that will overtake and amaze them on that great day!*

Genesis 4:4-5 Then Abel brought the first lamb born to one of his sheep, killed it and gave the best parts of it as an offering. The Lord was pleased with Abel and his offering, but he rejected Cain and his offering. Cain became furious and scowled in anger. Then the Lord said to Cain, "Why are you angry? Why that scowl on your face? If you had done the right thing, you would be smiling; but because you have done evil, sin is crouching at your door. It wants to rule you, but you must overcome it."

13

THE TROUBLE WITH CAIN

Something is wrong with the disposition of Cain. Both Abel and his brother Cain make an offering that is basically an acknowledgement of God. Able makes his offering from the heart and with reverent worship; within the offering of the first-born lamb from Abel's flock is honesty, respect, and love for the God, who has created all things, and within the authorship of all things it is understood that everything belongs to God. It is not the difference between the fruit of the earth (Cain's offering) and Abel's lamb that creates a wedge between acceptable and unacceptable; it is the act of offering done in a spirit of dishonesty that creates the difference in the eyes of God. Cain was not willing to sacrifice the fruit of his labors (he was a farmer and Able was a shepherd) to the one who makes all things grow.

Firsthand knowledge

Cain is the firstborn of humanity within the lineage recorded for us in the creation narrative that takes us all the way into the chosen people of God; that is, those who know him and follow his standards for living a life that is pleasing to him. As such, Cain received firsthand knowledge of the reality of God from the very first couple created! God speaks to Cain directly after he has murdered his brother. Cain doesn't appear to be shocked over the fact that God has revealed himself to him, which indicates that Cain was fully aware of the reality of God when he grudgingly made his offering.

In the book of Deuteronomy (chapter 8) we are warned to not forget the Lord. Forgetting the Lord is tantamount to a loss of faith, and a loss of faith, (especially forgetting all that God has done for us) is exceedingly hurtful to God. When even a small portion of the harvest God has given to us is grudgingly offered, it is on par with idolatry, and coveting. As such, God is pleased with the offering from Abel but displeased in the pretense offered by Cain. God never asked for oblations and/or sacrifices, as such one would expect an offering to be honestly presented. In the case of Cain's offering to the Lord it was all exterior; no different from the hypocrisy that was present in the religious during the time of Christ's ministry. ***Psalm 40:6 Sacrifice and offering you did not desire but my ears you have pierced; burnt offerings and sin offerings you did not require.*** *We are hearing the psalmist proclaim that God has completely given of himself to his creation unconditionally. He is also proclaiming the goodness of God, who has opened his ears, that is, "pierced" the unknowingness of man and replaced it with the knowledge of just how great our God is! Of course, all of us who are parents can understand this selfless posture; God is only concerned with our welfare.*

This aspect of his love is completely personified in the sacrifice of Jesus. God has done all the sacrificing for us! An oblation is a thing presented or offered to God; especially a voluntary gift. Herein we see the offering to God within a sacrifice or oblation an aspect of recognition that God had not required, but if one is to make an offering it is expected to be done from a genuine foundation. Earlier, in the fifth chapter of the book of Acts we saw the difference between the honest offering of a man named Joseph (Barnabas) and the contrasting offering from a man named Ananias and his wife; both Ananias and his wife lost their lives because they attempted to deceive the Holy Spirit. It is this same hypocrisy that found a home in the heart of Cain.

The aspect of knowing God is a reality that brings with it a great responsibility. It is one thing to not know such truth and live a life contrary to the will of God, and it is all-together a completely different set of circumstances when one knows the truth and fails to acknowledge such truth in both thought and deed. It is not the difference in tangible offerings, but it is the thought behind the offering that finds either acceptance or rejection from God. Setting aside an offering is an outward expression of faith and represents our understanding of God's provision for his creation.

Sacrifice

A sacrificial offering is a part of our self
Straightforward without hidden motive begrudging the act.
When evil attempts to hide, it shouts:
"Here I am! No need to look around."
God sees the lies, and hoopla, jumping about!
A plain and simple sacrifice is
Giftwrapped in honesty to God with love.
What is given did not begin with man
It is but reflection of what was placed into his hand.
All there is and all to come, shouts, "hallelujah!"
Loud and simple praise or whispered in the heart
God hears it all before the words of praise are wrought.

From the mountaintop of found
What was hidden, in the valleys
Darkness, night, and gloom
Is sent up into the heavens
To the throne of God.

Romans 12:1 So then, my brothers, because of God's great mercy to us I appeal to you: Offer yourselves as a living sacrifice to God, dedicated to his service and pleasing to him. This then is true worship that you should offer.

After the offerings are made

"The Lord was pleased with Able and his offering, but he rejected Cain and his offering." *The offering from Cain, being rejected by God finds Cain in a state of furiousness. God asks him why he is angry? As if to say, "Dear Cain you got caught with your hand in the cookie jar, you have no reason to be angry." Not only is Cain angry but his facial features give indication as to the depth of his being confronted with truth. It is at this point we must understand that all the conversation between God and Cain is taking place within Cain's conscience. Certainly, this exposition of wrong attitude when making an external offering to the Lord, has found the unexpected rejection surprising, but not one that will cause Cain to lose sleep. He may have been oblivious to the depth which conscience can convict and cause internal war between good and bad; now he is very much exposed when his true motives approach God. He deceived his brother Able, (even after being warned by God that he is making his intentions known within the brightest of light). God tells him, "sin is crouching at his door," and he must resist the thoughts accompanying unfounded and unrighteous anger; this conversation with God, made possible through conscience is completely and utterly disregarded. In the killing of Able we are given witness to the actual power of sin to totally dominate and enslave an individual, even when the individual knows that what he is doing is wrong.*

Pride will always initiate trouble

Cain takes issue with the favored status bestowed upon his brother's offering and decides to kill him! Able is completely trusting as he goes with his brother to his death. We know Adam and Eve were dispossessed from paradise (losing the ability to be in the presence of God), and, as consequence the knowledge of right and wrong made clear the difference between acceptance and rejection. As such, the conversation taking place between God and Cain is the very same conflict taking place in man since the advent of the very first sin. God asks Cain where his brother is and

Cain responds (probably with a smirk on his face), that, he didn't know and continues his response by asking, "Was I supposed to take care of my brother?" The pride of Cain, finding exposure of the hypocrisy dripping from the offering he made to the Lord, has transformed him into a sinner of the worst kind. Understanding that in this most serious transgression against what is right we find that Cain is not met with the serious judgment one would expect to find in an incidence of willful first-degree murder. God places a curse on Cain and makes it impossible for him to farm the soil. Eventually Cain moves away to a place called "Wandering." He has descendants and what we find is that there is no indication that he had ever lost a night's sleep over his brother's murder. We can safely say he was in possession of a depraved mind; given over to the evil that had been crouching at his door!

The right thing

God tells Cain, ***"If you had done the right thing, you would be smiling."*** *Anger and hate will always make it impossible for a smiling countenance to appear. Cain has an attitude that says, "My way or the highway!" The exposure of darkness thought to be hidden in the heart will never be receptive to criticism; not even if the negative remarks come from God. How many times in our lives have we found ourselves angry over our inability to do the right thing? How many times do we lament our former participation in things that were wrong and eventually such wrong proves to be a constant thorn in our lives? Perhaps just as the apostle Paul lamented the thorn in his side (this may very well be the memory of his former persecution of the church), so too it is we find remorse for the harm we had done to either others or ourselves. In the case of Cain there is no indication that he ever had any lamentations over the murder he committed; it is because of this lack of self-denouncement that I forwarded the thought that he had been given over to a depraved mind. Because he did not think the counsel of God's words something to be taken seriously he found himself absent any conscience. We see this kind of condition frequently today, as a perpetrator of some heinous act is led away* *in handcuffs, in front of the news cameras and there is a smile on his face. For others, they show acknowledgement of the wrong committed in the attempt to hide their faces from the cameras; a clear indication of what is going on internally.*

Romans 1:28-32 Because those people refuse to keep in mind the true knowledge about God he has given them over to corrupted minds, so that they do the things that they should not do. They are filled with all kinds of wickedness, evil, greed, and vice; they are full of jealously, murder, fighting, deceit, and malice. They gossip and speak evil of one another; they are hateful to God, insolent, proud, and boastful; they think of more ways to do evil; they disobey their parents; they have no conscience; they do not keep their promises, and they show no kindness or pity for others. They know that God's law says that people who live in this way deserve death. Yet, not only do they continue to do these things, but they even approve of others who do them.

It appears to us there are many who have been given over to a depraved or corrupted mind, having no conscience to intervene against the evil thoughts and deeds to guide them away from the levels of evil they have deliberately ventured into, and, also approve of these behaviors as they apply to others. This is pretty-much the mindset of secular humanist positions today that say to all, "Sin does not exist and do whatever you will, providing you do not infringe upon another godly realm."

No remorse

After all is, said and done, concerning the punishment of Cain, he is only concerned with the hardship he will suffer due to being banished from the land and the presence of God. He laments, **"This punishment is too hard for me."** *He's not concerned with anything but himself! He is concerned that someone may kill him, which he thinks is wrong but he did not think it wrong to kill his very own brother? I see the true depth of the teaching of Christ in this one* *example:* ***"Do unto others as you would have others do unto you."*** *Perhaps, this is but one reason we are told to love one another, for in doing so we do not allow anger (the crouching sin outside our door) entrance and rule over our house, that is, this earthly tent that our spirit has taken up residence within. As for the mark that God placed upon Cain it must have been evident that here was a man who has been placed under God's curse and no one is to suppose that he deserves death; God had already determined his punishment in this life, and of course in the judgment to come.*

Once we are brought into the events concerning the death of Able, and the consequence placed upon Cain, we don't hear anything about the sorrow that must have invaded the lives of Adam and Eve, except that Eve has another son that they name Seth. This the first recorded murder in the brief history of mankind, and we hear nothing concerning the emotional disposition of the parents of the victim? It is as if God had completely intervened and taken charge of the situation, in-order to spare Adam and Eve from having their sorrow become a spectacle. We see this same kind of protection displayed by Jesus as he denies a crowd desiring to accompany him to the home of the synagogue leader, whose daughter has died. The crowd wanted to know what Jesus would do? But Jesus respects the grief of the parents and only allows a few of his disciples to accompany him back to the home of the dead girl. However, the murder of Able will not be placed into an over and done situation by God declaring a death sentence upon Cain. Cain is sent out into the world clearly marked as a murderer in-order to advertise to the inhabitants the reality of having committed such an uncaring and vicious act; the murder of one's own brother. Yes, there are other people in the world containing great diversity, simply because God did not stop creating after Adam and Eve. Jesus said, ***"My Father is always working, and I must do the same."*** *We are given the linage of this one-particular "chosen" people as an example of how God interacts with mankind. Since God is unchanging with respect to judgment, justice and fairness, the lessons depicted for us throughout the bible are applicable to mankind forever.*

Unchanging

What is true for you may not be true for me.
You say, "I like spinach."
I may disagree.
You like fast cars and racing
I think walking is just amazing.
Tomorrow our choices can change
But God remains the same.
The list of what we consider likes and dislikes
Is unending, but when it comes to God
We find ourselves united and unbending.
Becoming one with reality is most beautiful
God is the only truth that is indisputable!

Acts 10:34-35 Peter began to speak: "I now know that it is true that God treats everyone on the same basis. Whoever fears him and does what is right is acceptable to him, no matter what race he belongs to."

Will God treat a man fairly, even if he does not know him or the salvation offered in Christ? Let's look at a hypothetical situation. There's a man living in a remote part of the world. He walks out of his hut and looks up into the night sky. He concludes within himself that there must be someone who created the magnificence he sees on display. He then feels frightened because he does not know what it is this someone may require of him. He then decides to live his life in a manner he believes this someone will approve of. Will God condemn him for not knowing Jesus? Will God treat a man fairly, even if the man does not know him or the salvation offered in Christ? Perhaps this recognition within himself declaring the reality of the God who made all things is this man's born- again moment? Certainly, it is truth that sets us free and such truth can emanate externally through hearing of the word of God, and, also such empowering truth can be formed within us. We understand faith comes through hearing and it is hearing the word of God that sets us free. However, we must recognize hearing can take place internally as well as from external sources. Thus, no matter where we are if we have been predestined by God to be among those he will save, it is easy for him to accomplish the communication aspect of the reception of truth.

I'm reminded of the conversation the Lord had with Abraham; the Lord had said he would not hide his intention to destroy the city of Sodom. Abraham ultimately asks the Lord if he would still destroy the city if there were only ten righteous persons living there? We hear God say that he would not destroy it. God will not destroy the innocent with the guilty, but more importantly what we find is the fact that God does not hide his intentions from his creation. Just as all of nature declares the majesty of God's creative talents and power, so it is there is no excuse for mankind not to recognize the reality of his existence. As such, for the one who comes to the truth because of the majesty displayed in nature, so it is such truth will also set him free to live in accordance with his conscience. Jesus is Truth. And so, indirectly when we recognize God's handiwork in nature we have come to Jesus. And anyone who comes to Christ he will in no way turn away.

Value of an offering

Luke 21:1-4 Jesus looked around and saw rich men dropping off their gifts in the temple treasury, and he also saw a very poor widow dropping in two little copper coins. He said, "I tell you that this poor widow put in more than all the others. For the others offered their gifts from what they had to spare of their riches; but she, as poor as she is, gave all she had to live on.

When we look at the comments of Jesus regarding the offerings of the rich we can clearly see a disapproving aspect of his comparing the rich to the widow's sacrifice. While it is not so much a tainted offering as the case with Cain, it is a clear demonstration of what the rich and the poor rely upon. The widow is totally reliant upon the provision of God and in her-offering, she is basically saying to him: "All that I have has always been yours, O Lord." The offering of the rich is truncated, held back, cut short, and kept in a reserve that says, "I must maintain my status, wealth, position and control of what determines who I am within society." It is this mindset that displays a lack of both faith-in God and the recognition that who we are is not dependent upon riches as the world understands and reasons. Rather, it is the spiritual poverty that is completely on display in the offering of the rich from the abundance of their material wealth. In the offerings of Cain and the rich men there is present a failure to understand the generosity of God. Clearly, we are made aware of this generosity when Jesus feeds the multitude with just five loaves of bread and a few fish; having twelve baskets of food left over. The offering of the fish and bread to the disciples and then to Jesus for the performance of the miracle demonstrates the reciprocal generosity of God toward those who have faith in him. This does not have anything to do with a tithing mentality.

All the poor

Matthew 5:3 "Happy are those who know they are spiritually poor; the kingdom of heaven belongs to them."

Luke 6:20 Jesus looked at his disciples and said, "Happy are you poor; the kingdom of God is yours!"

These excerpts from the Sermon on the Mount speaks to both the spiritually poor and the financially poor. To know we are spiritually poor is to recognize our faulty nature, and to be in poverty from a financial position is to gain reliance upon God. Many of the rich today are unaware of their spiritual poverty; just as the rich young ruler was told to sell all his possessions, give to the poor and then follow Jesus was too much of a sacrifice for him to fathom. He did not recognize that all he possessed had come from God's blessing and more importantly he could not see life having any meaning without his riches. He threw away what is eternal for what must perish. The financially poor are not all guaranteed ownership of the kingdom of heaven but they are more apt to recognize that it is God who provides for their needs. The more one succumbs to the illusion of self-sufficiency the more distant the reality of God's provision diminishes from our sight. The movement today for those in positions of power and authority to dispense the wealth of the nation have found political advantage in making people dependent upon government and in so doing they cement their positions within government. It has been said, "Give a man a ham sandwich and he will vote for you every time." This then is the key: We approach God in the same manner the innocence of a child possesses. Within this complete trust is the perfect offering of ourselves, and God will always find our presence and offering acceptable.

John 12:3-6 Then Mary took a whole pint of very expensive perfume made from pure nard, poured it on Jesus' feet, and wiped them with her hair. The smell of the perfume filled the whole house. One of Jesus' disciples, Judas Iscariot-the one who was going to betray him-said, "Why wasn't this perfume sold for three hundred silver coins and the money given to the poor?" He said this, not because he cared about the poor, but because he was a thief. He carried the money bag and would help himself from it.

The untruthful and dishonestly corrupt display of coveting the expensive perfume (the pretense of Judas), that spoke of aiding the needs of the poor was undeniable within the thieving character of Judas. It is this very same coveting that was displayed in the offering from Cain to God. In the case of Judas what we find is the attempt to stop a voluntary offering. I'm reminded of the complaints to Jesus about a man who was performing miracles in the name of Jesus, and the disciples reprimanded him and told him to stop doing what he was doing simply because he was not a member of their little circle. Jesus told them they were wrong in trying to stop the man. Doing good will never be met with resistance from the Lord. And so, whether it is Cain presenting his gift in an atmosphere of grudging dishonesty or Judas attempting to stop the woman from voluntarily offering a gift to Jesus, both are met with the pronouncement of unacceptable from God. The key to all our offerings and sacrifices being acceptable to God is the presentation giftwrapped in both honesty and love. So many of today's offerings made to church ministries have been tainted by the idea planted into the givers head that such donations will produce an abundant reciprocal response within the outpouring of blessings from God. As such, many offerings are made absent the honesty that does not expect a payback from God. Offering anything to God with the mindset that there is no net loss is to be deluded into thinking God to be, some kind, of securities portfolio manager!

Degree of unacceptability

"If you had done the right thing, you would be smiling; but because you have done evil, sin is crouching at your door. It wants to rule you, but you must overcome it." *Not only is the offering made to God by Cain unacceptable it is given the descriptive of "evil." Whenever there is a direct presentation of our self to God we must always understand that all of what comprises our existence is in full view. We stand naked before God just as Adam and Eve experienced after they sinned. Just as God had clothed them so too we are clothed in the righteousness of Christ. The only real gift we can offer to God is our love and loyalty. With love and loyalty truth will always be present to oversee our thoughts and actions. By declaring the sin of Cain to be evil we are brought into the understanding of degrees of unacceptability inherent in wrong. All of us are born with original sin, such sin within the inherent nature of humanity is not as detrimentally denounced as was the sin of Cain. Jesus has overlooked the sin of birth by stating that "Little children own the kingdom of God." It is only when we grow out of the innocence of childhood does sin have a serious pronouncement upon the projected outcome of a person's life; relative to eternal life through salvation or damnation through rejection of truth.*

Job 2:9-10 His wife said to him, "You are still as faithful as ever, aren't you? Why don't you curse God and die?" Job answered, "You are talking nonsense! When God sends us something good, we welcome it, can we complain when he sends us trouble?" Even in all this suffering Job said nothing against God.

14

LOYALTY

Loyal: *"Faithful to one's country, family, friends, beliefs etc." The level of loyalty to faith in God displayed in Job is admirable. Job's only reason for being tested by Satan was the pronouncement by God that Job was a faithful servant. Upon hearing this Satan seizes upon what he believes is his opportunity to prove God wrong in his evaluation of Job. Satan doesn't care if Job is a faithful and loyal servant, he wants to be able to point to a flaw in the judgment of God and in so doing remove the label of perfect from God, in-order to make his case to ascend to the throne of he who alone is worthy. Moreover, Satan is the opponent of mankind (his name means the opponent of human beings) and he is continually advancing accusations against God's faithful servants. At first Satan says the reason for Job being so faithful is because he is showered with wealth; he continues that if his wealth is removed he would curse God to his face! Indicating that Job is a faithful servant because he is getting paid very well for his faithfulness. Well we know that Job loses everything including his children through the testing of Satan. Once again Satan is frustrated and presents another scenario to the Lord, saying that Job would not be so faithful if his body were made to suffer. Again, God gives permission for Job to be tested with the caveat that limits Satan from taking his life.*

Opposites

Clearly, we are seeing a great difference in both Job and his wife. Job has suffered both emotional and physical assaults and he does not blame God for his misfortunes. His wife is not so tolerant and probably has already cursed God and wishes Job to also join her in her emotional distress. Job had seven sons and three daughters along with the fact that they were the richest couple in the East. It is becoming apparent that Job has been endowed with a tremendous outpouring of grace that has cemented the reality of God's goodness within the very marrow of his bones. Job knows whatever the reason for his misfortunes it is God who has granted permission for them to occur. His wife on the other hand is lacking the depth of understanding that strengthens Job.

Friends

Job has three friends who have heard of his troubles and had traveled some distances to lend whatever support they can. These are loyal friends and when they see Job from a distance they immediately began to weep and to wail and to tear their clothes; they completely joined in Job's sorrows. They sat down on the ground with Job for seven days and nights without saying a word because they saw how much he was suffering. Finally, Job speaks and his complaint to God is one that comes from the very depths of darkness and sorrow; he wants God to curse the day he was born and to make that day one of such darkness that it would blot out the sun. Job's friends want to find a remedy for his troubles and want him to understand that never has a righteous man suffered such punishment from God, as such, there must be some sin in Job's life that caused the catastrophic events to fall upon his head. While his friends are, well-meaning and have the best interests of Job at heart, they and Job, do not really-know the cause, except to recognize that everything is under the approval or disapproval of God and in this respect, it is inconceivable for the friends to understand the depth of testing that is taking place. Much later-on we hear Job's lamentation that expresses a desire to return to the days when God watched over him. He is fully aware of the change in his life and only wishes to return to a time when life was good and protected by the love of God. Throughout his suffering, Job desires to once again be accepted by God; he does not know of the Satanic testing designed to disprove God's judgment of Job's loyalty and dedication to the Lord, but he does not fail and proves God to be correct.

All of us find those times in life, perhaps not as severe as those that inflicted Job but nevertheless, we find occasion to look to the heavens and complain! We are no different than Job in that we are a part of God's family. Certainly, God had restored Job to the place he wanted restored and the same is true for us. No matter how much we may find troubles we understand that in the end God will make all things right. Just as Jesus had told Peter that Satan had been given permission to test him, so it is that many of the troubles we encounter stem from the close relationship we have with God.

Luke 22:31-32 "Simon, Simon! Listen! Satan has received permission to test all of you, to separate the good from the bad, as a farmer separates wheat from the chaff. But I have prayed for you, Simon, that your faith will not fail. And when you turn back to me you must strengthen your brothers." *It is coming into view that God is in charge but the accuser of man is continually testing both the judgment of God and the loyalty of those he has called his own. It is true that God disciplines those he loves but this aspect of testing is not a part of the discipline God would administer. What this tells us is profound! We are being alerted to the fact that Satan is not just testing humanity; he is prowling the earth seeking those he can devour; he has already been thrown out of heaven and the war rages upon the earth!*

We recognize the statement by our Lord, that he saw, "Satan fall from heaven like lightning," (upon the return of the seventy-two), to be both a retrospective, reflective utterance that brought to his mind the attempt by Satan (the dragon spoken of in the book of Revelation), to kill him (Jesus) through the devil's surrogate (Herod); and the devil's subsequent defeat by Michael and his angels; in defeat, he is thrown out of heaven quickly like lightning falling! It also marked the current ongoing defeat of evil shown to be a powerful weapon given to mankind and made evident in the accomplishments of his disciples. Certainly, it was a statement made in the knowledge of not only what will come to pass but a declaration of the power of God given to man, to fight and defeat the present and future testing of those God has saved. The power of God has been given to those who will embrace truth, and in such truth, all the evil schemes of the devil can and will be defeated. The healing of physical infirmities and the driving out of evil spirits are just the beginning of the signs of God's power available for mankind to overcome such a powerful enemy. Such power also provides the hope given to those who have come under severe testing. Let's not forget that it was Jesus who allowed himself to be tested in the desert for forty days, just prior to the beginning of his assault upon the deceptions of the world! As such our Lord, has shared in all the troubles plaguing humanity, except sin.

Revelation 12:7-10 Then war broke out in heaven. Michael and his angels fought against the dragon, who fought back with his angels; but the dragon was defeated, and he and his angels were not allowed to stay in heaven any longer. The huge dragon-the ancient serpent, named the Devil, or Satan, that deceived the whole world. He was thrown down to earth, and all his angels with him. *The devil is no longer the Tester in Chief but has assumed the role of a devouring lion. Until such time when the devil is totally defeated we are to resist the slings and arrows of the enemy. This understanding of Satan testing us brings a higher level of awareness to the urging by Paul for us to,* ***"Put on all the armor of God."*** *The warning given to us in* **Luke 22:31-32** *notifying Peter, and all the disciples, that Satan had been given permission to test them, (and all of us), clearly marks the defeat of the devil and his being thrown down to the earth; his being thrown out of the heavenly realm along with all of those who rebelled against God is a clear understanding that he is no longer adhering to the former restriction to not kill those who God has called a "faithful servant."*

We must always keep in mind the limits that God has placed upon the devil's testing; however, we are no longer being just tested but evil is actively seeking our demise. We are still finding temptations (tests) but the evil one is no longer abiding by the barrier placed upon him in the past. **1 Corinthians 10:12-13 *Whoever thinks he is standing firm had better be careful that he does not fall. Every test that you have experienced is the kind that normally comes to people. But God keeps his promise, and he will not allow you to be tested beyond your power to remain firm; at the time, you are put to the test.*** *We are hearing in this verse that even when the devil goes beyond the limitations placed upon him by God, God keeps his promise and will intervene in our behalf when the testing has reached beyond our limitation to bear.*

Again, **1 Peter 5:8-11 *Be alert, be on watch! Your enemy, the Devil, roams around like a roaring lion, looking for someone to devour. Be firm in your faith and resist him, because you know that your fellow-believers in all the world are going through the same kind of suffering. But after you have suffered for a little while, the God of all grace, who calls you to share his eternal glory in union with Christ, will himself perfect you and give you firmness, strength, and sure foundation. To him be the power forever! Amen.*** *GNB*

The reason we are told by Paul to put on the armor of God is because we are not only fighting against human beings; we are also fighting against, ***"The wicked spiritual- forces in the heavenly world, the rulers, authorities, and cosmic powers of this dark age."*** *This statement alerts us to the presence of these forces, who formerly inhabited the heavenly realms; such rulers, authorities and principalities, being present in the here and now upon the earth and seeking our downfall through all the schemes evil can muster. And since they are present on the earth now, we can extrapolate that their former residences have been vacated by being tossed out of them! As Peter said:* ***"The Devil is roaming around seeking to devour."*** *He has moved on from tester in chief to destroyer of those he can devour; not just Christians, but everyone he can. We may not see him and his spiritual surrogates, but we can see clearly* *the results of those suffering from the outpouring of evil actions throughout the earth; inflicted upon mankind by both the evil of mankind and the evil that has come down to earth from the heavenly realms.*

Fidelity

"Everything has a price" it is said.
Some things should never be sold,
bartered, traded, taken or loaned.
Testing in life wants us to deny truth.
Betrayal longs to hear us say:
"Run into darkness rebel against God and die."
But God is always with us through the darkest of times.
Never are we without his love and brightest of light.
Some things should never be disowned:
The trust of a friend.
The bond of love.
The soul of a man.
A child's trust.
The gift of wisdom.
The knowledge of plans
Must never be passed
From pocket to hand.
An atmosphere of loyal thought
Sees the border that must not be crossed.

Acts 20:29-30 I know that after I leave fierce wolves will come among you, and they will not spare the flock. The time will come when some men from your own group will tell lies to lead the believer away after them.

Many are the deceivers in the world who would test our faith. Not only the devil but those also who have been moved away from truth in-order to find a measure of wealth, power and adoration from those much weaker and those who have not had a sure foundation formed by the sacrifice and salvation made possible in Christ. What we have come to understand is simply that sin is always crouching just outside our door; we must develop a natural inclination to do the right thing.

Usually doing the right thing is instantly presented to us, but there may come times when we must weigh and contemplate not only what is right, but the degree of correctness achieved within the decisions we make; not all decisions are-cut and dry. Some present a degree of harm to someone and in this we might have to weigh our decisions to the act that produces the least amount of negative consequence. Fortunately, we are not alone in the decisions this life presents to us. For the one who truly seeks to know which way to travel, God is always willing to shine a light in such direction of higher approval. Certainly, the decision to unleash the atomic bombs on the cities of Japan was one that weighed the consequences that understood many more American lives would be lost if Japan continued its adamant stance of not surrendering.

Testing

The testing of our faith, loyalty to truth, along with everything that connects us to the reality we have been brought into is ongoing. The very moment that captured us within the clarity of our lives has always been under scrutiny. Those who knew us before conversion were awaiting the moment we would return to our former way of life. The evil that is continually crouching just outside our door is very patient in the belief that there is something in the world having ability to cause us to become unfaithful to the one who shed his blood for us. Once we recognize everything permitted and allowed, has already been decided by God via his approval or disapproval, we then recognize that even when some things happen to us, or to those we love, the underlying truth is that God can and will restore not only the so-called "lost-years" but every aspect of our lives will be completely made whole; all that seemed to be lost will be found and returned to us wrapped in the gift of eternal life.

<u>Constant proclamation</u>

Matthew 10:5-10 These twelve men were sent out by Jesus with the following instructions: "Do not go to any Gentile territory or any Samaritan towns. Instead, you are to go to those lost sheep, the people of Israel. Go and preach, 'The kingdom of heaven is near!' Heal the sick, bring the dead back to life, heal those who suffer from dreaded skin diseases, and drive out demons." *I'm imagining listening to Jesus and being told to do all these things that my logic is telling me is impossible. I know that Jesus has done all of this, in my sight, and he is now giving me the authority to do the same, and still, there is a struggle within me that is like a tug-of-war. I know the truth of the authority and the reality that comes with belief but still there is the doubt that intrudes and says: "Really? Is this (really) happening? It was one thing to see Jesus do all of this stuff, but now he expects me to do it?" Most of us go in the wrong direction of reality when we ask ourselves this last part. We forget that it is not "I" who's doing these things but it is the authority of God who has placed his trust in us to remain faithful to the bond established in love. Just as God had placed his trust in Job to remain a faithful servant, so too, Jesus had placed his authority in the twelve disciples and later he sent out the seventy-two in a full assault on the deceptions and sufferings of the people. The message of salvation available in the coming of the kingdom of heaven is still thwarting the evil schemes of the devil, and adding to the number of those God has blessed with being able to not only hear but to proclaim his truth. The proclamation of truth need not be within a formal setting as in a church building, but more often it is done just by the manner, in which we conduct our lives.*

For the one who conducts his life in the honesty and freedom that comes with the receipt and retention of truth, therein is the lamp that is not placed under a bowl, or the saltiness that hasn't lost its integrity. We can only imagine the joy and completeness of faith, within those who ventured out from the physical presence of Jesus, into the field of battle for the good of mankind, and finding the reality of the power of God, evermore increasing as the desire to do good mounted, must have been a taste of heaven itself! When the seventy-two return they were ecstatic from the victories accomplished in the name of Jesus. The words of Jesus as he witnessed the joy they presented, was a pictorial that painted and encapsulated the entire outcome of the attack's thrust: ***"I saw Satan fall from heaven like lightning."***

Even the smallest of victories, then and now, will find the exclamation from our Lord to be one of victory! These small or great victories have long lasting positive dividends for us who have denied temptation entrance through the doorway of our heart. We learn to fall back upon such memory of ability to overcome the schemes of evil and in this we find additional faith that not only strengthens but leads in the day to day decisions determining the outcome of another day in the Army of God. We come to realize that the evil crouching just outside our door has been reduced in potency by the presence of God living inside of us.

Victory

The call to battles lost lingers in the mind
It shouts, "defeat!" in crystal tones
At all attempts toward change.
Confident of victories past says:
"No escape remains!"
Trouble near within the heart
Despair the lot of man
Crushing laughter shouts, "No end!"
Hope sees not a friend.
Stone upon stone the sentry hushed
By rumors in the bones
Foundations quake and boulders break
At the sight of love.
The knowing look of lies rebuked
Take flight from temple cleansed
Silence, sweet silence, peace at last.
Change proclaimed to captive man
Soaring spirit sighs
At last deception is dragged into the light.
Truth is the key to freedom sought
Love is the victory cry!

1 John 5:5 Who is it that overcomes the world?
Only he who believes that Jesus is the Son of God.

No Surrender

There's a battle every day and with confidence to win
I call upon the Lord who strengthens and defends.
I can feel the struggle I can taste it in my teeth
The pulsing of desires raging at their peak.
They promise respite from the conflict "yes" and "no"
With lies designed for bondage to the things that hold and bind
To ball and chain submission to where we would not go
"No surrender!"
Is the message, says body, mind, and soul.

Philippians 4:13 I can do everything through him who gives me strength.

James 1:2-5 My friends, consider yourselves fortunate when all kinds of trials come your way, for you know that when your faith succeeds in facing such trials, the result is the ability to endure. Make sure that your endurance carries you all the way without failing, so that you may be perfect and complete, lacking nothing. But if any of you lack wisdom you should pray to God, who will give it to you; because God gives generously and graciously to all.

No pain no gain

The ability to endure is the progression of victories that lend confidence to our lives. Today I can bench press fifty pounds and tomorrow the ability to lift more is added through the building up of muscle, and in the case of faith-succeeding what we find are the same results. We are given the confidence to continue, enduring the momentary pain of denying the testing presented to us, on, a daily basis. James, is saying that when we recognize there is something lacking, and we are in need (such recognition is a sign of wisdom for it has defeated the self-pride that always fails to admit fault), we must ask seek and knock upon the reality that God gives generously and graciously, to everyone who understands the limitation of this natural life, we must endure. All the trials or testing that comes to us stems from several routes of travel: in the one there is our failure to do what is right and in this there is negative repercussion, and in the other there is the testing that comes from the natural aspect of life that calls upon everyone. Loss of youth, loved ones and employment are but a few of the negatives that are mostly unavoidable; but with God all things are possible for us to not only overcome but to rise above to the victory expected of those who have truth within their arsenal of weaponry designed to thwart the illusions of defeat that constantly plague the soldier in the field. The soldier in the field is given an array of defensive and offensive weaponry in-order to resist the evil designs of those who wish to only defeat the truth of God and the reality of eternal life for all who will accept such truth.

James 1:12-14 Happy are those who remain faithful under trials, because when they succeed in passing such a test, they will receive as their reward the life which God has promised to those who love him. If we are tempted by such trials, we must not say, "This temptation comes from God." For God cannot be tempted by evil, and he himself tempts no one. But we are tempted when we are drawn away and trapped by our own evil desires. *All of us have seen the presentation of an angel sitting on one shoulder and on the other the devil is whispering in the other ear for us to not heed the knowledge of what we know to be the right thing to do. Therein is the conflict in man that continually attempts to lead us in the path of wrong. We must recognize our own propensity to desire to do wrong and in this (recognition) we will begin to not only question the impulses that arise but we will gain the wisdom that takes into consideration the far-reaching implications of our unwise decision to permit action to accompany such desires. Wisdom is a great weapon in the arsenal given to us, like all other weaponry it comes from God alone. Let us not lose track of the reality that has already given to us the ability to say, "no" to all things contrary to the will of God. In this, victory, we will live our lives in the present, happy and free from the condemnations that are designed to steal* *away the truth we have been given, and the happiness that is always married to the truth and reality of the God who loves us.*

Luke 11:24-29 "When an evil spirit goes out of a person, it travels over dry country looking for a place to rest. If it can't find one, it says to itself, 'I will go back to my house.' So, it goes back and finds the house clean and all fixed up. Then it goes out and brings seven other spirits even worse than itself, and they come and live there. So when it is all over, that person is in worse shape than at the beginning." When Jesus had said this, a woman spoke up from the crowd and said to him, "How happy is the woman who bore you and nursed you!" But Jesus answered, "Rather, how happy are those who hear the word of God and obey it."

Disloyal

We have looked at the testing that comes to those who are faithful and love God, and now what we find are the sevenfold troubles that can overpower those who have received God's mercy, but failed to allow him entrance into their heart. It is almost inconceivable for us who have received God's love and mercy to fathom anyone who has also found freedom from the demons that plague, and in what can only be described as ingrate status, they have failed to invite God into their home. In the scripture-above, we find a man who has been freed from demonic possession and the demon flees to a dry place to rest, and collect himself, in effort to find another victim to plague, with whatever malady the demon finds most troubling to his prey. Apart from pure demonic possession we must understand that there are many who are plagued with compulsive behaviors that weigh heavily upon the one so afflicted by such addictions. Once freed from these and all of what had robbed us of our happiness, if the set-free soul should return to his former compulsion and/or addiction the outcome will be many times worse! The cast-out demon in the case of the one freed person in the above scripture finds himself in a dry place (a place that is not offering anything that would satisfy demonic purpose), and not finding refuge to his liking he goes back to his former habitat.

He is overjoyed to find his former home, from which he had been dispossessed to be completely rehabilitated and clean. He then goes and seeks others of his kind who were not so lucky to find an empty and clean habitat and he invites them to his new home! Thus, for the person who was set-free from the evil spirit and/or the entrapments of the world, his decline into greater captivity is rapid and seven times as bad as before; seven times greater indicates complete captivity! Jesus says to us he stands at the door and knocks. The door he is speaking of is our heart, and when we invite him into our heart and our lives, there is no chance of a relapse into darkness so long as he is with us. The evil crouching just outside our door continually finds it locked!

Self-affliction

Apart from the external trappings designed by others, there's the most detrimental assaults made upon us through our very own lifestyles! It is within these behaviors a twofold negative-consequence takes place; one is brought about by our failure to recognize foreseeable consequence, and the other is incurred because we have acted knowingly in a way that is apart from God (incurring the chastisement of God) and in this we find the judgment of God actively befalling the transgressor in our present day. Many a man has turned from his ways when the consequence of wrong appears without ambiguity; there's no question in the mind of the transgressor why such negative aftereffect exists. Many are the peoples who have received warning from God to turn from their wicked ways; some have listened and others have paid a terrible price. When an entire nation is given-warning regarding the judgment of God about to befall them, should they fail to listen, what was pronounced by the messenger from God takes place exactly as was described. This accuracy within the prophetic words of God should make everyone take notice and at least contemplate the reality spoken. Man, gives warning in a myriad of instances and everyone listens; the bridge needs maintenance; the water is contaminated and will be unfit for consumption should the present pollution continue, and the declaration of war from an enemy always finds the subjects of the declaration listening, and taking some sort of remedial action; but when we hear the voice of God spoken through his word or from those he chooses to carry his message, many are they who do not believe. Sadly, in every case of legitimate warning pronounced to man from God, his words are mostly unheeded. Within the bible there are numerous warnings that have gone unheeded and the consequence of such failure is still ringing true to this very day!

Romans 1:18-20 God's anger is revealed from heaven against all the sin and evil of the people whose evil ways prevent the truth from being known. God punishes them because what can be known about God is plain to them, for God himself made it plain. Ever since God created the world, his invisible qualities, both his eternal power and his divine nature, have been clearly seen; they are perceived in the things that God has made. So, those people have no excuse at all!

The reality of the existence of the one who created everything is clear. The complexity of nature and the life existing within our world should shout out to all: "God is!" Unfortunately, the greatest stumbling block existing for man is that the testimony bearing witness to the reality of the God who loves us, takes place within us; which is a twofold revelation: first, God is Spirit and in this he communicates directly to our spirit. Secondly, the fact that God does not herald the salvation of someone within great pomp and circumstance speaks to us of the great humility of our great God. Certainly, God can make wonderful miracles to take place, and in this there would be no doubt as to the reality being brought-to-mind, but, he speaks to us with the humility of love and in this we are drawn to the truth that sets us free. In this (freedom) we do all the heralding for him. As it is written: **Proverbs 27:2 Let other people praise you…even strangers; never do it yourself.** *GNB*

Again, unfortunately for the world humility is something that is not found in abundance; this flaw in humanity finds deception in those who heap praise upon themselves. They broadcast their resume as if it were something they accomplished without any outside influence. Unlike the assembly of the heavenly host, in the presence of God, continually singing of his greatness; they do so because they have complete knowledge of the God who rules with justice and judgment; unlike many of the elite rulers of the world who rule through lies, injustice and fear. Pride is the instrument that invites the judgment of God, in the hope that as such judgment is realized those who had strayed from the truth will be stirred back into the correct lifestyle approved by the creator. In the book of the prophet Jeremiah we read about how God used the Babylonian king (Nebuchadnezzar), to inflict his judgment upon an unfaithful people and their unwillingness to listen to correction. Even after God used the king against his unfaithful people he turns his attention to the king and pronounces judgment upon him for his transgressions against what is right; his captivity of the people of God for seventy years.

Jeremiah 25:12-14 "But when the seventy years are fulfilled, I will punish the king of Babylon and his nation, the land of the Babylonians, for their guilt," declares the Lord, "and I will make it desolate forever. I will bring upon that land all the things I have spoken against it, and that are written in the book and prophesied by Jeremiah against the nations. They themselves will be enslaved by many nations and great kings; I will repay them according to their deeds and the work of their hands." *If we look at the nation of Iraq today, we can clearly see that over the centuries it has not found blessing. This is a clear indicator that when a nation is pronounced as evil by God they will suffer greatly for great periods of time; even to the point of everlasting. It is clear, that the Middle East has been a melting pot for generations. It did not matter if ruled by kings, tyrants, despots or terrorists, the results with each regime change has been from bad, to worse! Absent God's blessing mankind will never find peace, as a nation or on an individual basis.*

Edge

Sometimes we are forced to the edge.
Sometimes we willingly take a chance.
Shaking earth, loose rocks shouting, "fall!"
Through it all we continue precariously close.
Grace is like a climber's rope held-fast to mountain rock
Denying a fall as light denies dark
Restoring life with a kindling spark.
Continued blessing as footfalls fail
A tumble a misstep a lost-focus stare
Finds forgiveness from he who understands.
Living on the edge is scary, but
It never has a definitive shout that says:
"You've reached the edge of God's love!"
Sin has some staying power
But in the-end will meet its final hour
On the edge of God's Sword!
Truth.

Isaiah 53:12 Therefore I will give him a portion among the great, and he will divide the spoils with the strong, because he poured out his life unto death, and was numbered with the transgressors. For he bore the sin of many and made intersession for the transgressors.

Keep enemies close and watch them closely

Just because someone is perceived as being close to God, it doesn't mean he or she is a loyal faithful servant. I suspect the origination of the above thought began with the enemy of both God and mankind, the devil. It has certainly held its position among true sayings when we see those who have been close to God and truth being recognized as enemies. We know that Jesus knew of the traitorous avaricious act lurking in the heart of Judas, that would lead to his being handed over to the Jewish authorities, and God certainly knew of the intentions of the devil from the very beginning of his being brought into existence. What can be derived from these two examples of disloyalty? Not all that claim to be positioned on the side of what is right and holy are in fact speaking truth. However, while it is true that we can be led to believe and trust a certain person who proves to be untrustworthy, God can never be deceived, and since this is a truth that is indivisible or unable to be separated from the all-knowing aspect attached only to God, it is our responsibility to remain in close contact with the one who will always give to us the necessary knowledge, so as, to not be deceived. No one wants to find they have placed trust in someone only to find they have misplaced such trust. This failure on our part will raise innumerable negatives as we move into the future of this life. We may build up artificial barriers within us, to not be easily misled in other aspects of life that require trusting others. Once we have found ourselves in the position of having been deceived we may find it extremely difficult to give to others the trust that they may deserve.

For instance, a pastor of a church I had attended, was been found to be a thief, and also, one who has been convicted of murdering both his first, and, second wives. In this venue, having placed our trust in the pastor to execute his duties as they apply to church resources, and, also his failure to remain faithful to the one he promised before God to love honor and obey, what we can expect to occur is a decline in membership in this particular-church. In this instance, what we find is not only a betrayal of the church congregation but a deception aimed at the heart of Christ! Moreover, there are some who will not only leave the church but they may also find themselves throwing the baby out with the bathwater. They may lose all respect for the reason to attend church worship. They will no longer find the trust to present themselves before the Lord. This is the greater sin incurred by the disloyalty of such a pastor. Jesus said: ***"Things that cause people to sin are bound to come, but woe to him who causes them to come. It would be better for him to have a millstone tied around his neck and drowned in the depths of the sea, then for him to cause one of these little ones to fall. So, watch yourselves.***

Covert betrayal

With regard, to both Satan and Judas, their seemingly stealth (they thought it was stealthy) desire to betray both God and Jesus was met with the confusion that will always find its way into the heart of those who think their hidden motives will go undetected. In the case of attempting to betray the only one who cannot be deceived, their actions were the most ignorant and foolish attempts ever recorded in both the creation of man and angels! Idiots! Both the devil and Judas knew they were challenging God and still they went ahead with their plans? These two examples are perhaps without rival, but betrayal can also find its way into existence by simply not believing truth. The wife of Abraham (Sarah) did not believe she was going to give birth to a son, and the father of John the Baptist also did not believe the angelic messenger of God's intent. Yes, this is a lesser sin than Satan or Judas committed, but disbelief is also filled with negative consequence.

Survival mechanism

Once mankind found reason to question visual appearances and oral presentations a negative disposition toward all things came into our determinate capacity. A "prove it" mentality prevailed and cynicism (a byproduct of sin) then inhabited the fabric of man. Where once trust, stood alone, distrust moved in. Wariness became wedded to a predisposed mindset for expecting deceit and calcified into a jaundiced response (an attitude of cynical hostility). The reaction to an exposed lie will always elicit hostility. Deception is never at ease with itself. Knowing that we have inherited such a distrusting disposition is a form of survival instinct that forces us to ask the question: "Is this the truth?" Because there is so much deception in the world it is almost a given fact that truth is a rarity within our everyday lives, that are subjected to not only advertisements filled with promise, but in just about every other venue of thought transmission we find either full blown deception and/or a moderated version of the lie. Having been made aware of the rampant usage of deception by man to further his agenda we can become weary of the constant assaults upon our faculties and in this we seek a rest from such bombardments. Fortunately for us there is a respite where millions of people have found not only truth but additional tools in which to determine truth; this is of course the Bible and all the content contained therein.

Just as Job had loyal friends so too there is a sense of friendship between those who are enamored, enriched, and advanced in the world by the usage of the lie. The usage of lies is much more than the failure of those to admit wrong; it is foremost a tool through which people can paint a picture of themselves that is far from the internal motivations thought to be kept hidden from others. Certainly, Judas and Satan thought they had pulled the wool over the eyes of God and there are many in this life who think they are so cunning that revelation of their inner self cannot be detected. Unfortunately for them, they are already standing in the light of truth that cannot be denied when we speak of the all-knowing quality of God to not only know what is taking place in the here and now but he was aware of all things before he brought into existence the foundations of the earth!

Trust

Who to trust and how much?
Family fails us at times and friends can be hard to find.
A multitude can produce one, but only if the one is not two.
We see the outer man and hope the inner man is the same.
It can get confusing-contemporary faith is often a bust.
Lord, may it come to pass, knowledge of
your goodness-enter hearts of men.
Within the being of man wrought from earth and dust
Within the flesh and sinew the spirit bone and blood
Shine light within the inner halls, make clear
as day the way we should call.
Let all who draw near to you find shelter in your thoughts
And find the dwelling place of he, who alone is God.
May sacrifice as Sabbath bread be offered up as praise
And bring to hearts the nourishment that comes with trust in grace.

Romans 9:33 As it is written: "See, I lay a stone in Zion that causes men to stumble and a rock that makes them fall, and the one who trusts in him will never be put to shame.

Friends

Apart from the most hateful form of betrayal that we see in the persons of Satan and Judas, there is the aspect of loyalty that forms between those whose basic foundations are cemented with the mortar of evil. For this example of evil uniting we will look at the secular rulers during the time of Christ; Herod and Pilate. Both men were formerly enemies but became friends, due to the distain they showed to Jesus.

Luke 23:11-12 "Herod and his soldiers made fun of Jesus and treated him with contempt; then they put a fine robe on him and sent him back to Pilate. On that day Herod and Pilate became friends." *Anytime a threat is presented apart from the existing power structure there will always be a pushback from those presently enjoying leadership and/or ruling positions. Prior to the disposition concerning Jesus, and determination from both Herod and Pilate, these power structures were at odds with each other. One was the figurehead king of the now occupied nation of Israel and the other was the representative of the occupier. As such there was a natural inclination for king Herod to at least appear to be confrontational with the Romans. In the case brought before Herod concerning Jesus there was no need for artificial resistance against Pilate, since the ruling religious had already joined forces with the secular occupiers. In this what we find is a trinity of evil united against the holiness presented in the person of Christ. Certainly, the declaration by Jesus prior to his arrest and subsequent hearing before all three of those who sat in judgment must have rang loud and clear in the ears of those privileged to have heard it.*

Mark 3:25-26 "If a household is divided according to loyalties, that household will not survive. Similarly, if Satan has suffered mutiny in his ranks, and is torn by dissention, he cannot endure;

he is finished." *In the same way, political parties in America have become unyielding, in their intent and ideology, and perhaps will remain in oppositional conflict until something threatens all-of their positions, as was the case during the time of Christ. You may ask, what was the threat made by Jesus to these secular and religious powers? The answer is simply that when truth is denied wickedness is brought forth. The truth that Jesus broadcast to the common man was that which exposes wickedness and sets free all of those who need only to embrace it. Having a foundation among the populace united through goodness and truth presented a clear threat to those whose agenda was never associated with either the good of the populace or the truth concerning the God who created all.*

Today the entire world is broken down into three main avenues of distinction: Those united with truth; those united with evil and those who have been kept in darkness by the evil that continually disallows truth to be uttered within any forums, unless such ruling authorities permit a dilute variety of truth, that no longer has ability to transform the lives of those listening. As Jesus said: ***"You are the salt of the earth, but if salt loses its saltiness it is no longer any good and will be trampled upon by men."*** *This is the case in many parts of the world, and yes, even in America. The movement on the part of some to erase God from public speech is a movement against truth. We are told of the "transparency" of government and for at least half of the nation what we understand that to mean is the lying nature of those in power is only the illusion of transparency, presented to pacify those who are eager to place their faith and loyalty in the declarations of a political party.*

Friends find the adhesiveness of loyalty to be constructed within the material and spiritual foundations of either good and/or evil. The evil that is formed and implemented within the darkness of hidden motives is accepted as a natural aspect of the war against good. With respect to "good" and the motivation to see it manifested there is no need for deception's entanglements; where there's good deception cannot be found. As it is written: ***Proverbs 12:19 A lie has a short life, but truth lives on forever.*** *Again,*

Proverbs 12: 3 Wickedness does not give security, but righteous people stand firm.

What is evil's allure, when it is clearly written in God's word that it will not prevail? I guess one could look at the shortcuts presented to the minds of those who seek the so-called riches of the world, and in their-reasoning conclude that through deception, thievery, murder and every other evil action they can achieve their heart's desire for the power and control that accompanies wealth. If this is the case, then we should recognize there is no fear of God in those so enamored by the temptations of both the world and their own evil desires. Of course, there is the possibility that they are nonbelievers in the God who created all things (including themselves), and in such-nonbelief they have concluded that there is no wrong, and when they die the wrongs they committed in life will not find consequence after death of the body. And so, what we have found is there are some who know, the truth of God and have no fear of him, and there are those who don't believe in the God of all creation, and in ignorance they continue to egregiously commit all kinds of sin, against both God and mankind. Sadly, even they have found others of like-minded evil to unite with in the shared bond of corruption, and lust for the world's offerings. They have not understood who it is they should fear.

Matthew 10:26-31 "So do not be afraid of people. Whatever is now covered up will be uncovered, and every secret will be made known. What I am telling you in the dark you must repeat in broad daylight, and what you have heard in private you must announce from the housetops. Do not be afraid of those who can kill the body but cannot kill the soul; rather be afraid of God, who can destroy both body and soul in hell. For only a penny you can buy two sparrows, yet not one sparrow falls to the ground without your Father's consent. As for you, even the hairs on your head have all been counted. So, do not be afraid; you are worth much more than many sparrows." *GNB*

Jesus makes known the limitation of man's evil, which clearly ends when the body meets the grave, and in this we understand that there's an afterlife that will be a wonderful experience for those who love God, and for those who do not there will be unimaginable horror for having sinned against both God and his creation. Even we who have been taken from the darkness of unknowing and brought into the light of truth, at times find it very difficult to understand how some people can knowingly rebel against God? This knowing rebellion becomes even more difficult to understand when we recognize that those who challenge God know that they will spend eternity within the fires of hell, or else, as Jesus said, God can destroy both body and soul.

Pretend friends

1 Corinthians 15:33 Do not be fooled. "Bad companions ruin good character." *The influences we permit entrance into our lives will have an impact upon our lives. It is for this reason we are to choose our friends wisely. Perhaps the best example of bad company causing generational harm and ruination is the association between Adam, Eve and the devil. From this (example) we not only find the scripture above to be truthful but it is one of tremendous warning. What was the motive for Satan wanting to ruin the perfection (perfection insofar as immortality is concerned) of the creation of mankind? Maybe he wanted to form a barrier between mankind and God? Certainly, this barrier is evident in the manifestation of mankind's sin against the Fatherly prohibition to not eat the fruit from the tree situated in the center of the garden. Even after they were told to not eat from this tree or even touch it, and if they should fail to comply with the warning they would surely die, they disobeyed and fell prey to the deception that they had not known existed. And in this act of disobedience to God the formal training associated with life, absent the very close association with God had begun. All the character traits that we associate with the good qualities of mankind began to be recognized through the hard times and suffering experienced by the human condition began. We learned of courage and compassion and mercy, along with empathy for those who grieve and those suffering from disease, all because we failed to heed the warning from he who created us. Certainly,* *we would have no comprehension for suffering or compassion for others since no one was suffering. Additionally, there would be no need for courage or mercy, since no one is being threatened or who has done wrong. It is becoming obvious to us that there was a need for us to sin, for us to fully understand the virtues associated with a loving God. This banishment from paradise was on par with a child reaching adulthood and leaving home, to experience the real-life presented to those who are no longer cared for by loving parents. In just the one aspect of salvation received through the suffering, death, and resurrection of our Lord, we gain tremendous understanding and depth, regarding the love of God. Not even the angels can understand as fully as we have been made to perceive; for them there is no salvation offered for transgression against God's prohibitions.*

What's in the name

Mankind has an enemy outside of his creation; not human.
He wages brutal war throughout life's duration.
Within the Holy Scriptures we are told his
name and weapons he employs
With purpose to defend ourselves with the armor God provides.
The enemy of humanity is named the Devil, and as for his weapons
They are easy for us to see-all we need to do is drop the "D."

Revelation 20:10 And the devil, who deceived them, was thrown into the lake of burning sulfur, where the beast and the false prophet were thrown.

Lessons learned

Lessons learned through our failure to heed warning and/or advice from those who have our best interest at heart, become embedded within us due to the unwanted consequence derived. We don't want to have to suffer the consequence of our former failure to heed wisdom's warning, and in this desire to not want to repeat such self-inflicted discomfort and/or harm we have the memory of the incident burned into our psyche. All the hard times and subsequent hard lessons presented to mankind are rooted in the very first deception that captured Adam and Eve. Is it a wonder why wisdom is thought to be found in the elderly? Someone at some point in time must have recognized that many of the mistakes made by mankind, have tendency to repeat themselves within the current younger generation; as such, the elderly were-consulted for their advice in matters presented as unknowing, by youth, and the possible outcome of actions discussed in-order to avoid consequence to unwise decisions, that appear, on the surface, to be fun, but underlying the fun, and hidden, there may be a serious price to pay.

Getting back to the motive(s) of the devil to desire the destruction of mankind, we can ask this question and perhaps never (really) find an answer that would justify the intent of such demonic evil. We can come to the realization that no matter how demonic evil has justified its actions there is never a valid reason why such action had been brought forth. In this we begin to understand that evil does not need a reason to perform the actions that represent its description. Demonic evil exists because it is the nature of the rebellious supernatural beings. When the evil is made manifest in the actions of mankind we can then begin to understand why such evil is made manifest. Looking at the second world war, the evil within the German dictator, Adolph Hitler, had his motives of world conquest, immeasurable power and unimaginable greed, made manifest in the hatred of the people of God. His motives are all formed from the hatred of God's creation; to the exclusion of those he deemed above the status he had considered to be dirt. Hitler, probably could not understand the love that God had made manifest throughout the history of the Jewish people, and may have thought it better to remove such a people (and in doing so their God also) in-order to establish a new religion that placed the devil at the altar of adoration and worship. This was the presentation made to Jesus while he was fasting in the desert for forty-days: ***"Worship me and I'll give to you all the kingdoms of the world."*** *Well it looks as if* *there has been many throughout the history of mankind who have knelt at the feet of evil, either knowingly or unaware, in the hope of conquering the world. How this is reconciled in the minds of those who choose evil, when it has been stated:* ***"What does it profit a man to gain the whole world and lose his soul?"***

As long, as, mankind remains blinded by the allurements of the world there will always be some who are motivated to achieve such offerings through any means. All of the attempts to conquer the whole world will prove to be fruitless, and still, there will come a time when the Antichrist will worship the Evil One and in this he will gain all of the kingdoms of the world, except for the nation of Israel, where, once again a despot will attempt to destroy God's people. It is interesting to note that because evil has chosen to achieve through even the most abominable means, such evil recognizes their desires will not be reached unless the-collective conscience of mankind is made to be numbed from the assaults; leading to a resignation by those who are troubled by such acts, that all the horrific acts of evil are just another part of the everyday life one must learn to tolerate! There is a belief in many that the present-day evil made manifest by terrorists is an aberration that will probably dissipate over a period-of-time, and in this, understanding, there is no need to confront it with the overwhelming power contained in the countries that can do so. The modern terrorists are united under the banner of evil but will not recognize such evil that has overtaken their lives. This is primarily due, to the fact that many of the followers of those who espouse a need for a religious theocracy, to fulfill their own prophesy, as well as ridding the world of what they describe as heathen nonbelievers, do so from the deepest depths of hatred. Thank God, for he will destroy all the evil made manifest in both mankind and the demonic forces arrayed against good.

The denial of evil, to the point of not even identifying terrorism, by many in the political class suggests several possibilities: They are a part of the evil that plagues the world or else they are completely ignorant! Additionally, there is the ostrich approach to such evil encroaching upon the populace of the earth. They bury their heads deep into darkness and hope it will go away. Denial of the problems within the world will never, on its own, cause them to go away. Just as the lie needs to be exposed and in the exposure to the light of truth finds destruction, so too, the evil acts throughout the world must be first recognized to exist and in this (admission) must find sufficient opposition to destroy those who will not live in accordance with what has been pronounced by God to be good.

Kingdoms

Within the scriptures, we are alerted to the existence of the kingdom of God and/or the kingdom of heaven. In one, instance, we are brought into the conversation between Jesus and a Pharisee named Nicodemus, who is told by Jesus that he must be born again and/or born from above, in-order to not only enter but to see the kingdom of God. (John 3:3). In another instance, we see Jesus being confronted by some Pharisees who declared that Jesus was-able to do miraculous feats because it is the chief of demons that has given to him the ability to do so.

Jesus responds by saying, ***Luke 11:17-18 "Any country that divides itself into groups which fight each other will not last very long; a family divided against itself falls apart. So, if Satan's kingdom has groups fighting against each other, how can it last?"*** *From this statement by Jesus, we are alerted to the fact that evil has established its own kingdom, in opposition to all that stands for truth and God. In life, we find opposites for just about everything. Up and down. east and west, good and bad, dirty and clean, blue sky or gray, and the list goes on. The kingdoms of God and Satan are also at odds with each other and completely opposite. These kingdoms of good and evil are not just inhabitants of the supernatural realm; they are also found to be manifestations in the natural world that we inhabit. There is no neutral ground in this war against God and his followers. The war is being fought on many fronts; beginning within our minds and hearts and extending outward onto the field of battle. From compromise with self to the manifest ugliness made apparent in the murderous acts of* *barbarism, perpetrated against all those who will not adhere to the demands made from a terrorist mentality, that must be recognized as evil, and not insane. Labeling such evil as insane lends to those who commit such acts the subtleness of "unknowing" what they are doing or the difference between right and wrong; there is no excuse for evil. Those who will not cry out against evil are a party to its existence! Both the kingdom of God and the kingdom of Satan are clearly made manifest throughout the world. For those who have been born again from above, God's kingdom has come to us. And for those who have worshipped a false god, (knowingly or not) whose mandate is to kill all who will not worship such a god, they are blinded by the evil that has promised everything that a meaningless life could lust after and hope to find as a reward for loyalty to evil. Criminal organizations, gangs trafficking in drugs, and other illegal contraband have their own code of loyalty, that promises extreme penalty for breaking such code of silence, thereby exposing to authorities, undeniable evidence of wrong, and permitting the ultimate judgment, according, to the laws of man. In both the evil initiated by man and that which is brought forth from the supernatural opposition to God and his creation, both are clearly seen by God. There are no backroom deals that go undetected; no-smoke-filled environment that precludes the activity from he who is fully aware of all things.*

Prize

Mankind sets traps, lays in wait,
Baits a hook expectantly
All the while it's he who's being led
As a sheep to slaughter
As a ram, a goat, or lamb
Still, he thinks it's he who's in command.
Warnings fill the air: "Judgment day is coming!"
And no one seems to care.
Barking at the dark, movement in the yard
He knows there's something there
Crouching, laying patiently, not wanting to be seen.
He will not heed the signs, the calls, the screams
Never will he ask: "What does it mean?"
A ship's horn, a train's whistle
A siren's piercing call
Alerting all who'll listen before the curtain falls:
"Wake up!"
The darkness that is evil
Disallows the warning signs
So, the man continues sleeping
While his life goes swiftly bye!
The now and tomorrow
Erased in the twinkling of an eye
If only he'd listened to the voices and the cry's.
"Eternal life."
Heard in whispers would have been
The captured prize!

Jeremiah 51:38-40 "The Babylonians all roar like lions and growl like lion cubs. Are they greedy? I will prepare them a feast and make them drunk and happy. They will go to sleep and never wake up. I will take them to be slaughtered, like rams, goats, and lambs. I, the Lord, have spoken."

In the above chapter of the book of the prophet and priest, the Lord, says, to Jeremiah, ***"You will see me repay Babylon for all***

the evil they did to Jerusalem. *There's no difference in the evil during the time of the prophet and our present day; all acts of evil will find the judgment of God. There is no place to run or to hide! It is frustrating for us to see criminals being set free due to a technicality in the law, or, because they have the resources to corrupt the justice system, but, there is no place for these same evil doers to evade the judgment of God and the punishment he will perfectly administer. Having the testimony from God outlined many times throughout the bible, that he will indeed punish evil, we also have the declaration that to be a member of the kingdom of God is to find reward.*

The apostle Paul declares, ***Philippians 3:14 So I run straight toward the goal in order-to win the prize, which is God's call through Christ Jesus to the life above. GNB*** *One of the many things about the writings of Paul that are clear for us to understand is the absolute declaration concerning eternal life, awaiting those of us who remain loyal to the one who saved us from judgment. Additionally, we are made aware through the many descriptive avenues approaching the reality of eternal life. <u>Example:</u> We are told in scripture that it has been,* ***"appointed unto man to die once."*** *Our understanding of death must be recognized beyond the bodily aspect of no longer functioning; death of the spirit (thinking ability) is the overall aspect of life, that exists in both the natural and supernatural dimensions, whereby without thought there cannot be life. As such, when we are told that man must die once we are being alerted to the need to be born again; to be in possession of a new spirit, for the old way of thinking has died. Just as supernatural is above the natural, so too it applies to the greater meaning of death being a definitive pronouncement when applied to the thought process and/or spirit. When we recognize that death of our old way of thinking, through the receipt of a new way, has fulfilled the biblical pronouncement that man must die once, we then are alerted to the reality of life after the body has died. Should a man not be born again while still alive in this body there cannot be an afterlife that awaits him; the only aspect of life after complete death of both body and spirit, that beckons to them is the second resurrection to judgment.*

Just as one would not categorize the convict kept in solitary confinement to be alive, a similar type of equating is found in those who have been condemned to hell; they cannot be described as alive, when all that they could hope for is death. This then is the kingdom of Satan; the kingdom of no hope for eternal life in Christ. The promised reward for the lost and rebellious of God's creation is hopelessness. Just as we are alerted to the reward awaiting the faithful servants of God, so too we are made aware of the verdict awaiting those who are not focused upon what is right and good. ***James 1:15 Then his evil desire conceives and gives birth to sin; and sin, when it is full-grown, gives birth to death. GNB*** *This unfocused, unaware and uncaring life, lived in the vacuum of self-centeredness, finds only complete darkness when the body and spirit meet the grave.*

James 1:12 Happy is the person who remains faithful under trials, because when he succeeds in passing such a test, he will receive as his reward the life which God has promised to those who love him. *It is apparent to those of us who have received a new spirit that we have received the reward of life in this the here and now, and such life will continue into the everlasting meant for God's children to enjoy. No more separation from loved ones, or pain, either physically or emotionally, just a constant meaningful life that I'm sure will challenge our human condition meant to seek knowledge and fulfillment within the things that are holy and good. Is it a wonder that Paul had wanted to be out of the body, to be home with the Lord? His desire to be home with the Lord, was made to be still because of his love for the church and his understanding that he had much more work to accomplish before he could claim the prize of eternal life, in Christ.*

Luke 11:18 So if Satan's kingdom has groups fighting each other, how can it last?"

15

HIDDEN KINGDOM

The hidden kingdom of darkness is the kingdom of evil. We can see the results of evil's impact upon the world but there is continual denial of such an orchestrated stronghold that reaches into the natural world of humanity. It is from this kingdom of evil we find manifested all the abhorrent actions plaguing humanity. A twofold manifestation is at work: the actions of those evil demonic spirits who have rebelled against God, and the evil desires in man that give way to deviant paths to achieve such desires for power and acquisition. Clearly, we are hearing in the words of our Lord, the existence of the kingdom of Satan. We are also hearing the correction of those who openly declared the actions of Jesus to be originated in the kingdom of Satan. We can understand the statement from those who deliberately pointed to evil as the power given to our Lord; it is they who are held captive in the denouncement of the good deeds, as was performed by Jesus. It is they who have found position power and wealth through the utilization of wickedness; why wouldn't they think good things come from the kingdom of the chief of demons? Perhaps this recognition of power to perform miracles was a statement by them meant to offer to Jesus membership in their group? As children of their father, the devil, they may have attempted to recruit our Lord, as the devil also tried at the outset of our Lord's ministry.

There is some confusion in the identification of the kingdom of evil; some think said kingdom is the place called hell; but, hell will not permit exit; it is eternal as in prison confinement and/ or the place wherein death is final. Thus, the kingdom of Satan is not the place spent in eternal lamentation, but is the realm wherein evil is brought forth from the supernatural into the natural world. I've written about this aspect of hell (its being permanent imprisonment or total death in a previous book titled, "Snapshots of Inspiration.") Additionally, I also believe the existence of hell as described in its depiction presented by Jesus, in the story of the rich man and Lazarus, to be a projected one; Jesus pointing to a place in the future that clearly is post judgment. It certainly does not make sense for us to imagine the unsaved being judged, upon death of the body and thrown into the lake of burning sulfur. The unsaved will more likely lose all consciousness (thinking ability) upon death of the body and such consciousness will not be restored until the second resurrection to judgment. Having said this, it is realistic to imagine the place called hell to be nonexistent, (at this, point in time) and unimaginable to declare hell to be the fortress of evil, in the here and now, wherein wickedness is brought forth into the natural world. In addition to this post judgment creation of hell understanding, we must recognize the devil has set up throne rooms in many places upon the earth; it is from these kingdoms, cities, governments, evil is brought forth. The hidden kingdom has found residency in the hearts of mankind. Just as we have invited God into our hearts, so too evil has been invited in the lives of the wicked. Jesus holds the keys to both death and the world of the dead. ***Revelation 1:18 "I am the living one! I was dead but now I am alive forever. I have authority over death and the world of the dead."*** *I think we can safely say that those who will be confined to eternity in hell qualify as residents of the world of the dead.*

I think anyone who is imprisoned would not describe their condition as being alive! As for the keys (authority) unlocking the condition of death there is the understanding that being made alive from a condition of death is taking place in the one who receives salvation, as well as the one who has experienced bodily death, and found the promised afterlife a reality in he who makes the decision to lock or unlock, said condition of life. Having a kingdom apart from the natural world and still having the ability to impact nature with extreme consequence is very difficult to imagine for those who have not been removed from the darkness of unknowing. They can see the impact of evil but refuse to acknowledge the avenues from which a tremendous amount of harm is brought forth. Here again, is a twofold manifestation: in the one it is disbelief (the absence of faith in God) in anything supernatural; that is, it is their belief that nothing exists apart from nature; and in the other manifestation it is the reality of evil itself continually denying itself to the world through deceptions.

There is more to evil than what lurks in the hearts of men; it is complete and undiluted in the hidden kingdom of Satan. Total evil wickedness is found in the unredeemable demonic beings and in many instances throughout mankind's history the same unforgivable behavior has revealed itself in the actions of men. For those of us who have placed our trust in the written word of God, there isn't any doubt concerning the existence of those demonic beings who have rebelled against God. A good portion of those fallen angelic host have been kept in darkness and confinement since before the days of Noah. ***Jude 1:6 Remember the angels who did not stay within the limits of their proper authority, but abandoned their own dwelling place: they are bound with eternal chains in the darkness below, where God is keeping them for the great Day on which they will be condemned.*** *This place of darkness-below is perhaps the place (the abyss) where the devil will be thrown into for a thousand years, and afterwards he must be released to once again deceive the world. This place is not hell, since there will be a time when the devil will be set loose to once again cause havoc through deception, upon the world. They will find themselves within the confines and prescribed torments deserving the evil that plagued all of creation (God is perfectly just) since the beginning of mankind's first sin of disobedience.*

<u>Evil continually denies itself</u>

Luke 11:14-15 Jesus was driving out a demon that could not talk; and when the demon went out, the man began to talk. The crowds were amazed, but some of the people said, it is Beelzebub, the chief of the demons who gives him the power to drive them out. *It is amazing for us to contemplate the good that was being done by Jesus, and the religious rulers make the determination that it is from the kingdom of Satan the power to cast out a demon has come. I guess we can say the deception in the world was so great that anything presenting a threat to existing authority, that thinks of itself as "righteous" could not be originating from good; it had to be from Satan. We can also imagine the consternation in those (because of the authority and power present in Jesus) who were stewards of the law, who interpreted the acceptable ways for living, within the pronouncements of the law of Moses. Unfortunately, the conclusion (that the devil gives his power for good), that evil can be the source of good, informs us of just how far into the darkness of unknowing God, these lost sheep of Israel had drifted away from truth. Even though the crowds were amazed by the miracle of driving out an evil spirit from a man, they wanted more! There were those who wanted to trap (test) Jesus by demanding a miracle showing that God approved of him. Just as we who have been set free, know of the power restoring us to new life, but, because this power is not experienced by others, it may prompt from them something more than our testimony to believe in our conversion; so too it was the case of those wanting to see a physical sign that a demon had been dispatched, other than the now ability of the man to speak. It is at this point Jesus injects the logic they were sorely missing:* ***"If Satan's kingdom has groups fighting each other how can it last?"*** *This injection of wisdom pronounced for the ears of the common man, and not exclusively for those trained in the religion of the day, finds its reality in all who have had family, friends, associations and all other unity dissolved within the advent of arguments, fighting and distrust.*

"Thy kingdom come"

Acts 2:17 "This is what I will do in the last days, God says: I will pour out my Spirit on everyone. Your sons and daughters will proclaim my message; your young men will see visions, and your old men will have dreams." *The kingdom of God has indeed come to mankind, and he has made of us a temple in which his Spirit dwells. We are also hearing that we are living in the last days! The hidden kingdom of evil had also come to mankind and as a counter punch, God has made us able to not only withstand the schemes of evil, but to be able to see through the lies and counterfeits competing for the attention of mankind.*

Acts 2:1-4 When the day of Pentecost came, all the believers were gathered together in one place. Suddenly there was a noise from the sky, which sounded like a strong wind blowing, and it filled the whole house where they were sitting. Then they saw what looked like tongues of fire which spread out and touched each person there. They were all filled with the Holy Spirit and began to talk in other languages. GNB *Before leaving the disciples to return to his Father's house, Jesus said that he would not leave them alone; he promised that another would come (The Helper, Counselor) to lead them into all knowledge; we see this promise fulfilled in the coming of the Holy Spirit on the day of Pentecost. It is now a twofold coming of the kingdom of God to man. At first it is in the person of Christ and the kingdom continues with the indwelling of the Holy Spirit in mankind. Clearly, the earth and its inhabitants are tightly engulfed in the war between these two kingdoms. No longer is the kingdom of those evil spirits denied reality; they are seen in both the actions of mankind and the infusion into society via corruption of all things ranging from dishonesty and immorality, to wickedness producing harm in every imaginable manner. It is now accepted as a normal occurrence for a permissiveness in both evil deeds and deceptions to be utilized for the achievement of personal goals. Deception used to be called a, "lie" but now it is applauded, expected and respected in those who can "spin doctor" an obvious denial of wrong. We now have doctors who can heal deception! It was from the lie that all manner of evil came forth!*

Kingdoms

It seems everyone wants a kingdom.
It has been said,
"Man, is king of his castle" and
"You must pass through hell to get to heaven."
Now it is said,
"The kingdom of heaven has come to man."
But does he know it?
Can we recognize a king from the puppet?
The free from the slave the living from the dead
The garden from the grave?
The innocent or guilty the present from the past
The future's song of victory or sighs within life's gasps?
Is there escape for the man living always in the dark?
Alas, God is forgiving to all admitting wrong
But for those who hide in darkness there is no hope.
"I never knew you!" is the sound of judgment
The Lord of lord's will bring!
The evil kingdom, for many is unseen
It's the way of deception behind a phony smile.
The kingdom of God is calling to all who go astray
Pointing into the darkness, revealing truthful ways
Nearing end of ages in these the final days!

John 1:4-5 The Word was the source of life, and this life brought light to mankind. The light shines in the darkness, and the darkness has never put it out. *GNB*

Irritant healing

There are things in life that are irritating, and when the discomfort becomes too great we either move away or tolerantly endure. In some things, there is no reprieve from the irritation that continually makes itself known. The Word of God is an irritant to darkness; its light constantly shines into the darkness, revealing all that is concealed. There is nothing the darkness can do to avoid the light that exposes all things contrary to truth and goodness. There is no place to run or to hide from the constant shining of truth into the consciousness of those who deliberately attempt to conceal their wickedness. The outward presentation of all things almost never is a complete picture of the whole. This is always true in the presentation of the lie; there is always a purpose behind or underneath that motivates a creative energy of denial. In most instances, it is an attempt to avoid correction and/or punishment. Being caught in a lie or arrested for a crime is never a reason to smile for the cameras, unless there is a complete loss of conscience. This is the level of evil that has ability to hold captive those who have been taken to this degree of wickedness.

Those who live life in the truth of God are an irritant to all who oppose truth; it is our declarations of right living that causes them to look inwardly and to confront the wrongs within their selves. In many it is the light of truth shining into the darkness that sets free, even those who are not aware of their captivity! Yes, the light of truth is that powerful! It may cause us to be uncomfortable at first, but it is this light that heals and makes us strong in the face of all adversity. Our first reaction to the appearance of light upon emerging from darkness may be the same as leaving a darkened movie theater and finding sunshine outside. After which, we become accustomed to the light and it is no longer an irritant but a great blessing for all who were made to be accustomed to darkness. It is not a mystery why there are those who would ban speech containing references to God and the bible; such speech cuts through the fog of denial and forces those held captive, or those who choose to be wicked, to understand that they are not hidden from God's light!

John 21:25 Jesus did many other things as well. If every one of them were written down, I suppose that even the whole world would not have room for the books that would be written. *Throughout the gospels, we are told of the wonderful things Jesus did; healing the sick, raising the dead and casting out demons who had invaded the sanctity of the human spirit. I'm sure not all of those who were recipients of the grace of God had such good deeds recorded in the gospels. John clearly acknowledges this fact. We* *must recognize that while the earth could not contain the books that could have been written, the deeds of Jesus are not confined to his ministry upon the earth. Having said that, the specific account of casting out demons appears to have been a common occurrence. We must not be confused by equating demonic possession with the common illnesses both then and now afflicting mankind. If we attempt to conflate the category of demonic possession and common illness we are admitting that Jesus did not know the difference between the two! Many people today, have done just that, either because they refuse to admit to demonic possession or else they simply deny the divinity of Christ.*

In today's world, almost all wickedness perpetrated against man is attributed to insanity on the part of those who have committed such heinous acts. What we may be witnessing is the evolution of evil's ability to conceal actual demonic possession, either by those willing to sell their soul for the promise of earthly wealth and power, or the actual housebreaking occurrence of demonic possession. In either one, what we are witnessing is the kingdom of Satan present in its current form. Just as the kingdom of God has come to mankind and has taken up residence in the individual, who answers to the knock, seeking entrance into a person's life, (Yes, Jesus says that he stands at the door and knocks, and if he is invited in he will sup with those who do so). Unlike demonic possession that will break down the door and take over the premises. Much of the wickedness we see today appears to be embraced and coveted by people with wicked intent. The teaching of Jesus also tells us, if a strongman (one who is aware of the possibility of evil's attack) knows of those who would break into his home, he makes ready for the invader's arrival and in this the invader is denied entrance. Along the same train of thought, we are told of the one who has had a demon cast out and the home (his freedom has been restored) is clean but no one is living there (meaning God has not been invited into the person's life, after the freedom of the man is restored). It is tantamount to hanging out a vacancy sign and blindly asking for a recurrence of the possession, but to a greater degree. And so, we have arrived at the conclusion that both the kingdom of God and the kingdom of Satan are vying for the possession of mankind's souls. Again, Jesus will always knock to gain entrance into a person's life, and for those who seek, to have him become a part of their lives, he will never deny them. On the other side of the spectrum is the forceful entrance, or it seems, in many cases, throughout human history there have been those who actively sought the kingdom of Satan and invited him into their lives. There are groups today who openly admit they worship Satan, which is equal to admitting that they embrace evil.

Revelation 2:12-13 "To the angel of the church in Pergamum write: These are the words of him who has the sharp, double-edged sword. I know where you live-where Satan has his throne. Yet you remain true to my name. You did not renounce your faith in me, even in the days of Antipas, my faithful witness, who was put to death in your city-where Satan lives." *Pergamum was an ancient Greek city located in modern day Turkey close to the Aegean Sea. Since it was a Greek city we can imply it was probably no different than Athens with respect to the myriad of gods, worshiped by the Greeks. The declaration in Scripture clearly defines this city as a place of many sinful activities. What we can surmise by the descriptive identifying this city as a place where Satan has his throne, is probably one that applies to all places where evil has become concentrated and tolerated by the greatest portion of the inhabitants. It is somewhat intriguing for us to understand that a small portion of the population had not succumbed to the lifestyles of debauchery and idolatry; for this, the loyal followers of Christ are applauded. Given the understanding that societal trends and adaptations to various styles in clothing, behavior and speech, will eventually find a place of permanence among large portions of populations, through many means of influencing compliance, it is paramount for us to remain focused upon not only what is taking place in our immediate surroundings but also within a worldwide movement as well. Certainly, when we imagine the activities that had taken place in a city like Sodom, it doesn't take much imagination to conclude that such a city is making available a throne room for Satan. There were also those* *cities during the time of Jesus, that because of their disbelief, were pronounced as already judged by Jesus, and heading in the direction of eternal damnation.*

Luke 10:13-15 "Woe to you, Korizin! Woe to you, Bethsaida! For if the miracles that were performed in you had been performed in Tyre and Sidon, they would have repented long ago, sitting in sackcloth and ashes. But it will be more bearable for Tyre and Sidon at the judgment than for you. And you Capernaum, will you be lifted-up to the skies? No, you will go down to the depths." *(the "depths" is a reference to hell, or in the Greek translation, Hades.) When the indisputable power of God is revealed in the healing of the sick, raising of the dead and the casting out of demons, such denial of apparent good is looked upon by our Lord as wickedness deserving of judgment. Such denial is internal as well as public denouncement of the presence of God. It is not the same as unknowing of the existence of God, since the residents of these towns were a part of the religious community that outwardly proclaimed allegiance to God, but their faith held captive, was such, that miraculous good deeds were not sufficient for recognition of Jesus.*

Mark 2:1 A few days later Jesus went back to Capernaum, and the news spread that he was home. *Capernaum was located on the shore of the Sea of Galilee and it is in this city that Jesus had made his home. We might want to ask why Jesus did not remain at home with his family? My guess is that while Jesus was actively involved in his ministry, of proclaiming the good news and performing miracles, he was also making a lot of enemies in the upper echelon of society; as such he was probably thinking of his family's safety when he moved into his own home, which was approximately forty miles away from Nazareth. It is one thing to witness something impossible for man, and scratch your head and walk away thinking, "O no, that is impossible!" but this town had Jesus living among them. I suppose it is true, "The prophet is never respected in his own home town." I also imagine that it was not only disbelief, but a certain amount of resentment and enmity that was held in the hearts of those Capernaum residents, for any number of reasons* *emanating from jealously and envy of one of the local boys making good. As such, there is the pronouncement by Jesus, that they had no excuse for their disbelief; in this they would pay a heavy price. Again, the kingdom of Satan had taken up residence in the hearts of those who were very close to Jesus, and this is very difficult for us to reconcile.*

It is one thing to deny the presence of holiness in the one who is given the power to achieve all that is good, and it is another thing to deny the goodness right in front of you; it is even more damaging to deny the darkness and sinfulness of one's own being. These inhabitants of Capernaum had demanded of Jesus a miracle. The devil also asked for a miracle from Jesus to prove that he was the Son of God. Isn't it amazing how we who have been the recipient of the grace of God, don't ask for proof of our salvation? The same conviction of reality was present in the miraculous deeds and teachings of Jesus, and still, the people rejected such apparent holiness and power by demanding more evidence! This is wickedness personified! Of course, those who were the actual recipients of the good deeds were totally made aware of the miracle that had taken place in their lives, and there was no doubt as to where the miracle came from. There was and is so much deception in the world that we can understand some to be unconvinced regarding what is taking place right before their eyes. It was so pervasive that Pilate asked Jesus: ***"What is truth?"*** *The blindness to truth is present in all levels of society; the powerless to the powerful can and are captured by deception's schemes. It is only with the advent of the kingdom of God, shining its light into the darkness of the captivity of unknowing, that the reality of life is made clearly recognizable.*

Two beasts

Revelation 13:13-15 This second beast performed great miracles, it made fire come down from out of heaven to earth in the sight of everyone. And it deceived all the people living on the earth by means of the miracles allowed to perform in the presence of the

first beast. The second beast was allowed, to breathe life into the first beast, so that the image could talk and put to death all that would not worship it.

Being labeled a "beast" by the apostle John is not a term-of-endearment; it is alluding to the total absence of conscience, along with a desire to kill and consume in effort to satisfy its nature.

Before we can begin to understand what is being said concerning the beasts, we must identify the meaning of this designation. We know that the dragon (Satan) gave his power to the first beast, described as having ten horns adorned with crowns, and seven heads, and in this giving of power and deception he receives a fatal wound.

There are those who believe the beast to be the son of Satan, and the opposite of the incarnation of good that was found in the Son of God. The ability for Mary to become pregnant with the Son of God was made possible by the Holy Spirit. There will not be a miraculous virgin birth regarding the antichrist. Satan does not have the power to perform such a task; he is a spirit who was himself created by God.

We hear the mention of two beasts, because it is likely the first beast (potential world leader) had failed and received a fatal wound. Perhaps, it is then that Satan (the dragon) seeks out another, perhaps with the same promise of receiving the kingdoms (governments) of the world, that had been offered to Jesus. This second beast unites or restores the first beast's government (breathes life into the first beast) and therein these two world leaders combine to deceive the world with miracles.

And so, the devil does not have ability to directly cause conception within the woman who gave birth to the beast; but the beast will willingly worship the devil and in turn will rise to the level of dictator of the world. This is done by deception as clearly stated: ***"And it deceived all of the people living on earth by means of the miracles allowed to perform."*** *The idea* *of deception, creating a world leader, should not come to us as shocking; deception has always been the primary tool in the devil's evil schemes. In the antichrist, we have a person who has completely given himself over to worship the devil. People being deceived is nothing new; especially when people applaud the magic tricks performed by magicians. In many of the magic tricks we see performed, the deception is so great that it is almost impossible for people to figure out how the trick was made possible. Some of the tricks appear to us as miraculous! The kingdom of Satan will find manifestation, not only within a government that bears the title of dictatorship, but will also infect and find adherents to Satan worship throughout the entire world. I guess we might say the old-adage of, "The world is going to hell!" is a truthful prophesy.*

Hidden kingdom

Deception, confusion, damaging costs
Foul and flagrant, paraded, naked and forced
It's the heart made of lies in the kingdom of lost.
Searching for homes empty of light manufactured
in darkness deep in the night
Cages and snares, weaving of tales absent
is truth conscience or cares.
The hidden kingdom lurks, captures detours and
grabs it's filled with screams and Failure's lament
for all who deny truth and its strength
Are left in a dream 'til placed in the grave
Never knowing the truth that releases the slave.

Revelation 20:10 And the devil, who deceived them, was thrown into the lake of burning sulfur, where the beast and the false prophet were thrown. *GNB*

The evil concealed in the hearts of men always thinks it is secure from being exposed. When it is exposed it comes as a great shock to the prideful who think their schemes are invisible to others; they are wrong. ***Matthew 22:18-19 But Jesus, knowing their evil intent, said, "You Hypocrites, why are you trying to***

trap me? Show me the coin used for paying the tax." *Jesus saw into their corrupt scheme to trap him within his own words, and with his exposure of their intent he traps them in their own scheme. They sought to present to him a question that no matter his answer he would find trouble. They ask him,* ***"Is it right to pay taxes to Caesar?"*** *If he says "yes" he incurs the wrath of everyone forced to pay such taxes to Caesar; and if he says "no" then he has placed a bullseye on his back, inviting conflict with Rome. Unfortunately for these Pharisees their belief in what was hidden in their hearts, could not be discovered, proved to be false. After Jesus tells them to render to, "Caesar what belongs to Caesar and give to God what belongs to him," they walk away from him amazed by his answer. These so-called teachers and supposedly possessors of high intellect, found not just amazement in the truth expressed by Jesus, but they were exposed to the light that permitted everyone an inside look, into the hearts of those who live in the hidden kingdom of Satan.*

There were other times wherein those positioned against Jesus found frustration by the answers he gave; ultimately, they gave up their attempts to trap or trick him by his own words; they did not, however, give up their intent to rid themselves of him. Probably the most damning in the eyes of the religious concerning the statements of Jesus is his straightforward declaration that he was the Son of God.

The religious knew Jesus was a man sent by God; this is revealed in the conversation between Jesus and a Pharisee named Nicodemus. ***John 3:2 "Rabbi, we know that you are a teacher sent by God. No one could perform the miracles you are doing unless God were with him." GNB*** *They knew he was a man sent by God and still they wanted him dead. Jesus was a threat to the hidden kingdom that had found residence in the hearts of the religious. This was not a brand-new residency lease; there is a great history of men sent by God and losing their lives because of the threat they made to the established powers of the day.*

Luke 11:47-48 How terrible for you! You make fine tombs for the prophets your ancestors murdered. You yourselves admit, then, that you approve of what your ancestors did; they murdered the prophets, and you build their tombs. *GNB It is plain to see that the darkness inherent in the kingdom of evil is constantly attacking all that is holy and good. It matters not if the attacks come from the religious, hiding behind piety, the government whose footprint declares it has the best interest at heart for the people, or the individual residing in said kingdom, the objective in every instance is to destroy the truth originating from the kingdom of God. There is no place to hide from the truth. God knows all things hidden in the heart, and in the time of his choosing he will disclose the evil that schemed and planned against his children and his kingdom!*

Shocked

Shocked shaken surprised
Like deer in the night
Blinded by light
So too the evil of men
And the kingdom of wrong
Will find no hiding place
When the gavel comes down!

John:18-20 Whoever believes in the Son is not judged; but whoever does not believe has already been judged, because he has not believed in God's only Son. This is how the judgment works: the light has come into the world, but people love the darkness rather than the light, because their deeds are evil. Anyone who does evil things hates the light and will not come to the light, because he does not want his evil deeds to be shown up. *GNB*

Nature

A cat doesn't woof.
A dog doesn't meow.
A sloth doesn't run.
A chicken's not a cow.
Nature.

The wicked run from light.
The proud have trouble bending.
Evil plans at night.
The lie's a way of life.
Eternity's unending.
Nature.

Depression tints landscapes
Nighttime darkens sky
Mourning shadow's peace
Grief runs and seeks to hide.
Nature.

Man's nature can be changed
From "penalty" to "saved."
He can find the days called, "wasted"
When wisdom had-not say.
When truth found-not the spot
To shine a focused ray
Into the mind and heart
Permitting righteous ways
In these, the final days
In this, the final age.
The final lasting stage.
Nature.

Romans 10:9-11 If you confess that Jesus is Lord, and believe that God raised him from death, you will be saved. For it is by faith that we are put right with God, it is by our confession that we are

saved. The scripture says, "Whoever believes in him will not be disappointed."

What is impossible for almost everything in nature does not apply to mankind. We are given a choice with respect to who we will follow or to what we shall be bound. The goodness presented to us in the person of the Son of God, and the promise of internal peace in this life, and in the life to come, is for us to choose or reject. And then, there is the false hope presented within the overtures of lies, wickedness, and evil, promising power and riches in the here and now, and denying the penalty in the hereafter, is also a choice. ***"To whichever you choose stretch forth your hand."***

John 3:17 For God did not send his Son into the world to be its judge, but to be its savior. *GNB*

16

ROCKS

It is refreshing for us to understand all that has transpired in our life; while a good portion is troubling to us, it is up to us to place such troubling memories into the past and keep them there! If God is willing to forgive, why then should we not forgive ourselves? There is a time when we are no longer troubled by the memories appearing as falling rocks, or piercing arrows upon our consciousness, but, there is also a time for those same rocks of condemnation to strike us again and again. Probably the most troubling of memories are those wherein we incurred, missed opportunity to do good, to save wisely and to share more time with family. I like to think having grandchildren is a second chance for all of us who have at some point in our lives gotten lost in and among the weeds, that blocked our vision; and like a maze denied to us a proper escape from the poor vision incurred by unknowing.

It is one thing for us to have to deal with the internal condemnations appearing as specters from the past, and it is very much different when being condemned by laws of man and the laws of religious rulers. Just as the laws of religion will find acceptability from a portion of the population, there will also be some laws that fail acceptance because they are both biased and intolerant of others, who are perceived as falling into the category of "sinner" for not following the rules of the religious. Certainly, tax collectors in the time of Christ were not only denounced as heathens, but were considered among the worst of sinners; outcasts from society.

When there is an imbedded way of thinking that says, "We have determined that you have met acceptability to both God and the laws of men, because you outwardly present a righteous non-sinner appearance (clean verses unclean), and in this your acquired self-righteousness can pass judgment upon others." What we may then find is a willingness from the people to not only adhere to the laws of the religious but to enforce the laws; even those declaring a death sentence. While there were certain things under the law of Moses that afforded remedial action, and in this restoration, a level of acceptability among society was once again permitted. However, for the sin of adultery there was only one remedy; death to the one breaking the law.

Law

There are few times in scripture where we observe someone about to be stoned to death in accord and agreement with the law of Moses; and since it was the law, people were more than willing participants to administer the punishment; even when it meant the stoning was to the death. Adultery is a breaking of a bond and a vow to be faithful in marriage; a vow to both the wife or husband and to God. Should a man or woman be caught in the act of adultery the injured spouse might be the first to throw a stone, of- condemnation.

John 8:3-11 The teachers of the Law and the Pharisees brought in a woman who had been caught committing adultery, and they made her stand before them all. "Teacher" they said to Jesus, "this woman was caught in the very act of committing adultery. In our Law Moses commanded that such a woman must be stoned to death. Now, what do you say?" They said this to trap Jesus so they could accuse him. But he bent over and wrote on the ground with his finger. As they stood there asking him questions he straightened up and said to them, "Whichever of you who has committed no sin may throw the first stone at her."

Here, once again we find the religious attempting to trick Jesus; if Jesus says, "Oh, well, it is the law so go ahead and let those rocks fly," he would be placing the purpose of his mission in jeopardy. Because his preaching had always, up until this point, been reflective of the inclusiveness of God's forgiveness, and, if he tells them not to stone her to death, they would naturally find reason to become indignant, outraged, annoyed and irate; after all, the religious are the determiners and adjudicators of the law; they just might ask, "Who is this person who attempts to change the law of Moses?" Everything Jesus said and did, potentially threatened the positions held by the religious rulers. Because Jesus was so popular among the people it was very difficult for the religious to openly attack him; because of his popularity, and performing of miracles that healed the sick, drove out demons, and raised the dead the religious had continually tried to trick him into a downfall from popularity; perhaps, with the initial intent for him to be the subject of a stoning to death?

Matthew 17:24-26 When Jesus and his disciples came to Capernaum, the collectors of the temple tax came to Peter and asked, "Does your teacher pay the temple tax?" "Of course," Peter answered. When Peter went into the house, Jesus spoke up first, "Simon, what is your opinion? Who pays duties or taxes to the kings of this world? The citizens of the country or the foreigners?" "The foreigner," answered Peter. "Well then," replied Jesus, "that means that the citizen does not have to pay. But go to the lake and drop a line. Pull up the first fish you hook, and in its-mouth you will find a coin, worth enough for my temple tax and yours. Take it and pay them our taxes." *Here once more we find those pesky tax collectors diligently racking in the cash! I suppose a failure to pay the temple tax might have been a serious enough offense in the eyes of the religious to bring charges against Jesus and his disciples? Any defamation of our Lord would add to the effort to show to others an unrighteousness displayed in the overt failure to not support the working of temple operations. I love the story of Peter being told to go fishing, no doubt in Lake Galilee. It is in Capernaum that Jesus had his home, and it was* *very close to the Sea (Lake) of Galilee as it was called. What must have been going through the mind of Peter? Not only when he was told to go fishing for the coin, but when he found it in the mouth of the fish, it had to have blown his mind! Pow! I assume these tax collectors were a part of the religious establishment, ordained and blessed with authority to collect the tax. But they were no doubt placed into the same unlikable category as those collecting tax for the occupying army of Caesar. The distance from Jerusalem to Capernaum was approximately one hundred and twenty miles. Capernaum was located on the northern shore of the Sea of Galilee; it seems the tax collectors had a large area to cover.*

Capital sin

Back to the woman caught in the capital sin of adultery: she is being pardoned by Jesus and the collective conscience of the crowd, including the religious who brought the woman before him; and the reasoning for the pardon is, no one was found-worthy or innocent to pass judgment upon another sinner. Additionally, what we are seeing is the taking back of the authority that belongs to God; (thou shalt not judge). I'm wondering why it is only the woman was brought before Jesus? Doesn't it take two to commit the act of adultery? I suppose we can say the man involved in the act was not married, and in this technicality within the law, a loophole of escape was exercised, avoiding condemnation for the man? However, we do know that stoning to death of a man is not outside the realm of possibility as we see in the case of Stephen; he was lied about and ultimately stoned to death, as Saul watched the proceedings.

This capital punishment decree initiated by Moses had run its course, and it was now time to focus upon the love of God and the mercy he's offering. Certainly, there was perhaps a need to institute severe punishment once the commandments had been given to the people. Just before making the commandments known, the people had not only entered-into an idolatrous relationship with a golden calf, made from the gold they had carried off from

Egypt, but they were also adulterous! Being unfaithful to one's spouse and unfaithful to God (remember, idolatry is looked upon by God as adultery, disloyalty, infidelity, falseness, treacherous and betrayal), is a serious infraction, for the one who has declared love and faithfulness to another. Remember, these same people were subjected to the evil intentions of the Egyptians for four hundred years! The Egyptians were heathen in their fornication and very sinful lifestyles, included in the worship of their gods. There is perhaps, no doubt, not only were the slaves subjected and forced to participate in the lustful advances of their masters, but over time they (the slaves) found adaptation of such sinful lifestyles acceptable and understood to be normal occurrences within everyday life. And so, when they are finally freed and left to their own desires, unattended for forty days, as Moses went to meet with God, they partied in such a fashion that might have initiated the "death for adultery" decree within the law of Moses?

Just as those of us who have married become one with our spouse, so it is the process of committing one's self to God brings about oneness. Jesus, in this instance, (the woman caught in adultery), is showing to the group gathered to uphold the death penalty, that they also are in-need of forgiveness, and in this he had in effect done away with the law that was most rigid, unyielding, stiff and unforgiving; completely opposed to the message of God's love for all who will come to the truth Jesus presented.

The people admitted internally that they also deserved punishment for the sins in their lives; they were confronted with truth presented by their own conscience. Their own conscience may very well have declared to them: "You didn't get caught with your hand in the cookie jar, but you know very well that you are a sinner, and no better than the woman standing before you." The woman endured an openly humiliating situation, because she got, "caught" but the people standing in judgment of her had also been caught and made to understand, whether caught red handed or finding ability to avoid the clutches of condemnation in the here and now, a time will come for all sinners to be in the same position of this woman; in need of forgiveness.

Blessed not Cursed

The beggars, the afflicted by dreaded skin disease, those pronounced as unrighteous, the demon possessed, and all other outcasts of society were labeled and judged in accordance with the law. If an elderly person (for instance), was dependent upon the mercy of others to survive, it meant to society-at-large that God has denied to him the social security system inherent in having caring children to look after him in his old age. Those inflicted by disease were also looked upon as outcasts of society; the disease reflected, (again) in the minds of others, an absence of blessing from God, attributed to either the sins of their parents or their own personal evils. By Jesus healing the sick, feeding the hungry and casting out demons from those so afflicted, he is saying to everyone, "The mercy of God is extended, offered and obtainable to all!"

A completely different way of thinking is presented to the people, wherein they are made to understand, their inclusiveness. Truly, for those who had little hope, brought about by being labeled as sinners and outcasts or anything below the self-righteousness presented by the religious, the words of our Lord broke through the constant feeling of being shot by arrows to the heart and being bombarded by falling rocks. The barriers that were erected by some, were broken down and replaced with the forgiving love of God. How wonderful it must have been for those looked upon as outcasts and below the status of religious righteousness, to finally know who they are in the eyes of God and the value he has placed upon them? The internal revelation of this truth continues today!

No one able to throw a stone

In this instance, the presentation of self-righteousness by the teachers of the law and the Pharisees is unmasked for all to understand there is no one who is righteous, no one who is sinless, and all are worthy of punishment, because everyone is a sinner! Jesus shows to the people the love of God in the act of forgiving the woman, and he tells her, "Since no one remains to condemn you neither will I." He continues by saying, "Go and sin no more." Of course, she will continue to sin, as all of us do every day, but it's probably a good bet she will not be involved in adultery any longer. All have thoughts that we regret; sometimes we get angry to the point we want to choke someone we have judged needing to be choked; in this, we find the line between good and bad being crossed over into sin. This example of adultery is a most hurtful infraction of a broken promise, and because we are given this example we must recognize that all other hurts and insults brought to bear are also recognized by God as pardonable sins; but, we must also recognize not all sin is pardonable.

Jesus told his disciples, if someone causes a "little one to fall" it will bring serious judgment; described as worse than having a, ***"Millstone tied around his neck and drowned in the depths of the sea."*** *Additionally, Jesus told the Pharisees they could be forgiven much, but to sin against the Holy Spirit would not be forgiven. The religious basically declared Jesus to be evil, by saying, he had been given authority to command demons because he had approval from the chief of demons; and by saying this, they sinned against the Holy Spirit; not very bright of them! This attempt to defame our Lord would not be tolerated then and will not be tolerated today.*

Simon the Pharisee and a woman's faith

Luke 7"37-38 "When a woman who had lived a sinful life in that town learned that Jesus was eating at the Pharisee's house, she brought an alabaster jar of perfume, and as she stood behind at his feet weeping, she began to wet his feet with her tears. Then she wiped them and poured perfume on them." *Upon his arrival at the home of the Pharisee, Simon failed to greet Jesus with the customary welcoming and the offering of water to wash his feet from the contaminants placed upon the roads by the unbelievers in the world. The woman however, not only washed our Lord's feet with her tears but she anointed him with expensive perfume. Simon is thinking to himself,* ***"If this man were really a prophet he would know the type of woman that is touching him."*** *The* *woman was clearly repentant of her sins and when she heard of the presence of Jesus in the home of the Pharisee, she leaps for the chance to be forgiven. The interesting aspect of Simon's thoughts is the fact that not only did Simon know this woman, the type she was, but she knew Simon and had no trouble finding entrance into his home. So, let's do a little recapping: adultery will cost a woman her life but prostitution will not; and those who visit the home of the prostitute are also not faced with being stoned to death? Apparently, the law of Moses had made allowances for both the rich religious fornicator, the single common man and the prostitute? How convenient for those who are the guardians of the righteousness of the law? The hypocrisy of those in power will never stop the truly repentant from gaining restoration through forgiveness from God.*

Modern day Pharisees

I've said this before, there are many in today's church, that by their actions bring defamation to the character of our Lord; they do not honestly represent him and they must know they will not be forgiven. An example of this was up front and in my face the other day when watching television. I listened intently to what was being said by the preacher and was certain I had seen his face before. When at some point in the show of Christian expression, they identified the host, while he was seeking a donation and pow! it was like getting hit with a rock. This very same television preacher had been incarcerated for embezzlement from his former television ministry (I use that term "ministry" very lightly), also for the crime of rape; he spent only five years in prison. He still owes (according, to the computer search of his name) six million dollars to the Internal Revenue Service. So what's up with that?

I suppose he deserves another bite of the apple, none of us are without sin, but maybe, he should not concentrate on ministry? Ministry is a sacred and most precious authority given to those who received blessing from God; betraying God's trust, in favor of greed and lust, along with a mindset that one is above both the laws of men and the laws of God (sounds just like the Pharisees and teachers of the law), is idolatry personified! It is perhaps an unpardonable sin, just as the betrayal of Jesus by Judas did not find forgiveness. Perhaps, we can surmise those who pretend to be sheep, but are really-wolves in disguise attempting deception, these will find a very harsh meeting with our Lord at the resurrection to judgment? Do you think so? It was no coincidence that he (the TV preacher) and his current wife were standing in front of a painting, depicting Jesus with outstretched hand holding a rock. The title of the painting is, ***"He who is without sin throw the first stone."***

Name it and Claim it

The electronic church of today brings pictures of worldly success
Their doctrine proclaimed is always the same:
"Claim to your heart's content."
We have witnessed television preachers
dragged off to prison in tears
Not of repentance but lamenting the sentence
deserving the doctrine they claimed.
There was he who gave a deadline to
congregations both present and home
Proclaiming that funds must be raised
or God will cut short his days.
Still another displayed great emotion in a forum of public devotion
His doctrine failing the test of desires presented to flesh.
Don't be misled by this poem not all of them are wrong
Some may be first rate.
God never promised material worth
Not kingdoms or riches on earth
But for those who believe him
Enough to receive him
Lat claim to new life in rebirth.

Luke 12:15 Then he said to them, "Watch out! Be on your guard against all kinds of greed; a man's life does not consist in the abundance of his possessions."

We should learn to forgive ourselves

Now, along with all the insults and ultimately the crucifixion of our Lord, shouldn't we at least give some attention to the sins we have failed to forgive ourselves? Jesus, while on the cross never wavered from his mission of forgiveness for mankind. Both the thief and the soldier who crucified him were forgiven. Jesus told the thief he would be in paradise with him; clearly indicating his salvation was secured; and with the exclamation by the soldier, saying, ***"Surely this man was the Son of God"*** *at the death of Jesus, the soldier's recognizing-exclamation points to his salvation; since no one can say that Jesus is the Son of God or that Jesus is Lord without the Holy Spirit bringing this truth into the consciousness of the one making the statement.* ***1 Corinthians 12:1-3 Now, concerning what you wrote about the gifts from the Holy Spirit. I want you to know the truth about them, my brothers. You know that while you were still heathen, you were led astray in many ways to the worship of worthless idols. I want you to know that no one who is led by God's Spirit can say, "A curse on Jesus!" and no one can confess "Jesus is Lord," unless he is guided by the Holy Spirit.***

Finding salvation and forgiveness of our past sins, mistakes, errors, faults and slipups is a renewal of our self-worth, because God has shown to us the tremendous value he has placed upon us; so much, that he sent his Son to suffer and die in effort to bring to us the truth of God's love, and the eternal life offered to all who will accept such truth. We have the Holy Spirit and this knowledge shields us from the falling rocks of condemnation. It is the indwelling of the Holy Spirit that identifies who we are as Christians; it is not theology that unites and identifies. Neither, is it a certain brand of Christian identity, raising the banner of the cross; it is the presence of God in our lives.

Again, ***Matthew 16:15-17 "What about you?" he asked them. "Who do you say I am?" Simon Peter answered, "You are the Messiah, the Son of the living God." "Good for you, Simon son of John!" answered Jesus. "For this truth, did not come to you from***

any human being, but it was given to you directly by my Father in heaven."

In the same way, the exclamation from the Roman soldier did not come to him from anywhere but the truth given by God the Father. Bringing all this understanding into the present time we also understand that we received the truth of who Jesus is from above. It is interesting for us to see the denial of truth in the religious Pharisees and others among the ruling religious, as they had openly admitted they, ***"knew he was a man, sent by God because no one could do the things he was doing if God were not with him."***

At another time, when they tried to trick him they began their conversation with our Lord by stating, ***"We know you are a truthful man"*** *before they asked him a question designed to trap him. They had asked a question concerning the resurrection as it pertained to the law of Moses. The law states that if a man dies his brother must marry his wife so she can have children that will be attributed to the dead husband. In this question, the dead man had several brothers and all of them had married her and died; they then asked, "Who will be her husband on the day of resurrection."*

I must give it to those deep-thinking Sadducees, most of their designed questions meant to trap, would have probably captured most people; but even when they admit they know Jesus to be a man sent by God, and a man who is truthful, they still, could not put the puzzle together; or else, they did not want to put the pieces together for fear they would lose their positions of authority and immunity from the very same law they imposed upon others. Jesus ends their attempt to trick him by saying, ***Matthew 22:29-33 "You are in error because you do not know the scriptures or the power of God. At the resurrection people, will neither marry or be given in marriage; they will be like the angels in heaven. But about the resurrection of the dead-have you not read what God said to you, "I am the God of Abraham, the God of Isaac, and the God of Jacob?" He is not the God of the dead but the living.*** *The Sadducees did not believe in a resurrection to life, and in this one short statement by Jesus he points out to them, whether they believe* *it or not the power of God is very much present (just as in the beginning) to grant life to those who will believe. While there is not a defining clarity or clear picture of the resurrection given to us in the Old Testament, and not until the advent of Jesus did we receive such clarity, there is the pronouncement of such action by God.* ***Psalm 16:9-11 And so I am thankful and glad, and I feel completely secure, because you protect me from the power of death, and the one you love you will not abandon to the world of the dead.*** *Again,* ***Job 14:13-14 If only you would hide me in the grave and conceal me until your anger has passed! If only you would set me a time and then remember me! If a man dies will he live again? All the days of my hard service I will wait for my renewal to come.*** *Jesus takes the Sadducees to school, when he said,* ***"Have you not read what God said?"*** *They did not believe in a resurrection of the dead and they refused to recognize all the prophesy pointing to the coming of the Son of God, and yet, they try to trick Jesus with a question about the afterlife? I suppose they thought this question was one that not only would stump Jesus, but just might put to rest the belief in the resurrection of the dead and the life to come? They were wrong, as some people were brought back to life by Jesus, and ultimately it was Jesus who proved the power of God to raise the dead by rising and pronouncing to the world?* ***"O death, where is thy sting?"***

Ingrained barrier

When some say that they know or believe something to be true and then they fail to do exactly what was presented to them in the person of our Lord, we must question the manner, in which such knowing had come about, and the barriers placed into their thinking process, that prohibits them from actually-putting the pieces of the puzzle together? The best example of this was revealed to me by a Muslim friend, when I asked him. "What does your faith tell you about Jesus?" His answer to me was very revealing. He said, "We recognize Jesus as a great prophet of God." I then asked him, "Is it possible for a great prophet of God to lie?" He answered strongly, "No, a great prophet of God cannot lie!" I then had to ask him, "Well, if that is the case, why don't you believe what Jesus had to say?" This was the same condition confronting the ruling religious at the time of Christ: they said, "they know he is a man sent by God" and they said, "they know he is a truthful man" and so, there is no excuse for those back then and those presently admitting to the truthful status of our Lord. Apparently, the age old ingrained and stubborn position adopted by those in many of the religions of the world remains the same: "this is my truth and while I can recognize the truth in what you say, I will not move from the traditions and footprint of my faith that has been handed down to me (even if it is wrong)." Sounds a lot like pride and the inability to surrender, and give to God the affirmation of his truth, belonging to him; failure of the religious of our day is no different from those in the time of Christ.

Vast communication media

The hurled rocks appearing in dreams have meaning that can condemn or uplift; we should pay attention to what we are being told: ***Acts 2:17 "This is what I will do in the last days," God says: "I will pour out my Spirit on everyone. Your sons and daughters will proclaim my message; your young men will see visions and your old men will have dreams.*** *We know from scripture that we are living in the last age (the age of forgiveness). From this understanding, we can recognize that there is value in our dreams, that can reveal what is necessary to either understand or to be prepared. We see in scripture where Joseph had a few dreams that made his brothers very angry with him; and they plotted to kill him. Daniel had prophetic visions that up to this day lends understanding to the end time events that will bring about the second coming of Christ. The apostle John was also gifted, exceptional and blessed with mystic-like ability as he was given insight into the events of the last days.*

These examples, and many more are presented to us within the outpouring of truth contained in the bible. The most enlightening of all prophetic utterances are those relating to the advent of Christ into the world of men. It makes sense for us to recognize that with the advent of such magnitude there would have to be foreknowledge of his arrival. Certainly, we can understand if our country sends an ambassador to a foreign country, they would expect advance-notice of not only who he is, but at what time he would arrive. All of this has been given to us within the pronouncements of scripture.

And so, our dreams alert us or condemn us, or else, bring-to-mind various other thoughts we should pay attention too, so we can find the meaning in what God is attempting to tell us. Sometimes we are given straightforward understanding and at other times we may have to seek answers to interpret meaning of dreams, prophetic utterance and visions. Asking is something we should be accustomed to do; all of us learn to ask at a young age and develop a really-good ability to do so; especially when the asking is of God so that we can understand. Every awareness that we are privileged to attain is a gift that builds us up into a better person; knowledge attained will always add to the foundation of truth we have been given. All understanding does not necessarily come to us in our waking hours, but, for those dreams that trouble our sleep with condemnation from the past, making of us a target for rocks thrown without care, we have ability to cast them right back into the depths of the subconscious; a very liberating aspect of God's forgiveness! Amen.

Falling Rocks

It feels like rain inside my head.
Hail the size of snowballs,
Embedded with weightiness.
Pain inflicted, internal singeing of thought
Hurt and dread stealing joy replaced with loss.

Crying out to memories, "Go away!"
Doesn't halt the cascade of hurt sadness and pain.
Our failure to know what wrong would cause
While living-life captive and lost
Doesn't deny God's grace forgiveness and love.
Only the love of God and the price he paid
Clears the vision of times called, "yesterday."

We've learned to shower in grace
Cleansing the heart
In the downpour of mercy peace and love.

No longer troubled by lamentation's rocks

Meant to deprive, remove, replace and insult
The sacrifice of God's only Son.

Proverbs 12:25 Worry can rob you of happiness, but kind words will cheer you up.

John 12:42-43 Yet at the same time many even among the leaders believed in him. But because of the Pharisees they would not openly acknowledge their faith for fear they would be put out of the synagogue; for they loved human praise rather than praise from God.

17

EXCOMMUNICATION

The religious, during the time of Christ and the established Christianity of today have excommunication in common. The word "excommunication" means to place a person or group out of the sacrament of communion. In some parts of Christianity, it means to be condemned, or banishment of the person or group because of a serious infraction against the laws or rules within a given faith. We can see from the above scripture there were perhaps many who had believed in Jesus, but because of the Pharisees they remained silent; they didn't want to be excommunicated or banished from the synagogues in their respective towns.

Community life was centered around synagogue activity, and effectively if someone was banished from religious life, they would more than likely become an outcast and shunned by all; perhaps, including his or her own family. The dictates of religious rule were very heavy-handed then, and in some instances even today. Fear was a tool utilized to keep the people in line; also, it was wielded in such a manner to keep those in positions of power from suffering any loss of their grip upon the people they oversaw.

The people were completely reliant upon the religious leaders and teachers of the law for instruction, as it pertained to the law of

Moses. It wasn't as if every household had a sacred scroll, or was rich enough to commission the writings of the prophets; they, like many in Christianity in the early years of the church, were without printed versions of the bible. In fact, it wasn't until the fourth century that the books of the bible were officially accepted by the church and declared to be the undisputed word of God. Centuries of contemplating the content of many accounts of the life of Christ had undergone church scrutiny. Both old and new testaments were settled upon and accepted by the church as the definitive word of God. It was, during this time the New Testament was sealed by the Catholic church, in a place called Hippo, which was, located in Africa.

Therein we find there was considerable time spent in the sorting out of the tremendous amount of gospel accounts. Certainly, there was no hurry on the part of church leaders, to make available to its members the written word. In fact, the printing press was not yet invented and all manuscripts were produced by scribes; as such not only was it time consuming but completely out of reach for the average man or woman to afford. It is in this vein we find the ability of the Jewish church leaders, during the time of Christ, and the early Christian church (393-397AD) having complete authority and ability to interpret the scriptures as they are applied to the laws of Moses or the teachings of Christ.

It wasn't until later when scriptures became more accessible, did people begin to question church doctrine. When people are not permitted to express their beliefs or doubts in a doctrinal presentation, there will always be those who will prevent freedom of thought away from such questioning endeavors, by denouncing them as either heretics or "free-thinkers." Their only purpose for denunciating contrary thought is to remain in a dominant position over the flocks they were entrusted to watch over; and to also preserve the thought of the church being perfect in its teachings concerning the life and purpose of Christ. This doctrinal presentation of infallibility on the part of the church has in many instances proven to be wrong; whether it is the doctrine of "Limbo" or others that clearly are contradicted by the words, contained in the scriptures, there will always be those who will attempt to present such contradictory doctrine as superior to the content of the bible. When a person, even in today's understanding of the truth presented in the word of God, speaks his mind in opposition to church doctrine, in-order to uphold the truth contained in biblical pronouncements, those in the religious positions of authority will not relent from the position of church doctrinal infallibility. One example of contradictory teaching, that is widely embraced, is portrayed with the wise men believed to be present at the birth of Jesus. The scriptures make it clear they were not present at the birth; they arrived at the house where Jesus was staying approximately two years after the birth.

We have seen the cruel unforgiving posture of the religious during the time of Christ as it pertained to the stoning of a transgressor to death; and we have been told of the persecutions initiated by the early church against those who the church had deemed heretical, unorthodox, profane and sacrilegious, in both thought and deed. In all of this we do not find the love of God and the forgiveness gained in the sacrifice of Christ. The sufferings of our Lord and the pain he withstood in order to bring to us the truth was absent in the early church centuries, because of the ambitions of man; nothing has changed; the fear that held the synagogue congregants in check, and did not allow them to acknowledge the advent of God's promise in the person of Jesus, was also present in the edict called excommunication or separation of those who find a way of thinking, that is not in line with the teachings of those in positions of power over others.

In many instances the religious stranglehold, upon people's thoughts appears to be one not only of intolerance, but one that closely resembles dictatorial regimes of our present time. We even see this within the political structures advocating "political correctness" that is really a device attempting to sculpt the thoughts of the young and unsuspecting. Perhaps this is an attempt on the part of governments to create perfection in the human condition, apart from the only one who can and will bring back to humanity the lost aspects of perfection and eternal life? During the Inquisition, sectarianism, which is not much different from racism, bigotry, discrimination and hatred, came into prominence within perceived differences between denominations of religion, nationalism, class or factions of a political movement. In all these differences, there is found the desire of those in power to remain above the common man status. From such desire, the message brought to the world in the person of Jesus is lost, and is replaced by atrocities against all who do not think and believe as do those within the established power structure.

We can see the desire of those seeking power over others in today's fanatical religious quest, aimed at dominating and removing all who do not think and believe like them; this is very evident in the evil unleashed in the Middle East, and increasingly present elsewhere. It appears this quest for power over others and desire to kill all who will not acquiesce to their demands, is not a new effort in the history of mankind. Whether it is the religious rulers in the time of Christ, or those propelling the Inquisition, to rid the world of heresy, or those in modern times seeking to torture, kill, destroy and dominate, the motivations are exactly, the same. The motives are always absent the love compassion and forgiveness proclaimed by Jesus. Not only does evil have many faces but it is disguised in the robes of many of the so-called religious.

Power

It's yours to choose, tight fist or open hand
To demonstrate understanding of what belongs to man.
Upward reaching embracing all in sight,
finds power given by the Light.
Tight fist closed mind cold heart blind eyes
Searching for a high place where privileged children play
Games of kings and queens, alas, but for a day.
Tight fist closed mind imprisoned spirit gropes
Fails to bring the power the unknowing hope
Will gain for them an audience affirming world acclaim
Find their race for power has placed upon them chains.
Stone upon stone, lock upon chain, down
beneath deep, rock and hard place
Tight fist to the grave arrogance stays, on top
of the bones as decorative death,
Meaningless!

Matthew 5:5 Blessed are the meek, for they will inherit the earth.

Even when we find there were those in leadership positions (synagogue leaders) who believed in Jesus they were dominated by the religious rulers through fear of losing their positions, ***"for they loved human praise rather than praise from God."*** *I'm reminded of the words of our Lord, pertaining to those who love this life, "they will lose it," rings so true! This love of life that Jesus spoke of was closely attached to the precepts of the world, and not at all connected to the truth contained in the virtues of love compassion and mercy. The opposite of the virtues will always find entrance into a person's life, or a groups footprint, or political aspirations, when the goodness of God is stripped and tossed into a pile, labeled as an unwanted hindrance to the desires of those so afflicted, by the call for power position and greed! Everyone it seems wants to be on stage to receive the adoring accolades of praise from the masses; nowhere is found the humility that recognizes the dependency upon God for his truth. Mankind is continually speaking the words: "That is your truth, I have my own!" Wherever we find the motivations* *of the wicked and their attempts to dominate the truth of God, violence will always be brought into the arena of broken lives and disappointing endings*

Choices

It's a legacy of sin, in part
Everyone has understanding up front and in the heart.
We all have knowledge of right and wrong,
and therein is the choice
To declare, "I'll do what I want!" or heed his righteous voice.
In the story of heaven and hell, Lazarus had no complaints
He was secure in the bosom of Abraham for eternity of days.
But nothing could crossover to the "rich man"
In life, he received his reward.
In hell, not even his name remains.

What price is paid for power riches and praise?
A hefty price indeed! In hell, nobody counts the days.
Nobody finds praise. No one finds applause or a pardon from pain.
Everything is empty dark mournful and bleak
For those who sold their souls to a promise and a dream!
There is no rest from the specters hidden in a life lived in the dark
Continually mocking and laughing at those who failed God's love.
And no one can find the light that was offered without cost!

John 3:19-20 This is the verdict" Light has come into the world, but men loved darkness instead of light because their deeds were evil. Everyone who does evil hates the light, and will not come into the light for fear his deeds will be exposed.

Matthew 23:1-7 Then Jesus said to the crowds and to his disciples: "The teachers of the law and the Pharisees sit in Moses' seat. So, you must obey them and do everything they tell you. But do not do what they do, for they do not practice what they preach. They tie up heavy loads and put them on men's shoulders, but they themselves are not willing to lift a finger to move them. Everything they do is for men to see: They make the phylacteries

wide and the tassels of their prayer shawls long; they love the place of honor at banquets and the most important seats in the synagogues; they love to be greeted in the marketplaces and to have men call them 'Rabbi.'

Note: The phylacteries were the boxes containing scripture verses, which were worn on the forehead or arms.

Here again, we are alerted to the hypocrisy that was running unchecked and unabashed, bold, brazen and shameless among those placed into leadership positions overseeing the laws of Moses. They were indeed blind guides! In the words of Jesus denouncing their hypocrisy, clearly heard by both the crowds and his disciples (there's no doubt the Pharisees and Scribes were also in attendance, for they were constantly looking to find fault with Jesus) there is the underlying invitation to those steeped in the offerings of the world to find forgiveness for their serious transgressions. They were exposed, uncovered for all to see, made visible and unprotected by their outward appearances in-order to allow them the opportunity to gain acceptance from God; but they failed because, ***"they loved human praise rather than the praise from God."***

Finding praise for a job well done is not a bad thing; we do care that the quality of our work be recognized (especially in the work place). But to be lifted-up and celebrated by the masses, in almost an idolatrous fashion, is crossing over into the dangerous area of narcissism. It is the love of self that gripped the evil one and caused him to think he should be worshiped and adored; it is this same feeling that causes many a political leader to think of "his legacy" as if it is he who has really accomplished something. Many are they who fail to realize that no one is placed into a position of authority without God giving approval, for his purpose and not the intentions of the one in such position. There is a difference between being placed into a position that God approves and the arrogance of some who take possession of a position through force and fear. Also, there is the person who, while not powerful enough to take a dominant position over others, there remains embedded within the thought that they deserve to be in that position! In the end, they find disappointment because they can never satisfy their desires and because ultimately, they will find the judgment they so richly deserve because of the wrongs committed in this life.

Might

The Potter breaks the clay for the defect it presents.
The Creator will send injustice into flight smashing it to pieces
By the power of what's right.
The lofty pride of man the evil in his hand,
the hidden things of hearts
And plans produced at night, will be brought
to justice by apocalyptic might!
Run to the mountains seek shelter in caves,
Now, the latent isles thought hidden from his gaze
Reveal the foolish measures of man in his last days.
The Lord of all creation has called an end to days
Of thought without the heart and of hearts absent praise!
"Look to the heavens he comes upon the clouds."
His kingdom to sustain, O man of foolish pride, repent!
It's your life to gain.
Before it's too late.
Before the Trumpets sound.
Before the Seals he breaks!

Revelation 19:11 I saw heaven standing open and there before me was a white horse, whose rider is called Faithful and True. With justice, he judges and makes war.

Matthew 13:13-15 This is, why I speak to them in parables: "Though seeing they do not see; though hearing they do not hear or understand. In them is fulfilled the prophesy of Isaiah: "You will be ever hearing and never understanding; you will be ever seeing but never perceiving. For this people's heart, has become calloused; they hardly hear with their ears, and they have closed their eyes. Otherwise they might see with their eyes, hear with their ears, understand with their hearts and turn, and I would heal them."

18

CALLOUSED HARDENED HEARTS

Jesus teaches in parables, and the disciples want to know why? They are told that some people are meant to understand; those whose hearts and eyes are open, they will be given the secrets of the kingdom of God. Those who refuse to see will remain blind and those who will not listen to truth, will never hear the good news of salvation being spoken in a language that only the attentiveness of man can understand. It is the inattentiveness of mankind that refuses to venture beyond personal intellect; pride envelops and disallows understanding in many of those holding positions of authority; they were clearly missing the understanding given to the common man whose willingness to see and to hear was not disappointed.

In the teaching of truth contained in the language of parables, Jesus speaks plainly to the hearts of those seeking to know God and his truth, but, to the hearts that have become calloused, hardened, and toughened within the public arena of, "the most spiritual and knowledgeable contests," the inability to allow truth to penetrate the darkness, finds understanding-denied the reality spoken by Jesus. Their woefully poor eyesight (miracles being performed right before their eyes), and deafness (deaf to the shouts of joy from those who were healed), precluded understanding of their own need, and made entrance into the heart impossible to receive the salvation presented. For those who could not understand the meanings contained in the parables there was certainly no excuse for not recognizing the product of good contained in the deeds of Christ.

This recognition of those who will not see and those who will not understand, shouts to us the truth spoken concerning God's knowledge of those who belong to him, and those who do not. God knew us before he created the foundations of the world, and in this predestination understanding we can see, and understand the wisdom of God not wasting time on those who refuse his message! He makes it impossible for them to know truth, otherwise they would turn to him and he would forgive them. Because they have adopted an all-knowing posture cemented in the pride that disallows light's entrance, they will continue to become calloused and thick headed, cold and uncaring, concerning all that is not originating within their hearts of stone. There were times when those unable to see and to hear found understanding when they recognized the parable was directed at them.

Matthew 21:45-46 When the chief priests and the Pharisees heard Jesus' parables, they knew he was talking about them. They looked for a way to arrest him, but they were afraid of the crowd because the people held that he was a prophet.

There were parables designed to bring into consciousness the truth concerning Jesus, but once the minds of many who had desired to arrest Jesus understood that their hypocrisy was being placed on display, their efforts to rid themselves of Jesus increased. Within the parable of the, "Wedding Banquet" we find all those who had been invited to the banquet making excuses for not attending; they went to take care of their businesses or else they went off to work in their fields, and others returned to their home and mistreated their servants, and in some instances, they killed them. There was not a question as to who Jesus was speaking about within the content of this parable; and the common man also understood the implication of the truth exposing the cold hardened hearts of the ruling religious.

Many were they who already understood the deception living in the hearts of the religious, but they were afraid of the repercussions that would certainly be brought to bear upon those who would dare to challenge their rule. It is true that within numbers there is strength, and Jesus had drawn many to his teaching because they were hearing the very words that they were afraid to say themselves! When power is threatened, there will always be a repercussion against whoever is making the threat. Because Jesus was speaking truth, an overt attack upon him during the brightness of day was made to be highly improbable, because of the support he received from the crowds attending his gatherings. There is no doubt the religious went into a tactical mode of war while the rest of the world was asleep; they planned against our Lord at night, and ultimately had him arrested at night and brought before them. This trial at night was completely forbidden by the law of Moses, but lawbreakers and those who believe they are above the law will never pay attention to what the law requires. Jesus drew large crowds, and within the crowds there were those who heard his message and were gladdened; there were also those who heard his message, but refused to accept his truth; and then there were those who were so deeply involved with the darkness of despicable evil, that they tried everything imaginable in-order to stop the advance of freedom that truth will always bring to a person. There was movement in the population, outward and away from the darkness contained in the lives they were forced to live.

Hope was being renewed as people asked themselves, ***"Could he be the Messiah?"*** *Hope found reality in the miraculous healings and good deeds that accompanied Jesus wherever he went. The hopelessness that was found in the limitations of man, was being made to bow in the acknowledgement, that, no longer was mankind to suffer within the unknowing reality of the God who loved them.*

There were many in our present time who gnashed their teeth and suffered fits of anger, from the realization that slaves under their rule were going to be set free, at, the conclusion of the war between the states. Whether it is the individual being set free by the mercy of God or entire groups of people finding liberation within the efforts of man, the rejoicing is never a silent affair! Neither will those who object to the freedom that truth can bring, fail to wail in silence! Just as they were successful (initially) in the crucifixion of our Lord, and in this they thought themselves to be quite cunning, so it was they also found the truth unable to be hidden, and their lives completely changed by the advent of the resurrection. Truth cannot be hidden or silenced and can never ultimately be denied!

At times Jesus spoke plainly and directly to the people, warning against the hypocrisy of the religious rulers. He says to them that because they sit in the seat of Moses they must listen to what they say. But when it comes to practicing what they do, "don't do it." Everything they do is for show-purposes and is a grand play upon the world stage; they were in effect eloquently dressed dummies, put out on display in-order for people to buy into their outward presentation. This practice of deception contained in the outward appearance of those occupying positions of power, in both the secular and religious spheres of society, has not lost much of its attraction to the unknowing and easily led portions of the population; no matter where in the world they may reside. There are many, who still proclaim the right manner in-which to live in accordance with the laws of both man and God, but they do not practice what they preach! Hypocrisy has not left the condition of sinful man; there is still the desire in many, to hide in the darkness in-order to prey upon trusting hearts, for, the purpose of self-gain. Ultimately, some will not find judgment in this life but cannot escape the judgment of God; and some will find judgment in both the here and now and the hereafter.

Sooner or Later

It cannot be hidden forever
The heart that seeks advantage
Will always find dismay
Will always find a door locked shut
A path filled with broken dreams
A lost chance for truthful love
When desire sends a fake smile
The projection is seen for many miles
Ending in ruin and horrid, realized, callous frowns.

Proverbs 26:28 You have-to hate someone to want to hurt him with lies. Insincere talk brings nothing but ruin.

When we (those of us apart from the secular and religious powers) understand the full implication of the word, "ruin" we begin to recognize a need to avoid it! We can imagine a desolate scene, or, destruction as it takes place outside of our impact zone, but when we see such ruination being applied to our self, the loss is magnified in meaning; the downward spiral embodying such ruin and loss is made more recognizable when the ruin is seen in terms that describe perdition and damnation.

When those who are so deeply invested in the lifestyles that continually place everything and everyone else beneath their own existence, are confronted by the inevitable outcome for such self-centered purpose, they either find their reasoning in total denial, or else, they adopt a more calloused and hardened defiance against truth. It is this posture of non-surrender that places chains, and restraints upon the heart and spirit of those being led into the jaws of perdition; from which there can be no pardon.

Warning

Matthew 24:4 Jesus answered: "Watch out that no one deceives you. For many will come in my name, claiming, 'I am

the Messiah,' and will deceive many." *Again,* ***Matthew 7:15-16 Watch out for false prophets. They come to you in sheep's clothing but inwardly they are ferocious wolves. By their fruit, you will recognize them.***

We can tell the type of tree by the fruit it bears, and we can tell the type of person only by the manner in-which a person lives life. Just as the religious in the time of Jesus spoke the truth concerning the law of Moses, but inwardly they did not apply it to their own lives, so it is there will always be those who lie, so they can deceive others for self- gain. The words of Jesus to the disciples are just as true today as they were two thousand years ago; we are to "watch out" that no one deceives us. Can we be deceived? Yes, we can be deceived in many areas of life, but when it comes to being deceived in matters of the truth given to us by Jesus, we cannot be led astray like unknowing sheep. Are we expected to know everything concerning the teachings of Jesus? No, but we are expected to be aware of the deceptions in the world meant to lead us away from the truth we have been given at great cost.

Whether it is prosperity churches preaching the benefit of tithing, or the television preacher hawking miraculous healing water for those who will send in a contribution, what we find underneath all the pitches to people, the terrains, arenas and fields of play, is the recognizable dishonesty of those presenting themselves as being sent into the world, to continue the work of Christ, but are really preaching the gospel for profit. Profit in both the arena of wealth and the platform that gives to them a voice in the world already filled to the point of overflowing with deception.

Hurry-Hurry

"Step right this way folks.
Special dispensations indulgences allowed
For all who have the price
Cures for all your ills, peace of mind and light.
Do your limbs fail to function?
No problem we can't solve
We have the healing water
And no sins we can't absolve!
It is we who hold the power to permit or bind your faith
Hurry-hurry before it is too late!
It's not the age of faith but splash for cash we're hawking
Is your body weak and broken?
Do you want to walk?
Smiles are cheap my friend
But it's cash that talks the talk!"

John 5:5-8 A man was there who had been sick for thirty-eight years. Jesus saw him lying there, and he knew that the man had been sick for such a long time; so he asked him, "Do you want to get well?" The sick man answered, "Sir, I don't have anyone here to put me in the pool when the water gets stirred up; while I am trying to get in somebody else gets there first." Jesus said to him, "Get up, pick up your mat and walk."

Wherever people gather there is potential for corruption. Where the purpose for gathering is self-preservation, desperation or need, corruption's potential is increased in proportion to the motivating need. Thematic occurrences within scripture are the norm and exemplify for us our need to be apprised of the workings of God and of man. The condition of man is highlighted throughout the history of God's chosen people. Recurring themes, of corrupt behavior, rebellion, chastisement and judgment, signal for us to recognize our need for vigilance to remain faithful to God, and to ourselves as it pertains to motives prompting all our actions. Woven throughout the magnificent history that is the word of God, we find good and evil, success and failure, truth and deception, exemplified in those who have had firsthand tutoring from God. The behaviors spotlighted in scripture, having failed or succeeded, hold multipurpose lessons that will stand out as beacons throughout the history of man; even until the end of the age.

So many illnesses and so little cures; such was the time of our Lord's entrance upon the scene of humanity. It was a time of faith and hope. There was hope in the faith that had proved to be viable within those who sought a healing from God. Many however, sought healing in the prescriptions put forth by the religious; one of which was the so-called healing pool in Jerusalem. The conditions surrounding the healing pool had prerequisites that excluded both the indigent, and those who could not possibly race to be first in the water, when it was announced that the angel of the Lord had stirred up the pool. Additionally, men could be hired to carry those who could not walk; this was sanctioned work (carrying the infirmed to the water) being performed on the Sabbath; but when the man was healed by Jesus he was immediately asked, why he was carrying his mat? Working on the Sabbath? They had to know who this man was, he had been in the pool brigade for thirty-eight years! They weren't concerned with his healing, or how it was accomplished; they knew it wasn't in the prescribed and sanctioned manner, and in this they were whipping out the law of Moses?

There is much within the gathering of the hopeful that runs counter to the love of God. Certainly, God would not place such healing parameters, restrictions and restraints upon those exercising their hope for a cure; neither would he deny such hope when he knows a denial will break the hearts of those gathered before him. The Pharisees however, were not touched by the sufferings of those in the healing pool arena. Maybe they were offering hope to those who had no hope available? Perhaps they understood that a man's faith in God alone, can heal, and if given a visible motivation to place faith into, then perhaps some might find a cure? Or else, they found an area that would place them in greater light, when those entering the troubled water of the healing pool found healing and in such healing the reputations of the religious grew? More likely, it was all staged. Even with the inclusion of an angel of the Lord being instrumental in the race to the pool, there was never the compassion of God on display for those in need to see. Thus, the religious improperly represented the mercy of God within the who's quickest contest, and they no doubt were the ones who determined the winner!

Yes, we are warned about those who pretend to be prophets, and those who pretend to be sheep, not only for our own wellbeing, but for those who are in-need of understanding the ways of God and the ways of man. Yes, everything depicted in scripture is true, but not everything depicted is representative of a truthful display of honesty, especially within those being fleeced by the modern-day charlatans at the Jerusalem healing pool!

Trust

Who to trust and how much?
Family fails us at times and friends can be hard to find.
A multitude may produce one, but only if the one is not two.
We see the outer man and hope the inner man is the same.
It can get confusing knowing where to place our trust.
Contemporary faith is sometimes a bust.

Lord, may it come to pass
Knowledge of your goodness enter hearts of men.
Wrought from earth and dust within the flesh and sinew
The spirit bone and blood, within the light of inner halls
Make clear to us the way that we should call
Let all who draw near to you find shelter in your thoughts
And find the dwelling place bringing peace into the heart.
May sacrifice as Sabbath Bread be offered up as praise
And bring to hearts the nourishment that comes with trust in grace.

Romans 9:33 "See, I lay a stone in Zion that causes men to stumble and a rock that makes them fall, and the one who trusts in him will never be put to shame."

Reward

Matthew 6:16:18 And when you fast do not put on a sad face as the hypocrites do. They neglect their appearance so that everyone will see that they are fasting. I assure you, they have already been paid in full. When you go without food wash your face and comb your hair, so that others cannot know that you are fasting-only your Father, who is unseen, will know. And your Father, who sees what you do in private, will reward you. *GNB*

Once again, the disciples are alerted to the hypocrisy within their society that for some it is perhaps one way in which to stand-out and gain points in the most spiritual contest. They are also alerted to the fact that God sees everything that we may think is hidden. For those who openly desire to be recognized as fasting (or any other form of sacrifice), Jesus says that they have already received their reward; their objective was never to please God, but to gain notice and find praise for their fasting effort. Jesus says that God sees their hypocrisy and permits them their earthly reward; they have nothing more in the form of reward from God, since their effort was never directly toward God. Their motive for fasting was not in any way meant to be a gain for others either; it would be one thing to fast secretly, and what was not eaten is then given to the poor, without the "O my gosh, look at how much I'm suffering" presentation. In the same way if the food not eaten was presented to the hungry within great fanfare, the offering would also find the poisoning of hypocrisy. And so, what we do whether in secret or in public is always presented before God; this should always cause us to recognize, not only a lack of heavenly reward for things that are adorned with hypocrisy but we must never forget, while there is no heavenly reward there will always be a consequence deserving deception. If we develop a mindset that is always seeking to please God we will dramatically curtail any urges that are seeking the praise of men; this is called humility, and our greatest role model is the Lord. So much so that in some instances where a healing was performed by him, he had instructed the healed person to keep quiet about the event. Of course, they could not remain silent, and so they continually praised God for the goodness they had experienced. It is wise to have others praise you, and foolish to be found praising yourself! As such, when we recognize the truth of just how limited we really are (we can't turn one hair on our head gray), life becomes, not one of seeking accolades or praise, but one that speaks quietly and humbly, ***"With God all things are possible."***

Humility

Eyes of love, seek truth
Step up with open arms
In grace, leave lots of space
And God will take his place.
Serve with all God bestows
Then step back in him
Allow the healing touch of God
From Christ to common man.
Keep pride in the rear
Listen to the voice of God
Whisper truth foremost
Hear the chorus from the heart
Sung by the Holy Ghost.
Choose the way of knowing bliss.
Wisdom from our Lord is as a flowing breeze
It enters marrow flesh and bone and calls
To those who have not known, humbleness.
Take the place of least importance
Give not a thought to stars whose night charade must fade.
Keep always mindful of the lost kept blind by starlight's rays.

Proverbs 16:18 Pride goes before destruction,
a haughty spirit before a fall.

Salami Vision

The Monk approached his brothers
To tell of his intent, "I shall fast for Lent!
A salami shall be purchased its purpose to suspend
From the ceiling of my room, my resolve to test!"
After many days, his hunger did increase
And so, began the practice, to the salami he would speak.
He paced in little circles beneath the enemy displayed
And with pangs of hunger mounting upon his knees he prayed.
Many days of sleepless nights, and fanciful flights
To banquets of the mind, as aroma beckoned, "Take a bite."

The fast was almost over and his brothers
watched as admiration burned.
With victory shouts increasing: "A feast the Monk has earned!"
Upon Good Friday morning, they heard a mournful shout
And found the Monk of mention with the salami in his mouth!

Though your intentions may be righteous take care not to start
To hang around with salami that will tempt you
And eventually break your heart.

I Corinthians 15:33 Do not be misled: "Bad company corrupts good character."

2 Thessalonians 2:1-5 Concerning the coming of our Lord Jesus Christ and our being gathered to him, we ask you, brothers, to not be easily unsettled or alarmed by some prophesy, report or letter supposed to have come from us, saying that the day of the Lord has already come. Don't let anyone deceive you in any way, for that day will not come until the rebellion occurs and the man of lawlessness is revealed, the man doomed to destruction. He opposes and exalts himself over everything that is called God or is worshipped, and even sets himself up in God's temple, proclaiming himself to be God.

2 Thessalonians 2:9-10 The coming of the lawless one will be in accordance with the work of Satan displayed in all kinds of counterfeit miracles, signs and wonders, and in every sort of evil that deceives those who are perishing.

19

MAGIC MAN

Deception has always been the tool of evil and during the end times, will be wielded with such convincing revelation, that all who are destined to perish will be led to the slaughter like sheep. All who have been forewarned of this deception will not be drawn to the spellbinding false miracles displayed by the advent of the antichrist. In addition to deceptive magic there will also be evil, covertly present in the person of such power on display. In and of itself deception is wickedness, but the wicked one will have packaged the evil-intent within the unawareness of those being deceived. We have been conditioned to the reality of magic and tricks; pick a card and place it back into the deck or pull a rabbit out of a hat, all of which is deception. The counterfeit magic, false miracles, signs and wonders presented by the devil's surrogate, will not be presented with the unreal caveat, forewarning or understanding qualifier, that such signs and wonders are fake; they will be understood to be a new reality presented to mankind. This is a condition that overcomes the world's disbelief in the supernatural. In one fell swoop the world is transformed into believers!

The wickedness within those during the time of Christ demanded of Jesus a sign; a simple miracle that would validate our Lord. Jesus responded to this by stating, ***"It is an evil generation that seeks a sign."*** *Jesus continues by saying the only sign they will get* *is the sign of Jonah, and with this they probably scratched their heads thinking, "What's he talking about?" The evil generation statement is twofold: one understanding is that such a demand is made by a group of persons that are evil, and the other is that the thought to ask for a sign is a generation from within the very core of darkness. "Just show us that you have the power and we will recognize an ability that comes from outside the limitations of mankind." It does not mean that those asking for the sign would then become good and faithful servants of the Lord. Not at all, it would only alert the evil that it is threatened by the reality of God's intervention in behalf of mankind against the deception present in the hearts of those in positions of authority over others.*

The world will be ripe for deception (just like today) because throughout the history of mankind there has never been someone who declares himself to be the ultimate power; in this the reception of such a person will be made more palatable with the added ingredient of fear; the understanding of those presently enjoying top-shelf governmental authority, that, by uniting with the miracle-maker they will keep their positions! The world has seen many who have promised, "hope and change" but, have always failed to deliver, simply because the hoped-for change in living conditions was purposely never defined. Jesus came to us in the authority of the Father, and in this the humility of our Lord is a visible character trait that will never be found in those who think they are the ultimate existence. ***John7:18 He who speaks on his own does so to gain honor for himself, but he who works for the honor of the one who sent him is a man of truth; there is nothing false about him.***

There is a correct way to think and in this the conclusions made are also correct, (absent conscience condemnation). When we hear of another person thinking and reasoning in the same way that we do, we accept what he has spoken and find a degree of unity. Just as there are those of us who know the truth of God and the salvation offered through Christ's suffering and death, there are those who reject God and the goodness proclaimed in the teaching and actions of Jesus. The world is basically divided into three groups: those who believe, those who refuse to believe and those who know the truth of God but rebel against him. For those who refuse to believe and those who know the truth but rebel they will be deceived by the false magical miracles presented by the antichrist; in this they will perish along with the devil and all his rebellious demonic spirits. I should add, mostly all magic is deception but there have been times in the scriptures where what is depicted appears to be actual occurrences. Example: ***I Samuel 28:5-8 When Saul saw the Philistine army, he was afraid; terror filled his heart. He inquired of the Lord, but the Lord did not answer him by dreams or Urim or prophets. Saul then said to his attendants, "Find me a woman who is a medium, so I may go and inquire of her." "There is one in Endor," they said. So, Saul disguised himself, putting on other clothes, and at night he and two other men went to the woman. "Consult a spirit for me," he said, "and bring up for me the one I name."*** *Saul had previously "cut off" the mediums and spirit consultants (witches) from the land but now we find him consulting one, and he gets an answer from Samuel; from the world of the dead.*

We can look at this depiction of consulting the dead in two ways: one is to say the Lord permitted the witch to summon Samuel's spirit from his deep sleep, or else, there was an actual utilization of magic that was outlawed by God. In the eighteenth chapter of the book of Deuteronomy we find prohibitions to this practice: ***Deuteronomy 18:10-11 Let no one be found among you who sacrifices his son or daughter in the fire, who practices divination or sorcery, interprets omens, engages in witchcraft, or casts spells, or is a medium or spiritist or who consults the dead. Anyone who does these things is detestable to the Lord.*** *My guess is there was a crossing of the line drawn by the Lord, by Saul. Remember, this prohibition against consulting the dead was written before Saul was king. As such, not only does he defy God but he breaks his own prohibition! Here again we find those in power thinking they are above the law.*

It is interesting for us to acknowledge the death of Samuel takes place before Saul goes to the one who consults the dead. It is with this information that we realize the intent of Saul is to enter, into God's prohibition, along with the understanding that when all else fails (or appears to fail), the desperate will resort to any measures that will bring a desired result. Saul is a king and it becomes apparent there is little tolerance for those who do not respond in a certain manner; even when the one not responding is God. By his action to seek guidance from a medium/witch Saul enters a world of deception, fully aware that he is in total disregard of God's prohibition. It is also apparent that Saul values his life and position more than his relationship with God. During Saul's battle with the Philistines he loses not only his life but the lives of his sons. How true, are the words of Jesus? ***"Those who love this life will surely lose it."***

And so, we know that Samuel is indeed dead at the time of Saul's transgression against God, and we know that Samuel's spirit is "brought up disturbed" asking why he (Saul) had done this? Saul laments that he has basically no place else to go and Samuel reminds Saul that he had moved into the camp of the enemy of God! In this instance involving witchcraft or magic we can conclude that it is indeed a reality of the time in mankind's history wherein the prohibited actions had not only been common knowledge throughout the world, with respect to its ability to gain something, but it was a time when the supernatural was an accepted reality within the minds of humanity; because of this belief the spiritual principle of faith, (always returning a dividend) was found to be most potent. Unfortunately for Saul he is finding occupancy in the world of the dead in very short order! Perhaps because there was this faith present is such abundance, evil did not have to resort to deception, and perhaps at the time of the antichrist's advent such former faith will no longer be available, and in this there is a need for ***"false miracles?"*** *Just as modern-day magicians use things to enhance their performance, the hat for the rabbit to be pulled out from, so it was during the days of Saul. We hear that he consulted the "Urim" which is a prop or visible part, for a form of divination; when we have materials used in rituals we can safely guess, the practice had been one of long standing.*

We should be reminded of the spiritual principle, of faith put into action will always be rewarded with a response, as such, God does not permit us to use our faith in areas that can only cause us harm via deception. Saul's defiance against God found defeat and death not only from the Philistines, but he lost his eternal life by totally defying and insulting God! The irony of Saul's outcome is that he takes his own life out of fear of being captured by his enemy; what he was so fearful of losing to the enemy he lost through his own action!

In summation, faith is a principle part of the Christian life and permits action and power within the lives of believers; faith is also a part of others who are entangled by false gods. When faith is exercised in Christ the resulting outcome will always be for the good of the individual. When faith is exercised in those things that are contrary, opposing and conflicting to the pronouncements of God, the outcome expected can always be understood to be bad.

Creation's limitation

It should be positively clear to our understanding that within everything in creation we will find limitation. Everything to include the ability of those angelic and demonic beings outside of the natural dimension that we inhabit. For an example of this limitation inherent in the supernatural realm let's look at the Exodus rendering of the plagues God had sent down upon Pharaoh. In the first three miraculous events presented to Pharaoh (The walking stick of Moses turning into a snake, the plague of blood and the frogs), we find that the magicians in the court of Pharaoh duplicate the miracles. After which what we find is that the magicians could do no more; God produces the plague of gnats and they are no longer in the, "I can do everything you can do" game. During the intervals of the first three miracles, not only is Pharaoh emboldened by the abilities of his magicians, but he is walking directly into the plan of God to completely ruin the Egyptians. Pharaoh is emboldened by the power of his magicians. He believed they did not have limitation, and he is also made by God to be stubbornly unreceptive to Moses and Aaron's demand for the people to be released in-order to worship their God.

In this presentation of limitations in the court of Pharaoh what we find is the limitation of the gods they served; there's no doubt it's the demonic spirits who had rebelled against God and found godlike status in the ignorance of Egypt. However, when we look at the duplication of the first three miracles, by the magicians, we must understand that it is God who had set such limitation in the ability of his creation, and so, indirectly it is God who permitted them to compete in the first three innings of the game! In this game of "My god is better than your God," not only the magicians but the gods of Egypt are put to shame.

In the context of the false miracles displayed within the advent of the antichrist there will also be limitation to the power given to the antichrist (just as was the case of power given to the magicians in Pharaoh's court), there will be limitation of ability. Additionally, deception has an ability to go beyond the inherent powers of man and the devil's surrogates. Where the power inherently given in creation finds limitation evil will always utilize deception. Like a blowfish attempting to present itself as bigger than life! Unlike the blowfish that says to predation, "Look how big I am, do you want to choke?" The puffing up in both the natural and supernatural find a different motive outside of self-preservation. Pride is always attempting to separate itself from others, for the sole reason of wanting and even needing to be adored by those they deem to be of lesser ability. Within this context of wanting and needing and even forcing others to present to them the adoration desired there is always something missing in the one desiring to be adored; love for anyone or anything outside of self is always made to be a difficult trait to find. In the case of the antichrist and the devil evil has filled the whole of their being, leaving no room for love.

Paul's letter to the Thessalonians speaks of the return of Jesus occurring when the rebellion occurs, and after the man of lawlessness is revealed. Paul is not speaking about "a" rebellion but he is referring to "the" rebellion. It is well known that throughout the history of mankind there have been those who rebel against God, but Paul is speaking (I believe) of the rebellion that takes place in heaven and in the outcome of such rebellion the devil and all other rebels are thrown down to the earth. The rebellion has already taken place and the devil has been thrown down to the earth, but the man of lawlessness is yet to be revealed and the temple where he will declare himself to be God has not been rebuilt. These aspects must be fulfilled before the return of Jesus. The curtain is then lifted (for all of us with foreknowledge), and the devil institutes his plan to takeover the earth. Fortunately for him (the devil) there is someone who will accept the offering of all the kingdoms of the world if only such person will worship him. It is at, this time we find the ability of deception to be at its peak. The generation of today is being taught the most secular, earthly, worldly and non-spiritual fundamentals; so much so that when the supernatural appearance of miracles is made to be most convincing and undeniable the world will be converted to the one performing such false miraculous signs. Added to this is the desire of world leaders to remain in their positions of power, and because they also have been deceived, they will perhaps immediately add their voices to the authenticity suspected by the general population. In this unifying act, the thought of "globalism" present in the hearts of many in positions of power will add to the movement toward a "one world government." A few years-ago I heard a young man state, he considers himself, "A citizen of the world and not just an American." We find this mentality already present and attempting to find a foothold in Europe. The initial attempt to unify Europe was to bring into existence the "Euro" that was meant to unite Europe in the commonality of sharing in the erasure of the most basic of identities; a singular monetary system that does not identify a specific country, as did the Lire in Italy or the Franc in France, and so forth.

Whether knowingly or unknowingly the world is moving in the direction that the devil is hoping to bring into fruition. Unfortunately for the devil God has had his plan laid out, in place and arranged since before the creation of the world. Just as a watch maker knows all the intricate details of his creation, along with the timing mechanism set for a predesignated time, so it is God knows everything about his creation. The watch was not meant to continue working forever without the input of maintenance from the watch maker, and this is also a fact in the creation of life; without God's maintenance upon his creation there can be no continuance of life, no matter what form of life is presented.

There's another example of limitation within the creation of God, that hopefully will seal the understanding that it is God alone who is omnipotent, all knowing, almighty and supreme, both within and apart from creation. Once again let's go back to the land of Egypt, some four-hundred years prior to the demands made upon Pharaoh by Moses and Aaron. At this, time we find Joseph the son of Jacob had been sold into slavery by his brothers, interpreting a dream for the Pharaoh. Pharaoh had been informed that Joseph had ability to interpret dreams and he summons Joseph from his unjust prison sentence. Prior to asking for Joseph to interpret his dream Pharaoh had consulted with his magicians and wise men and is told there is no one who can interpret the dreams. Pharaoh tells Joseph, that he heard he could interpret dreams and Joseph replies by saying, "I cannot, but God can." It is within this statement that gives glory to God that we find Joseph given the meaning of the dreams of Pharaoh.

Where all the magicians and wise men of Egypt had not even a clue to the meaning of the dreams, we find Joseph being elevated from prisoner to the second in command of all of Egypt! Once again where the limitation of man and magic has placed a barrier, we find God triumphant!

Limited life

When we look at everything in the natural world what we find is a limitation has been placed upon nature. The existence is temporary, as Paul has revealed to us, all that we see is temporary and what we do not see is eternal. The question I'm asking myself is does this eternal declaration apply to those within the supernatural realm of existence? Just as in the creation of man there was not a limitation of life; man was designed for eternity; no disease or criminal act was (even) conceived that would threaten the lifespan of mankind. But with the entrance of sin into creation, all bets were off; limitation was married to sin and they traveled together throughout the ages. I do think that with the advent of sin manifesting itself in the supernatural realm there was also a price to pay, with-regard to the loss immortality initially granted.

Just as man was denied access to the tree of life and the streams of life giving water, so it must have been for those whose existence was dependent upon connection to the very source of life. Jesus clearly states to us that we do not live by bread alone, but we are also dependent upon every word that issues forth from the mouth of God. We are dependent in two areas, the physical and the spiritual. We must eat and drink in-order to exist in this duality of bodily existence and spiritual; we must also be nourished by the words of God in-order to continue our existence in the spiritual realm. Angelic beings are not dependent upon bread or solid foods or life-giving water; as pure spiritual creations, they are not subjected to the same dependencies as are mankind and all other flesh and blood creatures upon the earth. The words that come forth from the mouth of God are to be understood as conditions, that once, if not followed will bring about a limitation to the angelic beings as well. Sin is a corruption bearer no matter where it exists. Just as we have within our justice system penalties for breaking the laws of man, either life in prison or a death penalty; so, it is conceivable that God will also determine who is cast into hell for eternity and who, will be completely-destroyed; no different from the determination by our Lord that, "It will be better for some on the day of judgment than for others." Rebellion against God will find severe punishment to the individual no matter if the rebellion takes place in the corporeal or spiritual realms of existence. How we treat the gift of eternal life is what determines existence of the gift; continued as initially designed or derailed from the path of eternity with the entrance of sin into the packaging. It is written: ***"Fire and water is placed at your feet, to whichever you choose stretch forth you hand."*** *Again,* ***Deuteronomy 30:15-18 See, I set before you today, life and prosperity, death and destruction. I command you to love the Lord***

your God, to walk in his ways, and to keep his commands, decrees and laws; then you will live and increase, and the Lord your God will bless you in the land you are entering to possess. But if your heart turns away and you are not obedient, and if you are drawn away to bow down to other gods and worship them, I declare to you this day that you will certainly be destroyed. *We are given the choice of life, represented in the offering of water, and within the offering of fire the inference is destruction. The creation of God often denies its part in ruination.*

Example: A teenager is arrested for a crime and when he is brought before the judge, his parent pleads with the judge to "not ruin his life!" There is a complete failure to recognize the reason for being brought before the judge in the first place; it is the crime committed that has attached to it the ability of life-ruination; the judge just follows the law set down by higher authority.

Revelation13:15 He was given power to give breath to the image of the first beast, so that it could speak and cause all who refused to worship the image to be killed. He also forced everyone, small and great, rich and poor, free and slave, to receive a mark on his right hand, so that no one could buy or sell unless he had the mark, which is the name of the beast or the number of his name.

Forced worship

At this point in the advent of the magic man we find the world being told what must be done. As with the case of all dictators the choice is clear; "Do what I say or die!" I look at the present state-of-affairs in the world and find there is also a do or die proclamation expressed in many areas of the world. I see the people in North Korea forced into clapping and showing external worship for the present dictator, who appears to be the only one in the country with the designation of being obese! If we look at the religious rulers in Iran there is the unmistakable threat made to the populace that speaks of imprisonment or death for all who will not do as the dictators-demand. As such there should be no shock with respect to the demands of the antichrist when he declares all will worship him or else they will die! I can imagine the thoughts of the people when this occurs: "God Almighty never forced us to worship him, he gave us a choice; but now we are faced with certain doom, not only in the present but in the near-future at the judgment of all who refused to acknowledge truth, and the mercy being offered through the sacrifice of the Son of God."

Revelation 12:7-9 And there was war in heaven, Michael and his angels fought against the dragon and his angels fought back. But he was not strong enough, and they lost their place in heaven. The great dragon was hurled down-that ancient serpent called the devil or Satan, who leads the whole world astray. He was hurled to the earth and his angels with him.

This war that beaks out in heaven is brought about by the deliberate attempt to kill the newborn Son of God. It is this outright attempt by the devil to thwart the Salvation plan of God that brings about the war in heaven, and in suffering the loss in the battle the devil and all of those who followed him are hurled down to the earth. Again, this war takes place at the very birth of Jesus. John's account in the book of Revelation is looking back in retrospect and remembrance of the war, and when Jesus says that, "he saw Satan fall from heaven like lightning" he is also looking back at the attempt upon his life as well as the subsequent successive defeat of evil demonstrated in the victories heralded by the returning seventy-two! The Apostle Peter confirms for us the time of the war breaking out, by telling us that Satan is roaming the earth like a hungry lion seeking those he can devour; clearly, he no longer is a resident of heaven. The implication of the usage of the wording that speaks of those being devoured by the evil one, make clear to us that he (the devil) is no longer the tester in chief, rather he has overtly disregarded the prohibition placed upon him by God that he must not kill. When he attempted to prove Job to be a disloyal servant of God he (Satan) was told, ***Job 2:6 The Lord said to Satan, "Very well, then, he is in your hands; but you must spare his life."*** *That restriction is long gone as we can see the evil in the world has no regard for the life of mankind.*

The devil's initial attempt to kill the Lord Jesus was no doubt when Herod ordered the innocence in the place of his birth to be put to death. For two thousand-years the devil has been devouring all that he can with the help of the evil inhabiting the hearts of mankind. The evil that is in the hearts of mankind must be attributed as a part of the overall forces arrayed against what is holy and good. We can understand this a little bit better when we look at the time the disciples complained to Jesus, about a man who was casting out demons in the name of Jesus and they were upset because this man was not a part of their little group. Basically, Jesus tells them not to try and stop this man because ***"Whoever is not against us is for us." Mark 9:39-41 "Do not stop him," Jesus said. "No one who performs a miracle in my name can in the next moment say anything bad about me, for whoever is not against us is for us. I tell you the truth, anyone who gives you a cup of water in my name because you belong to Christ will certainly not lose his reward."***

Hurled

The devil and his followers are not dispossessed from heaven, they are hurled, thrown, flung, tossed and evicted with great force, and with great speed! So much for the big bad menacing devil; he is shown to be a very limited creation when he attempts to usurp the position of holy-righteousness. Michael and his angels make a quick dispatch of this pretender and all of those who thought they were positioned to not only deceive God but to (actually) defeat him. This is clearly the height of stupidity on the part of those rebellious evil portions of creation. But then when we look at the continuous portion of the world's population choosing to be criminal instead of law abiding citizens we are convinced of the inherent stupidity always present in the ones who find the choice of wrong a most inviting alternative to correct living.

Luke 18:6-8 And the Lord said, "Listen to what the unjust judge says. And will not God bring about justice for his chosen ones, who cry out to him day and night? Will he keep putting

them off? I tell you he will see that they get justice and quickly. However, when the Son of Man comes, will he find faith on the earth?"

As I have said earlier, the deception exhibited by the antichrist will be so great the entire world will be deceived. Again, because of the falling away of the reality of God due to the efforts of the godless nonbelievers to erase God from the vocabulary of humanity, we find the secular, worldly, nonspiritual and materialistic has placed all faith in mankind's dependency upon the self-sufficient mindset that permeates the world. As such the answer to the question asked by Jesus, is when he returns he will not find the faith in God in the abundance enjoyed prior to the increased attacks upon mankind by the Evil One before he was tossed out of heaven. The world will have lost focus upon the reality of God and when the appearance of perceived unlimited ability is presented by the antichrist there will be a shockwave of conversion throughout the entire world. Once world power is in the hands of evil the forced worship and enslavement of humanity begins. Even then when Jesus returns and the wrath of God is sent down upon the earth, mankind will not turn from wickedness.

The Woman and the Dragon

Revelation 12:4 His tail swept a third of the stars out of the sky and flung them to the earth. The dragon stood in front of the woman who was about to give birth, so that he might devour her child the moment it was born.

It is becoming apparent to us that the devil is well versed in the Scriptures. He has been awaiting the arrival of the Christ Child in-order to destroy and prevent the salvation heralded throughout the word of God and among the heavenly host. The audacity, boldness and apparent uncaring attitude regarding the judgment that he knows will come and destroy him is the height of stupidity! This is the height of evil! We see this today in the totally mindless suicidal events brought upon peaceful societies by the evil entrenched in the terrorism perpetrated by Muslim extremists, who either fail to understand they are directed in their efforts by the evil god of this world, or else, they are fully aware of the initiating motivation of wickedness to which they willingly serve their master? In either case, knowingly or blindly they are going to be judged most harshly and without mercy, for they had no mercy upon those they destroyed! Self-preservation is one of the most compelling inherent safeguards built into humanity, and what we see in the very base evil is an uncaring for self when contemplating the destruction of another. This uncaring is engrained in both the fallen demonic spirits and in the wickedness found in the ones who have decided to aid the evil-one in his desire to destroy the works of God. This wickedness is present in the evil they serve, he (Satan) has no regard for the harm he brings so long as he finds pleasure in the destruction set forth. Indeed, all of those who embrace evil know they have invited the judgment of God and it appears they don't care.

Once again let us look at the desire of evil to cause forced worship from those they have enslaved. ***Daniel 3:4-6 Then the herald loudly declared, "This is what you are commanded to do, O peoples, nations and men of every language: As soon as you hear the sound of the horn, flute, zither, lyre, harp, pipes and all kinds of music, you must fall down and worship the image of gold that king Nebuchadnezzar has set up. Whoever who does not fall-down and worship will immediately be thrown into a blazing furnace.***

What's immediately revealed is the desire of those who want to return to the time that had no mention of the God of the Jews. They rush to the presence of the king and tell him of those who refuse to worship the gods of the king. At this point I'm wondering just how stupid is this king? He has been shown without doubt the reality of the God of the Jews, by Daniel interpreting his dream and still he manufactures a ninety-foot idol and forces everyone to worship it, under the penalty of death; not just any death, but being burned alive in a furnace! There must be something in the water of those who willingly refuse to accept the reality placed right into the palm of their hands! Evil seems to always have the same purpose, totally fixed upon the destruction of those who will not bend to their will. No different from the forced worship of the image of the beast we see repeated in the book of revelation written by the apostle John. I'm reminded of the words of Jesus,

Matthew 6:24 "No one can serve two masters. Either he will hate the one and love the other, or he will be devoted to one and despise the other. You cannot serve both God and money. *I'm understanding these words encompassing "no one" to mean no one in God's creation. As such, when there is a conflict within the core of a person that finds preference with one influence over the other, eventually there will come a time when any allegiance to God will have been diminished to the point of nonexistence. This is the case with people who find the offerings of the world to be most attractive and in this desire to acquire such offerings, all recognition of service to God is placed into a category of hatred, because God has prohibited idolatry of both the world's offerings and self.*

This declaration by Jesus is no less truthful when it is applied to the spiritual creation as well. Those angelic beings who have chosen to rebel against the Lord in favor of the offerings of the world, have also found hatred for all that is holy. Initially is was a lusting in the hearts of the ***"sons of God" Genesis 6:1-4 When men began to increase in numbers on the earth and daughters were born to them, the sons of God saw that the daughters of men were beautiful, and they married any of them they chose. Then the Lord said, "My Spirit will not contend with man forever, for he is mortal; his days will be a hundred and twenty years." The Nephilim were on the earth in those days-and also afterward-when the sons of God went to the daughters of men and had children by them.*** *The "sons of God" translated from the Hebrew language is understood to mean, "angels." However, I must ask myself this question: Can a totally spiritual being marry a woman and have children with her? Everything in my reasoning tells me that is not possible; even in the case of demonic possession it appears to be highly unlikely that such a union would produce a completely different form of being. The Nephilim are described as the "heroes of old" and "giants." As such, there is the possibility* *of other worldly beings of flesh and blood having disobeyed the prohibition of God, and in their lust brought a debauchery to the world that God hated and found to be an abomination; in this the ensuing flood killed everyone except for Noah and his family.*

Hatred of God's creation upon the earth has wide ranging and serious consequence for all who have chosen to rebel against the one who ultimately will destroy all who have aligned themselves with evil. Every descriptive of hatred is in opposition to LOVE HOLINESS AND JUSTICE: Hatred, loathing, detestation, dislike, distaste, abhorrence, abomination, enmity, animosity, revulsion and disgust! With all this working against holiness justice and love, is it a wonder why those who practice evil do the things they do to the innocence of the world? Evil knows it is destined to be judged, confined and tortured; this is especially true of those demonic spirits. When someone knows the outcome of their existence to be without hope of change, therein the understanding of hopelessness breeds a "nothing to lose" attitude unleashing every imaginable act that shouts of hatred.

Hate evil

Amos 5:14-15 Make it your aim to do what is right, not what is evil, so that you may live. Then the Lord God Almighty really will be with you, as you claim he is. Hate what is evil, love what is right, and see that justice prevails in the courts. *The words contained in the above scripture are advising us to hate evil. In addition, by avoiding- evil, doing what is right and insuring justice prevails we will not incur the wrath of God. We will be added to the list of those enjoying life.*

Love is stronger than hate

Even when we had done things that were frowned upon by God and were wrong, what we found is the love of God had overlooked our ignorance with love and forgiveness. We recognized our wrongs and repented (was deeply saddened) and in this moment of truth we found salvation. We were blessed by the love of God presented to us in the sacrifice of Christ. In this act of being forgiven we recognized the immeasurable strength of God's love for us. It must be a terrible place to inhabit knowing there is no hope for forgiveness? The ultimate standoff between love and hate will take place in the final chapter of the book called, "Man." It is here in the very cryptic book of the Apocalypse we find the final chapter revealing the end of evil-wickedness and justice pronounced upon all who had mocked and disregarded the warnings issued from the throne of God. The devil and the beast, along with the false prophets are dispatched into eternal damnation. The warnings contained in the Book of Revelation are certainly falling upon deaf ears, in both the hearing of mankind and the recalcitrant wayward disobedient and unruly mindset of those within demonic existence. Who knows for sure what type of life-forms the apostle Paul alluded to when he told us of the enemies arrayed against us; not only the adversaries inherent in mankind but also the rulers and principalities of the heavenly realms? They may not all be of the purely spiritual category, but it should be sufficient for us to know they are in existence and arrayed against all that finds favor with God. As such it is important for us to always resist the enemy with all the armor of God. Resistance of evil, for us, is very possible; we cannot say the same for all of those who resist the will of God; they are destined for the lake of fire without any chance of being pardoned.

The End

End of philosophies causing blindness of the mind
End of policing thought that handcuffed the heart
End of the ignorance keeping mankind from God
Gone are the old ways where evil caused us pain
Never shall that day advance to show itself again
End of time itself that step by stepped the grave
A condition whose time has come
And now in-turn is slain
End of the cover-ups
Spin-doctors velvet scripts
End of the liar's rug
That caused mankind to slip
End of the Viper's tongue
A hiss that won't be missed
End of hands feeding man false passion
Of children captured by a whim
In this the end of days
Adulthood calls to man
The end of death, it brought to us such sorrow
Say, "goodbye" to yesterday today and tomorrow
Amen. The end.

Revelation 22:12 Behold, I am coming soon! My reward is with me and I will give to everyone according to what he has done. I am the Alpha and the Omega, the First and the Last, the Beginning and the End.

Not only is Jesus telling us of the reward for those who have remained faithful to the love God and hate sin doctrine, but he is also speaking to those whose reward is judgment! All things begin and end in him. ***1 Timothy 4:1 The Spirit clearly says that in later times some will abandon the faith and follow deceiving spirits and things taught by demons.*** *I must admit to myself that it appears that we are now living in those "later times." When we see wholesale murder of the innocence in the womb of creation, and the reasoning for such abhorrent permissible evil, one must conclude that the* *so-called freedom to choose, life or death for the child in her womb, is just a teaching meant to sidestep the pronouncements of God. Nowhere is the love for the child displayed. As with all evil we will never see the appearance of love! Compounding this so-called right to choose is the fraud perpetrated against humanity within the global warning theology. Yes, it is a theology, for it has been pronounced by the gods of this world! In fact, one of the gods has openly advocated for the reduction of the human population to a manageable level of about five billion people; this he believes would lessen the global warming threat and ultimate destruction of the earth. I'm still waiting for him to be the first to sacrifice himself to the theory of impending doom!*

Acts 22:25-26 But when they had tied him up to be whipped, Paul said to the officer standing there, "Is it right for you to whip a Roman citizen who hasn't even been tried for any crime?" When the officer heard this, he went to the commander and asked him, "What are you going to do? This man is a Roman citizen."

20

CITIZEN

A simple case of "whip him" turns out to be much more complicated. Paul testifies before a crowd representative of a city in uproar. He is accused of teaching against the Jewish people, the temple, and as an afterthought he is accused of defiling the temple, by bringing Greeks into the temple area. This last part of the accusations really brings home the attitude within a belief system that fails to recognize their own sinful state as corrupt and unrighteous, but an outsider's sin causes them the most concern? They carried this "contact with Gentiles" mindset to a level of ridiculous. So much so, that because they could not ban Gentiles from walking along the roads (it was believed the Gentiles had defiled the roads through setting foot upon them), they established ritual washing of feet upon entering their homes. Of course, one may assume that everything in the world was contaminated by those apart from the Jewish community. Talk about an obsessive-compulsive behavior utilized in effort to make clean through religious law, as if, sin was some sort of contagious malady that only afflicted those living outside of the law of Moses.

Everyone living under the law had access to remedial action should a breach in law of unavoidable contact with the unholy cause or trigger a ritual cleansing or purification rite. There was even a prescribed length of time for the offender to be kept in isolation to be recognized as having been purified from the infraction of law and/or worldly contaminants. It was as if someone caught a cold and isolation was mandated to prevent the contagious virus from spreading out and into the general population. I suspect that had someone recognized the common usage of air the fear of Gentile contamination would have been raised to screaming proportions or at least equaling the outcry against Paul. The problem with laws becoming ridiculous, is inherent through the compounding of laws that attempt to reach perfection. Imperfect man seeking perfection back then, and-now, it is achieved through recognizing one's own godliness, in a world that denies the existence of God. If the world can deny God it surely will deny sin. In-order to deny sin the world must do away with the clear distinction between right and wrong, and in the process, it must then deny the present existence of societal law (since wrong does not exist). Most imposing to the worldly declarations is the conscience that is unrelenting in its recognition of all things contrary to what is right.

Paul is literally carried by the soldiers, away from the uproarious crowd in effort to find out the reason for the unrest; and when they reach the steps of the fort he asks the soldiers if he can address the crowd? Perfect timing. Paul has the high ground afforded to him by the steps leading up to the fort. The high ground lends psychological advantage, a kind of superior position. The steps set him apart as are actors upon a stage. Unfortunately, some actors believe the stage to be a rightful elevation that has nothing to do with presenting a view for all to see. After all, platforms are in existence for the mighty, right? Paul is now elevated above the mob and he assumes the position of those who have always talked down to crowds. It matters not if it is a dais, a mountain pulpit or a milk crate, the result is the same for the one assuming the position of authority. Additionally, people have always been drawn to the speaker or the performer and they naturally find silence in-order to hear what is being said. Everyone wants to get close to the power, either through actual proximity or being set apart as is the case in a private balcony seating arrangement, offset to the sides of the theater, affording a status that demands recognition of position, that silently shouts to those in the common seating arrangements, "I am special." In doing so the powerful do not have to bow or applaud, they need only to seem pleased by remaining for all to see them

The soldier wants to know what is causing the uproar, and he asks if Paul is the ***"Egyptian who started a revolt and led four thousand terrorists out into the desert some time ago?"*** *It appears terrorism was alive and well in the near east then, as it is today. Paul responds to the soldier by stating,* ***"I am a Jew, born in Tarsus in Cilicia, but brought up in this city. Under Gamaliel I was thoroughly trained in the law of our fathers and was just as zealous for God as any of you here today."*** *Paul had just pulled out a big political gun in the mentioning of Gamaliel, who was very well respected for his wisdom, leadership and teaching within the Sanhedrin. When we read the book of Acts what we find is persecution of the apostles by the High Priest, along with his companions and members of the Sadducee party; the apostles are arrested and placed into jail, but that night an angel of the Lord frees them and tells them to go to the temple and preach to the people concerning this new life they have found. Of course, these same apostles are arrested again and brought before the same persecutors. There is a heated discourse between the apostles and those who wanted them to cease preaching in the name of Jesus. Finally, the heat of the argument reached the boiling point and in this the religious rulers wanted to have the apostles put to death. It is at this point we hear from Gamaliel.* ***Acts 5:33-39 When they heard this they were so furious and wanted to put them to death. But a Pharisee named Gamaliel a teacher of the law who was honored by all the people, stood up in the Sanhedrin and ordered that the men be put outside for a little while. Then he addressed them: "Men of Israel consider carefully what you intend to do to these men. Some time ago Theudas appeared, claiming to be somebody and about four hundred men rallied to him. He was killed, and all his followers were dispersed, and it came to nothing. After him, Judas the Galilean appeared in the days of the***

census and led a band of people in revolt. He too was killed, and all his followers were scattered. Therefore, in the present case I advise you: Leave these men alone! For if their purpose or activity is of human origin it will fail. But if it is from God you will not be able to stop these men; you will only find yourselves fighting against God." *Well it looks like Gamaliel was correct, two thousand years later and it certainly must be concluded that the apostles did not fail.*

The warning by Gamaliel takes place sometime before Paul is causing uproar. Peter and the others are brought before the Sanhedrin primarily because the religious rulers are jealous of the attention the apostles are receiving from the people. They establish themselves as men sent by God and will not relent to the wishes and threats from those who would silence their message of Christ Crucified. They are filled with the Holy Spirit and are equipped for not only every good thing but also to defend themselves with the truthful words given to them by God.

Both Paul and the apostles were faced with the same reality; people wanted to kill them! In the case of Paul, he is not only a Jew with a glowing religious character reference exemplified in the association with Gamaliel, but he is also a Roman citizen by birth. He didn't have to purchase Roman citizenship. There is the question that absent Roman citizenship would he have escaped Jewish intent and the whip of Roman education? Certainly, the Jewish rulers and the angry mob couldn't touch him so long as God provided protection, and the Romans would have no power over him even if he were not a citizen. Religious freedom as God intends is rarely, if ever present when the leaders are referred to as, "rulers." Humanity has a way of transforming shepherds into "lords" who refuse to permit or even acknowledge oppositional thought, even when they know it is truth being spoken. It is the positions of privilege that are coveted, and in-order to maintain such positions men have always found violence to be a useful tool in cementing the status quo. Dictators, rulers, men of wealth and power will always adopt and cultivate an elitist projection of important persona based upon the ultimate usage of violence denouncing opposition through the usage of force. Nothing much has changed in the history of mankind. Elitism will always separate itself from the common man by temple guards, bodyguards or any other means necessary to continue self-serving pursuits without the bother of reprisal. I have always thought that by removal of those things that isolate, the powerful will think twice before placing self-interest above all else. Therein corruption is sustained by the sheer presence of isolation from those voices who will speak truth, but have no platform to be heard. So, it was with Paul who enjoyed his position of recognition as one who was well schooled in the law, but now we see him transformed from Saul of Tarsus, hitman for the established elitism, into Paul of Christ.

This transformation of Paul presented a particularly irritant window of exposure into the inner workings of the religious establishment. He was like an accountant for an organized crime family; he knew where all the corruption was hidden. Even those who perceived themselves immune from exposure did not want their self-righteous image tarnished. Paul had enough of corruption and deception as a legalist. He found grace in truth and would have no part in silencing its radiant healing warmth. Truth is always a threat to those whose activities are hidden from public scrutiny. These religious rulers were not much different from their Roman masters. However, to be a citizen of Rome was to be a member of the winning team, and since he was now in the custody of Roman jurisdiction he claimed his rights as a citizen of Rome! (He was also a citizen of the Kingdom of God). Thus, the report by the soldier to his superior, ***"What are you going to do? This man is a Roman citizen!"*** *So much for the corrective whipping! Those words pronouncing citizenship, were like claiming diplomatic immunity. The Jews couldn't touch him and the Soldiers could not administer their usual remedy for those stirring up trouble. Here we find Paul addressing the mob from a position of authority. He is wielding so much authority that the officer orders the Sanhedrin to assemble for the purpose, of finding the root cause of the disturbance; what crime was committed? He (Paul) rips into the Sanhedrin with truth and finds himself continually being referred to a higher authority.*

He finds himself brought before every rung of the ladder of higher voice and position; the Sanhedrin, a governor and king, and finally he is able to present the truth of God's offering to mankind all the way to Rome, where he enjoyed two years of unhindered preaching in his own rented home.

One must wonder why the religious rulers were so adamant in their attempt to silence and accuse Paul of a crime? After all, they had previously attempted to silence the apostles and were unsuccessful. Were they now willing to face the consequence of going to war against God? Even after hearing the wisdom of Gamaliel the rulers had the apostles whipped. Unfortunately for the apostles they were not citizens of Rome, and when there is no one to oversee madness disguised as righteousness violence is unleashed. The powerful will never tolerate the word, "no."

Almost every influential person in the Jewish religious and secular arenas wanted Paul dead and they were calling in favors to see his death come to fruition. All who view themselves as having reached the top of the ladder of worldly success and those who are placed upon a pedestal for viewing (the religious rulers loved to be seen in public arrayed in their robes of authority), had failed to realize the top of the ladder is the most dangerous place because it is where God resides. They received the accolades of man and refused to give to God the glory he deserves. They failed to recognize God must be acknowledged above all things otherwise a fatal fall is certain. When man seeks to elevate himself to the platform of ultimate authority he will soon be faced with the law of gravity.

Only once during his interrogation by the Sanhedrin did Paul call upon the presence of God; this occurred when he was struck in the mouth during this hearing. After he was struck he retaliated by saying, ***"God will strike you, you whitewashed wall!"*** *Paul had not realized he was speaking to the High Priest and so he repented his words. It was perhaps a good thing for the High Priest that he did pull himself back from calling upon God to strike him. There's no doubt in my mind that would have happened. Paul's testimony* *before the Sanhedrin is so brilliant that he causes an uproar between the two parties. As such the commander of the soldiers remove him from the premises, they had become fearful for his safety. Paul had declared himself to be a Pharisee and the son of a Pharisee. He states that his belief in a resurrection of the dead is the reason the Sanhedrin is ganging up on him. The Sadducees did not believe in a resurrection while the Pharisees did. It was tantamount to the vitriol, venom, bile, malice and hatred we see exhibited between opposing political parties. And just like modern day politicians who represent themselves, these religious rulers failed to represent God! It seems to me that nothing ever really changes unless people (religious or otherwise), truly recognize truth in both the creation of all things and the one who alone is God. Unless the heart is focused upon God man will remain lost in the darkness.*

Arrogance

Unwillingness to yield to truth suggests
A fool dressed in ignorance
Passing through testing's temperament
With violence as guide
Will find the well of arrogance is (really) dry
Wisdom's scalpel cuts to view inside
God pruning his garden and discarding what he will
He keeps the wheat and weeds are fed to flames
Eternal is the fire that never kneels or wanes
The grave is found unyielding
Where many lost their name.

Matthew 23:31-33 So you testify that you are the descendants of those who murdered the prophets. Fill up, then, the measure of the sin of your forefathers! You, snakes! You brood of Vipers! How will you escape being condemned to hell?

Calling

To be called to serve requires God's strength
Such strength is derived
From truth love and majesty
It's understanding given
To see hurt hunger and poverty
It's the vision that comes with forgiveness
It's really a call to live in the Kingdom
It's an offspring maker
A birthright-stamp
A kiss for common man
A blessing and kind of frightening
You see, such a call comes from God alone
Transforming flesh and bone into
Kingdom priest and home.

Acts 9:46 He fell to the ground and heard a voice say to him, "Saul, Saul, why do you persecute me?" "Who are you, Lord?" "I am Jesus whom you are persecuting," he replied. "Now get up and go into the city, and you will be told what you must do.

John 7:28-30 "Do you really know me and know where I'm from? I have not come on my own authority he who sent me however, is truthful. You do not know him, but I know him, because I came from him and he sent me." Then they tried to seize him, but no one laid a hand on him because his hour had not yet come.

21

HUMILITY

The festival of tabernacles is a feast wherein the people looked back to the time they spent forty-years in the wilderness fully aware that God was with them and providing for all their needs. It is fitting that we now see Jesus attending the celebration within the temple courts, also providing for their need to know the truth concerning God. While his disciples went to the commemoration celebration openly, he (Jesus) went covertly because the authorities were looking to arrest him. Of course, when Jesus began to speak there was no longer the undercover Jesus, who had entered the city covertly. There was much whispering about his good deeds, healing of the sick, freeing those held in the grip of evil and other miraculous signs. The people did not speak about him openly because they were fearful of the religious rulers. They asked one another, **"Is he the Messiah?" "Isn't he the man the authorities are trying to kill?"** *In addition, many believed him to be the Messiah, they asked each other,* **"When the Messiah comes will he perform more miracles than this man has?"** *After much speculation, he is found in the temple courts saying,* ***"Do you really know me?"***

So much for the undercover Jesus, it is now within the temple courts surrounded by people hungering to hear him speak, knowing that the Jewish authorities were looking to arrest him, we hear

Jesus tell the crowd that they do not know him or the Father who sent him. The temple guards sent to arrest Jesus had placed their mission aside so that they also could hear firsthand the preaching of our Lord. They were so enthralled by his preaching they had discounted the urgency of the task placed upon them by the chief priests and permitted themselves the experience of learning directly from Jesus. People are still asking themselves the questions that permeated the air two-thousand years ago. Many of the doubters of our Lord have spread lies (just as back then), and some have even walked a narrow line by agreeing that Jesus was indeed a "great prophet of God." This acknowledgement is especially relevant in the Muslim faith, wherein they acknowledge Jesus to be a great prophet of God, but when asked, if this is your belief, why don't you believe what he had to say? Additionally, there is this account among the Muslim community, that Jesus was not crucified; they say, he was substituted by someone else and in this projected fallacy, myth, delusion and error they have found reason to deny the sacrifice of the cross? The entire account of the crucifixion of Jesus, depicted in not only the gospels, but in the writings of historians of the time, we find a complete denial of truth in those who will not look past their own accounting of events, that fails to recognize there was no Muslim representation in the entire world, at, this time in history! It may be that when the antichrist appears they will be first to embrace his deceptions as well? The bestowing of the title, "great prophet of God" begs the question, "Can a great prophet of God lie?"

When they answer no, we must ask why then do you not believe him?" But if they say, "yes he can lie" then it may be time they checked on the great prophet they have looked to for truth.

<u>No one can boast in the presence of God</u>

1 Corinthians 1:26-29 Now remember what you were, my friends, when God called you. From the human point of view few of you were wise or powerful or of high social standing. God purposely chose what the world considers nonsense in-order to shame the

wise, and he chose what the world considers weak in-order to shame the powerful. He chose what the world looks down on and despises and thinks is nothing, in order-to destroy what the world thinks is important. This means that no one can boast in God's presence.

Since no one can boast in the presence of God, that means boasting and prideful attitudes cannot be allowed anywhere! The omnipresent ability of God precludes everyone the ability to boast, since they are not the greatest in attendance! Whenever we hear in scripture of someone who has become confused by words of wisdom, we rejoice in the knowledge that God's wisdom was used to confuse the so-called wise, and in-turn illuminate the perceived unlearned or the common man. God confuses the wise so they can see they are not the wealth of knowledge they suppose everyone should account to them, because of their schooling or training. Secondly, God wants them to understand there is so much more wisdom outside of their cloistered or otherwise confined existence that cries out to them as well. He confuses the so-called wise and narrow-minded, elite thinkers, so that they who have constructed a high tower of worldly pride can see there is something more to amaze outside of their own intellect. In simple terms, it is God who wishes none to be destroyed, (even the so-called wise), and so it is we find Jesus teaching in the temple courts even when he knows the authorities are looking for him. A man known to have no formal religious training within the halls of higher learning, is teaching in a manner never-before heard from any of the known accredited teachers of the law, says to those who have a desire to choose God's will as their way of life, as their lampstand of righteousness and illumination, ***"Whoever is willing to do what God wants will know whether what I teach comes from God.*** *God's wisdom is always accompanied by humility in the one representing him. It is this facet of truth that spotlights the truth spoken by our Lord, when he states that he is the representative of God's will and it is God's teaching he is revealing. The one who represents himself is seeking glory for himself, but Jesus is seeking glory for God.*

As a boy, Jesus is found conversing with the elders in the temple courts and they are amazed by the wealth of wisdom contained in one so young. On the day of Pentecost all of those who heard the apostles proclaim the wonders of God accomplished by the man called Jesus, ask of themselves the same question concerning the apostles. ***Acts 2:7 In amazement and wonder they exclaimed, "These people who are talking like this are Galileans! How is it, that all of us hear them speaking in our own native language?"*** *This is basically the same question made by those hearing Jesus, at, this time in the temple courts,* ***"How did this man get such learning?"*** *The answer to this is that wisdom and all teaching of truth comes from God alone, it originates from the beginning from the mouth of God. Jesus says to the people,* ***"My teaching is not my own."*** *In speaking in this manner, he is giving honor to God. Jesus challenges those listening by saying,* ***John 7:17-18 Whoever is willing to do what God wants will know whether what I teach comes from God or whether I speak on my own authority. Those who speak on their own authority are trying to gain glory for themselves. But he who wants glory for the one who sent him is honest, and there is nothing false in him.***

Wow! This statement exposing the lack of humility in the teachers of the law must have had the chief priests running for the armory! By Jesus speaking in this manner, (giving glory to God), he is not only speaking to the intellect of man, but he is speaking to the truthfulness that all men know resides within their own hearts. Speaking in this manner awakens in us the understanding that it is God speaking directly to us on a level that cannot be denied internally. In the same way, Jesus spoke to all of those who wanted to stone to death the woman caught in adultery. He says, ***"Whoever is without sin cast the first stone."*** *This truth held deep in the heart of everyone is the same truth that Jesus reveals by saying, he does not speak on his own authority, but he speaks in the name of the one who sent him. Those speaking in a manner absent humility (perhaps unknowingly) do so not only under a cloud of suspicion that must accompany pride, but their spoken words have tendency to close ears and hearts, rather than to incur attraction to self-aggrandizing* *hot air. More than not we will be repelled by dishonesty and pride, even if what is being spoken seems to make sense.*

When man is amazed by the words of wisdom, never-before contemplated within his inner core, and the words spoken are from one who has not had the opportunities of the so-called "learned" he then must ask himself, "How can this be?" By asking this question he is then embarked upon the road leading to God. Within the teaching of Jesus (parables and straightforward speech), we find always present the emphasis upon humility and truth, without having to announce its presence to all who want to do what God requires; the realization of the truth spoken is automatically perceived. Jesus speaks to his disciples in this manner, ***Matthew 23:11-12 "But he that is greatest among you shall be your servant. And whosoever shall exalt himself shall be abased, and he that shall humble himself shall be exalted."*** *Again,* ***Luke 14:8-9 "When someone invites you to a wedding feast, do not sit down in the best place. It could happen that someone more important than you, has been invited, and your host, who invited both of you, would have to come and say to you, 'let him have this place.' Then you would be embarrassed and have to sit in the lowest place."***

This marriage between humility and truthfulness is as lasting as eternity, and in this understanding, we can see where humility is absent, especially noteworthy, within the context of the world stage, we can be assured of the absence of truth. Here then is the humility of wisdom speaking truth: Our worth originates in Christ, and in Christ God finds us acceptable and important. When man heaps upon himself accolades, seeks glory, and sets himself above others (others can also include God) he then may begin to believe his existence and self-worth comes from his ability to be self-sufficient, independent, and above the thoughts and hardships suffered by the common man. Within this self-assured reasoning, the flower of pride blooms, and from its root corruption finds avenue to destroy the rightful place God wants us to reside. This self-important attitude causes others to understand they are looking upon someone who is a glory seeker. Because there is so much glory seeking in the world, about as much interest in the things being said will amount to the excitement of being in attendance to view a silent movie made in the beginning of the last century! All the teaching of Jesus is meant for us to take a step-back attitude in effort to make us recognize the greatness of God. When we place God first (his rightful place), we are then removed from the worldly race for greatness, which is translated to mean pride, position, power along with their sister greed. Absent these worldly pursuits we become reliant upon God in the same manner the feast of tabernacles had represented to the ancient Hebrew people.

Humility

Make way for he alone is reserved the highest place
Serve God with all that he bestows
Deep within the heart and mind
And deeper still, the soul.
Allow his healing touch
To make a flower grow
Glory and praise are the things
That must be given.
Put pride behind, keep it in the rear
Listen to his voice
Whisper truth foremost
Hear the chorus in the heart
Sung as heaven's host
"Doing what is right and good
Is what God loves the most."
Choose the way of God
Welcome knowing bliss
As it enters, into heart
With strength of humbleness.
At the Wedding Feast of Christ
All will live in peace.
United then forever
Under banners truth and love
Humbleness is true strength
That needs-not primp about.

Proverbs 16:18 Pride goes before destruction,
a haughty spirit before a fall.

Crowns

Kings and queens of royalty
Of pride and vanity displayed
Of countless ventures, high atop
The common man arrayed
Will come to naught
When life is brought
Gentle to the grave.

Knowledge of our rightful place
Says, "Take these things away."
Humility transforms and calms
The rush of worldly ways.
May all the crowns
Kiss the ground
At the feet of Lord and King
He who holds head held high
Be humbled by God's grace
And enter, into paradise
To receive a rightful place.

Revelation 4:9-11 The four living creatures give glory, honor and thanks to him who sits on the throne and who lives forever and ever, the twenty-four elders fall-down before him who lives forever and ever. They lay their crowns before the throne and say, "You are worthy, our Lord and God, to receive glory and honor and power, for you created all things, and by your will they were created and have their being.

John 7:37-39 On the last and greatest day of the feast, Jesus stood and said in a loud voice, "If a man is thirsty, let him come to me and drink. Whoever believes in me, as the Scriptures said, streams of living water will flow from within him." By this he meant the Spirit, whom those who believed in him were later to

receive. Up to that time the Spirit had not been given, since Jesus had not yet been glorified.

Last day of the feast

On the last day of the feast (we are still at the feast of tabernacles) Jesus is speaking in a loud voice, inviting all who believe in him to drink of living water. As we have looked at earlier the Spirit given to us when we are born again is the Spirit of new life and assures us of continued life when the body dies. In the present state of most of the world's population this new spirit of awareness that convinces of truth in the words of Christ, and convicts us of our sins remains unknown. As such, the spirit of man is handicapped. No matter how smart or how smart others may think we are, we remain unknowingly wanting and needing the truth of God. Until our thinking is changed by the transformation made possible by the Holy Spirit we remain empty inside and like men in a land of darkness we are compelled to search for the offerings of the world to satisfy this spiritual thirst. We cannot satisfy a spiritual need with a physical prescription. The Holy Spirit (Streams of living water) is what's missing in our lives that makes a blind man see.

The feast of tabernacles lasted from seven or eight days and we must assume Jesus spoke to the people on every day of the festival. It must have been frustrating for those chief priests who wanted Jesus arrested, but because it was not his time to be taken into custody and because the people would have shown their displeasure at such an attempt, they (the chief priests) had to grin and bear it! I'm reminded of the time Jesus said he was thirsty while on the cross and everyone thought he was speaking of a physical thirst, but in truth, he very well may have been thirsting for the streams of living water which he had been separated from, as he took upon himself the sins of the world. What a magnificent sacrifice! Jesus offered himself for the sinful condition of mankind absent the fanfare of pomp and circumstance; no trumpets announcing the sacrifice; just the presence of humility and truth bearing witness to the love of God.

Evil's frustration and the abuse of truth

The frustration caused by Jesus speaking truth within the temple courts was probably causing severe acid indigestion, in those who have found their time for raking in the cash somewhat interrupted because of all the attention Jesus had been attracting during the whole time of celebrating how far they have come as a people since their hard times of having to live in the wilderness, within huts or tents. I remember as a child in Brooklyn New York, in, the neighborhood of Borough Park (a predominately orthodox Jewish neighborhood), the people would erect makeshift wooden huts on their fire escapes, in remembrance of the feast of tabernacles. I didn't understand it back then but it showed to me the dedication and importance of remembering all that God has done for us. As we look back on the celebration of this festival where Jesus was speaking to the people and we envision the hatred focused on Jesus by the chief priests (you really must hate someone to want to kill him), we can recognize that no matter where authority is threatened by truth those in power will always resort to violence. The insecurity of those in positions of rule over others was most evident in the desire of those who wanted Jesus dead. Jesus was also not happy with them as they had openly made their intentions known and flaunted their positions through the conversion of the House of God into a money changing and animal sacrifice exchange. Power over others is perhaps the most alluring and tempting of all the offerings of the world. Such power offered to the sinful condition of man, made manifest in greater expectation with the accompanying wealth associated with power, misleads many into thinking they can do all things a mortal man can conceive of. The allure of power is not much different today; the craving for political power and accolades received in the arena of worldly recognition are always with us when humility is trampled into the dust, in favor of the offering of the world. Many people know the truth of God but they have no voice that can reach beyond their own interactions with others. Should we decide to support another with voice, we almost always find disappointment when we recognize they are preaching the gospel of and for profit! The disadvantage of relying upon others to voice our beliefs in the truth given by Jesus, is very often found to be weakened by those entrusted with ministry, due to the allurement of the world catching and making a mockery of the truth of Christ, as some of these acclaimed preachers are dragged off to prison in tears.

Love is always outward looking and selfless

For some the desire for power does not always translate into a need to acquire worldly riches; but can also manifest itself in a desire to control others. This is of course one of the main reasons why Jesus is causing others to want him dead! No matter what a country's political structure may fall into it will always have those who do not want to release their grip upon the common man. Serving others without desiring accolades and applause from adoring fans and followers is a selfless and Christ like attitude. After all what else could be our real motives within the context of serving others, if not from a truthful desire to better the lives of those we serve? When love and desire to improve others is absent what we find is corruption and lies underlining the outward display of altruism. This was of course the condition of those within the religious structure during the time of Christ's ministry. Pride and the accompanying desires for acquisition always hold the potential for flash flooding, and drowning everyone caught in the eruption of anger designed to remove truth from the view of those held in captivity of lies. The impurity of hypocrisy and pride attempts to deceive and keep hidden the reality of those living in a land of self-aggrandizement. The riches and power of those in religious leadership positions were not going to stand for their corrupt motives being exposed.

All dressed up for judgment

Acts 12: 20-23 Herod was very angry with the people of Tyre and Sidon, so they went in a group to see him. First, they convinced Blastus, the man in charge of the palace, that

he should help them. Then they went to Herod and asked him for peace, because their country got their food supplies from the king's country. On a chosen day Herod put on his royal robes, sat on his throne, and made a speech to the people. "It isn't a man speaking, but a god!" they shouted. At once the angel of the Lord struck Herod down, because he did not give honor to God. He was eaten by worms and died.

Nothing is hidden from God. No matter what our thoughts may be, they are always presented to God, and in this show of prideful narcissistic admiration of his self, Herod finds the knockout punch of death administered by the angel of the Lord. The city of Sidon was one hundred and twenty-four miles away from Jerusalem, and Tyre was a bit closer. These cities were dependent upon Herod's continued trade with their countries. We hear that Herod is angry with them and they petition him for peace. The idea that they convinced Blastus, with reasoning, is probably not accurate; more than likely it was a bribe offered to him that ensured their addition to the listing of those who the king would honor with his presence. There was not an ounce of humility within the makeup of Herod. He was a ruthless tyrant who beheaded John the Baptist. Let's not forget he was totally devoid of any sense of morality! I'm attempting to envision the look upon the faces of those who shouted out the god like status of Herod, when, like the unfruitful fig tree that withered and died instantly, Herod is consumed by worms and when they had their fill he dies! He died after they finished consuming him; eaten alive! That must have been one heck of an audience reaction; do they say, "Oops, guess he wasn't a god?" Or do they slowly exit the throne room of the now very pride filled stack of worms? In this instance, we find the accolades heaped upon Herod were accepted by him and in this aggrandizement, bordering on worship we find the increasing of the worth of Herod to the status of divinity something that he does not deny. In fact, he probably gloated and basked in the accolades from those who were dependent upon his trade. We can safely say, "Herod was a fool."

Glitter

The flower of pride blooms and takes on
a color that captures the scene
Its fragrance, apart from the earth is neither wholesome
Or strength-filled like honesty of dirt.
Its roots seek to command,
Binding and holding the posture of man.
Denial of truth primping vision projected
Clear are the motives attached to pride!
The end is not cared for or left with, "goodbye"
Only the present is thought to survive.
Outside it glitters and plastic the smiles.
Designed to endear, external beauty belies
The content beneath the falsehood of pride.
Shined shoes, pressed pants, hat whose top is sky-high
Stands out in the rain naked and plain,
with truth the beacon that shines.
Awards from the masses congrats from kings, celebrity status
And all of it brings, not a day older or peace for the mind
Glitter of pride is commanded, "You too must die!"
In the order of things lofty and high, lowly and weak
Everything is accepted absent pride.
An ocean's volume and depth is unknown
Can only be fathomed by the Master of Storms.
The sun and the moon the universe wide
Were all made without the glitter of pride.

Proverbs 8:12-14 "I, wisdom, dwell together with prudence; I possess knowledge and direction. To fear the Lord is to hate evil; I hate pride and arrogance, evil behavior and perverse speech. Counsel and sound judgment are mine."

Wisdom hates pride, evil, arrogance and perverse speech. Perverse: "Obstinately or unreasonably wrong; refusing to do right. Or to admit error; self-willed." At times, I am so confused by the prideful arrogance of evil contained in those whose speech is contrived and corrupt. It is applauded because of their ability to avoid telling the truth! They are applauded for their ability to evade justice! What's more confusing is that the powerful know there is no consequence for them and still when caught they exclaim, "I take full responsibility." Sadly, when they are brought before the Ultimate Judge the consequence they avoided will seem very mild compared to the sentence handed down by wisdom. I suppose the arrogance of pride has convinced itself there is no one to fear; not even God? Big mistake.

Revelation 21:1-2 Then I saw a new heaven and a new earth. The first heaven and the first earth disappeared, and the sea vanished.

22

JUDGMENT ON THE INSTALLMENT PLAN

I am struck by the words of the apostle John, especially the emphasis upon a new heaven and a new earth. I'm not one who studies the heavens and have very little knowledge and (even less) understanding of what is taking place in both the heavens and the earth. However, there is one thing that shouts out to me like an avalanche of provocative thought: all the planets in our solar system appear to be without life. This absence of life leads me to ask why that should be? Certainly, everything in nature has purpose and I suppose we can say the purpose of the planets in our system are to show to us the marvelous handiwork of God? Perhaps there is unknown and yet to be discovered contributory aspects in the overall design of our system we do not yet understand? Certainly, such intricacies within the solar system are present with purpose other than to just show to us the wonderful creativeness of God. But then it may be our recognition of reality (God's handiwork), being so much more intricate, that it surpasses even the most famous of artists that have portrayed the magnificence in nature throughout the ages. Our view of nature is not a depiction but is the reality of God's handiwork on display for all to see and understand, with evermore awe as each piece of the universe is brought to our attention; the magnificence of quantity alone shouts out to us, and we must retreat from our observation simply because we do not understand all that is presented.

I suspect there is something more, in the form of ominous warning presented in the absence of life apart from the planet earth. Could it be these planets at one-time supported life, and did not appear as they do today? What I'm hinting at is the possibility that such planets were inhabited, and with the decline of the resident population's faith and failure to heed the warnings of God they found destruction, leaving only the tombstone of former existence? God is holy and what he creates must reflect his character; when his creation ceases to reflect his goodness the decline of life is rapid; rapid insomuch as what was intended for life to last throughout eternity. If the planets were once conducive to life, and in fact permitted life to flourish, what then could have happened? Perhaps it is the same dilemma that faces the earth today (a falling away from truth), and in time God will send forth his judgment upon the earth and all its inhabitants who failed to live in accord with the precepts, principals, teachings and rules of God. We have been given ample warning, not only in the words of scripture pointing to the wrath of God being sent down upon the earth, but it is perhaps within the visible absence of life we also find warning for us to ***"return to your first love"*** *and to,* ***"strengthen the things that remain."*** *These other worlds may have found judgment in the same way that the city of Sodom found itself eliminated from the face of the earth? In the pronouncement of John concerning the old being replaced by the new heaven and earth, what we hear him say is the* ***"sea vanished."*** *Evaporation would certainly be expected when engulfed in flames.*

We believe the word of God when it states, everything in nature will disappear and all things will then be made new. This is an awesome thought in both power and liberating recognition. Yes, just the idea of existence that no longer contains injustice and corruption is sufficient for us to shout for joy!

What's coming

Now, having looked, at the planets at one time being inhabited, and the obvious absence of such life today, the purpose of such planets remains unclear unless the former inhabitants faced an apocalyptic event. A progression of judgment is not unimaginable. It shouts to the inhabitants of creation; "Repent or else find the garden given to you uninhabitable." Just as Sodom was an example to the people of the earth, in the display of God's awesome power, so too it is for all of creation to take notice of the planets that no longer can sustain life. It may be that we on the planet earth are the last inhabitants of our solar system? Well, at least some of us recognize the end is coming to sin's influence; an end is coming to injustice, to the mocking of God and all that is holy through God's inescapable justice.

That there is life apart from the earth is a certainty, for we have been given the testimony from biblical pronouncements, as well as eyewitness accounts of alien sightings throughout mankind's history. However, it is not evident in the solar system where we reside, except for reported visitations from either angelic-spiritual (pure spiritual beings) or corporeal life forms. For the believer, there is no doubting the existence of either spiritual or corporeal beings as both are represented to us within the books of the bible.

We believe heaven occupies a place in the physical universe, simply because it is told to us that the first heaven will pass away and the new heaven will come down to the earth. Jesus was taken up to heaven in bodily form and his purpose (in-part) was to prepare a place for us.

The Sun

Another mystery to me is the sun. Like a great torch giving light and warmth to the earth we are told it is a continuously burning, erupting and immeasurably powerful mass of combustible matter; for want of a better explanation, a ball of fire. Even more mysterious is the known fact that there are billions of stars in our galaxy alone, not to mention the entirety of the ever-expanding creation of God, throughout the expanse of eternity! I understand for fire to exist upon the earth there must be temperature, oxygen and of course flammable materials. The meaning of the term "solar system" simply means that we are kept operational by the existence of the sun and all that it provides to the earth. The sun is classified as a star, and there are (minimally) fifty billion stars in our galaxy alone! The reality of what stars do, appears to me to be a miracle of combustion; and they are not everlasting. Science has observed supernovas wherein the life of a star has come to an end. It certainly takes incredible design to calculate the lifespan of a sun; especially when it is we who are so dependent upon our own. In fact, it is we who are in the greater context dependent upon the grace of God for our continued existence. Still, it is a marvel to contemplate the enormous calculation within the lifespan of our star. I don't know how a definitive explanation for such a magnificent display of awesome power can be determined by science, simply because of the great distance our star is placed away from us in the system. Ninety-three million miles away (93,000,000) is not a short junket; but then in comparison to eternity it is not even worth mentioning!

Why recreate everything

Revelation 21:5 He who is seated on the throne said, "I am making all things new!" Then he said, "Write this down, for these words are thrust worthy and true." *By saying, "all things" what we find is an all-inclusive statement encompassing everything in creation. The natural question we would want to answer is this: if all things in in our solar system are absent life (indeed all of creation) why then would God determine that all things must be destroyed and made new? It may be that with the advent, the beginning and the arrival of sin into the creation of God it made a lasting stain that required everything that it touched be made new, even the memory of sin will be made no longer to exist. Perhaps the only place of sin's remembrance will be found in the creation of hell, where all of those destined for eternal torment will reside? I can only imagine why the planets are awaiting a new creation, because if there was not a problem with them why would God recreate? There must have been a falling away from their original* *condition, leaving them devoid, barren, empty and without life? Yes, it seems to me that God would want to erase all things touched and consequently infected by sin; even the thought of sin will have been removed. Therein we can recognize the great chasm, gulf and gap separating all of what has been renewed from what has been retained from the former existence; all of those who have earned the judgment of eternal hell! The place called hell will be the single repository of such remembrance of sin. It is staggering to contemplate the progression of sin in the concept of encompassing the entire order of creation! What is even more mind boggling, is the ability of God to not only make new all his original design, but to remove any trace of the cause of its decline.*

<u>We are not alone</u>

I have come to the belief that we are not alone. Jesus said, ***"My Father is always working and I must do the same."*** *It seems to me that the work of creating life and matter is one aspect of God's work that is ongoing. It is only logical to recognize other lifeforms, to do otherwise would be to crown mankind with the mantle of hubris, pride, conceit and self-importance; and there certainly seems to be a lot of that present in the world today! It is logical to conclude other lifeforms would also be endowed with the good characteristics of God, and it is also logical that such others have also found judgment with the advent of sin, contaminating, infecting and falsely representing the one who created everything in nature; all life and matter! Therein we can understand that as such influence of sin had reached epidemic proportions, radical surgery was necessary for its removal; life was removed and all that remained was the emptiness of where once life had inhabited. Contained in all this supposition is the knowledge that nothing lasts forever, as perhaps, was the original design, but with the advent of sin the timeclock of life began to unwind. Nothing can survive except for what God decides shall not pass away.*

Signs of oceans past

Getting back to what the apostle John said concerning the sea vanishing, we don't know of any water being present on these planets but science tells us there are indications that they very well may have had oceans at one time in the past. Throughout the Book of Revelation, we hear of a steady flow of warning and subsequent judgment befalling the inhabitants of the earth. There is a continuous downpour in between intervals meant to bring acknowledgement to the earth's population, that they are in-need of reform! We see the seals that are opened and with each there is announced the impending catastrophic event that is visited upon the earth and the inhabitants. And then as if a drumroll demanding silence, a seventh seal is broken and the wrath of God is thrown down to the earth in the form of earthquakes and fire. We then see another announcement heralded by trumpets and each succeeding one bringing additional horror upon the earth. Again, the culmination of these announcements is heralded in the seventh trumpet's call, proclaiming, **"The power to rule over the world belongs now to our Lord and Messiah,"** *It is now becoming obvious to us that judgment is pronounced in stages, not the least of which is the plagues and the bowls of God's anger that follows the seals and trumpets. Having viewed this pattern of specifically increasing judgment, we can assume such incremental judgment may have been realized elsewhere within the expanse of God's creation, where the inhabitants had fallen into greater sin until finally God's patience and outrage had been provoked. Such incremental judgment is meant to capture the attention of those who are moving quickly toward destruction. We are told by John that even after all the horrors inflicted upon the earth and its inhabitants, mankind refused to turn from their evil ways.* ***Revelation 9:20-21 "The rest of mankind who had not been killed by these plagues, did not turn away from what they themselves had made. They did not stop worshiping demons, nor idols of gold, silver, bronze, stone, and wood, which cannot see, hear, or talk. Nor did they repent of their murders. Their magic, their sexual immorality or their stealing.*** *God has always given warning* *of impending doom, and so it may be that those living elsewhere within the expanse of creation may have also not heeded the calls to repent from evil?*

To the people of Israel, they were continually warned of their failure to heed the way of the Lord through the prophets; and even in the city of Sodom the inhabitants were given warning against attempting to corrupt the holy angels who had entered the city to warn Lot of its impending doom. The inhabitants of Sodom were struck blind when they attempted to take hold of the visitors. This should have been sufficient warning to the inhabitants of the city that something big was about to happen! The simplest form of second chances incorporated in the teaching of God is the renewal of our baby teeth. In this incorporation allowing for another set of teeth, God may be saying, "I will provide for all of your needs if you will but trust in me. If you will heed the warning of such loss attributed to the excess of uninformed youth, all other ancillary, secondary or auxiliary- support will not be necessary, for I have designed into my creation the longevity necessary for mankind to fulfill his purpose." ***Proverbs 22:6 Teach a child how he should live, and he will remember it all of his life."***

Additional purpose

Acts 2:19-21 "I will perform miracles in the sky above and wonders in the earth below. There will be blood, fire and thick smoke; the sun and the moon will be darkened, and the moon will turn red as blood, before the great and glorious day of the Lord comes. And then whoever calls out to the Lord for help will be saved." *Within this declaration by the Apostle Peter we see additional purpose assigned to the heavenly lights. It is an indirect form of communication from God to mankind, meant for us to heed their meanings. For those who heed the signs their salvation is made manifest. Additionally, we have found other meaning in the heavenly fixtures, for our good; the greatest of which is perhaps the prophesy that would announce the arrival of the Messiah into the world. The* *star appeared and they (wise men) were led to the land of Israel to inquire where the foretold King was to be born?*

Warnings

Warnings are not whispers in the dark. God does not want anyone to miss the events that are announced, because they are important! And so, we find a heralding in prophetic utterances materializing in the heavens, as either good news (the birth of Jesus), or else, we find warnings of impending judgment. In all aspects of prophetic fulfillment or warning we find God has not hidden his intention for mankind. There are no favorites in the plan of God for the salvation of mankind. It is written, ***Hebrews 3:15 "If you hear God's voice today, do not be stubborn as your ancestors were when they rebelled against God."*** *So many voices and signs and still the world is deaf and blind. What will it take to awaken mankind from his stupor? Has the wall of pride been built so high that even the majestic handiwork of God is cast off as so much accidental occurrence?* ***Hebrews 2:7-8 You made him for a little while lower than the angels; you crowned him with glory and honor, and made him ruler over all things."*** *This scripture quote is referring to mankind, and is pointing to how powerless we have become! Man cannot even take control of himself, let alone rule over all things! Let us heed the vocal signs displayed in the heavens in-order to live in freedom and gain eternal life!*

Warning

I admit, I don't hold all the pieces of the puzzle.
Some things are kept hidden from my sight.
The sun moon and spheres all appear so bright.
Why is there no life?
Could it be, sometime past footprints dotted Mars?
Did Saturn spin a different way, were roads built for cars?
Could Jupiter be found with excavation lines"
Did planes speed across its sky?
All within creation will find upward and then down
Some will find eternity and others wear a frown.
Disconnection from the one who made us all
Finds incremental judgment knocking on the door.
I see it plain and clear within solar system's light
The planets hang as globes but
Absent is the laughter that comes from joyful life.
A giant jigsaw puzzle moving dot to dot
What was and is to come has definition not.
Conjecture is a trying thing like intended sport
It takes us up and down the field and sometimes truth is scored.
The mind of man was made for playful thought.
Imagine this or that and see where it leads and ends
A rabbit's hole mysterious filled with twists and bends.
It would be nice to understand why the planets seem to stare
Lifeless as a statue, saying, "There's nothing living here."

Revelation 11"1-3 I was given a stick that looked like a measuring rod, and was told, "Go and measure the temple of God and the altar, and count those worshiping there. But do not measure the outer courts, because they have been given to the heathen, who will trample on the Holy City for forty-two months. I will send two witnesses dressed in sackcloth, and they will proclaim God's message during those 1,260 days."

It appears God has not left anything to chance. Not only are we given heavenly signs and wonders but we are given warning from the two-witnesses proclaiming God's message for mankind to turn from his wicked ways. Throughout the history of mankind, we find direct intervention by the hand of God into the affairs of man, when the conditions reach outcry proportions. These can represent to us both God's love of his creation and incremental desire in the form of chastisement, to capture our disbelief and return us to the place of God's initial intent for man. Ultimately the total-destruction of the planet and all of creation will come to pass and then be made new. This is a previously determined fact pronounced by the word of God. Just as the Lord did not hide from Abraham what he was about to do to the city of Sodom, so it is on a grander scale he does not hide his intent for creation. It is up to us to listen to truth and heed the warning of the coming storms.

Signs

So many signs and voices and still the world is blind.
It's an amazing thing, even in today's light.
We have leaders speaking lies and scandals day and night
And still some people think their voices will not lie?
Woe to you for bowing to gods of gold and cash
Of idols made of stone and statues made of brass
For worship at the altar of murder, magic, lust,
Indeed, your bones shall rot and no longer will you strut!

With the world's deceptive-tactics it appears easy to hide truth.
A cannon blast of truth will not turn a head
It will not make a path away from wrong or wickedness
If it's cold and dark and mind and heart are dead.
Even when the heavens bleed and thick smoke fills the air
When the sun and moon are darkened, when fire spreads like flares
When the moon's blood-soaked eye has a vacant stare
Still, they will not listen to the signs and wonders clear.
"Turn away from wicked ways judgment day has come
In this the end of days there's no place to hide or run!"

Revelation 13:1-4 Then I saw a beast coming up out of the sea. It had ten horns and seven heads, each of its horns was a crown, and on each of its heads was a name that was insulting to God.

The beast looked like a leopard, with feet like a bears-feet and a mouth like a lion's mouth. The dragon gave the beast its power, his throne, and his vast authority. One of the heads of the beast seemed to have been fatally wounded, but the wound had healed. The whole earth was amazed and followed the beast. Everyone worshipped the dragon because he has given his authority to the beast. *GNB*

It is amazing to me that when the beast displays false signs and wonders the whole world is instantly converted to worshiping the beast! This is not a new-phenomena simply because history has a way of repeating itself. With all the plagues and miracles set loose upon the Egyptians for failing to free the people of God, they still needed to be destroyed in-order for the message from God to sink in and cause them to relent. Now, it is one thing when the magicians in the court of Pharaoh, showed their power in the usage of magic with help from the demonic gods they worshipped, and once their magic reached its limitation they had to let God's people go. But within the end time judgment what we find is a total recalcitrant, wayward, disobedient, unruly and intractable stubbornness has invaded the hearts of mankind; so much so that just as the city of Sodom was unmovable in its sinful display of arrogance toward God, so it will be for the world at the time of judgment.

Ecclesiastes 9:4 But anyone who is alive in the world of the living has hope; a live dog is better off than a dead lion."

23

LIVE DOG DEAD LION

The words of the "Philosopher" tell us of the hope that should be present in all those alive in the world of the living. Even within the most desperate of times and circumstances there will always be hope in deliverance from such conditions. It, doesn't matter, whether rich or poor servant or king, we are called upon to be mindful of death. Within today's understanding of salvation available to those who will receive the offering in the sacrifice of the Son of God, the hope of eternal life is the greatest hope ever presented to mankind!

Hope is not a forever aspect, feature or part of our lives; we don't hope for what we can see, for what has been realized is no longer hope, it has become reality. Hope is present for us, when what is hoped for has not materialized. We can hope for the things of the world and to be delivered from the hardships that constantly seem to appear without notice, and when they appear we hope they have a short-lived life. Or else, we may hope for the ultimate appearance in the second coming of Christ. All hope falls into basically two different categories; good, upright moral and virtuous, and bad. For those of us who have received God's grace through Christ's sacrifice we know of the reality presented to us. There is no hope available for the inhabitants of the world of the dead. While alive in our body, no matter, rich or poor ruler or slave, there is the offering of hope to all who will recognize the offering.

All hope for eternal life is offered to those alive in the land of the living. Live dog (what the world considers to be nothing), or lions, those on the top of society's ladder, eat what they will and suffer little if any consequence for infractions against the laws of man. Those who have died in the hope of life, (those who have embraced and accepted truth), after the body has died, are rewarded for their recognition of the truth presented to them, in, salvation received while in the land of the living; they will not be disappointed. For those who do not have such hope in the life to come, it must be a terrible burden when they believe they shall be separated from those they love forever! I'm not sure they have thought of this aspect of disbelief, hopelessness and desperateness that must be accompanied by despair, for, if they had thought about the condition they have embraced, they just might want to look at those who have received not only the hoped for offering of eternal life but have been blessed in the knowledge, that those we love and who love us will continue our bond throughout eternity! What may be most pressing on the minds of those aged, old and elderly lions, might be the nagging reality that they cannot take their riches with them; a mountain of gold will not purchase another beat of the heart.

THE BETTER END

Cling not to me endurance friend
For gray the hairs upon my head
Point clearly to a better end.

Holdfast not days of youth
It's better now with nuisance aches
Better now at reduced pace
Much better now with love and grace.

O flesh and bone, to no avail or reward your moan
Conformity is right, with hands upraised to God in praise
Hope's goodness ability and promise is in sight
And all our cares are washed away
By the promises of Christ.

Ecclesiastes 7:1 A good name is better than precious ointment, and the day of death is better than the day of one's birth.

John 5:25 "I am telling you the truth: the time is coming-the time has already come-when the dead will hear the voice of the Son of God, and those who hear it will come to life." *While we are alive in this body without the knowledge of salvation pulsing within our veins, we are a part of the walking dead. This understanding is made clear to us in the words of Jesus when one of his disciples wanted to leave him for a short period of time in-order to bury his father; he is told to,* **"Let the dead bury the dead."** *If we are not alive in Christ now, in this life, there is no hope for forgiveness when leaving the land of the living for the world of the dead! Anyone who is living can hear the truth of salvation, offering eternal life. You may be a very important person in this life, and society may erect a great monument in appreciation for the things you have accomplished, but none of it matters if you are residing in the world of the dead. If you gain the whole world and lose your soul what then does it matter? If we are captured by the race to acquire the things of this world, so-called riches, fame and power, they will not last, and will be given to another upon your entrance into the world of the dead! When captured by the pursuit of worldly offering we cannot see the offering of eternal life, that is given freely to all who will only accept the truth of God and the sacrifice of his Son.*

Luke 6:37-38 "Do not judge others, and God will not judge you; do not condemn others and God will not condemn you; forgive others and God will forgive you. Give to others and God will give to you. Indeed, you will receive a full measure, a generous helping, poured into your hands-all that you can hold. The measure you use for others is the one God will use for you."

24

GIVING

The above scripture quote from the gospel of Luke, relates to us the words of Jesus as he is teaching about a primary principal of heaven, expressed elsewhere in the Lord's prayer, ***"Forgive us our trespasses as we forgive those who trespass against us."*** *How we treat others is what we can expect from God. Let's look at how Jesus answers a question from the apostle Peter:* ***Matthew 18:21-30 Then Peter came to Jesus and asked, "Lord, if my brother keeps on sinning against me how many times do I have to forgive him? "Seven times?" "No, not seven times," answered Jesus, "but seventy times seven, because the kingdom of heaven is like this. Once there was a king who decided to check on his servants' accounts. He had just begun to do so when one of them was brought in who owed him millions of dollars. The servant did not have enough to pay his debt, so the king ordered him to be sold as a slave with his wife and his children and all that he had, in-order to pay the debt. The servant fell on his knees before the king. 'Be patient with me' he begged, 'and I will pay you everything!' The king felt sorry for him, so he forgave him the debt and let him go. Then the man went out and met one of his fellow servants who owed him a few dollars. He grabbed him and started choking him. 'Pay back what you owe me!' he said. His fellow servant fell-down***

and begged him, 'be patient with me and I will pay you back.' But he refused; instead he had him thrown into jail until he should pay the debt.

The story goes on to say that the other servants witnessed the manner their fellow servant was treated and went and told the king everything that had happened. The king calls the servant and declares to him that he is worthless, and given all that he had been forgiven he should have forgiven his fellow servant, just as he had received mercy! Of course, the king sends the worthless servant to prison until he should pay him the debt he was now, once again, responsible for. **"Do unto others as you would have others do unto you."** *This was something the worthless servant had to learn the hard way! There is no limit to the times we should forgive others, and Jesus makes this plain to Peter when he says to him to forgive your brother seventy times seven. It is becoming clear to us that the posture of unlimited care for others is described in the, characteristic, distinguishing attribute of love. God is Love, and in this understanding, we are to emulate his patience and forgiving attitude toward those who have hurt us. For us to do otherwise is to enter-into a condition wherein we leave ourselves open to be judged in a very harsh manner; the same way we had treated those who sought from us mercy, compassion, forgiveness, understanding and love! God wants us to treat others in the same way we would want to be treated. We are given the ultimate presentation of forgiveness in the sacrifice of Christ; we are given understanding, that it is not our place to judge, but. we are to forgive others as we have been forgiven.*

If we think about what is really being told to us, it simply means, everything belongs to God and he has shown to us the proper way we should treat what he has given. He wants us to understand the virtuous condition of giving. He gives to us totally and this should be evident in his children. All of nature shouts out to us. The sun and the moon and the stars give their light; the earth produces a great bounty, and trees, a myriad of fruit; animal life gives and the oceans and all of creation gives, even the air we breathe is continually offering to us the unlimited generosity of God. God is saying to us, within his creation, "I want you, mankind, to be responsible to one another and responsive to me." Within mankind we find the condition of seeking a comfort zone wherein we amass wealth and storage of goods (a condition that can be always looking inward for what "I" need, as opposed to what our neighbor may be needing), and in the process, we fail to look to God for our needs.

GIVING

The sun the moon and sky
Air threes birds and bees
Earth and oceans bend a knee
To God's voice above
All in nature finds its way
Giving without measure

A hungry man cannot share
What he does not have
And if he finds charity
Within another's heart
He'll remember what was done
And to others he'll show love.

"Give and it will be given to you."
What we receive is not ours alone
It's blessing from above
For us to give and share with those
Who do not know God's love.

Matthew 5:6-7 "Happy are those whose greatest desire is to do what God requires; God will satisfy them fully! Happy are those who are merciful to others; God will be merciful to them.!"

Judges 14:1-6 One day, Samson went to Timnah, where he noticed a certain young Philistine woman. He went back home and told his father and mother, "there's a Philistine woman down in Timnah who caught my attention. Go get her for me; I want to marry her." But his father and mother asked him, "Why do you have to go to those heathen Philistines to get a wife? Can't you find someone in our own clan, among all our people?" But Samson told his father, "She is the one I want you to get for me, I like her." His parents did not know that it was the Lord who was leading Samson to do this, for the Lord was looking for a chance to fight the Philistines. So, Samson went down to Timnah with his father and mother. As they were going through the vineyards there, he heard a young lion roaring. Suddenly the power of the Lord made Samson strong, and he tore the lion apart with his bare hands, as if it were a young goat. But he did not tell his parents what he had done.

25

ENTER THE LION

It appears Samson has become accustomed to getting what he wants. He tells his parents to go and get her for him! (So much for equal opportunity for women, and they say women's rights have not improved?) Samson's parents did not know what was taking place, had been designed by God to render a knockout blow to the Philistine pride that had ruled over the people of God. During this time, the Philistines had ruled the people of God, but their grip on them was about to be loosened. Both Samson and the Philistines understood strength. The Philistines derived their strength from the point of the sword and Samson received his from the Lord.

Something appears to have happened to Samson, he forgot who he was or who he is supposed to represent, or more likely he was distracted by the temptations present in the- lifestyles inherent in Philistine culture? The Philistines were definitely-lost in the offerings of the world, and the "anything goes" mindset still very much prevalent in the world today. Even though there may have been a strong sword control law enacted by the Philistines, Samson had no need for a sword, but he should never have drifted from the Sword of the Spirit; the truth of God living in him.

Samson is seeking a wife and apparently the wedding had been arranged. At the wedding festivities, it was customary for the bridegroom to offer to those attending a riddle, along with a wager which would be paid to the happy couple should the riddle not be solved. I suspect that in every instance the guests would purposely not solve the riddle, because it was an avenue through which they could shower the happy couple with gifts. In this instance of stumping the guests the groom could (at least in this one time) appear to not only be intelligent in his choice of a bride but in worldly matters as well. Samson had joined with the Philistines and somehow had lost focus upon the communication between he and God. This is unfortunate because these guests were not Samson's family. Samson was moving into a neighborhood that was uninviting and hostile! Those who rule always think it is they who are endowed with the ability to think. They will threaten and carry out threats in-order to maintain this persona and identifying role of superiority over those they rule.

While we are told that Samson's parents did not know of the plans of God seeking a chance to fight with the Philistines, we can also recognize that neither did Samson know he was being used as an instrument of God's judgment upon those who had mistreated the people of God. ***Judges 14:10-14 His father went to the woman's house and Samson gave a banquet there. This was a custom among the young men. When the Philistines saw him, they sent thirty young men to stay with him. Samson said to them, "Let me tell you a riddle. I'll bet each one of you a piece of fine linen and a change of fine clothes that you can't tell me its meaning***

before the seven days of the wedding feast are over." Tell us your riddle they said. "Let's hear it." He said, "Out of the eater came something to eat. Out of the strong came something sweet." *Three days later they still had not been able to understand the riddle, and so they approached Samson's wife, encouraging her to trick her husband into revealing to her the meaning of the riddle.*

They had threatened to burn down her father's house and then to burn both her and her father to death. Well she succeeds in finding out the meaning of the riddle and passes the knowledge on to those who had threatened her life. They guess the riddle and as what would be expected, Samson figures out what had happened and he is furious! He pays the wager by striking down thirty men of Ashkelon. He killed them and strips them of their clothing. He feels betrayed by his wife and storms off to cool down. Sometime later he returns and finds that his wife has been given to his best man at the wedding. Perhaps this is where the custom of "best man" originated? Samson is not making good decisions and displays a lack of prudence in his choice of friends. (Again, so much for a woman's rights). This sounds, so much like slavery! Samson continues his furious state in an-attempt to satisfy his anger by burning down the wheat fields and the olive groves of the Philistines. He is focused upon the Philistines as the cause of his troubles; but if you don't want to be burned it is prudent to stand away from the flame. It is also wise not to start the fire to begin with. Unaware of God's intention for him he begins to make this a personal vendetta.

Naturally the Philistines want to know who it was that burned their fields. They are told it is Samson the son-in-law of the Timnite woman. After hearing this the Philistines murder the father and wife of Samson by burning them to death. Apparently, they did not hear of the "best man" taking over the husband spot that formerly belonged to Samson? "You burned my fields so we'll burn your family!" These Philistines seem to be fixated upon burning people to death; apparently it is a great motivator for solving problems. Samson vows revenge and slaughters many of the Philistines. It is not surprising that the Philistines realize they have a big problem concerning Samson; he just slaughtered many of them. They don't want to confront Samson directly so they do what comes natural to them; they set up an encampment in the-neighborhood of the people of Judah. The men of Judah ask. ***"Why have you come to fight us?"*** *The people of Judah don't want to fight with the Philistines (the outcome for them was obvious). The people hand Samson over to the Philistines and this gesture placates the anger of those wishing to find an excuse to fight and kill them. When the Philistines see Samson being brought to them bound with new rope they are overjoyed! They are shouting for joy, but Samson breaks the ropes and kills a thousand Philistines with the fresh bone of a donkey.*

The fresh bone had not been deprived of its strength as if it had been buried in the earth for any length of time. All this back and forth violence is heading in the direction of mutual destruction, but Samson is showing a weakness that the enemy will exploit. It becomes obvious that the Philistines had been observing Samson in some sort of clandestine manner; in-order to recognize his behavior to be such that it may prove to be his undoing. Samson is being exposed to the corrosive element of sin. He visits a prostitute in Gaza and the people decide they will capture and kill him in the morning when he attempts to leave; but Samson departs in the middle of the night and as a parting gesture he rips off the doors to the city gate along with two doorposts and carries them off with him!

When we see the usage of the words "door" or "gate" in scripture it can sometimes imply underlying understanding that alludes to the opening or closing of one's heart or mind. I think in this instance we can safely say it means that Samson blew their minds to pieces! Shortly thereafter we find Samson falling in love. Unfortunately, it is a woman named Delilah, who prostitutes herself for large sums of money, offered by the Philistines who are determined to find the cause of Samson's great strength. Samson's mother was warned by the angel of the Lord concerning the prohibition of wine consumption; but Samson is acting out of his desires and not the prudence of one who has been dedicated to the Lord and his purpose. Perhaps while under the influence of wine and lust he reveals to Delilah the source of his great strength. Samson loses his hair and strength, no doubt while he is asleep from the overindulgence of wine. Samson had entered the darkness of the world's enticements with an air of invulnerability, but he is made vulnerable by the trust he had placed in someone who was really-unknown to him.

Samson had an identity crisis. He is vocally declaring that he is a child of God and he does so while being entertained in a brothel! Once he compromised and negotiated with his conscience concerning what he knew to be wrong, he displayed the weakness that has plagued humanity throughout the ages! He had the wine and the woman, and I would not be surprised if he was found singing, "This little light of mine" within the entrapment designed for his demise.

Strength is one of those words that like a coin is double sided, and presents to us a choice to rely upon for identity. On one side, there is physical strength and on the other is the spiritual strength having the ability to overcome where brute force is not applicable. The apostle Paul tells us that physical strength is fine but spiritual strength is more important. Physical strength is not lasting, and spiritual strength is our connection to God. Upon his capture, the first thing the Philistines do is to make his expedition into the world of darkness permanent; they gouge-out and make his eye sockets vacant and hollow! He is made blind. By blinding Samson, they inadvertently began to walk upon- the road heading toward their own demise. They believed that once Samson's hair had grown back they would be safe in the knowledge that unfocused strength is not a threat to them. In fact, when his hair returned they had him perform in a manner one would expect from a circus strongman; they had him perform for their entertainment!

Long hair and everything else taken into consideration the bottom line is that Samson's strength came from the Lord. These Philistines must have all started to grow long hair, thinking they could then enter a muscle builder's contest! They did not want to kill

Samson, no, that would be too easy. They wanted to see him suffer! They wanted to delight in mocking him and the God he served. The Philistines had no knowledge of Samson's God, for if they did they might have not gone as far as they had. They mocked the Most High by crediting their god "Dagon"" the "nothing" god they outwardly worshipped for delivering Samson into their hands. They knew exactly how Samson was defeated, but it was politically a good thing to have a god that defeated the God of those they ruled over. The rulers could not afford to appear weak in any way that would place their subjects in a more powerful light. Failure to dominate one of the judges of Israel would leave an opening of doubt concerning the appearance of their absolute dominance over their subjects. (When we hear of the Book of Judges, we should not think of one who sits and contemplates the guilt or innocence of those sent before them. Rather, judges in this context is better understood as one who is a hero of the people). Failure to dominate Samson would also allow hope for freedom to be born in the thoughts of those who were subjected to Philistine rule. Anything that would threaten or bring doubt to the absolute rule of evil will always be attacked in a most vicious manner.

Failure then and now is shunned denied and treated as though it were anathema, a curse and abomination to those who present themselves as victorious in all arenas of life. On a deeper level below the surface of the Philistines lived the cunning stealth of evil. When mankind manufactures a god, or thinks of itself as a god it is evil! To think of yourself as a god is idolatry and this mindset has not gone away, for there are many in today's world who believe they are above the common man in both intelligence and abilities! In fact, within today's new-age religion, it is offered to all who will acknowledge their godlike condition within the illusion of self-determination. They are awarded the mantle of gods within the illusion manufactured by deception and tyranny. Deception is never a good thing, for those being deceived; it is even more damaging when we deceive ourselves! Within darkness all things can be imagined to-exist, and all things can be made to support the denial of truth.

Samson began the deliverance of Israel from the hands of the Philistines and God finished the fight, by toppling that which they had placed their trust. Their manufactured god and the tip of the sword were both shown to be worthless when God is the one who is being opposed! The people of God had found themselves in the unwanted forty-year sentence for rebelling against God; in favor of their will and desires, and what they found was the change they sought after was really a curse; and, once again, they found themselves the recipients of a forty-year sentence pronounced by God and administered by the hands of the Philistines. The mention of God is thought of as "clinging to hope" by those who deny the God given rights inherent in mankind; there will always be those who will attempt to destroy such hope and distort truth, but they have a great surprise about to fall-down upon their heads!

Slavery

"I wonder how this came about?"
A tribal chief says,
"Let's get some people to do our work."
"Sure," says the other,
"But they will not work for free."
"Slavery demands sacrifice on both sides" says, the chief.
"Some must die, on our side" says, the chief.
"It's the only way to make our tribe stronger."
"By getting killed in the process?" says, the other.
"Don't worry," says the chief
"We are strong now, but we will be stronger."
"How does that make us stronger?" says, the other.
"Trust me it will, we will have more time to care for our tribe."
"I see," says, the other. "People are now a
commodity to be traded or sold.
What's to prevent others from selling us?"

Slavery has not gone away; it has moved deeper into darkness.
The greatest form of slavery is to be denied the knowledge of God.
Knowledge of God removes the chains of slavery.
Deception finds no place to hide from truth.
Slavery is still with us in many forms
But God is triumphant over all that can make us fall.

Judges 17:23-28 The Philistine kings met together to celebrate and offer a great sacrifice to their god Dagon. They sang, "Our god has given us victory over our enemy Samson!" They were enjoying themselves, and so they said, "Call Samson and let's make him entertain us!" When they brought Samson out of the prison they made him entertain them and made him stand between the columns. When the people saw him, they sang praise to their god: "Our god has given us victory over our enemy, who devastated our land and killed so many of us!" Samson said to the boy who was leading him by the hand, "Let me touch the columns that hold up the building. I want to lean on them." The building was crowded with both men and women. All five Philistine kings

were there, and there were about three thousand men and women on the roof, watching Samson entertain them. Then Samson prayed, "Sovereign Lord, please remember me; please God, give me my strength just this one time more, so that with this one blow I can get even with the Philistines, for putting out my two eyes.

Samson's prayer was answered and he brought God's judgment upon this evil people. Those who enslave others have a terrible fate awaiting them! Let us always find the strength to look to the heavens and to allow God to defeat all those things that intend to harm and enslave. Amen.

THE LION

The lion has such strength within his teeth and claws
All who view his majesty fall from his gaze
King has been his title throughout all his days.

Protector of the pride he is a royal beast
And none can snatch away his feast.
He lives life free from all attack
And with confident ability
He shows enemies his back.

Revelation 5:5 Then one of the elders said to me, "Do not weep! See the Lion of Judah, the root of David, has triumphed; he is able to open the scroll and the seven seals."

1 Peter 5:8 Be self-controlled. Your enemy the devil prowls around like a roaring lion looking for someone to devour.

When we look back on the opening scripture in Judges we find Samson encounters a young lion who reveals himself to Samson with a roar. Samson dispatches the lion and his parents are not aware of the danger that had been prowling in the vineyards. The threat had been quickly removed by the strength of the Lord manifesting itself in the person of Samson. Samson may well be a prophetic vision of the true Lion of Judah (Jesus), who will put an end to this devil who roams the earth seeking the downfall of all.

Revelation 17:13-15 They have one purpose and will give their power and authority to the beast. They will make war against the Lamb, but the Lamb will overcome them because he is the Lord of lords and King of kings-and with him will be his called-chosen and faithful followers. *Again,* ***Revelation 20:10 And the devil, who deceived them, was thrown into the lake of burning sulfur, where the beast and the false prophet were thrown. They will be tormented day and night for ever and ever.*** *It is clear, that the power and strength of God has no rivals.*

Samson was humiliated and faced death willingly (it was he who toppled the columns), and in death he saw his enemies defeated; crushed by the arrogance and evil pulsing within their hearts. Similarly, Jesus willingly faced death and was humiliated; in death, he triumphs over all the enemies of both God and mankind! The greatest enemy of mankind was sin and death; the greatest enemy of God is to be denied by those who he has created.

Power is defined in both the physical and spiritual aspect of creation, and is made to be greatest in the power of God, because in God, we find not only the apex, peak and perfection of such power, but where there is truth, love and desire to do good we find the highest level of all. Almighty God! The Lion of Judah! The Lord of lords! The King of kings! Jesus.

Jonah 2:1-10 From inside the fish Jonah prayed to the Lord his God. "In my distress, I called to the Lord, and he answered me. From the depths of the grave I called for help, and you listened to my cry. You hurled me into the deep, into the very heart of the seas, and the currents swirled about me; all your waves and breakers swept over me. I said, 'I have been banished from your sight; yet I will look again toward your holy temple.' The engulfing waters threatened me; seaweed was wrapped around my head. To the roots of the mountains I sank down; and the earth beneath barred me for forever. But you brought my life up from the pit, O Lord my God."

26

SIGN OF THE PROPHET

In some there is the belief that Jonah did not die bodily, and as consequence was not resurrected. Why this conclusion is doubtful for the events surrounding the death of Jonah, is made manifest in the words of Jesus when he answers those who had demanded of him a miraculous sign, to prove not only the authority of his teaching, but his representation of God himself. Jesus responds that the only sign they will be given is the sign of Jonah; Jonah was in the grave for three days (in the belly of a great fish), and after which was brought back to the land of the living, for the main purpose of bringing to the citizens of the city of Nineveh the warning from God to turn away from their sinful ways. Instead of going to the city of Nineveh as he was initially instructed, he runs south to the seaport city of Joppa and boards a ship bound for Spain! The distance between Israel and Spain is two-thousand and three miles. The distance between Israel and Nineveh which was located near the modern city of Mosul in Iraq, was approximately five-hundred-sixty miles. In those times both distances were great undertakings, but Jonah wanted to get as far away from the Lord as possible! Unfortunately for Jonah, he had to find out the hard way; not even death could shield him from the eyes of God.

Jonah is hurled into the sea, he is drowned and becomes lunch for a great fish; he falls to the root of the mountains; a long way down. It is interesting for us to recognize that this is before undersea mapmaking was invented and the bible speaks of undersea mountains. The account of the rebellion of Jonah and his subsequent death and resurrection is important for us to understand because within his death and resurrection he prefigures the death and resurrection of Jesus. I suspect when Jesus told those seeking a sign that they would get the sign of Jonah in-order to prove to them his validity, they may have looked at each other with a dumbfounded look, as if saying, "Say what?" ***Matthew 16:1-4 The Pharisees and Sadducees came to Jesus and tested him by asking him to show them a miraculous sign from heaven. He replied, "When evening comes, you say, 'It will be fair weather for the sky is red,' and in the morning, 'Today it will be stormy, for the sky is red and overcast.' You know how to interpret the appearance of the sky, but you cannot interpret the signs of the times. A wicked and adulterous generation looks for a miraculous sign, but none will be given it except the sign of Jonah."***

Why do we suppose Jesus had reacted in this manner, to those who had asked for a miraculous sign? I suspect it is like asking for proof that God exists. These Pharisees and Sadducees were the ruling religious; the top shelves of belief in the Almighty (at least that is what they portrayed themselves to be), and they wanted proof of the existence of God (proof that Jesus was acting on the instructions from God), even when they were witnesses to the miracles Jesus had already performed! Jesus healed the sick, raised the dead and set free all of those held in the grip of evil; these religious could not or would not accept the reality of Emmanuel (God with us), even when all that Jesus accomplished was, "good."

Isaiah 7:11-14 Again the Lord spoke to Ahaz, "Ask the Lord your God for a sign, whether in the deepest depths or in the highest heights." But Ahaz said, "I will not ask; I will not put the Lord to the test." Then Isaiah said, "Hear now, you house of David! Is it not enough to try the patience of men? Will you try the patience of God also? Therefore, the Lord himself will give you a sign: The virgin will be with child and will give birth to a son, and will call him Emmanuel."

Ahaz was the son of king Uzziah, and he (Ahaz) was now the king of Judah, at the time Isaiah spoke these words to the house of David, concerning a miraculous sign that the Lord himself will give to the people. Ahaz, however, is not as dumb as those future Pharisees and Sadducees, in their bold attempt to tempt or put to the test the authority of Jesus. Perhaps they were very fortunate in not receiving a response that might have turned the group of them into crispy critters? The thing that shouts to us of the boldness of those who would test God is their open admittance to the reality of God, and all that he has accomplished for the "good" of mankind and all of creation. As such, what we realize is those seeking a sign were really those who had no faith in the God they so openly worshipped and preached to others concerning their need, to not only believe, but to heed the pronouncements of the Almighty. It is here that we see the sign God had prophesied to the house of David (in the person of Jesus), and even with a sign from God himself, they refused to acknowledge our Lord; even with all the miracles producing goodness they could not or would not complete the puzzle they had perceived to be so complicated, and yet, so easy for the common man to see.

Matthew 12:38-39 Then some teachers of the Law and some Pharisees spoke up. "Teacher," they said, "we want to see you perform a miracle." "How evil and godless are the people of this day!" Jesus exclaimed. "You ask me for a miracle? No! The only miracle you will be given is the miracle of the prophet Jonah. In the same way that Jonah spent three days and three nights in the big fish, so will the Son of Man spend three days and nights in the depths of the earth. On the Judgment Day, the people of

Nineveh will stand up and accuse you, because they turned from their sins when they heard Jonah preach; and I tell you there is something here that is greater than Jonah! On the Judgment Day, the Queen of Sheba will stand up and accuse you, because she travelled all the way from her country to listen to king Solomon's wise teaching; and I assure you there is something here greater than Solomon!"

The above scripture is the first time (in the gospel of Matthew) that the Pharisees and teachers of the law attempted to test Jesus by demanding a miraculous sign; later-on, (chapter sixteen) the Pharisees are joined by some Sadducees, and once again, we find them demanding a sign of miraculous exhibition. Truly they were the sons of their father, the devil, for when the antichrist appears with counterfeit miracles and wonders the people of the earth will find it within themselves to believe in the supernatural presentations, and in this they will fall to the greatest of deceptions ever performed for the eyes of man. Perhaps these religious rulers were so blinded by their own reflection and evaluation of themselves that they really could not see the wonders being performed throughout the entire region by our Lord? The Sadducees accompanying the Pharisees at this attempt to have Jesus bow to their demand for a sign, had come to the meeting with an already predisposed and inclined leaning belief, that the dead will not rise from the grave. As such, even if they understood what Jesus meant by using the miracle of the Prophet Jonah as a sign, they would have dismissed it out of hand.

It is not as if Jesus had totally refused their demand for a miracle; no, not at all, he told them they will witness the same miracle that raised Jonah from the dead, but, apparently that was not sufficiently demonstrative for them. Jesus told them he would be raised from the dead, and in this declaration, he also told them he was fully aware of their intent to kill him! They refused to accept the truth in the miracles he had already performed; they were special, and were accustomed and expectant of everyone bowing to their determinations and will. Surely, this upstart of a religious teacher was troubling to those who could not relent to the freedom being presented to mankind, that was totally apart from the very unforgiving rule of those who not only taught the law of Moses, but, also determined who was or wasn't in compliance. They judged who was the sinner without ever looking at themselves.

Nowhere to Run

He fell to the root of the mountains because he attempted to flee
From God who had commanded, "In Nineveh, you must be."
His life passed quickly before him and by a fish of the deep
Was consumed in great strife, and after three
days of death was given new life.
Without further debate the news he did
break to the city of intended fate
"Impending doom for those having no room,
to heed words from he who is great."

Jonah 2:7-10 When my life was ebbing away from me, I remembered you, Lord, and my prayer rose to you, to your holy temple. Those who cling to worthless idols forfeit the grace that could be theirs. But I, with a song of thanksgiving, will sacrifice to you. What I have vowed I will make good. Salvation comes from the Lord. And the Lord commanded the fish, and it vomited Jonah onto dry land.

Even in his dying breath Jonah found the Lord was listening to his cry. This is a very special revelation for all of us to recognize, for even in our last breath God will hear us and for all who call out to him they will not be disappointed! Listen to what the Apostle Peter says on the Day of Pentecost to a large crowd gathered to hear whatever they (the apostles) had to say.

Acts 2:19-21 In the last days God says, "I will pour out my Spirit in those days, and they will prophesy. I will show wonders in the heavens above and in the earth below, blood and fire and billows of smoke. The sun will be turned to darkness, and the moon to blood before the coming of the great and glorious day of the Lord, and everyone who calls upon the Lord will be saved." *Peter is* *referencing a well-known scripture from the book of Joel; he is saying that the pouring out of God's Spirit on men has taken place, and it is now that all who call upon the mercy of God will be saved.*

Art Vision

The world is depicted through great works of art
Captured perceptions not commonly thought
Observations from those whose view is expansive
Insightful discernment on canvas presented
A statue of clay, a bright shining day, a sparrow at play
Exquisite viewing, showing the world peerless truth
God made it all from His Eternal Word
And still, we, who cannot paint draw or sculpt
See the truth that's presented in the heavens above!

The works of man are but copies
Inspired by God
Who painted the heavens
The colors of thought
The universe wrought, shaped bent and fashioned
To inspire the books of wondrous verse
For all to see the works of His hand
The work of his Word and marvelous plan.

Psalm 19:1 The heavens declare the glory of God; the skies proclaim the work of his hands.

Revelation 1:9-11 I, John, your brother and companion in the suffering and kingdom and patient endurance that are ours in Jesus, was on the island of Patmos because of the word of God and the testimony of Jesus. On the Lord's Day, I was in the Spirit and I heard behind me a loud voice like a trumpet, which said, "Write on a scroll what you see and send it to the seven churches: to Ephesus, Smyrna, Pergamum. Thyatira, Sardis, Philadelphia and Laodicea.

27

IN THE SPIRIT

The apostle John along with Paul and others have had mystic like occurrences in their lives and such occurrences are-described as being in the Spirit. The simple definition for mysticism is a joining of man with God in love. Within this special unity God permits us knowledge not normally accessible to the intellect. In every instance of God bringing us into a special awareness there is a gaining of understanding that is difficult to comprehend while disconnected from a "being in the Spirit" moment in time. Certainly, we have had these moments of recognizing the presence of God, while in prayer and praise, but to be taken, set aside and placed apart from the normal activity of body and mind, that is, to say, our everyday life, is to find awareness that otherwise we could not fathom. Additionally, there is always multiple purpose for such occurrences, apart from bringing to us a clearer picture of reality; there is perhaps always the underlining desire of God to make us aware of what is available to us when we combine both faith and love.

Dreams

There are dreams that cause us fear as in nightmares and those that we cannot remember, either because we did not have a dream or the dream itself did not make a pronounced impression upon our soul. Some of the most impressionable aspects of a dream state, find a pathway that is lasting into our consciousness. It is these very impressionable instances wherein, upon remembrance, we seek to find the deeper understanding and ultimately the purpose for being, "in the Spirit."

The cause for adding this chapter occurred last night while asleep; upon awakening I did not remember a thing about a dream or other impressionable thought, but later in the day I was reminded of the very impressionable incident that can only be attributed as being "in the Spirit." I found myself outdoors in a desolate dry place and there I saw a young black child on the ground apparently in need of help. There was no one else to be seen and I approached the young boy who was obviously in pain and crying. I went down to his level and held him in my arms and laying my hand upon his head I prayed to God for his mercy upon this young and very much in-need person. As if miraculously, the young boy opened his eyes and appeared to gain strength in his countenance. He got up and walked away, as if completely healed from whatever was afflicting him.

I have come to understand and realize, that a healing had taken place because the love of God was transferred through me and into the young boy. It is the love of God that makes all our endeavors possible; we can do nothing if only lip-service is present. As Jesus had freed a young boy from demonic possession, and his disciples asked, ***"How is it we could not?"*** *The response from Jesus,* ***"This kind requires prayer,"*** *speaks to us that our desire to do the will of God, united in the bond of love (Spirit) must be present to alleviate the sufferings of others.* ***Romans 8:1 Therefore there is now no condemnation for those who are in Christ Jesus, because through Christ Jesus the law of the Spirit of life set me free from the law***

of sin and death. *Again,* ***Proverbs 16:24 Pleasant words are a honeycomb, sweet to the soul and healing to the bones.***

The law of the Spirit of life, sets us free from everything that captures! No matter what it may be that captures us, whether, it is demonic possession as was the case with the young boy freed by Jesus, or captured by our inability to choose what is right, and in this condition continually find ourselves doing what we do not want to do, there is freedom present in the love we show to others. ***Proverbs 17:22 A cheerful heart is good medicine, and a crushed spirit dries up the bones.*** *When we hear of a cheerful heart we recognize that it's the heart that contains love, and love is most potent when the presence of clouds and downpours render us into a state of disbelief in the ability of God, to once again make cheerfulness appear in the place it is most desired. When we are positioned in the love of God and the cheerfulness that comes with the knowledge, of not only the belief in the ability of God to accomplish (through us) what is impossible for man, but our knowing of his ability to be a reality is like faith on steroids! It is the ability for not only us but for others to become free from whatever ails, troubles, pains, distresses, or has captured and robbed our cheerfulness of the heart! Being set free is total healing and receipt of life, for the law of sin and death that bound our heart and spirit in sadness is no longer the specter of hopelessness, for the law of the Spirit of life has made itself known!*

LOVE

It was love that walked the cobblestones of fear
Embracing pain and sorrow for a world that had not room
To understand the drama: "Salvation's time has come."
It was love that shook trembled and silently withstood the pain
That called to God Almighty to forgive the ways of man.
It was love embracing a solitary fate and
still love calls triumphantly
"Repent, O man, repent, from sinful ways."
It is love that speaks to the hardened hearts of clay
Made brittle and unyielding from hurtful pains today
Saying, "Bring your empty jars and place them at my feet
The water that I'll give will satisfy your needs."
As water flows life grows for filling is acceptance
Of God who heals the weak.

2 Corinthians 4:7 But we have this treasure in jars of clay to show that this all surpassing power is from God and not from us.

We have seen where pleasant words are like sweetness and healing, and, it must be recognized that being unpleasant and destructive will come into being when vitriol, bitterness and hatred is brought forth. The most recent hateful speech was used to describe half of the country, by a Presidential candidate. The word "deplorable" was used to describe half of the country or all of those who do not think like her. Many have not even taken the time to grasp the full implication of what was being said. The word "deplorable," was meant to convey to those who supported her side of politics, to mean, persons who are disgraceful, terrible, awful, appalling, unacceptable, improper, unsuitable, inappropriate, undesirable, insufferable, obnoxious, unredeemable, and unfit to be included in humanity! Now, who says politicians don't mean what they say? When this kind of hateful speech is evident we can always find a designed effort to divide one section of humanity from another. Just as we have believers and unbelievers, we have haters and lovers of the works of God. To purposely agitate and desire to bring into existence an atmosphere of evil design is clearly not intended to heal whatever wounds may be experienced by the nation.

Bitter Sweet

Mountains wear a blanket of pristine crystal snow
Adding sweetness to the valleys through
the way all things must flow.
The sky stores up its moisture until it feels the
strain to release the blessing of rain.
Deep within the earth are springs of water great
Travelling through the gravel seeking rivers to create.
There will come a time not given to man,
When the Lamb of Glory breaks the Seventh Seal by hand
When thrice the trumpet calls a star shall fall as planned
Bringing bitterness to springs that flow over one third the land.
There's a time for bitterness and a time for love
There's a time for forgiveness and of judgment from above
What is sown is reaped and what we do is seen
What is hidden in the heart is plain for all to see
When the spoken word is of hatred evil speech.
Be the same on the outside as a soaring bird in flight
All who look upon him know the purpose of his life.

Revelation 8:10-11 The third angel sounded his trumpet, and a great star, blazing like a torch, fell from the sky on a third of the rivers and on the springs of water-the name of the star is Wormwood. A third of the waters turned bitter, and many people died from the waters that had become bitter.

Luke 23:32-43 Two other men, both, of them criminals, were also led out to be put to death with Jesus. When they came to the place called "The Skull" they crucified Jesus there, and the two criminals, one on his right and the other on his left. Jesus said, "Forgive them, Father! They don't know what they are doing." They divided his clothes among themselves by throwing dice. The people stood there watching while the Jewish leaders made fun of him: "He saved others; let him save himself if he is the Messiah whom God has chosen!" The soldiers also made fun of him: they came up to him and offered him cheap wine, and said, "Save yourself if you are the king of the Jews! Above him were written these words: "This is the king of the Jews." One of the criminals hanging there, hurled insults at him: "Aren't you the Messiah? Save yourself and us!" The other one, however, rebuked him, saying, "Don't you fear God? You received the same sentence he did. Ours however, is only right because we are getting what we deserve for what we did; but he has done no wrong." And he said to Jesus, "Remember me, Jesus, when you come as King!" Jesus said to him, "I promise you that today you will be in paradise with me.

28

ONE ON THE RIGHT-THE OTHER ON THE LEFT

There is such an intricate weave presented to us within the presentation of the crucifixion event, that if we rush past the sight (it is normal for us to not want to remain fixed upon our Lord's suffering), we may miss the underlying implications deliberately designed into the holy weave that is the bible. Let us first recognize that within both criminals there is the divide that depicts acceptance of eternal life and denial. Both criminals represent to us the entire world in need of the forgiveness that Jesus had asked of the Father. Even the soldiers who mocked him found fear and trepidation, anxiety and apprehension at Christ's death, for the events that followed made clear to all witnessing the event a greater power was also present! The soldier had exclaimed, ***"Surely this man was the Son of God!"*** *Unfortunately for those religious who had also mocked our Lord we hear nothing from them that would affirm the truth of Christ. Therein, we find the divide between saved and unsaved doesn't have limitation for just the secular world, there is also the religious who will be faced with the Judgment for not rendering to God what is rightfully his! So, we see one of the criminals is promised salvation and the other is only thinking about getting out of his present predicament. There's no acknowledgement of his deserving such harsh punishment and there is no indication that if he were to be forgiven on the spot he would repent and no longer live the life of a criminal. There is a blending or synergism of cooperation between Old and New Testament declarations; it is mind boggling to consider the impact of both prophesy and heralding, that foreshadows, anticipates and prefigures the reality of the arrival of Jesus.*

Matthew 27:15-18 At every Passover Festival the Roman governor was in the habit of setting free any one prisoner the crowd asked for. At that time, there was a well-known prisoner named Barabbas. So, when the crowd gathered, Pilate asked them, "Which one do you want me to set free to you? Barabbas or Jesus called the Messiah?" He knew very well that the Jewish authorities had handed Jesus over to him because they were jealous.

Just as we saw the salvation of the thief being crucified next to Jesus, we now witness the setting free of one who was also deserving of prison. When we go back into the Old Testament in the Book of Leviticus we also find a heralding of what was to come in the person of Christ. One goat is offered as a sacrifice to the Lord and the other is set free. ***Leviticus 16:7-10 Then he is to take the two goats and present them before the Lord at the entrance to the***

Tent of Meeting. He is to cast lots for the two goats-one lot for the Lord and the other for the scapegoat. Aaron shall bring the goat whose lot falls to the Lord and sacrifice it for a sin offering. But the goat chosen by lot as the scapegoat shall be presented alive before the Lord to be used for making atonement by sending it into the desert as a scapegoat.

The goat that is sacrificed to the point of being killed is a sin offering. It appears the price for sin has always meant someone or something must pay the price for the infraction. As for the goat set free, it is also placed into the category of making atonement. Making atonement is placed into the compensation, penitence, punishment and making amends category; the goat sent into the desert is not heading for a field of milk and honey. Along with the atonement aspect represented by the set-free goat what we recognize is there's also a sacrificial aspect made by the people since they are all made a bit poorer by the loss of the set-free goat. Perhaps, in the case of Barabbas, if he went back to his criminal ways someone was going to be made poorer also? But with the death of the sacrificial goat what we find is an overshadowing or covering over of the sins of the nation, which basically is an acknowledgement of the nation's sins and not an attempt to deny the reality of the imperfection of man. Just as the bible states, **"There are none who are righteous, no, not one."** *It is within this recognition that the people find acceptance from God and the promise of one who will remove the stain of sin from creation forever! How wonderful is it for us who not only know of the promises of Christ, but have seen and experienced his forgiveness come into fruition within us? The sacrificing of goats took place on the Day of Atonement which is very closely related to the Day of Passover; in fact, it is pointing to the true Passover Lamb. "The Lamb of God who takes away the sins of the world." This life that we live was always meant to be peaceful, but with the advent of sin we found the cousin of sin called "pain."*

PEACE AND PAIN

From the beginning the start of man's days
Innocent thoughts and innocent ways
Capture a leaf as it sails on the breeze
Sleep in the shade or bathe on a beach
Speak with a lion or swim in the deep
All this and more was given to man
From the beginning as strength in a friend
Grace and peace was always the plan.

Decent into bondage distrusting grew
We looked upon others with cynical stares
We carried the burden of failure to listen
We stumbled in darkness without healing rays
From the slip and the fall came the wrong and the pain.

Genesis 2:15-17 Then the Lord God placed the man in the Garden of Eden to cultivate it and to guard it. "You may eat the fruit of any tree in the garden except the tree that gives knowledge of what is good and what is bad. You must not eat the fruit of that tree; if you do, you will die the same day.

Higher need

The higher need of the ruling religious that was being threatened by Jesus was jealously! They were jealous of the rightfully directed accolades pointing to the good deeds performed by our Lord. The rival to the condition of narcissism existing in the hearts of the religious, was also present in the heart of their father, the devil. They so loved to be adored and idolized for their burdensome task of upholding the law of Moses. From the perspective of the common man the religious had sacrificed much to live a sin free life. Now, not only are they being exposed as sinners, just like the rest of humanity but they are also being exposed as corrupt judges, no different than the ruling power of Rome, but more importantly they are revealed to the common man who had followed, witnessed and received much goodness from Jesus in both words and deeds. **Matthew 27:18 For he knew it was out of envy that they handed Jesus over to him.** *Not only does Pilate know of the motivating hatred of those who brought Jesus to him, for the-purpose of putting Jesus to death; even the wife of Pilate knew this was an innocent man.*

The insecurity of those in religious power was most evident in the time of Christ. Power over others and the status bordering on a living idol in the eyes of society, is a majestic way to produce a fool! Perhaps the most tempting of all to the human condition, made manifest in conjunction with one's wealth and political power leads persons into thinking they can do all things a mortal man may conceive.

The allurement of power and wealth and the desire to be adored by the masses is not much different today, except for the fact that we no longer feed people to the lions! But the craving for political power and accolades in the arena of worldly recognition will always be with us, so long as humanity continually tramples into the dust the truth of God in favor of the offerings of the world. Many people know the truth of God but their voices are denied a podium. The individual cannot broadcast the good news from his front porch as effectively as a local television network. But in some cases, that may not be the case, since some of the television stations preaching the word of God, have squandered their opportunity in favor of preaching the word for profit.

Therein the disadvantage of voice leaves truth weakened, not much different from those who killed Jesus in effort to suppress truth. Even in the secular world of politics truth is the enemy of those who would rule and in many instances, it appears that they lord-it-over those they are supposed to represent. Nothing has changed. The Christian today (Just like Jesus), is constantly attacked for his beliefs and even the symbolism of such faith is continually finding those whose psyche is offended by just the appearance of a cross! The main reason Christianity suffers such unacceptance from those who outwardly declare, "There is no God" is because they live in the darkness of wanting their lives to remain hidden and secret; the light of truth is always an irritant to them! Just as those evil people who crucified our Lord will one day find out that none of their hidden exploits, deeds or activities can remain concealed, so it will be for everyone. What was true in the time of Christ is true today. Those who persecuted him knew he was a man sent by God, **"Because no one could do the things you are doing without God."** *If we take a longer look at just what was going on in the time of Jesus and in the world today, we can reach the conclusion that the world has never desired to alleviate the sufferings of people in any way. So long as people are suffering the evil in the world is happy; it matters not if the suffering is poverty or slavery or sadness caused by devastation, or the most heinous of atrocities, the evil in the world has been on a wartime setting since the very beginning of the corruption of mankind; it became most pronounced when Herod the Great attempted to kill our Lord, acting as a surrogate for the devil. He slaughtered the innocence in his desire to deny the birth of one who would rule. Moving forward, we find Herod Antipas a coconspirator in the actual killing of Jesus. There was a trinity of evil arrayed against our Lord; the Roman occupying rulers, the religious rulers and the titular ruling king, Herod (Antipas). Later-on, after the death and resurrection of Jesus we find another king (Agrippa) and he has been infected with the very same narcissistic lineage that invades the hearts of those who (really) think of themselves as gods! This king Herod (Agrippa) was eaten alive by worms when the people who were praising his speech said that he was not a man but a god! It was then that he entered the arena of death, believing he belonged in the arena of the divine; so dumb!*

BLINDNESS

It's one thing to not understand her call.
In this we can certainly ask, "Who are you?"
It's another thing to pretend to be her friend and then ignore her.
Wisdom's soul resides in Truth a complete covering for the earth.
In this the heart will soar to unimagined heights
Will capture thought as pearls shining in the light, she'll say,
"I'm glad to meet you here in the dark
Now, no longer will you have to step uninformed
Along life's road, as if atop a rotting bridge"
Wisdom's arrival may cause a covering
of the eyes denial or surprise
Like exiting a darkened room confronted by sunlight.
Some may seek to go back inside where ignorance hides.
She may cause a hardening inviting pride to reign
It's a failure to learn as rocks repel the rain.
As flame gives way to burn, man's hand is pulled away
Allowing wisdom's song to ease and comfort pain.
"Better to hide in the dark with imagination" they say.
Defense of illusion is a cardboard smile, picture perfect, but dead!
A cry without sound is found wanting
As a caged lion sees his prey jaunting
A painted landscape has neither height nor width or depth
And illusion finds a viewer where desire should not tread.
Traps set and longing to bite and rip and shred
All who fail to understand Wisdom's call so blessed.
Ignorance of God is true blindness
It's just a step away from mindless
"Have courage," we say,
"God answers all at Wisdom's dawning
None are turned away
As sure as daytime sees the morning
And birds chirp and fly
The soul of man will sing a song
When blindness says, "goodbye."

Job 28:28 And he said to the man, "The fear of the Lord-that is wisdom, and to shun evil is understanding."

Exodus 12:7 Then they are to take some of the blood and put it on the sides and the tops of the doorframes of the homes where they eat the lambs.

Mark the entrance to the homes with blood

In the above scripture from Exodus we are hearing the instructions given to the people on the very first Passover. It is here on the Passover that the Lord will kill all the firstborn sons of the Egyptians. This will be the final miracle that breaks the backs of those who had refused to recognize the evidence placed before them, regarding God who is demanding they release the people held captive. Their concept of gods was such, that they also believed themselves included in this category! Surprise! It took a long time for the ability of such truth to strip away their pride! Yes, it is true, God made Pharaoh stubborn so he could continue punishing the Egyptians for their cruel treatment of the people for four-hundred-years! Still, it is said, "Even a blind squirrel finds a nut" but, these Egyptians were not only blind but they were filled with the very same narcissistic illness that has produced so many fools throughout history.

Once again, we're allowed to see the heralding of the coming of the true Passover Lamb in the instructions given to the people as to how they must mark their homes, so as, to not be killed by the Lord, when he exacts and obtains justice for the people who had been treated so cruel for such a long time. The most visible sign of the coming of the true Passover Lamb is in the instruction for the people to mark the entrances to their homes- with the blood of the lamb. Let's imagine an ancient doorway to the homes of the people. A horizontal beam on the top and bottom of the doorway; and two vertical beams on either side of the entrance forming a vertical rectangle. Now let's mark all four beams beams with the blood of the lamb, and the message is clear as soon as we connect the dots! Top to bottom and left to right and we have drawn a cross.

Life was never a free ride

Genesis 2:15-17 Then the Lord God placed the man in the Garden of Eden to cultivate it and to guard it. *Some of us have the impression that life in the Garden of Eden (the world), was comparable to a couple of panda bears sitting around and chewing on an inexhaustible supply of good things to eat. However, what we are clearly hearing in this quote from Genesis is that we were given responsibility to cultivate and guard (care for) the world we have been given. We were not told to manufacture great destructive weapons and do everything in our power to destroy paradise. I guess we thought of that on our own as competing societies determined it was in their best interest to dominate everyone and everything in creation? We can understand the shortcomings inherent in humanity, and we can hope to be enlightened by truth, so that we do not repeat our sins, failures and falls from acceptability; but, when we recognize there is an enemy, apart from humanity that seeks our destruction, the hatefulness in the world becomes very much clearer for us to see. Our enemy is the devil, and while we do not actually see him, we do see the results of his influence upon us. Perhaps this is one reason why Jesus prayed,* ***"Father, forgive them because they don't know what they are doing."***

BLOOD SWEAT FEAR AND JOYFUL TEARS

I saw the Lord, his face upturned to heaven,
saying, "Father take this cup from me."
Human fear divine tears sweat in precious
blood, I tremble, and marvel at the Lord.
In the moment I thought weak, again, I heard
him speak, "It's your will I seek."
Just the other day I heard "Hosanna's" ringing through the streets.
Palm branches paved the road and children strained to see
The coming of the, "Savior King" the, "Man from Galilee."
Glistening spears in torchlit night seeking one called, "Christ."
I see a friend walking with this band, pointing with a kiss.
Armor has its sound and silver has a ting
But only Jesus knows the sound betrayal brings.
I remember many things but there's little I understand.
Only he knew, it was hidden in the brilliant light of day.
The first Passover, lintel and doorposts, set apart by blood.
Head hands and feet pierced with great
pain, but greater was his love.
The blood of the Lamb stood guard at the doors
Pointing to salvation denying death and sorrow's pain
As it had always been before the Lamb was slain.
Manna sent from heaven, rich in mercy's ways
Seeking out the lost and captured by the grave.
The blind and deaf found meaning and
the dumb spoke words of love.
Miracles and good deeds producing great expectant joy
Proclaiming to the world, "Jesus Christ is Lord."
As in the beginning and will be at the end
I see a new day dawning-sunshine's ray as song
I remember Isaiah's voice saying, "A child to us is born!"
I remember many things that come to me in waves
But nothing overshadows,
Resurrection's morning and the souls he saved.
I remember many things, now, and marvel
at the complex simplicity of God.

Luke 18:31-34 Jesus took the twelve disciples aside and said to them, "Listen! We are going to Jerusalem where everything the prophets wrote about the Son of Man will come true. He will be handed over to the Gentiles, who will make fun of him, insult him, and spit on him. They will whip him and kill him, but three days later he will rise to life." But the disciples did not understand any of these things; the meaning of the words was hidden from them, and they did not know what Jesus was talking about.

Genesis 3:2-5 The woman said to the serpent, "We may eat fruit from the trees in the garden, but God did say, "You must not eat fruit from the tree in the middle of the garden, and you must not touch it, or you will die.'" "You will not surely die." The serpent said to the woman. "For God knows that when you eat of it your eyes will be opened, and you will be like God, knowing good and evil."

Half-truth is not truth

This serpent is a seriously stupid individual; it is one thing to deceive the infant creation of God but it is awfully interesting to listen to this devil lie about the words of God. God told the man and woman not to eat from the tree in the center of the garden or else they will die; in fact, they were told to not even touch it. This sounds like the mother of all poisons and it (actually) was very toxic. I'm wondering why it is, since they (Adam and Eve) were curious enough to disobey and distrust the instructions of God that they did not question the serpent concerning the difference between "good and evil?" Why didn't they ask for the meaning of death? Of course, we understand God was fully aware of the failure that would take place on the part of his creation. He knew they would be tempted to eat the fruit and all this knowledge would be added to the mind of man along with the necessary ingredient we have come to know as "conscience." As we have discussed earlier, concerning the necessity of our failure so as, to, gain knowledge, that can only be fully understood by experiencing hard times and suffering. Meaning, who, can understand courage, without being threatened? Or, who can feel compassion, can empathize, sympathize or relate to suffering, without first experiencing it ourselves? Truly a marvelous plan of God to instill in us both a knowledge of good and evil as well as the emotions that bring to us a reality of the character of our great God! The devil denies the truth in the words of God by saying, **"You will not surely die."** *However, he half-truth's them (he lies about death being a consequence), of what to expect with respect to obtaining the knowledge of "good and evil." Not only does he lie to Adam and Eve but in the commission of the lie he labels God as a liar! This half-truth tactic used by the devil is not a one-time usage; he tried it on Jesus when he asked Jesus to jump from the high place, adding that God's angels will not allow him to stub his toe. Jesus responds by saying, it is written,* **"You shall not tempt the Lord your God."** *This is one major reason why we are to know the truth contained in the bible. The bible is our foundation by which we can judge all aspects of life placed before us, and all pronouncements from the lips of man are also placed into either acceptance or conflict with God's word.*

SWEET LIES

No matter how we arrive at the truth
There's always one thing that eventually happens: "Healing."
It's always better to hear a caustic truth
then to ingest a "sweet lie."
So many songs written, past and present, asking for "sweet lies."
We want to avoid rejection, and in the process,
we hurt ourselves with a "sweet lie."
There's so much rejection in the world,
even a "sweet lie" is accepted.
This is really-cruel confusion denying what lives underneath.
Poison's purpose is illusion gift wrapped in smiles.
Diluted presentation made acceptable because
it is now the possessor of "Sweetness?"
Healing comes with the warmth of reality
Whose weight of truth stands tall and binds all wounds.
The hurts and cares of this life's trials are captured by the truth
Seized within its breath and released in loving eyes
Reality doesn't come in increments designed to duck and hide.
Truth is courage and empowerment that lives in the Light of Christ.
Truth lives within the heart of God and the soul of the blessed
Rejecting a "comfort zone" to avoid certainty
in a world afraid naked and stressed.
"Sweet lies" are but a buffer added to a pill
Disguising pain's discomfort as a bandit seeks to hide
Dishonest speech and fraud concealed deep inside
With the help, support and service, from a tiny sweet filled lie.

Proverbs 12:3 A man cannot be established through wickedness, but the righteous cannot be uprooted.

The reality of truth is not limited to what we may send out into the world from within us, but, we should not ever try to deceive ourselves. Recognition of truth contains more than we could ever imagine; its rewards are perhaps always giving, and in the giving we do not know the extent of its content or the depth of its generosity. Within truth there is reality; just as the repentant thief realized that he was receiving what he deserved and as consequence he also received what he did not deserve. He received the promise of entrance into paradise; the place we were dispossessed from in the very beginning of man's disobedience to God. The other thief, refused to understand or recognize that he was receiving the judgment of man and deservedly so; he wanted to escape his present predicament and no doubt he would have continued his criminal lifestyle. He certainly would not have any respect for the prohibitions set-forth by God, because he had no respect for the laws of man, and so it is probably accurate to assume he would continue his life of crime. Again, it is one thing to be deceived by the abundance of lies in the world but it is perhaps always more detrimental to deceive ourselves!

Uprooted-displaced-evacuated

The righteous cannot be uprooted, simply means God will not deny justice to those who love and believe his word. Being uprooted also means the unrighteous will find judgment for failing to heed his truth. There is no argument mankind can present in the defense of wrong. We did not come into being on our own; it was not accidental! We were created for God's purpose. Just as the potter creates a pot for any number of reasons; holding water, grain etc. the pot was not made to fly or jump and so it is with mankind, we were made with purpose by God. There is a certain kind of behavior that goes over the line and when it is done we can expect a rebuke from God, up to and including destruction; we can also be gladdened to recognize that God will not destroy the righteous with the unrighteous. The example that shouts to us this truth is found in, ***Genesis 18:32 Then he said, "May the Lord not be angry, but let me speak just once more. What if only ten can be found there?" He answered, "For the sake of the ten, I will not destroy it."*** *After this discourse with the Lord, Abraham returned home and both Sodom and Gomorrah were destroyed because of their egregious lifestyles; there were none who were righteous or living an acceptable life in the judgment of God. God knows we are not perfect, and there is much that he overlooks (at* *least to the point of not imposing immediate judgment), but in the end of time we will have to answer for all our sins and failures. Being answerable for ourselves with respect to our sins (in the case of the saved) does not mean eternal damnation, but it does mean we will be reminded of just how lost we were; and how fortunate we have become! Are we righteous? No, but we are clothed in the righteousness of Christ, and, while adorned in this fashion we are found to be acceptable to God and permitted into his presence. It is as if we are the "scapegoats" receiving what we did not earn; receiving freedom instead of death. Jesus went to the cross of death for us to receive the gift of life!*

It is reassuring for us to recognize there is and never has been something we could do to earn salvation. The only thing required for us to do is recognize the price that was paid, and what a price it was! The mind of man is very imaginable and creative in every aspect conceivable in both good and evil. Certainly, the crucifixion of man was a truly evil and wicked generation from the depths of a depraved, debauched and immoral heart. The courage shown to us in the willing acceptance of crucifixion by our Lord is indescribably great and inexpressible within the language of man. It can only be expressed and peripherally understood when we love with the depth of both forgiveness and freedom.

LIMITED VISION

How can I express this love in my heart?
"Hallelujah!" can't begin to convey
The joyful refrain passing in waves
Again, and again and again!
How can I express the joy abundantly stored?
I must confess, "I can't do it, Lord."

But you have not limits confined as are mine
So, send forth your Spirit to help me to pray,
To help me to say,
"Father, I love you!"
In just the right way.

Romans 8:26 In the same way, the Spirit helps us in our weakness. We do not know what we ought to pray, but the Spirit himself intercedes for us with groans that words cannot express.

A man can see with his heart, better than an eagle flying high above the earth. We are not confined within these bodies. We travel great distances with great speed; the speed of thought. Having said that let's go back in time and imagine the destruction taking place in the time of Noah and the great flood, and the destruction of Sodom and Gomorrah, as just a few of the most noted examples of God's wrath being sent down upon the earth. It is within these monumental events that we must remind ourselves that God is Just and will not destroy the innocent with the guilty. The only innocence that God continually recognizes is the trust that lives in the heart of a child. Jesus said, ***Matthew 19:14 Jesus said, "Let the little children come to me, and do not hinder them, for the kingdom of heaven belongs to such as these."*** *It now becomes apparent that within the destruction events highlighted above there were no innocent lives lost in the actions brought upon the evil in the world; God did not destroy children. Logic should allow us to look at the declaration of God that all the firstborn sons of the Egyptians would be killed during the first Passover. This same logic (the fact that God is and always has been just), must lead us to the conclusion that all the firstborn sons were no longer in their childhood when death came knocking to collect the price for the evil committed.*

Exodus 1:15-16 The king of Egypt said to the Hebrew midwives, whose names were, Shiphrah and Puah. "When you help the Hebrew women in childbirth and observe them on the delivery stool. If it is a boy, kill him; but if it is a girl let her live."

It appears to us the Egyptian king was totally depraved and I suspect God's punishment of killing all the firstborn sons of Egypt was an event that struck into the Egyptians an acknowledgement to their minds and hearts the evil they had inflicted upon the Hebrews, and now, they will experience the total strength of God as he restores to the people their freedom!

In four hundred years of captivity, it is imaginable to our logic that many of the Hebrew slaves had willingly submitted to the evil lifestyles that were a natural part of Egyptian life. As such, just like the thief that was promised paradise because he had recognized his own guilt, so too it was with the Hebrew people. When the reality of God was made manifest to them in the miracles produced by God's messengers, they understood their guilt and inwardly they repented and in time were brought to the promised land.

REMEDY

They thought it was the end of love,
something they knew little about.
"All will remain blind" and "We will remain in power.
When the cross has done it work, at this un-godly-hour."
The vision of the cross would soon confuse their lives.
In the span of three short days the world would be surprised.
"He is risen!" came the cry.
And still proof is demanded to satisfy their eyes.
Are men still demanding proof?
Sure, they are, nothing's changed.
Some have put the question to bed.
"There is no God and Christ is dead!"
This is the depth of the lost.

Truth is self-evident it stands alone.
Demanding proof is like saying, "Turn stone to bread,"
No matter, the stones have a greater chance of praising God
Than those whose stone hearts mark the entrances to grave yards.
His eyes closed shut, earth rumbled forth its ire
Tombs gave up the dead and the sky became a pyre.
Earthquakes parted ground and tremors rushed the source
And laid awaiting movement at the foot of the cross.
Heads lifted-up to the sky, angry clouds and feathered cries.
The dripping of his blood had now its turn to speak:
"It is finished,
Will you now believe."

Isaiah 61:13 The Spirit of the Sovereign Lord is on me. Because the Lord had anointed me to preach good news to the poor. He has sent me to bind up the brokenhearted. To proclaim freedom to the captives and release for the prisoners, to proclaim the year of the Lord's favor and the day of vengeance of our God, to comfort all who mourn, and provide for all who mourn in Zion-to bestow on them the crown of glory instead of ashes, the oil of gladness instead of mourning, and a garment of praise instead of a spirit of despair.

In the same way, we recognize the reality of God being Just and Fair and completely Honest in his pronouncements against humanity, we are also given recognition of the injustice within the evil hearts of those who have no compassion for innocence; they only possess a passion to control and dominate, kill and inflict tremendous harm. Evil will not hold children in a place of security; no, they will hide behind them as shields. Those who mourn now will be comforted and those who are evil will be sent to the place of eternal darkness or eternal torture! It is not only those who are totally debased corrupt and spoiled, by the offerings of the world, but it is all of those who stand with them who commit such atrocities, and actions of evil without the slightest hint of remorse for the harm they have brought upon the innocence! God is the only person who can exactly determine the punishment deserved.

Ephesians 5:11-14 Have nothing to do with fruitless deeds of darkness, but rather expose them. For it is shameful to even mention what the disobedient do in secret. But everything exposed by the light becomes visible, for it is light that makes everything visible. This is, why, it is said: "Wake up! O sleeper, rise from the dead, and Christ will shine on you."

29

DRUG ADDICTION A BRICKS WITHOUT STRAW AFFLICTION

Many of us seek to find a measure of peace in a world of war. We will always have wars in one of its many forms. Countries will make war against one another. Consumers will search to find a bargain that has not overtly taken advantage of their finances, and physical desires are constantly in a warlike setting produced by influences presented daily. Some of these desires appeal to both the physical and spiritual characteristics of man. When man is captured on both-of-these levels he is lost. When saved, his objective for the remainder of his days on this earth is to not be overcome by the onetime formidable enemy of sin.

Entire countries live in the tyranny imposed by a few, and those finding a measure of physical freedom must be constantly vigilant against the erosion of freedoms-enjoyed. It is no different for those of us who have received God's grace; vigilance is required. In addition to tyrannical schemes, addictions are designed to dominate the thoughts and actions of man. There's the internal conflict that strives to control, as would dictatorial lords, striving with ruthless motivation to subjugate the desire for freedom within the slave. It is to this reality that the apostle Paul warns us against fruitless deeds of darkness, needing to be exposed by the light of Christ. Paul is also telling us to be true to ourselves and to recognize the condition of falling asleep for increasingly longer periods of time; until we are lulled into an existence that is in total denial of the truth of our lives. Captive again! There are good and bad deeds and perhaps the first fruitless deed originated in the "Garden of Eden?" From this infraction, (disobedience to the instructions of God) came into existence all manner of fruitless existence.

Troubles in life come to us mostly through our unwillingness to recognize and heed the pronouncements of God. Substance abuse or drug addictions become the dictatorial lord of our lives in place of God when we fail to both heed his words and recognize the troubles involved in a life that we are not in control of. All parents look forward to the day their children become independent to a certain degree, but no parent wants to hear they are no longer needed. God is no different, because he knows for us to declare independence in all things is to find the cold edge of reality poised to come crashing down upon us. ***"Have nothing to do with the fruitless deeds of darkness."*** *Deeds of darkness are those that produce nothing good and we don't want to be exposed to the light of day; even if we are not ashamed of them we still would not want them revealed.*

Light doesn't allow discretionary revelation. Without notice, whatever was hidden by the dark is revealed. The light of truth illuminates in a way all can see what had been concealed. It uncovers hidden things within us that we were not aware of. It exposes uncovers discovers and forces recognition through bathing in its presence. It shouts a wake-up call for us to realize nothing can be hidden from the light of God. Truth brings sight and in the gaining of sight all things are transformed in its light. What was secret is no longer hidden. And what is right and pleasing to God is highlighted, for all to see, as it contrasts with things that are wrong and evil in the pronouncements of God. Jesus is the light of the world.

The life we live can often bring to us troubles. If we are not promoting problems for ourselves there is always someone eager to lead us into the so-called "jackpot." A rock and hard place situation affording no visible hope for reversal until the intervention of light points the way to freedom. The apostle Paul says it this way, **Ephesians 1:18 I pray also that the eyes of your heart may be enlightened in order that you may know the hope to which he has called you, the riches of his glorious inheritance in the saints.** *To have our hearts and eyes enlightened is to have truth clear away life's distractions, that, when we are focused upon such distractions we ultimately find ourselves lost in the illusions and pretense of freedom. We lose our freedom to say "no" to everything we deem to be not in our best interest when we are enslaved. The two areas that tend to be the most evident, causing slavery, are living in a cruel dictatorship where there is imposed upon us great threats of torture or death, and living under the dictatorship of self-imposed addiction to the myriad of drugs provided by the world, that claims to be a diversion from the everyday troubles and problems that haunt us, with the question, asking, "When will worldly demands be met?" Of course, when we are very young there is not the pronounced worldly demands of adulthood; there is only the exploration of life and the offerings presented. Unfortunately for the young there is always someone who will bring to their conscious awareness the "great experience" of "getting high!"*

The world has already begun to condone the usage of Marijuana, and again, what we find is a half-truth embedded within the objective of enslaving those who have not had the heart and eyes enlightened by truth. Apparently, (I don't know for sure) there is some sort of medicinal benefit derived by the usage of Marijuana for those with a specific medical problem; it doesn't cure anything, only is said to alleviate the symptoms. I've seen a documentary wherein a child is given a derivative from the plant and a relief of some sort is derived. I believe this to be a true presentation of a medicinal benefit from the plant. However, the wholesale usage of the drug has always been described as a "gateway" to the hardcore drugs that grip a person and tears away the will to break free from the constant call for, "More!"

The other kind of enslavement is pronounced to our consciousness when we view the ancient Hebrew people enslaved by the Egyptians for four-centuries! In both forms of slavery there is never a place for the captive to say, "no." At the time of Moses he had asked of the Pharaoh to allow the people to go out into the desert and worship God. Pharaoh thought this to be a ruse, a con or scam for the people to attempt to escape. Pharaoh had declared that the people were lazy,

Exodus 5:6-9 That same day Pharaoh gave this order to the slave drivers and foremen in charge of the people: "You are no longer to supply the people with straw for making bricks; let them go and gather their own straw. But require them to make the same number of bricks as before; don't reduce the quota. They are lazy; that is why they are crying out, 'let us go and sacrifice to our God.' Make the work harder for the men so that they keep working and pay no attention to lies.

Many a slave is kept working to fulfill the desires generated within, by our nature, and as in the case of the Hebrew slaves they were forced to endure because of the evil that held them against their will. In both cases of slavery, internally imposed or externally forced through threats, there is a desire for freedom and a longing to offer (sacrifice) one's self to God. The thirst for freedom is unrelenting and will seek even illusory measures in effort to quell the reality of a slave condition, that sees no hope of escape. Within the illusion of freedom physical bondage still exists; it is made to appear and feel more bearable through the construction of a mental barricade that separates, for the moment, the constant deliberation upon a slave condition. A meaningless life appears to gain direction and purpose through escape routes formed in the darkness of pockets in the mind; the only conceivable place for retreat.

The people saw hope in the words of Moses, but Pharaoh fought back with tenacity, calling the words of God, "lies." They believed in the message that God was concerned for them and the initial breaking of the chains of slavery began in their hearts. From that point on it was just a matter of bending the back of Pharaoh with heavy burdens the Lord God would place upon him. Hope, then, is the switch that turns on the light making a way for all to see the route from which freedom is found and made permanent, no matter who or what may threaten; all that the Lord has set free remains free!

The problems we may find ourselves confronted with, can be similar too, a "make bricks without straw" condition of slavery, imposed by not only others but may mostly materialize when we do not recognize the initial overtures concealed in the motive to enslave. The fears and feelings of hopelessness are as real as the shackles placed upon the feet of the ancient slaves in Egypt or in the past of our own nation. The enslavers are unknowingly no better off than the brick makers. Until recognition of God's light shines into their hearts as well. All of us are or were trapped by sin taking us to our permanent death! Gambling, drug addiction, immorality, and a host of others are but traps designed to keep us in bondage, and in service to others for their enrichment. Some people have unwittingly rejected the reality of sin, because darkness and deception keeps them ignorant to the good news of Christ. Some people purposely deny prohibitions of wrong in-order to pursue an agenda positioned against the positions of God. These are the people whose deeds are fruitless and shameful and must be exposed because they have fallen into the very deep quagmire of sin. It is one thing to fall into sin and is completely different when others plan to trap and enslave us for their own gain. Those producing bad fruit have declared themselves to be a god! Perhaps the Evil One was the very first narcissist? Perhaps it is he who started the first of many false religions? It used to be only a Pharaoh or a Caesar was looked upon as a god, but now it is offered to all who will but accept it.

The purpose of false religion has always been to deny to us the truth that will set us free from all slavery no matter, if it is the internal desire for drugs, or the external pain from the task master's whip! Celebrities are made to shine as stars high above us in the heavens; unlike the wise men following the star provided by God, the bright lights and stars are meant to lead us away from the reality that is God, and the truth he provides. The stars of the world present an existence of having no prohibitions, limitations, or responsibilities imposed upon their actions, because their manmade godlike status precludes the world's justice. When a star is found flawed (guilty) he or she is immediately rehabbed and restored to their former place of brilliance, in-order to guide us into the perceptions that all things are good, and can be explained away without accepting responsibility. The star is applauded and adored even more by bowing to restorative measures. We have teen idols and screen and print projections of what is declared as perfection; stars that are given as role models to emulate and recognize as free and uninhibited by the hardships afflicting the common man. Truly it is the blind leading the blind! Restoration is done skillfully by "spin-doctors" but in-truth they are liars. These masters of the lie speak a language of duplicitous two-faced and tricky ambiguity that never allows for or solidifies an answer without backdoor plausibility, purposely designed to deny truth. Liars refuse a response of "yes" or "no" to probing questions which is the equivalent of drawing the blinds to deny the entrance of light. If we continue to conceal the things we know to be wrong it is indicative of a self-serving agenda. There are those who clean pigeon droppings from park statues and this is also a form of restoration, but the statues are as dead as those who deny truth. By resisting the presentation of truth for fear we will be exposed is of itself condemnation igniting the war within us-the "conflict in man" spoken of by the apostle Paul.

Attractions of the world are a hope for change

The world's attractions promise us a measure of peace from the condemnations of conscience, and hope for freedom from a slave's existence; it is a lie manifesting itself in the temporary disconnects of drug addiction. These send us off into altered states of consciousness that tell us, "It's all good!" With tones of mocking captivity that bite into the fabric of marrow and bone, as chains would wear upon flesh; and both the spirit and flesh endure the punishing captivity of slavery to the various substances designed for such purpose! Substance abuse is not the cure for the life of a slave;

it is deception designed to keep the chains of slavery fixed and tight upon those so afflicted.

Instability

Instability of life is caused in-part by our nature dictating itself against the knowledge of what we know to be right and correct, by a desire to break free from a condition we are not in control of and by the cumulative impact of this duality that adds rapidity to our increasing descent into darkness! Instability turns us upside down, headlong into deeper solitude manufactured by darkness, denying to us an upward view. Having the ability to set us free. Instability increases the speed in which we experience life and increases our chances for missing critical signs of danger.

Stability

When we first taste the goodness of God stability becomes able to deny the dictates of all things negative, undesirable harmful and wrong! It is then that the chains that rendered us impotent, powerless and weak, are broken; we are then permitted to say, "no" to all the things that held us captive and denied to us the life God desires for his children. This is joyful and cause for all of those who love us to celebrate with us, but it does not end there. The light of truth and the healing warmth it affords begins to construct the foundation that brings to us stability to our new life in Christ. STABILITY IN OUR LIFE BEGINS WITH RECOGNITION OF THE TRUTH CONTAINED IN OUR LIFE AND IS REINFORCED AND STRENGTHENED MORE AND MORE AS WE BATHE IN THE REALITY OF GOD'S LOVE FOR US! It is truth that arrests and places the dictates of a slave condition, into a used-to-be way of life. Failure to recognize truth (God) as the ultimate source of freedom is a chief enslaver.

For those who are seeking a way out of slavery, other than the light of truth, what is found does not come without cost. Failure to recognize God places mankind at the godhead of existence and is not baggage free. The belief in the nonexistence of sin is the beginning of the denial of the existence of God. One such responsibility that clings to the "independence from sin philosophy" is to find contentment happiness, gladness, peace and satisfaction through a value oriented rating of success. "Your life is a success when you can shape your identity through your possessions. Life becomes a rock of stability when your possessions declare independence from the hardships of life." When the outward appearance of a person is dishonest, expressing an inner condition of peace, where there is none, it is easy to conclude by those wishing to break-free from the constant desire for "more" that materialism solves all our problems cares and hardships. We know this to be a false presentation because it is written, ***"Human desires are like the world of the dead, there's always room for more."*** *Human desires must be put to death through the receipt of a new spirit. As Jesus told the Pharisee named Nicodemus, that he must be born again to be able to not only enter the kingdom of God but to see it as well, so too it is with us. Being in possession of a new spirit is a complete change in our thinking process; we know truth and it has set us free! No longer do we desire a- substitute promising contentment and peace for we have found the reality of God who loves us! There will always be a carrot promising to arrest the hunger in man. A drug addict may be sitting on a mountain of drugs and still, there is the desire for, "More!" Embracing a world-view of "anything goes" within a mindset of self-sufficiency captures both the rich and the poor.*

People who cannot admit to dependency will certainly find it difficult to seek God; they have embraced an independent and prideful position that declares, their existence, free from all things having an absolute label attached. Rejection of God is the ultimate denial of he who is the, absolute authority. Those who will not admit to substance abuse are destined to continually seek spiritual and physical freedom for the remainder of their days. Curiously, the world accepts death as an absolute and therein resides the contradiction generating encapsulation within the mindset of man, but is unrecognized by him, until the light of truth shines into the darkness that held him enslaved.

The battle within, between right and wrong leads to battle fatigue, which is an emotional disturbance in the heart of man. Acceptance of truth concerning God and our- acknowledgement of need are the first steps toward stability in our lives, that not only removes the lies, buy injects truth of everlasting life in Christ; our great hope. Again, we must admit that God is right and we are not. When we exist in a slave reality, that discounts truth, what we are really saying is, "I don't want to do it!" This is denouncement of "Thy will be done." When we are in rebellion against the rightful authority of God, in pursuit of our own desires and dictates it is then encapsulated into the "me, myself and I" syndrome, that captures and makes central the sole purpose of our existence. There are perhaps many reasons for some to build or allow a wall to be constructed around the heart, but the windows and doors are always locked from within. Therein the isolation of captivity deepens and impacts most negatively upon all aspects of our lives. Spiritual and physical illnesses must always follow the life of a slave.

We can see the results of captivity and somehow fail to recognize the cause, to be "Plain old-fashioned sin!" It's no wonder, why the world denies the existence of sin. It is the chief enslaver! We have all experienced the war within us. We recognized our ability to know what is right, but have always failed to do it, as one who is held in bondage by a ruling power. Somehow our captivity is looked upon a just another speedbump along the road of life filled with trials and troubles. EVEN A MUFFLED CRY FROM WITHIN AN ENCAPSULATED HEART WILL BRING THE LIGHT OF TRUTH INTO THE DARKNESS OF CAPTIVITY. ANNOUNCING BOLDLY TO ALL THAT HELD US WITHIN ITS GRIP "FREEDOM!"

PRISM

The nature of light reveals
In darkness, all is concealed
A forest of night a room without light
A candle of wax absent wick
Inhibited movement caution advised
What good is beauty without light?
Corrective lens high wattage bulb
Movement captured by the timing of strobe
Fly to the paper moth to the flame
The nature of man does the same
Within the rainbow nothing's concealed
In the spectrum of light all is revealed
All must be tested and where there is darkness
Its movement arrested.

1 John 4:1 Dear friends, do not believe every spirit, but test the spirits to see if they are from God, because many false prophets have gone out into the world.

The apostle John is not speaking of the appearance of angelic beings bringing to us a message; no, he is reminding us to be careful with those we place our trust. Many false prophets, priests and ministers of the word have proven to be false; inwardly they have an agenda that is aligned with the desires of the world, and if we are not conscious of the fact that these kinds of persons are prolific in the world we may find ourselves deceived.

DAYLIGHT SAVING

Supporting cast is ready with labels bathed in light
For us to choose the company in this, the falling night.
Heightened pews where elbows come to rest
Lend solitary respite from worldly cares and stress.
Somber figures passing within the lifted glass
Touch the deep recesses of future, present, past.
Conversations flowing to the cadence of "refill"
Ever dim bulbs glowing within the hallowed zone
Emotions searching the troubled homes of bone.

Within each daylight morning that whispers, "saving grace"
Like liquid crystal pouring through night's veil for us to gain
The hope that is renewal's bliss to wash away the pain
That kept life passing quickly, down through open drains.

Psalm 18:28-29 You, O Lord, keep my lamp burning; my God turns my darkness into light. With your help, I can advance against a troop. With my God, I can scale a wall.

Bricks of condemnation

Once we have been permitted to see the truth of our lives we must get in the habit of looking forward. To focus upon the past is to invite self-condemnation and within it there is the ability to slow spiritual growth. This spiritual growth aspect has to do with developing confidence in the grace of God, and reliance upon him in the face of all adversity; even when our past transgressions shake us to the bone. These boneshaking thoughts can wake us in the night and disallow sleep. When they appear, it is like an accusing finger pointing directly at our heart. There is the underlining presentation that we are not worthy of the mercy we have received; prompting us to run from the surety of grace. At times, it doesn't matter that we understand we are clothed in the righteousness of Christ; the flashback brings us to a time regrettable, and mocks our present day with what is dead and buried! We cannot forget but we must recognize the truth concerning compulsion; what we were forced to do as slaves is not our fault. We should not dwell upon buried memories for they are dead in the eyes of Christ. We know that to look back on the past is to lose focus upon the prize of life; we sometimes forget just how big a prize that is.

COMPULSION

To go where we do not want and do what we should not do
Compelled by an inner voice that has no time for life
Its purpose is to satisfy that which cannot be eased
Cannot be told to rest a while or to get some sleep
Cannot be put into a box or stored upon a shelf
Or made to go away, by hiding in a darkened room
As a man within a cage.
And all this time he's wondering,
"How to quell this rage?"
Pacing this way that always in confusion
He cannot understand what is truth and what's illusion.
He cannot hear freedom knocking just outside his ear.
To quench the thirst within
He's bowing to compulsion to gather-up the straw
To make the bricks of passion
Placed at deception's door.

Romans 8:6-8 The mind of the sinful man is death, but the mind controlled by the Spirit is life and peace; the sinful mind is hostile to God. It does not submit to God's law, nor can it do so. Those controlled by the sinful nature cannot please God.

Renewal is something that is taking place throughout all of nature. Everything in nature has a building up and tearing down process; God needs only to renew us once! Along with the words of Jesus who tells us not to worry over the things we cannot change, we must recognize the things set into motion by God and include ourselves in the master plan, which translates into eternal life. We cannot forget our past but the cross of Christ sends those bad memories back to the deep place of darkness. Within God's truth one job done well buries a multitude of mistakes. As such, when those bottom dwellers appear unexpectedly as blasts from the past, with expectation of causing us to turn inward. Remember Jesus, and send the bad memory packing.

CONSCIENCE REPLAY

Who can stand this weight upon the soul?
I would do all I could to undo the dye cast.
I would do all I could, but who can undo the past?
Like the dead who can repay them?
All that I possess is nothing compared to the pain
That attacks in the middle of the night.
Who can count my youthful transgressions?
They assault me without notice.
Like daggers close-in upon my soul.
As the grave remains cold even in summer's day
So too the inner recesses of my life.
O Lord, allow me to forgive myself.
Even the knowledge of you, at times runs away from me.
I don't scorn your forgiveness Lord,
But how can I forget and forgive myself?
How can I stop replaying the past?
Renew my joy and trust,
That I may declare with strength to the shroud
Surrounding my heart
"God loves me, depart!"

Philippians 3:13-14 Brothers, I do not consider myself yet to have taken hold of it. But one thing I do: Forgetting what is behind and straining toward what is ahead.

Romans 10:9-10 That if you confess with your mouth, "Jesus is Lord," and believe in your heart that God raised him from the dead, you will be saved. For it is with your heart that you believe and are justified, and it is with your mouth that you confess and are saved.

30

CHOICE

Entrance into the world is not by choice. Once we are born we begin to grow in knowledge and understanding and we choose to either comply with or reject the laws of nature and society. We must comply with some laws of nature or else there will be serious consequence; gravity doesn't ask us if we want to deny the consequence of falling to the ground from a high place. There is no choice involved with gravity; we will fall. With respect to the laws of man, there is always someone who will think they can defy society without consequence, and the prisons are filled with such lawbreakers. There are societal laws that in some instances reflect the hierarchy of law throughout the universe. All of creation is bound by the laws contained within its existence; no matter, if upon the earth or throughout the heavens there are laws that govern. We can choose to have distain for nature, society or God, (any infraction against law placed into existence by God is an infraction against him), but within all law there is consequence. Justice, like truth is a double-edged sword, cutting both ways. On one edge of the sword, is receipt of what is deserved and on the other it is making the injured whole. Truth is the foundation of the laws of God; crime begets punishment, reprimand and sentencing; every choice (right or wrong), has two sides, reflecting guilt or innocence, worthy or unworthy, disgraced or honored, clothed or naked; bringing into the light our condition of need for mercy, because there are none who are righteous. Truth relating to our need within a system of perfect law (the laws of God), and the lower-case derivatives riddled with corruption and flaws alerts us to the reality of he who established all law above mankind.

Because we are not living within an existence of perfection, with respect to the laws of society, there will always be an inclination by some to scrap the entire system and live by their own rules, guidelines and laws. Criminals, who know they will be convicted in a court of law, are often given a choice to "plea bargain," but, just as we do not have a choice concerning entrance into life there will not be a choice for those who defy the truth of God. We don't have a choice upon entry, but we do have a choice in where we are going when we exit! Unfortunately, many do not recognize this choice and fail to receive the mercy extended in the sacrifice of Christ. All of us have heard of "Judgment Day," and even with this belief extending throughout the world there are those who will not recognize or are kept blindfolded from such heralded reality. We are told, if we believe in the heart, we will be saved; this is a wonderful way to express truth. Within our heart we will truly know, if we love someone or not; we may have varying degrees or levels of love and it is with this same conviction that we know if we are saved or not. With respect to confessing with our mouth that, "Jesus is Lord," what we find is the truth, that God has called all his children to be communicators. We can say many things, but we will not believe what we say, unless the heart confirms it! Maybe the heart (love) works closely with conscience, with truth as an unbreakable binding? Love and Truth are the same.

VIEW OF THE HEART

Happy sad glad hurt
Chapters contained in the heart
Water rains from the sky
The head bows eyes cry
Tears of mercy regret guilt or shame
All are from the choices we make.
Love truth reality fact
Denial of these is a hurtful smack
To the "Heart of Creation"
First and Last Beginning and End
A view of the heart is truth's best friend.
Eyes focused without twists or bends
Love moves stirs and reaches
For all that is good is what the heart teaches.

Psalm 37:31-32 The mouth of the righteous man utters wisdom, and his tongue speaks what is just. The law of his God is in his heart; his feet do not slip.

Complex simplicity

Just as we can understand the attributes, qualities and traits of love and truth designed into the heart of mankind, we must also recognize the heart can be corrupted and the lie brought into the prominent position of a person's life for the self-gain within the world's offerings. Clearly, we see this throughout the world's governments and its leaders. Telling the truth has become an anathema, abomination and loathing to those whose objectives are formed by an inward focus, leaving no room for anything extending to the good of mankind; only a resemblance reflection and untruthful presentation is given to deceive those who have been duped by displays absent the love authenticating the heart's purpose.

*Some have started out in positions of authority with the intentions of truth and love present in the heart. But, power and greed for the world's offerings, finds the system of achievement is so much easier, when the rules of corruption are accepted and honed to a level of skillful deception; the compromise within begins its advance toward total corruption. This is perhaps one reason why it is written, "**Guard your heart for it is the wellspring of life."** The "wellspring of life" simply means it is the source of life and if- and when, the heart stops-beating life is lost; and when the heart no longer loves, deception, dishonesty and the lie has moved a person into the, "Day of Judgment" side of the coin. Lost or saved are the only results having eternal meaning in the final analysis of a person's life. The only thing having lasting value in life is the gift of eternity, for those who will accept the truth of God and honestly focus upon pleasing him and not ourselves. Although, when we please ourselves, by choosing correctly, absent conscience condemnation we are pleasing God.*

1 John 3:19:22 This then is how we know that we belong to the truth, and how we set our hearts at rest in his presence whenever our hearts condemn us. For God is greater than our hearts and he knows everything. Dear friends if our hearts do not condemn us, we have confidence before God and receive from him anything we ask, because we obey his commands and do what pleases him. *Again, everything in life can be understood to bring forth reward or consequence depending upon how we choose our actions; in addition, there are also emotions and thoughts that can come to us without notice; anger, hatred, and a host of others which are not only displeasing to God but harmful to us. When they appear to our awareness within emotions or thought, we can choose to remain in this incorrect focus, or else, we choose to change our focus into areas that are not displeasing to God. For us to do otherwise is to invite consequence. There can be times when anger in-particular can grab-hold of us and drag us into a hateful revengeful mode; it is at these times we are to remember,* ***Hebrews 10:30-31 For we know him who said, "It is mine to avenge; I will repay," and again,***

"The Lord will judge his people." It is a dreadful thing to fall into the hands of the living God.

When my attention is brought to the evil in the world, there are times I feel like, "This is too much! Just bomb them out of existence!" This is especially true when innocent children are made to suffer or die. We understand through biblical presentation that there will be a point in time that God will bring forth his righteous judgments upon the earth. I'm not speaking of our right to defend ourselves against such evil in the world. When Jesus told us to turn the other cheek, he was not telling us to let our enemies kill us. In the same way, we are not to kill (murder) others, we are not to let others kill us. **"Do not kill,"** *presents to us, once again, that double edged sword that yields reward or consequence in the appropriate choice presented to us. If we go out and judge others to be deserving of murder by our own hands, then we should expect others to come to the same conclusion regarding their right to judge us as also worthy to be murdered. This concept of murder has nothing to do with the right to self-defense since no one has the right to take a life unjustifiably.*

And so, as was the case when I was driving my youngest grandson (Jacob), home from his preschool I had gotten involved in a road rage incident where the driver behind me took exception to my braking and steering to avoid hitting an animal in the road. Had she not been almost glued to my rear bumper, perhaps her anger would not have provoked her male companion to act so foolishly? At the traffic light, the passenger in the vehicle, had gotten out of the vehicle and came to the passenger side of my car with a bayonet in his hand. Had he made a threating move apart from the clearly visible presentation of his weapon, and I had shot him to defend not only myself but my grandson it would have been justified in the eyes of God and society.

BUTTONS

Natural and synthetic materials are used in making buttons.
Power buttons that start and stop the machines we use each day.
Pushbuttons that call our friends to play.
But the buttons that cause us to explode
Must be discarded in a way
Assuring a final resting place
Where the choice of right and good
Does not tread the edge of rage.

Proverbs 16:32 Better a patient man than a warrior, a man who controls his temper than one who takes a city.

It is almost always better to be patient instead of making rash, impulsive and thoughtless decisions. Sometimes we don't have the luxury of patience, affording contemplative time for choosing correctly. If we are attacked by someone, absent provocation, it is then that the self-preservation aspect of, "life is precious" and must be protected kicks into play. Since we do have this self-preservation instinct and/or predisposition for preserving our lives proves to us the desire of God that none should perish.

2 Peter 3:9-10 The Lord is not slow in keeping his promise, as some understand slowness. He is patient with you, not wanting anyone to perish, but everyone to come to repentance. *Since God is patience with us, with all our shortcomings, shouldn't we also follow his example of patience? We are urged to not only follow the commandments but to also follow Jesus in the manner-in-which he lived this life and the teachings he presented to us; shouldn't he (Jesus) and the example of his life be in the forefront of how we should also live? Following Jesus is hierarchically the most important aspect of a Christian's life. Jesus exercised much patience (this was not the first time he had entered the temple), with those who had created an atmosphere resembling a den of thieves, in the house of God.*

Matthew 21:12-15 Jesus entered the temple area and drove out all who were buying and selling there. He overturned the tables of the money changers and the benches of those selling doves. "It is written," he said to them, "'My house will be called a house of prayer,' but you are making it a 'den of robbers.'" The blind and the lame came to him and he healed them. But when the chief priests and the teachers of the law saw the wonderful things he did and the children shouting in the temple area, "Hosanna to the son of David," they were indignant. *The chief priests and the teachers of the law became, "indignant." Because Jesus was doing all things good, these temple officials became filled with wrath, scorn and contempt for him. I guess if he had done nothing but bad things they still would be indignant? In their determination, no matter what Jesus did he was upsetting their cash cow!*

Let's look at the time within Jesus' ministry that this event took place. He is well into his ministry and only six chapters in the gospel of Matthew remain, before he is crucified. It does look like Jesus exercised great patience, before he took the action of cleansing the temple. However, the chief priests and the teachers of the law, up until this time in the ministry of our Lord had set-out upon every devious avenue to stop him. It wasn't until they realize their carnival atmosphere of filling the temple treasury, has come to an end that we hear of their, "indignant" posture. Yes, they were not happy with our Lord prior to this incident but they had thought they could demote his popularity through deceptive tactics, but now, they no longer are able to hide their disdain, contempt and hatred for our Lord. I'm visualizing the great, "Day of Judgment" and the look on the faces of these hateful hypocrites. I guess they could not understand the meaning of, vengeance belonging to God? The commandment, **"Thou shalt not kill,"** *must have also been a puzzling pronouncement since everywhere they looked murder was being committed? They willfully committed murder, and we can assume the murder of Jesus was not the only time in the history of the ruling religious, that they condone and/or pursued the death of those they held in disdain. Their decision and choice to go to war against goodness must be the dumbest decision in the history of mankind! We understand-everything* *concerning the permissiveness of evil acts, was preordained by God, within his plan for salvation, and so, we also understand that they were destined to be condemned at the Judgment.*

CLARITY

For every truth, a counterfeit appears.
Truth is a clear voice pronouncing what is right.
Truth transforms darkness into light searching for those
Seeking freedom's peace.
Understanding, like a trumpet's call
Awakens and informs.

Worldly chatter is a clutter atop horizon's crest
Unknowing is like a vacuum humming
Filling the room with noise.
Truth makes the skies open
Puzzle pieces fall upon the ground
As understanding captures hearts
With a soft-sung sound.

Clarity comes to those who seek.
It climbs-not what's too steep.
It soars within the heart of all
And truth understands its call.

Mark 4:11 He told them, "The secret of the kingdom of God has been given to you."

Justification via end-result

"For it is with your heart you are justified." *Having already equated the heart with truth and love, what we are hearing, is there's no doubt in the hearts of those who have been set free by truth; that we have been justified by the sacrifice of Christ. This justification appears to mean those of us who have been saved will not be judged. Hallelujah! There are beliefs present in the* *world appearing to be true, but, they are not a blanket covering for all situations. For instance, "The end justifies the means." The meaning of this phrase, or expressive idiom, is sometimes true, but not so the case in all instances. It certainly does not represent all things good. The religious rulers felt justified in the crucifixion of Jesus; the murder, was a necessary means for them to remain within their elite positions. From this we can deduce, if you are wrong in the way you decide you are right, you are still wrong! "The end justifies the means," is a presentation brought forth by the world, its meaning is stated to be, "It is acceptable to kill (murder) one person to save many." The appearance of the actions of those religious, seeking the death of Jesus, does not, on the surface appear to be much different from this modern-day expression.*

John 18:14 Caiaphas was the one who advised the Jews that it would be good if one man died for the people. *Before bringing Jesus to Caiaphas (who was the high priest), they had brought him the Annas, who was the father-in-law of Caiaphas, and Annas turns Jesus over to Caiaphas. During the interrogation of Jesus (this was never a truth-seeking mission on the part of the Jews), they were already filled with contempt for our Lord. Jesus is brought before the high priest and false witnesses and testimony was charged against him. He is asked by the high priest about the testimony of the false witnesses and Jesus remains silent. It is then that the high priest says,* ***Matthew 26:63-66 But Jesus remained silent. Then the high priest stood up and said to Jesus, "Are you going to answer? What is this testimony that these men are bringing against you?" Then the high priest said to him, "I charge you under oath by the living God: Tell us if you are the Christ, the Son of God." "Yes, it is as you say," Jesus replied, "but I say to all of you: In the future, you will see the Son of Man sitting at the right hand of the Mighty One and coming on the clouds of heaven. Then the high priest tore his clothes and said, "He has spoken blasphemy! Why do we need any more witnesses? Look, now you have heard the blasphemy. What do you think?" "He is worthy of death," they answered.***

Apart from Jesus declaring that he is the Christ, the most damning of words spoken at this false trial are the words of Caiaphas, **"Why do we need any more witnesses?"** *With the inclusion by Caiaphas of the word, "we," what we find is the entire trial was corrupt, and the outcome was never in doubt in the hearts of those who had determined they needed to kill Jesus. Caiaphas had no clue to the truth he had spoken, by saying it is better for one man to die for the people. Had he known the most immediate truth pronounced down through the centuries, and now, present before him, would he still have condemned Jesus to death? Yes, Jesus spoke in parables during his preaching, so that they would not be able to see or understand the truth concerning himself. Self-centeredness makes people blind to the happenings of truth, beyond their own perceived aura of ability to judge and make choices righteously.*

If you, **"believe in your heart that God raised him from the dead, you will be saved."** *This portion of the quote from Romans, is a most powerful statement. It is powerful because we are also told in the parable of the,* **"rich man and Lazarus"** *that even if the dead were to come back to life people would still not believe. The rich man wanted someone to go and warn his brothers of the misery he was now experiencing in hell; Abraham basically says, people have evidence through the scriptures and the prophets, but still they will not believe. If this is so, (and we understand it is), how powerful is the advent of truth (the work of the Holy Spirit) in our lives that proves to us the sin in our lives, and convinces us of the resurrection of Jesus? Let's remember, even after the resurrection of Jesus there were some of his own disciples who doubted, even when they had Jesus right in front of them! As I have stated before, once we have convinced ourselves that something is impossible, we will find it very difficult, if not impossible to believe. We have tendency to deny the reality of the truth contained in, "nothing is impossible for God." However, we have been blessed and saved by the hand of God and with the Holy Spirit making entrance into our lives, which were formerly in darkness, we received the ability to believe and know of this truth concerning, "nothing is impossible* *for God."* ***Matthew 19:26 Jesus looked at them and said, "With man this is impossible, but with God all things are possible."*** *Jesus had just finished telling his disciples that it was,* ***"easier to put a camel through the eye of a needle than for someone who is rich to enter the kingdom of God."***

It's a good thing for us to understand the limitations of man and the infinite abilities of God. When we recognize our limitations we then begin to find reliance upon those who are apart from ourselves; the ultimate person of reliance upon is God. Within our families, friends and society, we find a need to rely upon each other within the vocations, jobs and skills we bring to the job market, this diversity of skills strengthens us and overcomes the shortcomings of being alone; but together as a society we can thrive, flourish and prosper, in both specific and general terms. When the ability of togetherness finds limitation, there is the need to reach-out and call upon God for help. We really don't wait until we find the need great enough to approach God; it is he who knows in advance what we need, and he provides for us in ways that often cause us to say, "Wow!" I do think God gets a great kick out of our being adorned with the face of, "Wow!" Point of interest: At the time Jesus told his disciples the parable, depicting the rich man in hell and Lazarus safe in the bosom of Abraham, he (Jesus), was perfectly correct in stating, that even if someone would come back from the dead they still would not believe. At the time of this telling the Holy Spirit had not been given to the church; but with the advent of the Holy Spirit, after the Ascension of Jesus, the church (us) became empowered, and in this, we were able to know truth. When we hear of the Holy Spirit leading us into all truth, it is also depicting a confirmation of all truth we have been given as well!

John 16:13-14 But when he, the Spirit of truth, comes, he will guide you into all truth. He will not speak on his own; he will speak only what he hears, and he will tell you what is yet to come. He will bring glory to me by taking what is mine and making it known to you. All that belongs to the Father is mine. That is why I said the Spirit will take from what is mine and make it known to you.

Another point of interest: In the same way that Jesus did not come to us speaking and declaring his own authority, so it is we see that the Holy Spirit will also come to the church and give to the church the understanding of all that Jesus had already given. This is once again, the humility of God on display; unlike the one who is to come, and represent himself as the ultimate authority, filled with the pride that is so evident in many throughout the world. This antichrist will find acceptance from the world because they will see the deceptive wonders and not only believe, but they will approve of him because he represents all that they have embraced since the beginning of deception's emergence upon the doorstep of mankind!

SAY WHAT

I sometimes stop to ponder how it was devised
This talent of the world for telling bold face lies?
I live half of life, "too young" and in the latter part of life
They tell me, "I'm too old?"
I admit, I once sought a happy place in time
Where it would come together bringing peace to my mind.
To my chagrin, I'll begin to tell of this farce
There are no ideal settings upon the earth.
No age the suit will fit, no special date of birth
No limit for bull-dinghy to clog receiving ears
With efforts to confuse with earthly fears.
The world is a battlefield of intense bitter fibs
And the faster we find truth the sooner we can live.

John 8:43-44 Why is my language not clear to you? Because you are unable to hear what I say. You belong to your father, the devil and you want to carry out your father's desire. He was a murderer from the beginning, not holding to the truth, for there is no truth in him. When he lies, he speaks his native language, for he is a liar and the father of lies.

BOOK 2

Emergency 911

In remembrance of Sept. 11, 2001
Never Forget.

Once the sound of peaceful pace, busy feet from place to place.
Within an instant hope is forced to halt in silent marvel gaze
At courage racing in the Brave.
In the Finest thoughts as flint
Faced the beast for innocence.
EMT's healing hands joined the Boldest in the task
Presented to the Tower's Best.
Bells and Preacher disbelief forestall movement of the feet.
"All, is well, return remain," halts the flight of downward gain.
Hope lay stricken bound in tears as truth
in windows gripped despair.
Heart to heart and eye to eye as a beggar's bowl advanced
Ignites the bond in common man.

Determined feet in turnout coats through
the heat and blinding smoke.
Hope renewed in just a glance of axe and strength in hero's hand!
Of light in crowded stairwell floors, of
steadfast hearts beating grace
Into the maw of hell, they raced, to meet the beast face to face!

Angels marveled in refrain:
"No greater love can man display."
Flashing lights and sirens prayed as courage faced the beast.
Falling beams of crippled steel as arrows to the heart.
Concrete sighs afflict the eye and all things fed the heat.
Flashing lights and sirens prayed as courage faced the beast.
A moment in the sun's retreat children's laughter turned to gray
"O my God!" all voices speak through
crashing sounds and panicked feet!
Flashing lights and sirens prayed as courage faced the beast.
"Haul away now lads, haul away fast

With hope in your helmets and strength in your hands!
Haul away now lads haul away fast,
From the top of the rubble to a pocket of chance."
Remember, truth is freedom's key.
Hold to the breast thoughts long past of what life used to be.
Captured thoughts of what was lost is food to keep us free.
The mind reason's, "Separation brief."
Yes, in paradise united, but still the heart weeps.
Have mercy, O Lord, on us who remain and into your kingdom
Embrace the Brave.

Proverbs 11:21 Be sure of this: The wicked will not go unpunished, but those who are righteous will go free.

Justice

In remembrance of Sept. 11, 2001

Suffering and shock stuns the soul, but justice
like a clock, ticks ever in the bones.
Resolute in purpose recompense assured by
God who is Judge, Strength and Sword.
Mourn to break the knot of pain barbed awareness in the veins
Free the spirit from the cold as a dagger rending flesh
As an arrow pierces storm
As light defeats the dark
Mourn to break the knot.
Mourn for the souls who fled to heaven's door.
Mourn for the heroes who are no more.
Mourn for all creatures and birds upon the wing.
Mourn for the earth that had not a voice
Convulsing from the life that ran into fertile ground
In rivulets of crimson that made-not a mourning sound.

Within the ash of the grave voices call as crashing waves.
Resonant the sound to hands stretched forth to flame.
"Swift is judgment to hearts of stone and evil ways!"
To eyes in darkness light is shone as eagle wings take flight.
Wisdom as her guiding force fed by silenced lives.
Voices free of mourning moans cry, "Justice" at God's throne.

It's love that's feared in fortress stone sending tremors to the bones.
Breaking boulders at the root with the hammer strength of truth.
Announcing boldly, "Time to pay!
There's nowhere to run and no hiding place!"

Isaiah 9:7-8 He will reign on David's throne and over his kingdom, establishing and upholding it with justice and righteousness forever.

Healing

In remembrance of Sept. 11, 2001

Into the mist of cloud filled skies
The heart descends and spirit cries
Tremors race to temple's brace
Purchase heavy whispers, "Break."
Defense born at marrow's gate
Enter still, the crashing waves of yesterday.

A shade a shroud a coffin pall ending day in westward fall.
Wisp of cloud bows above, through it all love remains
The healer of souls.

With truth comes sweet surrender, to walk on water in the storm.
To holdfast hope we have known.
To see the fruit upon the vine
With leaves of green in sunlight reign
Etched into each the precious name of all
God has saved.

Revelation 19:9 Then the angel said to me: "Write: Blessed are those who are invited to the wedding supper of the Lamb!" And he added, "These are the true words of God."

Heat

Volcanic undercurrents releasing poison's heat.
Vocal breath advancing threats chalkboard screech
Clanging bells emptiness of thought
From conflicts of the flesh friction's heat is wrought.

A fire stoked by hateful flames
No thought is given to earth ground trees
Or the fate of those who mourn and bleed.

The heat continues in battle's fray.
Until the flame of anger dies and smoke is cleared away.
It's then and only then it's said, "What a price to pay!"
A landscape of insanity not fit for man or beast
The promise of a robin's song cannot be heard or seen
When the battle of the mind exits with its heat!

Matthew 5:44 But I tell you love your enemies and pray for those who persecute you, that you may be sons of your Father in heaven.

It is probably the most difficult thing for us to accept. Let's think about what is being asked of us by our Lord. Jesus is asking us to not only pray for those who would kill us but he is telling us to love them! It is not as if Jesus didn't show to us his willingness to forgive and pray for his enemies; he set the stage and expects us to follow. ***"Father forgive them for they know not what they are doing."*** *If we are bitten by a rabid dog, do we harbor hate and hope it dies? I would like to think that we would understand the dog's action is based upon the sickness, not actually giving serious thought to bite us. It hasn't thought about the consequences for either the person bitten or itself. I guess we can say that it does not know what it is doing! I suppose some people are just like the rabid dog? They don't know what the heck they are doing! The condition of sin reaching the level of evil may be equated to a person becoming rabid.*

Again, it is not easy for us to grab hold of a love for our enemies and perhaps just as much a desire to pray for them, but if those who crucified our Lord didn't know what they were doing it is easy to extrapolate the same for modern man; some of us don't have a clue! And so, while we are attempting to forgive our enemies and to pray for them, let us pray also for ourselves, that we may at least try to understand the hatred of others. Keeping all of this in mind let's not forget that some things are classified as "unpardonable" sins. Sin against the Holy Spirit and/or to purposefully cause, ***"one of these little ones to fall"*** *is to be recognized as the enemies of both God and innocence. The ones who hurt children are those who have a depraved mind, and they have already been given over to their evil ways. The devil will not be forgiven and this is also true for the evil in men's hearts. Is there a limit to which we should, "love our enemies?" Loving our enemies does not mean we are to permit them free passage to murder us. We have within our creation a "self-preservation" response. This is the inherent knowledge that life is precious and should be protected from all harm. When Jesus tells us to turn the other cheek if we are struck by our enemy, he is not telling us to lay down and die; he is speaking to us in a way that exemplifies tolerance for those who don't know what they are doing. We assume this position of knowing simply because we have been brought into the light of understanding. Such understanding is the recognition of God; his permissible declarations as too how life should be lived, and our understanding that we also were once in the very same darkness, that currently clouds and veils the minds and hearts of our enemies. When we are told to love our enemies, we must also understand that it is a generality that encompasses all that is against goodness. As such, what we find is the deeper implication that is not limited to a physical affront, but in a broader view such enemy is recognized as against God; an ideology inherently opposed to anything that presents a barrier to evil's intent. When one is antigod it does not necessarily mean that he recognizes the reality of the Almighty. Rather, it is a twofold descriptive that understands both aspects of evil; that which is recognition of God and purposefully against all that he stands for, and those who are ignorant of such reality but are lost in the* *wilderness of clouded and wrong lifestyles, that have set-loose a sinful permissiveness in the heart and mind, accurately describing that which is in opposition of holy and good.*

Forgiveness

As we have received so too we must offer.
Of all the hurtful-things we've done to others we should love
And later, find remorse that's stirred to advance an offering
Of reconciling salve, refusal of the offering is just as bad.

Matthew 6:12 Forgive us our debts as
we have forgiven our debtors

Freedom

What does it mean?
Freedom is the state of being complete
Within our self in the home and in the streets
Where the heart and thoughts are free to roam
Wherever thought is right, and it does no harm.
Freedom is a gift from God to man.
It must be protected in the heart and in the land.
When freedom is attacked, a change is ushered in
By those who would be kings, their rule of law is sin.
When freedom is found in all its forms
The boulder is lifted from the center of each breath
Where deep within a tear-filled rain, sadness came to rest
God spoke a whispered thought, set the spirit free
And filled a vacant heart.
O shower of light and love that rains upon the soul
Mercy brought forth freedom in its richest form
It's the knowledge of you, O Lord, in a man who is reborn!

Psalm 95:7-9 "Today if you hear his voice, do not harden your hearts."

"The land of the free." When we think of freedom our thoughts are focused upon what it may have meant to have been a slave, or perhaps we might associate freedom with an ability to lay claim to our hearts desires, because money is not an obstacle. Many are those who recognize slavery in the form of addictions to substances, and others find they are compelled by influences that force compliance to the desires of others as was the case in the days, whole segments of society were condemned to a life of servitude to others who held forceful power over them. All these and many more examples of a lack of freedom are present in these days and times of our lives. However, unless a man is set free by the truth of God and the reality of the hope he has given to us, no matter what our station in this life may be, freedom in all of its glory can never be truly had, understood or appreciated.

There are many countries today where freedom is unknown, and the populace can only imagine how life could be if allowed to express themselves in a manner acceptable to both God and self. However, even in totalitarian societies people have heard the truth of God and the sacrifice of Christ, and in this they have been set free; more so, than many in our own land who are free to live in accord with the laws of man, but have not been given the experience, of being without the chains that keeps the spirit bound and gagged in the deep dark recesses of our soul. To be free in both one's country and in one's own inner self is the true freedom God desires for all of those who call upon his name.

Crossroads

The straight road is easy to follow
Sun by day and lamp by night
There's nothing to balance upon the scales of life.
A troubled man seeks a way out, up and down, east and west
The crossroad beckons, saying, "This way is best."
All roads are but testing for footfalls solid
Listening to off roads inviting a rest
Wandering the backroads away from the straight path
Snowfalls that follow erase all our steps.
A wayward point alone isolation
Captures visions presented in time
Entraps the journey as dead-end signs
Slows the rhythm underbrush grabbing
Crossroads deny that life can mean sadness.
Life is hard.

A painted sun gives not warmth.
We know there is sweet and sour courage and fear
Right and wrong laughter and tears
Weak and strong hatred and love
On the crossroads of life, the road gets tough.
For those who have left the safety of narrow
The Crossroad speaks, "It is better tomorrow."
The straight path is the shortest of lines
No intersections or impossible climbs
Decisions come with sunshine or rain
But many a storm is for man's gain.

Proverbs 12-28 In the way of the righteous there is life; along that path is immortality.

With today's technology incorporated within a ground positioning system we very rarely lose our way, when traveling from, "A" to point, "B" but still, there are times when we are given a choice or forced into a direction of travel. Many a man has struck-out on his own without a GPS to guide him and found himself lost! For the most-part the GPS is a very useful tool that, can save us from becoming lost, especially if we are lost in a state other than the one in which we reside. What this traveling is telling us is: No matter where we are we must always know where we are going or else we will be forced to try and read the map that we have buried in the trunk of the car. Does anyone remember maps? Many roads traveled promise clear driving without roadwork or monster delays; but a sure thing is worth more than the promises from roads we have never traveled. Life is filled with chances; if we choose the off road, or crossroad only to find the decision to do so was a mistake there is consequence; or else, if we make a good choice then so much the better. Losing focus upon the directions to eternal life needs more than a ground positioning system, we need God's Positioning System. Jesus; he's the Way.

Nightmare

I dreamt I was rich, they toppled the system.
I slept in a room filled with cash, it was locked from the outside.
I won a lottery and had a mansion built
with a great wall surrounding it.
The finest of electronic surveillance was installed inside the wall.
A moat with drawbridge encircled the wall.
The firemen waved.
The trunk of my car was filled with gold bars, it was repossessed.
I found a brown paper bag filled with bearer bonds.
In a cold articulate voice, I heard, "This is a stickup!"
While diving, I spied a treasure chest.
Hundreds of sharks suddenly appeared.
Lastly, I found myself poor, the telephone rang only to remind me.
I had so many bills I kidnapped my mailbox.
This I knew all too well, sleep at last, thank God.

Matthew 6:19-21 Do not store up for yourself treasures on earth, where moth and rust destroy, and where thieves break in and steal. But store up for yourselves treasures in heaven, where moth and rust do not destroy, and where thieves do not break in and steal. For where your treasure is there your heart will be. *It's a fact of life, treasure in this life is fleeting. One day a dollar is in your hand and the next it calls someone else, "friend." Some have attempted to stop the constant ebb and tide of finances only to find that the offerings of the world and the desire to acquire are too much of a challenge. However, there is a time for us to save and become responsible in the way we either acquire wealth (planning for retirement) or in the way we squander it. Focusing on either extreme takes our focus away from where it counts.* ***"What good is it for a man to gain the whole world and then lose his soul?"*** *Here again in the words of Jesus what we find is the reality of true treasures. What would a man pay for eternal life? I'm reminded of the story of the* ***"Rich young ruler."*** *He wanted to know what else, in addition to the commandments, he should do to gain eternal life. He had become so obsessed with his riches* *that when he was told to sell all he had and to give the money to the poor, he walked away from Jesus very sad. He could not do it because his heart was fixed upon his earthly riches, not devoted to finding eternal life. I'm wondering just how this young man continued-on with his life? We know that he went away from Jesus very sad by finding out that he had to stop loving worldly riches and in its place focus upon the treasures promised to us by Christ. Did he have sleepless nights? Did he continually attempt to reassure himself of his own self-righteousness to stop hearing the words of Jesus that in his reasoning would have reduced him to poverty? Certainly, he couldn't see his present state of spiritual poverty and in this, he could only imagine true poverty to exist in the one who cannot acquire. He could not focus upon God when his heart was fixed upon his riches.* ***Proverbs 28:22 A stingy man is eager to get rich and is unaware that poverty awaits him. Proverbs 28:27 He who gives to the poor will lack nothing.*** *This is exactly what Jesus meant when he said,* ***"Sell all you have and give to the poor, then follow me."*** *He couldn't understand that God would provide for his needs.*

Bedtime

"Now I lay me down to sleep" aware of places deep.
Reality the pillowed bed mindful places dark and dread.
Conscious dwelling fixed as flint, sealed within deep with strength.
Nothing fancy straight and plain, "Reside with me, O Holy Name."

Faith in grace steadfast shield
Humble truth dispatch with haste
Evil from this place.
Spirit Sword knowledge swift
Steadfast love upon my lips
Readiness in my feet
Helmet fastened slumber sweet.
"I pray the Lord, my soul to keep."

Revelation 2:12-13 To the angel of the church in Pergamum write: These are the words of him who has the sharp-double edged sword. I know where you live-where Satan has his throne. Yet you remain true to my name.

Insomnia is a condition that denies sleep. Even if we are not directly and physically affected by the pressures placed upon us in a world that seems constantly in conflict, it can cause us to lose sleep. I'm reminded of the warning given to the apostle Peter that Satan had been given permission to test him; but Jesus said that he prayed for him to pass the test. We are constantly being tested by the world and the evil contained within the hearts of others, as such we must recognize the testing originates with the chief of demonic activity and in this, we are told by the apostle Paul to, ***"Pray constantly."*** *The more revealing aspect of this advice is for us to remain in contact with Jesus. It is when we are distracted and lose focus upon the purpose of life, what we then find are the temptations (testing) of life seeking to gain entrance into the place where God resides; within us. None of us are perfect, but if we want to lessen the impact of sin upon our lives, especially as it disturbs our sleep, we should* *pray, and in this we will find an attraction to do good, opposing the pull of the world that is never meant for our well-being.*

In addition to the sleepless nights that can be derived by improper living there is the attempt to indebt us to the world's system of, "Get now and pay later mindset." The world's systems are utilizing the understanding that human desires can never be made to say, "Enough." As such we are led into enslaving debt that denies to us sleep, and in such a lack of rest we will find additional detrimental aspects arising within our physical health. Keeping up with the Jones's was a well-known saying that basically meant that to not have what your neighbor has is to be considered a failure. In this mind set we will never find a restful night's sleep; all of this is within the plan to do harm to the creation of God.

Opened Books

Recordings and books, look-into the
matter, searchers digging to find
All that transpired throughout eons of time.
It can't be done with the hands of man, not
with printing of great books.
Not by professors with endless discourse neither
stone carvings or markings with pen.
The mind records all actions deeds and thoughts of men.
Opened books are read with praise or shock
All things must end when time cannot find a clock.
At the restoration of man seals are unlocked
Books are opened names are read heads uplifted or hung in regret.
All that was done in the soul of a man
Is seen in an instant without picture printer or pen.
The spirit-mind imprints life with vision and breath
First thought to last, unfading, simply weighing, life.
The spirit speaks in language well-known
It cheers from the heart cries and/or moans.
The book of life is not written in stone
Not printed with ink or stored in great tomes.
The life of a man is much more than flesh
When books are opened, a light is revealed
Shone into darkness where nothing's concealed!
Deceptive corruption ragged and soiled
Thoughts hidden from others in pockets sewn deep
Shocked and confused amazed to find
Unfolding of records thought privately owned
Searches the past as a miner seeks gold.

Revelation 20:11-15 Next I saw a large white throne and the one who was sitting on it. The earth and the sky fled from his presence and there was no place for them. I saw the dead the great and the lowly, standing before the throne, and scrolls were opened. Then another scroll was opened, the book of life. The dead were judged according to their deeds, by what was written in

the scrolls. The sea gave up its dead; then Death and Hades were thrown into the pool of fire. (This is the second death.) Anyone whose name was not found written in the book of life was thrown into the fire.

I do believe we are these opened books. I am so impressed by the forceful wording of this passage; it speaks of those who are not going to be given eternal life as being thrown into the fire! The spirit of man is not limited by space available. There are times when we are taken so far back in our lives by a memory, it is this memory aspect of the spirit that speaks to us of recording every thought and deed. We may not be able to remember everything, but the memory is there waiting to be unveiled in the end of time. This alone should give us pause, and lead us to recognize that nothing escapes the vision of God. This is a frightful thought even for us who have been saved; but more than the fright is the realization that all evil people will not escape their due punishment. Perhaps this is, why, we are told to love our enemies? Hatred is a waste of time.

Shining Ray

Hard knock, hard place, hard luck hard case.
Shining ray descends with grace.
Hope is special it's a gift from God to man
A river never ending until we see God's plan
Wide as the universe or tiny like a spark
It confirms the truth of him by bringing home what's lost.
A shining ray pierces darkest night
And calls to God Almighty, "Make what's wrong right."
It's the cradle where faith in him is borne.
It's strength within clay vessels
Where emptiness was thought.
A constant where defeat in man abounds
Until what was thought forever lost
Is forever found!

Colossians 1:27 To them God chose to make known to the Gentiles the glorious riches of this mystery, which is Christ in you, the hope of glory.

"The hope of glory." *Glory can be understood as someone having an excellent reputation, and this is exactly how God looks at us when in fact we are clothed in the righteousness of Christ. This hope is a reality not only for the future, but it is evident in the life we have been given now, through the unveiling of the deceptions of the world. Such conviction in our faith permits us to see truth and reality of the great hope for eternal life. We might ask ourselves what is this thing called hope? Why should we find hope present in just about every aspect of life? The answer may not be as complicated as we might think. Simply explained, it is the realization that something is possible and even probable when we have been led to believe it will take place; it will come into fruition. Hope is not a forever aspect of life, because once hope has materialized there is no need to continue hoping. I see myself in a snowstorm waiting for a bus to arrive in the dead of night. I hope it will arrive soon because it is very cold outside, suddenly* *the headlights of the bus appear in the distance and I am no longer hoping for it because I see it! The same is true with our great hope in Christ, simply because we have been given the* ***"down payment"*** *toward this great hope by the entrance of the Holy Spirit into our lives.* ***Proverbs 10:28 "The prospect of the righteous is joy, but the hopes of the wicked come to nothing."***

Hurricane

The hurricane breathing strong captures wistful wind of souls.
Desire soaring captured by the storm.
Beat and battered by debris within the forceful flight.
Tumbling ever downward no end of depth in sight.
Contact with the world crash of flesh and bone
Scattered fragments faulty sight
Caustic visions haunting nights
Echo loudly, "Grief and Strife!"
Mercy's mission healing touch upon marrow's moan
Cradled hope in forward steps seizes strength unknown.
Truth of life ingrained complete, freedom's breath sustained
By drinking deeply water pure that calms the hurricane.

Taste the goodness of the Lord, praise his holy name.
Sing to him a joyful song
O redeemed from hurricanes!

Mark 6:51 Then he got into the boat with them and the wind died down.

Having spent four years in the U.S. Navy, I can testify that being in a hurricane in the middle of the Atlantic Ocean is not fun. In fact, depending on just how severe the roll of the ship became, many of those having no faith in God were instantly converted! Just as threatening are the internal hurricanes that will not give to us a moment of peace, until we permit Jesus to Captain our ship. It is only then the storms are told to, "Go away!"

How mighty is the power of God? When we place out trust in God, to rectify the torrential waves, threatening to capsize and sink our vessel of life, it is only he who can repair the structural damage, done by the continuous pounding of unforgiving waves. It is also the internal damage produced by the constant movement that adds tremendous stress to the interior compartments. A ship will always find the best repairs are made when it returns to the dry dock from which it was constructed, there is then no question as to the expertise contained in the skills present within such a safe-haven.

Wind

The internal wind
Carries us to places we would not go.
We are driven like a leaf in its downward fall
Lifted high into the sky just to fall again
What is this force within me from which I can't defend?

How long can we live like the wind?
Not knowing where we're going
Not caring where we've been.
Racing-round in circles downward spiral's end
Torn by constant movement alone in troubled times
Captured held in bondage by blindfolds of the mind.
Denied within the core the truth of sunshine's breath
Will we keep on running until this life does end?
Fire and rain flakes and frost cannot hold the wind
It travels hither-yon knowing not a friend.
We are like the wind when we don't have a home
Where thoughts of coming danger are given to the strong.
When shall we hush the wind and live life's intent from God?

Hosea 8:7 "When they sew the wind they will reap a storm."

Just as we can understand what may be fatal for the physical has no impact upon the spiritual (so long as we are in Christ), so too we must understand the poisons of this life can have a lasting impact upon the afterlife. It is difficult to breathe in a windstorm and even more difficult is to live a meaningful life with the conflicts that force us to go where we would not go. Such forces toss us about spit us out and when we recover they do it all again! How long will we keep on racing? As long, as, we deny the truth of God we will never find the peace that calms the storms of life. Our thoughts and deeds comprise the quality of life. When we are not in control we are reduced to a slave made to comply with the dictates of our nature. That is, when the thinking faculty is reduced to a slave's position there can be no thought given to the things we are forced to do. The collective specter of condemning conscience brings to us nightmares that we are not responsible for. When the sinful nature rules there is the realization that it is not thought or reasoning in command; it is the desires of the body that demands of us compliance. ***Romans 7:21-25 So I find this law at work: When I want to do good, evil is right there with me. For in my inner being I delight in God's law; but I see another law at work in the members of my body, waging war against the law of my mind and making me a prisoner of the law of sin at work in my members. What a wretched man I am! Who will rescue me from this body of death? Thanks, be to God-through Jesus Christ our Lord! So then, I, myself in my mind am a slave to God's law, but in my sinful nature a slave to the law of sin.*** *It can be like a windstorm when we are not focused upon the weather; we know the storms are out there, not only in the world but internally, we can and do cause many to appear, it's our duty (with God's help) to keep the wind of wrong from blowing us away!*

Fat Cats

The love of power is a product of pride.
The power of love speaks gentle and wise.
The love of standing applause
Cannot hear truth calling out to the lost.
Titans of industry tycoons and heirs
Show us a picture at times without care.
Facades of perfection faces aglow
Behind the projection lives darkness below.
Hollywood hammers celebrity nails
Erecting the sets designed to fail.
Seekers of office like sails of a ship
Dip into the wind and flow with its grip.
Deceiving pulpits lofty and high
Declare to the masses financial praise.
"Demons plaguing our days
Are conquered by capital raised."
"Everything has a price," it is said.
Some things should never be sold:
The faith of a friend, the bond of love
The soul of a man a child's trust.
The gift of wisdom and knowledge of plans
Should never be passed from pocket to hand.
An atmosphere free of shallow thoughts
Sees a border that must not be crossed.
Some cats are wearing thick glasses
But still, everyone gets his cut
It's not vision needing correction
It's the heart!
Many fail what is just, ignoring the law
They acquire positions and manipulate flaws.
Never addressing sidestepping ways
They pack opportunity as a bigot stores rage.
Greed erects great walls and circles
Absent only is the barbed wire.
The homes of some are beautiful prisons.

What is sown is reaped and nothing's for keeps.
Time drifting toward tomorrow
Suddenly arriving to collect what was borrowed.
Not power coin or pride can revive a silent heart.
Cold cash in the freezer no matter how many grand,
Will turn over as clothes in a dryer as combat demands
Hand to hand.
The cycle ending in accord God's plan.
Mercy accepted or fiery end.

James 3:13-16 Who is wise and understanding among you? Let him show it by his good life, by deeds done in humility that comes from wisdom. But if you harbor bitter envy or selfish ambitions in your hearts, do not boast about it or deny the truth. Such wisdom does not come down from heaven but is earthly, unspiritual, of the devil. For where you have envy and selfish ambition, there you find disorder and every evil practice.

Today's world leaders, celebrities and the exceedingly wealthy confirm the above scripture without leaving any doubt regarding the truth expressed by the apostle James. We find corruption in just about every aspect of humanity but nowhere is it more pronounced than in the aspirations of those who seek the twofold power of money and political position. Neither the secular and/or the religious spheres of influence are immune to the pull of the world that promises a better existence for the one so enriched by both power and money. We have had celebrities from the arts cross over to the political spectrum and what they found is a world even more artificial than the one they previously inhabited.

The hope of those who believe they will find the satisfaction sought after in either of the spheres of influence, is sadly dashed upon the rocks of shipwrecked shores. The belief that combining both celebrity and finance to unite in the purpose of collecting power over others is a myth. Many a man has endeavored to achieve such status and in finally reaching such mountain top they find themselves even more confined, by the realization that they can go nowhere without bodyguards and extreme safety measures.

They live in beautiful prisons no less confining than the totalitarian societies of the world. They disguise themselves to hide who they are in efforts to deny the constant flash of cameras seeking to capture an image, to sell to the legions of adoring fans, (read as idol worshipers). At some point in time many move out of the country to remote and isolated mansions, only to find there is no commutation of sentence; no parole from the life they have fought so hard to achieve.

Some of those who have fallen into such traps have realized they need help to return to a normal way of life that permitted them freedom to travel without being surrounded and threatened by both photographers and/or the insane. Can we imagine a president of the United States having to live in a gated community and protected by the Secret Service for the remainder of his days? I wonder how many times they asked themselves, "What the heck was I thinking?" Of course, we applaud their sacrifice even when we have not agreed with their political determinations. There is only one avenue of escape for those wishing to find the freedom they relinquished when at-first they began the quest for power. Yes, it is only God who can bring to them the sense of freedom and peace while still here in this life; the knowledge of the afterlife is a great comfort to those who have wasted this life on the illusions presented by the world's offerings. ***Proverbs 4:7 Wisdom is supreme; therefore, get wisdom. Though it cost all you have, get understanding.*** *Many are the powerful and rich who have gone to the grave instantly understanding all that they worked for means nothing without the promise of eternal life. Many are they who have found such success as described by the world, only to find their destruction in the unending demands of human nature's cry, saying, "More!"*

Thirst

Power greed position, vanity anger lies
Paint a plastic face on man to hide the dark inside.
High atop the mountain egos gloat and grow
They laugh aloud at people living in lands below.
A thirst for wealth and power is a thirst for escape
Away from those whose motives
Strike-out at us like snakes.
Contaminating venom has a tasty bit of hate
That speaks like wealth and power, saying,
"A snake's life is great!"
Jutting jaw hissing sounds send-out great alarm.
No matter the condition, living on a lake or mountain top
The snake of wealth and power will never quench his thirst.
He's tasted lying venom from the pool of vain pursuits
And fallen into ruin that promised him the earth
By consuming poison's sickness
That has done to him its worst.
There's longing in the soul of man
That seems to scream and shout
Constant is the sound it makes, saying,
"Get me something now!"
When power greed and vanity
Leads lies and pride at night
They'll be no need avoiding a serpent's bite
For the snake of wealth and power
Has converted another to its ranks.

Romans 12:20 Rather, "If your enemy is hungry give him something to eat; if he is thirsty, give him something to drink; for by doing so you will heap, burning coals upon his head." Do not be conquered by evil but conquer evil with good. *Do not join with the evil in-order to escape it, rather, show kindness to the evil in-order to conquer it. I think the internal heat produced by receipt of kindness, is something our enemies would never expect to be the equivalent of a burning coal. The offering of kindness to* *those devoid of love for others, (except for those they accept and love) is like a powerful beam of light shone into the darkness of hearts, never expecting to receive from those labeled by them as, "enemies." We are told to basically not be excited into wars, rather, to do good to avoid conflict produced by hatred. The underlying understanding of the above instruction is this: if it is we who are doing the offering to our enemies, it is they who have already been defeated by good. Their defeat was completed as soon they tasted the lying venom of the world; love is the cure for the poison of snakes. Their defeat is understood by us in this: unless they recognize the punishment that awaits, an unkind response would then be meaningless long term. God wants to convert evil into good through forgiveness and wisdom; just as evil attempts to convert what's good to evil through hatred and ignorance.*

Reputation

It seems everyone wants recognition
Normal behavior or weird the aim is the same,
Notoriety and fame!
No one thinks of reputation
Until it is shredded
Once it has been ruined
How can we go back and get it?
Celebrity and stardom often asks a hefty price.
"Do what I ask and I'll put your name up in lights."
Symbolic power in blackened limousines
Stakes a claim, "role model" to emulate and achieve.
In the glitter of existence, the heart finds no reprieve
From the prideful stings and blisters
The put-on passion of the weeds.
The glory of God is his excellent reputation.
Why then, is he not the role model for all generations?

Ephesians 4:17-18 I tell you this and insist on it in the Lord, that you must no longer live as the Gentiles do, in the futility of their thinking. They are darkened in their understanding and separated from God because of the ignorance that is in them due to the hardening of their hearts. *Paul is writing to the church in Ephesus and he's reminding them they are to no longer live as do the Gentiles; a godless state of existence. They are also reminded that their thinking and their hearts have been converted to focus upon the reality of salvation afforded in Christ. Within the Book of Revelation, we also find a message given to the church in Ephesus, and mostly it is a glowing review of their faithfulness to hard work, good deeds and hatred of wickedness. Apparently, Paul's letter written to the church some time before the message from John had a lasting imprint. Ephesus was an ancient Greek city located in modern day Turkey. It was built in the 10th century BC.* ***Revelation 2:2 I know your deeds, your hard work and your perseverance. I know that you cannot tolerate wicked people, that you have tested those who claimed to be apostles and are not, and have***

found them false. *In this letter to the Ephesian church, as are, all the churches mentioned in the book, it is addressed to the angel guarding over the church. I point this out because it is the angel (God's messenger) who always has access to God. God is always aware of what is going on in the churches. It is important for us to understand that we also are always in the presence of God, and in this there is or should be a sense of peace attending within our cognitive awareness. We are no longer kept in the ignorance of the world that believes it can evade judgment and punishment, from any authority so long as they are stealthy, devious and maintain an appearance of innocence. If we do not have this sense of peace or feel exposed when we are not truthful, we should then examine ourselves to see if we are still in the faith. It is always prudent for us to check ourselves and in checking, make the necessary corrections as may be necessary for restoration to the intent of God for us.*

Priority

Pay for the car or wear out the feet, buy medicine or eat.
Send a man to the moon, cure mankind's ills head to feet.
Capture a sparrow and study its walk,
clothed the naked with burial cloth.
Feed the hungry a musical dirge, take the limo
for a final lap cover the loss with dirt.
Celebrity shakedown champion's a cause, all
is as smoke that billows and chokes
Caught in the wind of bluster and chatter,
churning a fly in with the batter.
Struggles in life are denied attention, as ears
plugged with cotton and glasses tinted.
Efforts to solve the ills of the day are but
footnotes in priority's way.
Give to the poor and still they're forgotten,
angels of mercy dispense the crumbs.
Research grants for ridiculous things are
unaware of chemotherapy's stings.
Who can deny the hunger of a child? It's easier
at night when the world is asleep.
The sun is shining and the snoring is deep.
Research looks like a pickpocket in many subjects and topics.
Push the cash examine a dream filled with
heartbreak and a cavern of screams.

Hooray for the children abortion is free! Hooray for the children.
They gave their lives for a grand plan, examine
their cells for the good of man?
Hooray for the children, they never had a
chance against hypocrisy's dance.
Does priority end at the property line?
Build a fence where it leans jump!
Watch out for that stump, a reminder of what was.

1 Timothy 4:1 The Spirit clearly says that in latter times some will abandon the faith and follow deceiving spirits and things taught by demons. *Choosing to make the right decision is sometimes aligned with our beliefs. If there are those in power who believe that studying the movement of shrimp or the mating habits of kangaroos should take place before we feed the hungry or before we defend the helpless, they are fools. But if they do not believe in those priorities, then we can safely say they are the representatives of evil. We have come to expect such decisions from our politicians, but perhaps the most damaging decisions are those that impact us directly. These are mostly made by us and are brought into negative and often unintended consequences simply because we did not choose wisely. This is not something that we can avoid, we are not perfect and we can expect to make a poor decision at some point in our lives. Hopefully we can recover from the negative impact such decisions brought to us. When we know that there are those who purposely deny to others the necessary things that they cannot provide for themselves we must not deny to ourselves the truth of the world; that this is just another decision made from the corrupting hearts of those placed into positions of power. Fortunately, we live in a democracy (well at least it is still called that) and we regularly are given the opportunity to vote for those who have promised to correct such poor decisions made unknowingly or because corruption had reached into its pocket and bought its way into vital decisions affecting the lives of others. We can only pray and hope that injustice in these areas of allocating resources of the nation into ridiculous endeavors will be made to cease; if they do not there is the realization that ultimately, they must answer to the Ultimate Judge. Even a fool understands basic needs. Both the foolish and the wicked understand importance; there's no excuse for either one!*

Charcoal Dreams

Charcoal has it rough its life is hard.
Suffering's an offshoot of discord trouble strife.
Charcoal dreams of becoming diamond escaping from this life
It schemes of finding peace by any means but love.
Always there is suffering on both sides of the track
And both know of movement forward and/or back
Always there's a contest to dominate and
bind the naked and the blind.
A power play of subtlety from those who fear
Revealing of the wickedness that stays awake to snare
Unsuspecting travelers who enter starlight's
glare of promises of treasure
To quench the heat within, embers burning
quickly singeing at the skin.

Producing neither diamond or a chest of gold all of man's desire
Cannot bring a cup or drop, not barrier moat
or wall can halt prevent or stall
Wishes dressed as promises upon the road a
man is bent, motive fed by haughtiness
In shadow sister greed decisions weighing
heavy for what is sown is reaped.
When the peak is conquered the price of folly is in sight
Shining lures find capture like the fruit of thorny pride!
Conscience of the spirit sings a mournful song

When notes put into action rise then fall with wrong.
Fruit declares the worth of trees a river's flow says, "Fresh"
Air is in the sky above the sun and moon play catch
Oceans teem with many things with benefit to man
And still the charcoal dreams to become a diamond of the land.

Proverbs 15:21 Folly delights a man who lacks judgment, but a man of understanding keeps a straight course. *All too often people find themselves dissatisfied with their station in life. It is* *as if a lump of anthracite coal dreams of becoming a diamond, no longer to be held captive in the confines of the earth. It dreams of being displayed and admired by all who view its exquisite facets. Some of the aspirations will seek to be valued even more than the current market will bear. It is when the aspirations and dreams along with the schemes concocted in the dead of night are placed into action does the fruition of wickedness come into being. Of course, we recognize that coal has a useful purpose that a diamond cannot achieve. A diamond cannot heat a home or produce the fire necessary to turn water into steam and in turn power the machinery that makes living upon this earth so much more tolerable. A lump of coal may not sound as luxurious as does a diamond but its purpose is still of value. People aspire to heights that would make dreams envious. At times people demand to be uplifted by the laws of the land to be recognized as special, and worthy to be given every opportunity to become something of greater value; after all, it is no fun being a lump of coal. Unfortunately, unless a person recognizes honestly his own value, he will never find it given by others. No matter how many laws are passed the person seeking elevation will never find satisfaction unless he first recognizes both his purpose and value placed upon him by God.*

Government Gods

A dictator's slogan: "No man no problem"
A government god: "No man no cost"
A dictator's title: "Dear leader"
A government god: "Servant master"
A dictator's scheme: "Brown shirts"
A government god's dream: "National police force"
A dictator's solution: "Firing squads"
A government god: "Death panels"
Numbering of man's days has already been decided by God.
Permissiveness is illusion's song when, right
is denounced instead of wrong.
When foolishness no longer shocks, shakes
or tumbles political stock.
Dependency is slavery to the hand that writes the check.
An honest man still says, "I worked for this."
Society has labored long and hard to bring us laws of good.
"We care for you with many allotment beats per heart."
So-generous are the limits the government gods set forth!
A rooster-crows with each new day waking us from sleep,
A factory-whistle signals, "Work" or "Cease"
A government god pretends unknown is
the language that we speak.
A school bell sings a special song serving food so bland
And nothing on the cold steel tray speaks of God's great plan.
A government god offers, "hope and change"
nothing has depth and all is staged!
Nodding heads, cardboard stares, prison
walls with windows made of lies.
Beautiful landscape paintings, mechanical
breeze, woven as if mortared
Sewn and weaved as thread blinded by
illusion and all within are dead.
A servant denies his master and his worth
plummets like lightning falls
Surely the master's spoken but he does not heed his call.

We call them "politicians" but that's much
too kind; leaches have a nature
And parasites we understand, politicians have a
choice, to bend a knee or upright stand.
To be blind makes not a fool but a fool is surely blind
His hand can feel the fire sending truth up to the mind
But still he can't withdraw while immersed in flames of pride.
A gilded cage denies flight, a beautiful prison
appoints inmate guards, what's changed?
Freedom.

Revelation 13:16 The beast forced all people, small and great, rich and poor, slave and free, to have a mark placed on their right hands or on their foreheads. No one could buy or sell without this mark that is the beast's name or the number that stands for the name. *Today's prideful attitudes within some government officials lends to the appearance of the biblical prediction, that speaks of bringing about captivity for the entire world, as not only close, but many are longing for the advent of this antichrist! They do so because they are already on the side of evil, this is evident throughout the entire world. Again, all governments are corrupt and such corruption engulfs those who may want to lead a righteous life. In order, to compete with the lies from those who promise everything the formerly honest man is ensnared by what he reason's is the only way to compete. A former President of the United States recently said, "Government is corrupt." It was kind of startling to hear a former President revealing this truth! This is probably a mortal sin among the political ranks, but then, a few days after the statement was brought to the attention of the public, it was revealed that he is suffering from the disease of Cancer, in this the latter portion of his life. Many people upon hearing of this illness threatening his remaining days (he is 90 plus, years old), looked upon what he had revealed in the same way the legal system views a, "deathbed confession." With respect to the statement I made concerning, "all" governments being corrupt, it is based upon the fact that Jesus was offered the "kingdoms of the world" (governments) if only he would worship the devil.* ***Luke 4:5-6 The***

devil led him up to a high place and showed him in an instant all the kingdoms of the world. And he said to him. "I will give you all of their authority and splendor; it has been given to me; and I can give it to you, if you worship me. It will all be yours. *Well there you have it, the devil is in control of the earthly authority of man, and now we understand how it is that some of the leaders of the world remain in power. They have submitted to the request by the devil to worship him! What this means is that the lure of riches and power instilled in man, (in many cases because they do not believe in any power above their own) has without their knowing it, signed the contract that ensures ownership of their souls to the devil!*

At this point in the conversation between Jesus and the devil, the devil wants proof that Jesus is the, "Son of God." Jesus is then led to the highest point of the temple and told to jump! The devil reasons to himself that if Jesus is not the "Son of God" he will have a bloodstain on the temple grounds and in this the "No man no problem" mindset will have removed someone who threatens to upset the applecart. However, had Jesus proven that he is indeed the "Son of God" by performing the miracle of flight, the devil would have been placed on notice that he is directly competing with the Lord! This pronouncement by the devil, that the kingdoms of the world had been given to him is an interesting thought.

The devil is always attempting to prove God wrong; a classic example of this is the attempt by the devil to force Job to denounce God. In this instance, the devil is given the earth because he probably said he could do a better job of earth's administration than God. At some point in the future God will reclaim the earth and his people, when it has been sufficiently demonstrated that governments under the influence of evil are not working properly. The truth is, with the advent of Jesus the process of earth's reclamation and its inhabitants had begun.

The unification aspect of evil is constantly moving the world's governments closer to each other, so much so that there will come a time where not only a world government will be brought about but also a world leader shall emerge! The bible speaks clearly on this subject and predicts the antichrist to be that person designated as the world's leader. What may be forgotten is the ultimate ability of God to take back what is rightfully his, once his plan for mankind has reached its conclusion and the boasting of the devil is silenced for good!

Revelation 2:3-4 I saw the Holy City, the New Jerusalem, coming down out of heaven from God, prepared as a bride beautifully dressed for her husband. And I heard a loud voice from the throne saying, "Look! God's dwelling place is now among people, and he will dwell with them." *Everyone loves happy endings, in the movies, in the lives of those we love and in the final happy ending when the beast and the false prophet and the dragon are thrown into hell, for eternity! No devil no problem!*

Another way of interpreting the offering to Jesus of all the kingdoms of the world if he would only worship the devil is to understand that the devil is a liar! He is saying that the kingdoms of the world and the accompanying authority had been given to him. That statement may not be accurate, inasmuch, as the devil had so corrupted the earthly authorities that he, by the default of man, had become the chief influence among those who ruled (as was the case in said kingdoms at the time of the offering). Within today's description of governments defined as democracies, socialism, communism, dictatorships and theocratic governments there are none able to escape of the devil's corrupting influences. As such there is the implication that the devil had by default inherited the authority given to man. In this instance, what we are seeing on the part of the devil, is the offering of giving back to mankind (in the person of Christ) the authority initially given to man prior to the advent of sin.

Mankind was initially in charge of all that God had given to him; he was instructed to be fruitful and to multiply. "Fruitful," is also an implication to being able to bear "good fruit" within the structure of the earth's management; not just to increase in numbers as is the primary implication in the instruction from God. The underlying intent of evil has always been to have mankind worship the devil; to subordinate mankind to the authority of the devil that had been laid at his feet due to the separation that occurred between God and man. Satan is attempting to fill the void that sin brought about; he wants mankind to recognize him as God! He does not want to be just a god, rather, he wants to be God! Such aspiration of the devil is closely associated with those who seek after wealth and power. This should not come as a surprise, because we are aware that there are those who Jesus had labeled as, ***"Children of their father, the devil."*** *At the time, Jesus said this to the Pharisees they had claimed to be the children of Abraham, and they were corrected by our Lord by his telling them if they were the children of Abraham they would know where he (Jesus) had gotten the power to do the things he had accomplished. Once again in the history of mankind the offering will be made by the devil and it will be accepted by the man we have come to identify as "the antichrist," he will be given control of the governments of the world through deception (all that Jesus had rejected) except for Israel. Israel will not bow to the antichrist in the same manner that Jesus would not acquiesce to the advances of the devil. Throughout history there have been many who have desired to dominate the world, and in all of them there is the pronounced presence of evil. It didn't matter who it was that attempted to be king of the world; the Roman emperors, Alexander the Great or Hitler, all of them possessed the desire to possess all that is contained in the world, their only huge mistake was to fail to recognize the price that must be paid throughout eternity; the loss of their very souls!*

The revealing view of the kingdoms of the world was probably thought to be a new revelation being brought into the eyesight and cognitive awareness of Jesus. The high place he had taken Jesus was perhaps one that showed to our Lord the entire earth from a mountaintop perspective. A view of all the kingdoms of the world was something that had not been possible during the time of the offering. We are told that mankind did not know of the spherical footprint of the earth at that time and so the devil may have thought he was adding tremendous incentive to the offering. Although it is written, ***Isaiah 40:22-23 He sits enthroned above the circle of the***

earth, and its people are like grasshoppers. He stretches out the heavens like a canopy, and spreads them out like a tent to live in. He brings princes to nothing and reduces the rulers of this world to nothing. *Again, "****What does it prosper a man to gain the whole world and lose his soul?"*** *So, what is implied is this: greed and the desire for power is a major cause for someone to lose his soul.*

Caveman

It takes a lot of faith to believe in random chance.
"Early from the primal soup emerged that old caveman." They say.
Knuckle dragging hairy cat carnal living brute with bat.
Tiny little pea size brain hunter of the smaller game.
"Treetop swinging early man had lots of fortitude." They say.
He must have had a bad day to make him act so rude.
Knuckle dragging forehead slope, I can't see
resemblance in these caveman folks.
Halls of higher learning echo clarity sincere
Enough to brave an octave strong advancing from the rear.
They're aware of the willingness of ears, spoon fed
primal soup mixed with lies and fear. The world's
motives are kept hidden for if the truth was known
Their lies would be forbidden.
"Evolving toward euphoric state" so say
those who think they're great.
Absent roadside warnings or intent to brake
lacking all stability attached to only faith.
The gods upon the earth command demand threaten,
"We know what's best for you so don't you be forgetting!"
They tell us, "Only we can solve the problems you perceive."
They never admit, "It is we who make the
problems that we make you believe!"
They pick and choose who lives and dies
based upon the wallet size.
Is it a mystery why cash is idolized?
"Choose a clinic take a pill don't you worry about the bill
We will care for caveman needs, just remember vote for me!"
Manufactured crisis one after the other keeping
godless gods above the dusty roads
A caveman must travel and carry heavy
loads; lies one after another
Piled high and deep is weight enough for
any man to want to rest and sleep.
Thank God for his clarity that makes them look like clowns

These jesters primp and proper on the outside wearing smiles
But deep inside their blackened core corruption there is found
The haughtiness of pride and silence made from shrouds.

2 Timothy 3:1-5 Remember there will be difficult times in the last days. People will be greedy, boastful, and conceited; they will be insulting, disobedient to their parents, ungrateful, and irreligious; they will be unkind, merciless, slanderers, violent and fierce; they will hate the good; they will be treacherous, reckless, and swollen with pride; they will hold to the outward form of our religion, but reject its real power. *There is a mindset within many who fill positions of power and wealth; they believe they are advanced along the evolutionary ladder and with this belief they openly tell us, in so many words, that it is they who are called to lead! They are filled with all the negatives described in Paul's letter to Timothy; this is obvious to all who have ability to see. Given all this evidence that tells us of the motives of people desiring position and power over others, clearly, we find deception in the demands from them to "level the playing field" and/or "share the wealth" in-order to give all an equal opportunity, without divesting their selves of the positions of power and wealth in-order to level the field, (share the wealth). Hypocrisy is most blatant when it is smiling!*

It's interesting for us to observe those wanting to "level the playing field" in that they never divest their selves of their foundations, companies, businesses, bank accounts, mansions, and all other material structures that set them apart from the playing field! They are content to remain off the field and in this capacity, control the activities taking place on the field. Another way of expressing this is to say that they are removed from the world's entrapments because it is they who have set the traps!

A contributor to the belief that there is a certain kind of person that is acceptable to lead comes from the vanity that embraces a difference in the life contained in humanity. There are those who believe they are so far advanced along the evolutionary chain, that it is their duty to step forward and dedicate their lives in service to the lesser lifeforms, the uninformed and the destitute of acumen for the good of mankind. And then there are those who believe it is their turn to be placed into the highest office in the land, because they have been singled out and labeled as the smartest man or woman alive! Tragically they believe their own propaganda. I've mentioned this before but it is mindboggling to think that people in positions of power and wealth have willingly given themselves over to a life encapsulated within a beautiful prison. They are confined because it is understood there are people who will attempt to take their lives; as such they live the remainder of their days surrounded by secret service personnel. Private planes, limo's and everything that sets them apart from the common man is theirs to roam within, but never to experience the freedom enjoyed by the common man.

A great sense of narcissism has invaded and found a home in many, and at times they reveal their inner thoughts without realizing they have lifted the curtain and allowed light into their true self. A small but telling example of this was demonstrated by a film maker who had spoken vitriol and disdain against police officers at a demonstration against police. He had said that it was his duty to call the "murdered-murdered and the murderers-murderers." Later-on, he said, "It is the responsibility of a person of his stature to speak truth." It is one thing for society to anoint someone with a "stature" designation, but to bestow this upon yourself is pure elitist thinking! From my point of view he may be one of those lesser evolved individuals! If a person does not see the wisdom in humility that person has been captivated by his own evaluation and has no concept of what is of real value to a person's life. **Ecclesiastes 10:5 "Here is an injustice I have seen in the world-an injustice caused by rulers. Stupid people are given positions of authority while the rich are ignored."** *GNB* **Psalm 53:1 Fools say to themselves, "There is no God." They are corrupt, and they have done terrible things; there is no one who does what is right.** *GNB*

Concrete Soldiers

Warmed over graves dead men walking
Eyeballs bulging sockets depressed
Heartbeats shouting, "Race for the quest!"
Stone soldiers seeking rest for the head
Mark time in movement silent as death.
Gather in doorways and subways at night
Avoiding the light.
Cash in hand hope in a spoon
The bayonet hungers searching for food.
A nickel a dime a compromise
Brings rest for the body and sleep for the eyes.

Reveille stings a monotone call
"Rise up with the masses and sing the same song."
The body is passing slowly away
The concrete soldier doesn't notice the fade.
Daytime awakens the dead like thunder
and lightning inside the head.
Demanding compliance surrender of
dreams when the mess kit is empty
The body shakes, the mind screams, "Please!"
They won't gain trust, parades or monuments
The concrete soldier has numbered his days.

Isaiah 61:1-3 The Sovereign Lord has filled me with his Spirit. He has chosen me and sent me to bring good news to the poor, to heal the broken-hearted, to announce release to captives and freedom to those in prison. He has sent me to proclaim that the time has come when the Lord will save his people and defeat their enemies. He has sent me to comfort all who mourn, to those who mourn in Zion joy and gladness instead of grief, a song of praise instead of sorrow. They will be like trees the Lord himself has planted. They will all do what is right, and God will be praised for what he has done. *GNB*

There are so many things in life that are intended to capture and make of humanity slaves. It would be difficult to even attempt to list all the evil designs of men. For this endeavor, I will look at the substances that cause addiction in the person so enamored into taking a trip into the illusion of drug induced promise. Many a man and woman have fallen into the traps designed by evil; lawbreakers and those who want to legitimize drugs under the initial offering of medical applications, in bold announcement is declared, "some drugs should be allowed simply as a recreational endeavor." Drug addiction, gambling and anything having the possibility to capture will always find a political aspirant for approval of legalization. A former governor of Pennsylvania had openly stated that it was better for the state to collect monies generated from legalized casinos, rather than have illegal gambling take it without paying taxes. He went on to further state that the gambling addicts (pronounced as suckers) were going to lose it anyway, so the state should be the beneficiary of their addiction. Should we wonder why politicians are held in such disdain?

Fool's Gold

Gold stabilizes countries as a currency of worth.
It is fashioned into jewelry for those who wish to state,
"I am wealthy and that makes me great!"
Look at all this stuff that's draped pierced and worn
That's put on for display with a message that is known.
"Success is acquisition and it takes me where I want!"

In some designer's fashion, lives religious overtones
Declaring allegiance where none is ever found
The worth of faith and action that brings to man a crown.
Mixed and confused are the steps of the proud
Where outside is displayed jewels and coinage-round,
Shouting, "shine and sparkle" but nowhere is it found
Truth within the heart outshining gold's renown.
Rings and things and gold capped teeth says to all with sight
"This is what I advertise!" Like a lying smile.
Trust in gold lasts only for a while, it's a
substance like others, saying,
"Unfaithful will I be and from your hand shall pass
For the-moment all is well with struggles more or less

But absent what's most precious the house is left bereft!"
Honesty.
A whitewashed wall a gold chain's talk a swaggering crucifix
Denounce the deeper meaning of the structure's true intent.
Beneath the holy pretext of signals mixed and bent
Is found a cobweb teeming, with unwanted guests!
Deception and hypocrisy blend as ornaments
And vie against each other in reflection's hollow stance.
Outwardly needing is the picture opulence.
Understanding is not found in facet glint or ray
What is meant to capture, isn't put on display
Not weighed coveted or fathomed
A man's best appearance is not found in gold or diamond.
Unless wisdom is the crown placed upon his head

It is just a picture of what will not last.
There's nothing that comes with us save the spirit's onward quest
For the river ever flowing through the streets of gold so blessed
Be mindful of the signals sent to those we meet
For in the end they find arrival at the Savior's feet.

Exodus 32:2-4 Aaron answered them. Take off your gold earrings that your wives, your sons, and your daughters are wearing, and bring them to me. So all of the people took off their earrings and brought them to Aaron. He took what they handed him and made it into an idol cast in the shape of a calf, fashioning it with a tool. Then he said, "These are your gods, O Israel, who brought you up out of Egypt.

And so, the ancient Hebrew people left Egypt with much gold and wealth. They left with the wealth of Egypt, not only worn as ornamental jewelry but I'm sure they had loaded down the animals to carry all that could be taken. It was kind of like a payday that took over four-hundred-years to finally find compensation for all the hard work and suffering that must naturally accompany those held captive by the evil designs of others. What's almost mind blowing is the fact that these freed people knew who it was that had freed them from such slavery; only God's intervention could make it possible and they knew it was God who had not only saved them from a torturous life but he continually provided for them all the time that they were without a home in the wilderness. God brought forth manna from heaven and water from stone and still, it appears they had not learned a thing about the worshiping of false gods.

In today's world, there are many whose appearance is made of outward displays of wealth, which in and of itself is not necessarily a bad thing. If a person wants to be adorned with the trinkets of the world that is his choice; certainly, a woman with earrings is not something that should shock us, and men have been wearing earrings for a long time as well. This should not make us think, "Say what?" It is not what is taking place on the outside of a person that is troubling to God; he's only interested in what is taking place on the inside of us. Naturally the perfect union will be when we are the same on the inside as on the outside. If there is no pretense on the inside there is nothing to worry about in the-manner, we dress and/or adorn ourselves with rings and things that glitter and shine. So long as the light inside of us shines the brightest, then everything else is seen in the best of ways.

There is a lesson to be understood in the rebellion against God, by the people he had freed from the yoke of oppression, placed upon them by the Egyptians. They have been compensated for their suffering in more than just the gold they had carried away from their former masters. They left Egypt in the knowledge that God had completely ruined the nation and a sense of stability had been instilled within them; they had never- before seen the power of God; they may have heard of God but as far as they were concerned he was a long-ago God of their forefathers and all hope that may have been placed in him had long ago vanished under the oppressions of slavery. I can't imagine the impact of reality as God made his presence known to the rulers of Egypt and to the captive people. In the one there is consternation over the fact that they were made to recognize a power greater than not only themselves but of the gods they worshipped! In the other the impact of God's truth must have been pure uninhibited joy!

What happened to these people in such a short period that made them abandon the God who freed them, and then replace him with an idol made of gold? Moses goes to the mountain to meet with the Lord, to receive God's laws (the way in which the Lord finds acceptable for his people to live) and in the short span of just forty days without Moses they demand of Aaron to basically create for them a god. It appears there is very little hesitation on Aaron's part in this idolatrous request. He readily finds a solution and instructs the people to divest themselves of their gold and in turn he manufacture's the god! Moses is gone and the people party! They entered the depths of depravity in the belief that both God and Moses were no longer around. The people had come very close to annihilation by the God they had forgotten in just the short period of forty days, and without Moses being present to them. If we think about this we may reach the conclusion that this may very well be the reason why, "patience is a virtue." It was the impatience of the people that caused them to seek avoidance from the constant guidance of those God had placed into positions of leadership. They wanted to be free to follow their base desires, but they did not understand that even freedom has limits that must be adhered too. Four hundred years of slavery and now there's a God who is going to tell them how they should live? Forty days was long enough for them to declare Moses to be gone and with him the God who had brought them to this place! They did however find it in their cognitive awareness to want a god to represent for them a license to sin! A golden calf, how innocent? The calf was lifted-up in the eyes of the world because it was made of gold! It had value in the eyes of man and in this those who viewed the god of the Israelites, saw a god who has prospered in a world of weights and measures! This outward presentation was thought to be a reflection, of the people who worshipped such a golden god, and in this it may have been thought to bring in converts to the glitter of gold's allure?

When leadership fails the people, the people fail leadership and they are found seeking another to follow. Moses is conversing with the Lord, and as soon as Aaron is confronted by the mob that wants to party, he finds it in his best interest to give to them what they are demanding; a golden calf to worship. It is not just symbolism that is being worshipped; the people have placed what they value most (gold) into the form of an animal but underlying such symbolism of a god taking the shape of a living creature, there is the invested power inherently present in gold. Gold, then and now offers to man the desires of his heart. As such, wealth is idolized just as much today as it was yesterday. Such a value system is easily shattered by the realization that no amount of gold can restore a heart that has grown cold. There are no wealthy people in the grave; all are reduced to the same fate when anything but God is recognized in this life; when anything is idolized in God's place, the poverty of the one so lost, knows no end to his fall into the depths of unknowing darkness. Perhaps, this is, why, we are urged to place our riches in heaven, where they cannot be ruined by moths or stolen by thieves? Everything in this world that is held in high esteem, because man has placed value upon it will not last. Everything that is unseen has found a home in eternity. Unfortunately for those people who rejected God and placed a golden calf in his place what they found very quickly was the truth that there is no place to spend such idolized gold when caressing the grave. We are told that we cannot serve two masters, we will hate one and love the other. There is only one God and the sooner we understand this the faster we can begin to live free. The permissiveness (imagined freedom) that gold invited is the real idol that was constructed by Aaron for the people, who were demanding freedom from the confines of everything that said, "no" to the desires of the flesh and the desires of everything counter to the precepts of God. Ultimately almost none of these rebellious people went into the promised land. It was only to their descendants that God permitted entrance. The parallels of then and now are strikingly alike, in the manner that mankind has gone off in different directions to find satisfaction in the offering of freedom believed to be present in position power and wealth. For those who have tasted the sweetness of power, to lord over others and the positions that afford head of the line status, and the availability of the things that can only be imagined by the financially poor, for these what we find is a never-ending quest by them to find both freedom and satisfaction in a world that offers nothing that cures the search. The search for freedom is not confined to the physical aspect of life; it is the spiritual that cries out the loudest and it is the spiritual that is constantly denied recognition within a world that only recognizes what can be seen. The line of sight to the offerings of the world is uninhibited when there is no one to correct the vision of those who think they can see!

Inside Calling

Hunger thirst or pain I cannot see
But still there is no doubt concerning these three.
To thirst brings awareness of our need
And hunger sends a warning
With rumblings from within
Pain is most pronounced
When it's sharp and narrow!
The insistence of thirst will cry very loud
When the absence of our need is beyond our reach
It is then that our speech is defined by the scream and moan
The very same sounds made by the spirit alone.
Without thirst being quenched the body will fade
Into the night where no one can see
The truth of this life or the meaning of, "free."
All need has an insistent call
Everything is the same in both body and soul
The spirit cries a whispered want
For God's grace to fill the heart
With that which is forever
And wells that don't run dry
The spirit calls with urgency
For he who is Most High.
Heed the call of all our needs
And listen to their cries
But never listen to the shouts
That promise all with lies!

Isaiah 55:1-2 "Come to me all of you who are thirsty, come to the waters; and you who have no money, come, buy and eat! Come buy wine and milk without money and without cost. Why spend money on what is not bread, and your labor on what does not satisfy? Listen, listen to me, and eat what is good and your soul will delight in the richest of fare."

Depression

The spirit calls out to be found
Confusion denies the joys of life
We tell ourselves, "It's not so bad."
Still we walk in the dark and think so sad.

A negative mind
Will only allow internal sight
Denying reality and the strength of truth.
A voice within is speaking,
"In darkness, there's escaping
Into a private comfort zone
Absent the confusion
That clings to doubt and wrong
Without windows doors or walls
Without dangerous storms or ruin."
But still, the somber veil lays heavy on the heart
It finds a way inside and bit by bit resumes
The agony and pain that was never (really) gone.
No matter where we hide a hurting heart still cries,
"O God! Bring me to an avenue where your light shines
And lift the heavy weightiness from body soul and mind.

1 Samuel 1:15-18 "No, I'm not drunk sir," she answered. "I haven't been drinking! I am desperate, and I have been praying, pouring out my troubles to the Lord. Don't think I am a worthless woman. I have been praying like this because I am so miserable." "Go in peace," Eli said, "and may the God of Israel give you what you have asked him for." "May you always think kindly of me," she replied. Then she went away, ate some food and was no longer sad.

In the scripture above we find a woman depressed and saddened because she has up until this point in her marriage been unable to conceive. Adding to this failure, she is married to a man who has another wife. This other wife has not only given birth but she mocks the inability of wife number two. This, places the woman in a state of sadness that can only be cured by the intervention of God. Her prayers are eventually answered and she gives birth to a son. She dedicates her son (Samuel) to God. Not only does she find the fulfillment of her life through becoming a mother but she has secured the life of her son, who grows to become a prophet of God. Becoming a parent is so much more than just going through the process of conception and giving birth. It is a lifelong dedication to ensuring the betterment of those we love. Certainly, there will come times in life where we feel discouraged and saddened by circumstances brought about by conditions we have no control over. There are also those consequences that are caused by our direct aid; these could have been avoided had we only taken the time to think! In all the negative aspects that bring to us sadness or depression there is always the hope in the knowledge that God can alleviate or remove altogether everything that causes us pain. It is even when we do not receive the hope of our prayers immediately, we are still aware that all things will be made right! This last aspect of not being delivered from the immediate circumstance must be understood apart from the concept of time. Our prayer, and cry for help, to be rescued from the circumstance that has brought to us the pain of sadness has not gone out from us unheard. No, not at all, God has heard and has placed into action the necessary response that will bring to us the joy that was thought to be lost forever. This is the wonderful quality of knowing that God is always with us. Many times, in the lives of the apostles we have read about their sufferings and hardships and through it all in the final analysis it is they who have overcome everything that the world had laid upon their doorstep. It was by God's grace that they were able, to overcome the hardships contained in the life of those whose message of salvation was much more valuable than the suffering they experienced. Their suffering was in some instances worn as a badge of honor! Apart from the hardships experienced by those sent out into the world to proclaim the good news of Christ, what we are faced with are perhaps the same arrows that penetrate and bring hurt to our heart and pain to our soul. Through it all God has never left us. In this there is the hope that can never fail.

It is said that time heals all the troubles and heartaches entering-into our lives. A wound at first will be most pronounced in both pain and its unexpected arrival. Over time the wound will heal, the pain will cease but the scar attached to memory will always be with us. It is only when we are healed by the grace of God's love that we find a completeness in the injury; a total healing of both body and soul. It is only truth that says to us, "No one that we love has been lost forever." There is nothing that God cannot heal or make whole once again. This is such a reassuring statement that is infused with not only truth but with the strength that brings to us the courage to face another day! The example of Christ to face the cold uncaring cross of torment reminds us that even death is no problem for God to overcome! There is nothing beyond the ability of God. We cannot imagine anything that places limit upon the ability of God; just as we cannot envision an end to eternity, so it is we cannot place a stop sign upon the abilities of he who created everything! As the old hymn asks, "How great is our God?" It is a mind exploding question that cannot be placed into any form of understanding. Given this aspect of God's unlimited abilities, is there anything that can keep us from the joy he desires for us? Is there anything that we should allow to bring to us depressing thoughts or make us think there is no possibility of escaping our present condition? Sadness will come to us all, but truth can overcome anything. It is written, ***"I can do all things with Christ who strengthens me."*** *Again,* ***"All things are possible with God."***

O God

It would be nice to put an end to lots of stuff
The lies from crooked tongues
Wars against all life, injustice grief and strife
An end for unknowing the wealth contained in truth
An end to politics that tell us what's correct
We know what's good so what use is there for this?

A man must be competitive to achieve
And one must find the truth of life to believe.
O God, bring an end to time itself that step by stepped the grave
It has seen the sun come up and settle in the west

And now it must be told,
"No longer are you needed, be gone with all the mess."
An end to cover ups spin doctor's velvet scripts
Surely, it's a viper's tongue that caused us all to slip.
Bring an end to hands of false passion and desire
And bring an end to all that says, "This will heal and cure."
So-say the street physicians whose offerings endure
The wind and rain and weather as a plague upon the poor!
Hands inviting capture of children's hearts at play
Demanding attention as the whistling of a train

Speeding toward the end without promise of escape
Marching toward affliction to the place they know not where
As cattle led to slaughter in confusion and despair
Knowing something's wrong in the way they're made to bow
To the drugs of broken promise on the streets of here and now!

Say goodbye to yesterday today and tomorrow
Say goodbye to heartache pain and sorrow
When you come again in splendor strength and truth
Bring an end to all that is and begin again anew!
Amen.

Isaiah 61:13 The Spirit of the sovereign Lord is on me, because the Lord has anointed me to preach good news to the poor. He has sent me to bind up the brokenhearted, to proclaim freedom for the captives and release for the prisoners, to proclaim the year of the Lord's favor and the day of vengeance of our God, to comfort all who mourn, and provide for those who grieve in Zion-to bestow on them a crown of beauty instead of ashes the oil of gladness instead of mourning, and a garment of praise instead of a spirit of despair. *It has happened only once in the entire history of man, and in this we finally taste the fruit of victory over death. With the resurrection to life by our Lord Jesus Christ, the specter of death which had forever hung over the heads of all life, had finally met the truth of its existence. Everything that had surrounded death has also been done away with. What had always been temporary has now been elevated to eternal status. Life eternal, absent the negatives has now been given permanency. With this, what we shall find is still unknown. We do know that our nature is one that continually asks to be challenged, and in this, I do believe God has specific plans for every one of his children. This is an exciting aspect of post limited life that lends itself to much speculation. I do think there will be a time wherein we are praising God in what may seem to be endless deserving praise, but at some measure in time we will be told what we must do to continue God's plan for creation. Who can guess at the reality of such a life to come? While it is intriguing to surmise our life at some point in the eternal future, it is probably God's plan to keep as a surprise the full content of our new lives in Christ. Certainly, the new beginning will be absent, the negatives that plagued mankind from the inception of life have no longer any power over us; they no longer exist. What a thought, no longer must we give a great portion of time to the defense against the natural inclinations of the flesh. We have been set free to do God's work unencumbered by distractions that have only one purpose: to delay, stop or otherwise corrupt in some fashion the intent of holiness.*

Just the thought of evil no longer lurking in the darkness of men's hearts planning to hurt harm sadden and kill the innocence that was initially installed in all children of the world, is enough for us to scream, "Thank you!" to God who loves us. The promise that we hear from the prophet Isaiah, is the very same scriptural quote that Jesus made at the beginning of his ministry. He quotes Isaiah, and then tells the listeners that the scripture is fulfilled in their hearing it spoken by him. What a message of hope and joy along with release from the bondage that is also very much alive and well in today's daily life. We get up in the morning, go to work get paid, pay the bills feed the kids and keep a roof overhead. These tasks alone are more than enough for many a man or woman to deal with, it becomes increasingly more difficult when we believe we must do it all alone. The declaration by Jesus to those listeners and to us is one that frees us through the recognition that there is one who has been sent to alleviate our most difficult tasks. Bind up the brokenhearted, proclaim freedom for those held captive by the world's designs and a host of other difficulties that only God can alleviate. Hope spoken in this manner from one who knows his purpose and objectives is like lightning striking into the heart of despair! It is not just words that are heard but it is the power and truth contained in the one who declares, ***"The Lord has anointed me to preach good news to the poor."***

Was Jesus speaking of the financially poor? Sure, he was, but more to the point he is addressing the spiritual poverty of those whose hearts have been disappointed by the suffering and death that continually invades and steals away the joy attached to loved ones. Ultimately Jesus reveals his true purpose to also include eternal life and no more suffering or broken hearts for everyone who will accept the message that God loves them and is willing to offer himself as a sacrifice for their sins. Those of us today who have heard the message of redemption and have received it into our hearts have found peace in this world that always seems to be attempting to deny to us such peaceful existence. Unfortunately, there is the constant evil that desires to kill the peaceful hearts of those who have replaced hatred with love; only to find hatred attempting to once again deny to us the truth of what will certainly come into fruition, when God declares an end to all injustice and evil! Let all God's children say, "Come, Lord Jesus!" Amen.

Material Thing

"Listen man, in this life you call, 'yours' you lose!
You scramble for pay and pay with your life's work.
The winter of your days are laden with loss and then you die!
'Eat drink and be merry' from sun up 'til down
There is no right or wrong or conscience to be found.
Take your fill today there's nothing in the ground.
There is no afterlife or judgment of the proud
There's not a step beyond there's only here and now!
A moment in the sunshine says, 'all things are allowed'
Don't let the moment pass lest darkness weave a shroud.
Come, take hold my hand 'til mourning sounds ring loud.
Life is just a moment what is done is gone
There's nothing to regret when you go underground."

"Well, Material Thing, it sounds like you have it all together.
But when will you understand your vision
is omitting God's great plan.
Illusion and poor vision is what you offer to man.
Nothing is for keeps except the soul God gave
A man must find the truth of life to be saved.
Yes, the body meets the ground but then the spirit soars
To heights we can't imagine, to meet the risen Lord.
How correct were those long-gone kings lavished in everything?
Pyramid tombs secret rooms with a window to the stars
Dead man's bones misplaced hope most precious truth not met
When their eyes closed, they failed this earthly test.
The weight of gold or silver did not add a breath.
Pay attention, O voice that shouts, 'Collect and get!'
Many have felt your pull and fallen for your lies
But truth declares to everyone, 'Open up your eyes!'
Materialism will not ease a fire's breath
Will not bring an end to desire's nagging call
For, 'more and more and more!'
Hunger seeks not rest until the curtain falls!
Dead man's schemes lavish dreams and calls for, 'more'
Will perish in the dust with the lies you told to us!"

Luke 22:31-32 Simon, Simon! Listen! Satan has received permission to test all of you, to separate the good from the bad, as a farmer separates the wheat from the chaff. But I have prayed for you, Simon that your faith will not fail. And when you turn back to me, you must strengthen your brothers.

In this scripture, what we are finding is similar, to the injection of doubt by the devil as it pertained to the servant of God named Job. Satan was permitted to test the judgment of God as it pertained to the declaration by God that Job was a good and faithful servant. Here again what we are seeing is the devil intruding into the decisions made by Jesus regarding those he had chosen to be his disciples, followers and ultimately his apostles. We recognize that all had passed the testing of the devil except for the one who was destined to betray our Lord. We should look carefully at the specific pull of the world (attraction) that captured Judas and ultimately led him to the grave. Yes, it was the thoughts of money and all that it can purchase that had captured the imagination of him. He is no different than any of us if we should let our imaginations run wild in the field of dreams painted with the illusion of satisfaction and peace. There is no one on this earth who has found peace within himself because of the material wealth the world offers. Only when a man recognizes the reality of God and the promises of afterlife does he find the peace to live abundantly in this life now given. There is a balance of pain and suffering along with periods of the absence of such intrusions into the daily aspects of life. The wealthy may not have to experience hunger and the effects of homelessness but there's sufficient irritants for everyone in this life. Physical illnesses show no favorites to either the wealthy or the poor; as such we find such intrusions upon life discounting the allurement of material things in the very present moment of life. One may be sleeping in a king size bed and covered with expensive comforters only to find the comfort is not to be found due to the angry intrusion of pain that cannot be quelled. I've said it before and now again. "We cannot satisfy a spiritual need with a material thing."

Understand that we are not asked to live a life of poverty, devoid of even the barest of necessities; not at all, but we are told that we cannot serve two masters, because we will love one and hate the other. We cannot love God and the things of the world; we will be devoted to one and in the other only unkind thoughts will be found. It is impossible to serve both God and money! As such we must choose the truth of God and his love for us, or else, we will find God to be an intrusion into the physical desires that continually tell us, "There is no need to feel guilt or self-condemnation because everything in life ends when the body meets the grave!" Let's ask ourselves this question: If there is no such thing as wrong why then do we have a conscience telling us of the wrong some refuse to recognize? I look at the daytime sky and not only do I see the sun but I feel its heat radiating down upon the earth. Clearly as this is not placed into doubt so it is that we recognize the truth in what is acceptable and/or unacceptable behavior throughout all of creation. We find abnormalities in all forms of life but these are apart from the normal expectations because of a defect or illness within such presentations of life. A rabid dog, an insane person and even the demonically possessed are apart from the expectations normally attributed to such unacceptable examples. However, where there is no outside interference directly causing aberrant behavior what is left must be the choice of the individual to indulge in the offerings of the world that will ultimately lead to evil's corrupting influences. There is a great difference between the corruption of the body and the corruption of the soul. All flesh will find corruption in death. In the other (spiritual aspect of life) there can be redemption and eternal life, or judgment to eternal hell or death; mankind is given a choice. It is written: ***"To whichever you choose, stretch forth your hand."***

Unending

I see no difference above or below the ground
Dead is dead if no one's home.
An empty shell finds little worth
Nighttime bows to morning and daytime has its song
Echoes fade as drifting clouds portraits of the mind
The life of man is unfulfilled bleak and oft times wrong
Until his course is altered and he's rescued from life's storms.
A man hears laughter mocking, "Life is brief."
Until he finds himself he cannot be complete.
Until someone he finds understands the way he thinks
Life is just a journey ending in defeat.
Could it be life is more than, "Start and finish?"
Could it be continuous as thought?
More than just a passing breeze in summer's heat and rays?
More than shelter from the cold in winter's falling flakes?
Eternal breath is captured outpacing reach and length
Upon the wind is carried beyond laughter's mocking breath.
Everlasting has not broken lines.
Forever is removed from the concept of space and time.
No need for a rewind to keep the counting strong
Unending ever stretching beyond finite leaps and bounds
Expressed within the Prodigal's acknowledgement of love
Unending finds beginning in God who gave man life.
Air permits breathing connecting inside and without
So too the voice of wisdom, saying, "Unending is God's love."
As in the beginning where death had not a sting
Truth is everlasting and life to man it brings.

John 3:16 For God so loved the world that he gave his one and only Son, that whoever believes in him shall not perish but have everlasting life. *Trying to wrap our hands around eternity is a chase after the wind. Is like trying to put the universe into our rearview mirror. Even if we could imagine outracing existence and reaching the outer edge of all that exists, what then would we see? Having said this what is derived by this mind game? The thing that* *must stand out as reality is the factual recognition of the unending eternal expanse of creation. As such eternity is not just some imaginary concept but is in fact a reality that points to the truth in the promise for man to attain eternal life. It is God who created all, and it is he who declares to us that to believe in the redemption within the sacrifice of his only Son is to find the beginning of eternal life. The clock no longer is counting down to the inevitable death of a man but instead is marching off into the everlasting, wherein all the things that hurt and saddened a man are no longer of any consequence. A reuniting with all of those we have loved and who have loved us is an explosion of joy that is only part of the promise of everlasting life. Such a promise made in the environment of truth contained in creation should immediately bring a person to his senses, exclaiming, "Yes, Lord! I believe you!"*

Blackened Core

It's a part of us at birth and learns with tiny roars.
As a poisoned-rain it wears and tests its claws.
Sinful ways grow freely without a need to hide.
Works of dreadful hurt as if a caustic bath
Burns away the innocence and swiftly grips and bends.
Deceptive hiss from viper's lips intending only harm
Caring peace and love washed away by rising tides
Washed away in turmoil made by ambition greed and pride.
Like the growth of trees wide ranging they become
So too the sinful life of man that beckons him, "Succumb."
Reaching with its branches and digging with its roots
Holding tight upon a man from his head down to his boots.
The snake between the leaves is then revealed to man
No longer pretense needed evil then declares:
"I am the darkest night you chose in place of truth.
The poisoned blackened core of lies pretending good.
You gave away God's light in favor, "hope and change"
And now are left bereft in shackles made of shame.
Don't act surprised or as if you didn't know
You tasted rebel stew and allowed a curtain call.
Now you live in memory of when you had your way
Alas, the days of prominence are gone away to stay.
'Misery loves company' and there's 'always room for more'
In this the blackened core where you first learned to roar."

Job 28:28 And he said to man, "The fear of the Lord-that is wisdom, and to shun evil is understanding."

There are so many things in life that once begun find additional strength in the continuance of the initial action. This is especially true of wrongs. Smoking cigarettes may seem to be not so bad at first, but once it has tightened its grip is very difficult to quit. Ask any drug addicted person if he or she has tried to quit the never-ending quest to satisfy the constant cry to "get-high," and you will certainly find the greatest response of answers to be, "I try but always fail." In the case of the drug addicted there is a complete capturing of the individual on both levels of body and spirit. The sinful life will never lead to freedom or satisfaction; it will only leave a person destroyed in both this life and the life to come. In the beginning sin hides in the dark, decides it is not wanting to be identified as inhabiting a person's life; eventually it can no longer be kept hidden and no longer does it care if it is exposed; the incubation period has been completed and in this the person exposed to the poison of its venom is like an empty shell; dead inside and out. This blackened core begins at our birth; we are born with a nature that is inherited; one that has been handed down from the first of mankind. Although our nature is sinful we are still looked upon as innocent in the eyes of our Lord. Jesus had declared little children possessors of the kingdom of heaven.

Matthew 19:13-15 Then little children were brought to Jesus for him to place his hands on them and pray for them. But the disciples rebuked those who brought them. Jesus said, "Let the little children come to me, and do not hinder them, for the kingdom of heaven belongs to such as these." When he had placed his hands on them he went on from there. *Such innocence is slowly stolen from us by sin, embedded in our nature. As we grow into adulthood our innocence is no longer able to ward off growth within the blackened core of our being. We become in need of a Savior to restore to us the innocence lost. In truth, we had slowly become slaves to our nature and in need of the freedom that can only be restored to us by receipt of a new spirit with ability to say, "no!" to the formerly dictatorial nature of our birth. This is done for us in the sacrifice of Jesus, wherein he willingly gave himself to the suffering and death that we as sinful human beings deserved. Upon receipt of the mercy inherent in the sacrifice of Christ we no longer are faced with the judgment of God. God invites all of us to be washed clean in the blood of Christ, and to once again find acceptance within his kingdom as do, little children. The world is corrupt and it corrupts everyone slowly. There is no age that determines and/or declares, "innocence lost;" it is determined by* *the actual removal from childhood into the greater understanding of adulthood. That is, to say, when we understand the separation existing between right and wrong and the implications attached to doing wrong we find ourselves lost. Yes, the innocence lost had created the condition of the lost that needs to be rescued. All of us fall into this category, because there is no one who is righteous; there is no adult in the entire human race that is absent the need to be saved, salvaged and set-free to once again find admittance into the household of God. We are again able to start over with a new spirit which is a new way of thinking, apart from the corrupting ways and sinful influences of our old and forceful nature. We are no longer a slave to the dictates and impulses of our old way of thinking, and the rebuilding process is ongoing throughout the remainder of our days upon the earth. Our growth, unlike before is not negatively influenced; with the light of truth we are now able to see the pitfalls arrayed throughout the darkness that is pervasive in the world of the lost.*

Lions Of Stone

Fire and water is there at your feet
Life or death is for you to decide
Believe in God's Son or simply deny.
Lions guarding the door are but stone
They stare straight ahead and cannot roar.
They can't hunt the living or rest in the shade
Tear away flesh growl or stalk prey.
They cannot move have no need for rest
Not bothered by heat because they don't sweat.
We have a choice to become alive
Or stay as stone with the appearance of life.

Lions of stone neither flesh nor bone
They have no cares for heaven or hell
No troubles in life to ponder or tell
No choices to make of consequence binding
No God to obey or to heaven find climbing.

Lions of stone are not intended to praise
The God of the living the Savior of man
To be sinful or holy was not meant for them.
They had nothing to lose from the beginning
It was never a question of losing or winning.
We are not stone our purpose is clear
Accept the forgiveness that shower's the soul
Stretch forth your hand and in water you'll find
A life of peace and love that's divine.
In fire destruction, a terrible choice
Like a lion of stone
No heart.
No soul.
No voice.

Matthew 12:13 Then he said to the man, "Stretch out your hand." So, he stretched it out and it was completely restored, just as

sound as the other. *There's a story of a lion in a marble stone. Each day a young boy would walk past the sculptor's shop and each day he would see a bit more of the piece being sculpted by the artist. One day as he was going to school he looked-into the window and saw a magnificently sculpted lion in the artist's showroom. He entered the workshop and told the artist that he had created a wonderfully impressive lion from the marble. The sculptor replied to the child that he did not create the lion, but that the lion was always in the stone, he had only helped to bring it out. It is in this same way that God frees us from the confines of the world's imprisoning tactics and permits us to come out and into the light of truth. We are then looked upon by those who knew us (before being freed from the confining dictates of life), as someone who has been set free. We are looked upon as a magnificent work of art; no one knew the person hidden inside the interior of the external façade except for the one who created with the purpose of one day setting us free.*

Life

Marble clay stone
Flesh blood sinew bone
It matters not
If locked inside a cold uncaring world.
If told to stay inside while the sun is shining bright
It matters not to anyone when we're locked inside.

What would you like to be?
A lion made of stone unable to roam free
Or a man whose life is peace and victory?
Stretch out your hand and in this tiny gesture find
God who will sculpt a new and satisfying life.
Will carve out from sinew blood and bone
A meaningful existence where the truth of life is known.

John 3:3 Jesus answered, "I tell you the truth, unless a man is born again, he cannot see the kingdom of God."

Faith Anchors

Placed into our lives, stable as truth
The presence of God is a wind at our back
A sail filled with hope and courage to match
Such are the anchors placed deep in our hearts
Preventing drift in days filled with fog.
We know truth and the presence of God
We know he is with us when life appears hard
We know he is here in sunshine or rain
It's then he is smiling giving us strength
To walk upon water or swim in the deep
To soar with the eagle or march along sand
Always he's there with his open hand
Lifting us up when hurt pulls us down
Planting the seed of knowing in man.
Faith anchors are given
Mile markers presenting the truth that is Christ
Onto a pedestal reminding and lighting our way
At the start of new life and the end of our days.
A man's attention is sometimes distracted
By hard times and the unexpected
It's then the anchors keep him held-fast
Against the wind and the rain and deceptions of man.

Hebrews 6:19-20 We have this hope as an anchor for our lives. It is safe and sure and goes through the heavenly temple into the heavenly sanctuary. On our behalf Jesus has gone in there before us and has become a high priest forever, in the priestly order of Melchizedek.

The term "faith anchors" represents those times in our lives that we were sure of the presence of God. It is at these times that the faith of an individual is made stronger and given the ability to resist, the constant attempts of both external deception and the internal doubts that can and do occur when we are drawn away from the light of truth, due to the withdrawing that takes place when we sin. The following represents the times in my life when there was no mistaking that the presence of God was made known to me.

God-The Tree-Mother And Me

It was during the summer of nineteen-hundred and fifty-four at the age of seven, that I received the first of many faith anchors. This one summer's day was very hot and humid outside; and my mother determined that it was better for me to remain indoors. I protested, but to no avail. As I stood in the kitchen of our third-floor apartment in the borough of Brooklyn, I watched as mom washed our clothing in the washing machine that was perhaps equipped with the latest of modern attachments, including the dual rollers that were used to squeeze the water from the clothing once the machine finished the agitation cycle. We didn't have all the soap products that are present in today's market; mostly it was a large bar of brown soap that was tossed into the open tub as the clothes were tossed around by the agitating motion of the machine.

After watching the wash proceedings for a while I once again advanced the desire to go downstairs and at least sit on the high stoop that all the neighborhood brownstone buildings have incorporated in their structure and design. Once again, I was told it was too hot outside and that I should look out of the window and ask God to play a game with me. The view from the top floor window was one of a large fig tree growing in the back yard of the house, and in this I thought of a game that we could play. I told God that I would pick a leaf on the magnificently leafy tree and it would be his challenge to find the one leaf that I had picked. "Okay, God, I picked it, now you try to find it." After several minutes, I complained to mom that God did not want to play with me, but she insisted that I continue the game and to forget about going outside. At last, I announced to God that he had one last chance to find the leaf or else he would lose the game. I stared at the leaf for what seemed to be a long time but just as I was going to complain again to mom, I watched as the leaf of my choice was plucked away from the branch and both fear and awe filled me as I watched the leaf slowly fall to the ground from the very top of the tree! It was at this-time, I looked away from the tree and focused upon the Williamsburg Savings Bank that constantly let just about everyone in Brooklyn know the time of day, by its great clocks that faced all directions. As I looked at the clock, I said in a loud voice, "No! God, not me!" I did not fully know the meaning of this thought but I knew that if the leaf could be made to fall so too the bank could also. And I did not want to play this game any longer!

I'm looking back on this event and realize all the work it took just to wash clothes. There wasn't a clothes dryer and, as-long as the sun was shining and the outside temperature was above freezing the clothes could be hung out to dry upon the clothesline. When it was raining or other weather condition precluded hang drying mom would hang the clothes on the hallway bannister and the steel ladder leading up to the roof. Life today seems so much easier because of the advances in modern conveniences. And let me not forget the washboard that was utilized to wash small items of clothing, like socks, that did not warrant a complete setup for a full load of clothing. Some of today's mothers find doing the laundry not all that is offered within technology. Some have had to cart the laundry to the laundromat, wash dry and fold the clothes and get home before the kids return from school! Serious planning!

GOD, THE TREE, MOTHER AND ME

Activating faith in a child is wonderful to see.
The summer of fifty-four had a day I'll not forget
It was so very hot breathing caused a sweat.
Mother said:
"You can't go outside today.
Look out the window at the fig tree on display
And if you ask him God will come to play."
Thus, the game was devised.
I'll pick the leaf that God must find.
After a few minutes, I cried
"Mom, God does not want to play with me!"
Her answer was the same.
"In the house, you must stay."
Declaring at last, "God, you have one last chance!"
It was at the age of seven I first met the God of heaven
He picked the leaf right off the branch with his very last chance.

Matthew 19:14 "Let the children come to me, and do not hinder them, for the kingdom of heaven belongs to such as these.

Proverbs 1:8 Listen my son, to your father's instruction and do not forsake your mother's teaching.

Lord Please Send A Taxi

It was during a day that I had planned to have the afternoon devoted to peace quiet and prayer. Rosalie and her sister Marie (a devout Christian) had made plans to take the children to the movies. Everything was going according-to-plan when suddenly the sky opened-up with a tremendous downpour. Rosalie had called every car service in the neighborhood, and was told there would be a long wait before a car could be made available. Ordinarily this would not be a problem but the movie was scheduled to start in about a half hour and this meant that a good portion of the show would be missed if they waited for the car to arrive. Walking to the movie house was out of the question due to the heavy rain and so my wife called off the plans for the afternoon to the disappointment of the kids and me. As they were undressing the kids I stopped them and said, "I'll get a car for you, just wait a minute while I ask God for a taxi."

Of course, my sister-in-law laughed and my wife looked at me with that knowing glance that said "Okay, we will wait." I should add (at-this time, in our lives) none of us had a car or even a driver's license, probably, because the public transportation system in the city was good and reliable. Owning a car was made to be very difficult due to the constant hunt for parking space, and the parking regulations that forced the movement of the vehicles on the street, (in order) to make way for the street sweeping vehicles, that caused everyone to move the cars to the other side of the street. It wasn't until some fifteen years later, after leaving the confines of New York City and moving to Pennsylvania, did I, at the age of fifty finally recognize a need to both drive and own a car.

Now, having asked for them to wait a minute I ran to the back of the house and fell upon my knees and asked God to please send a car service. Arising from the prayer position and walking back into the front of the house I began to move everyone to the front door. Just then there was a car horn sounding right outside of the house. I told them it was their car service and out they ran and got into the car, and off they went to the much-anticipated theater. I thanked God and went straight into my afternoon of prayer.

When everyone returned from the movie house I was told the rest of the story. I asked my wife if they enjoyed the movie and was told that they did. Rosalie continued by saying she had asked the driver of the car how it was he had come to know we were looking for a car? The driver said, he had just dropped off a fare from Manhattan and he was not familiar with the neighborhood; and so, he stopped in front of our house to bring his paper work up to date and too try and get his route planned for his return to Manhattan. He had accidently sounded the horn of the car when he laid his clipboard on the steering wheel and the rest was history.

As I look back on this answered prayer the thought of God being so much in-tune with the everyday happenings of our lives is a tremendous awe-inspiring awareness! ***Psalm 118:7 The Lord is with me; he is my helper.***

Plans

"Forget it! It's starting to rain.
The weather outside is hitting the roof
Like a snowstorm in winter
With ice and hard times
Needing boots and a shovel
Digging quickly in time.
Car service has a long waiting list
It's looks to me like the show will be missed!"

"God, please send a taxi
For peace in this place
The kids are excited
Car service has failed
The wife is unhappy
Her sister's in doubt
I'm looking to you
To make a way forward
Despite the rain and the
Down pointing frowns
At this place in time
Bring a ride and the smiles!
Amen."

Matthew 21:21-22 Jesus replied, "I tell you the truth if you have faith and do not doubt, not only can you do what was done to the fig tree, but also you can say to this mountain, 'Go, throw yourself into the sea,' and it will be done. If you believe, you will receive whatever you ask for in prayer."

Psalm 145:17-20 The Lord is righteous in all his ways and loving toward all he has made. The Lord is near to all who call on him, to all who call on him in truth. He fulfills the desires of those who fear him; he hears their cry and saves them. The Lord watches over all who love him, but all the wicked he will destroy.

Desire

There is perhaps in every aspect of life two sides needing to be explored; the good and the bad is most pronounced when examining our desires. Sometimes we are led into a situation that on the surface does not reveal the end-product. Where the initial or preliminary desire is originated in the good, remaining focused will bring about a most unexpected joyful outcome. The same is true when the negative desire of bad, initiates and motivates, an unimaginable outcome of ill feelings will be made manifest.

The stronger the desire the greater the reward or the consequence. Just as the laws of man do not pronounce a life sentence in solitary confinement for all infractions of the laws, so it is also true for the wrongs expressed in our negative desires. With respect to our righteous desire to show our love for others and for God there is the positive outcomes that are derived from the initial presentation of love. This positive outcome whether in the physical (as in doing something nice for someone), or the spiritual presentation of love for God within our times of prayer, will almost always produce the most joyous of outcomes.

One of these most cherished moments within a prayerful setting occurred when my desire to express my love for God took place in the early years of my new life in Christ. I found myself at the foot of the cross and was moved to great sorrow by the sights and sounds of those also present. The mockers and disbelievers had already left the tiny hill of crucifixion and those remaining were filled with both sorrow and a kind of hope-filled anticipation brought about by the unspoken knowledge that the death of Christ had not meant the end of his life. A heaviness pressed upon my entire body as I lay prostrate at the foot of the cross. I was unwilling to raise my head and look upon our Lord, for the sight of him hanging there, I'm sure, would have been too much for me to bear.

I was removed from the deep and all too real presentation of the crucifixion by the sounds of my family returning home from a school function. The experience of these precious moments, made manifest by the desire to know and to feel, the anguish of those present at the time of our Lord's crucifixion, have remained with me as a sure foundation; a sure faith anchor.

Philippians 1:7 It is right for me to feel this way about all of you, since I have you in my heart; for whether I am in chains or defending or confirming the gospel, all of you share in God's grace with me.

Confirming Truth

There are times when we are given confirmation regarding the working of the Holy Spirit in our lives. One such occasion took place some thirty years ago, when I was deeply involved in all lay ministries in the Catholic church, and was also, a member of the prayer and bible study group that met every Thursday night in the basement of the church. At some time during the week just prior to the prayer group's meeting I was led to write down some suggestions for the group, that were aimed at enhancing the meeting's overall purpose; the praise and worship of God and the sorting out of scripture references that were quoted while we were in prayer.

The normal activity during the group meeting was for individuals to quote a scripture verse as they are led to do so by the Spirit, and, at-the-conclusion of the meeting the moderator of the group who was also the pastor of the church would tie together the night's events. On this one particular-night I had come to the group with several pages of hand written notes that were planned to be given to the pastor as suggestions. My surprise came at the end of the meeting when the pastor began his presentation by reading from a packet of notes that he had written. His notes were almost a verbatim recital, a literally letter-perfect reading, to the ones I had written down prior to the meeting. As he continued to read I could not keep my seat and began waving my notes because I knew that they were the very same things that he was now saying! When he had concluded his time at the lectern I found that there was only one paragraph left in my notes that he had not mentioned. I was asked to now speak concerning my clearly excited demeanor and as I stood in front of the lectern I handed my notes to the pastor, who began to smile in recognition of what had taken place. I just looked out at the group and said there was nothing more to add to the comments of the pastor, except to say that sometimes what we are led to do finds tremendous confirmation, and it is then that we understand, God is making his presence known to those who look to him.

WINDOWS OF LIGHT

A stone tossed into the sky seizes the moment to fly
It brings back to earth a far greater worth
for its vision was that of a tree.
If it returns to a lake upon the water it
makes a statement suggestive of he
Who, gave to the stone the vision of trees.
We too get windows of light, sometimes from wondrous heights
And the things that we see cause ripples of glee
In hearts where lived only night.

2 Samuel 22:20 You are my lamp O Lord; the Lord turns my darkness into light.

John 21:5-6 He called out to them, "Friends haven't you any fish?" "No," they answered. He said, "Throw out your net on the right side of the boat and you will find some."

The Great Fishing Expedition

Brooklyn New York 1980.

Some neighborhoods have sparse plantings of trees along the sidewalks while others are unaware of the shade trees produce. Some trees were planted in backyards by our grandparents, who brought with them the seeds of immigration. My wife's grandparents had a fig tree in their backyard and when fruit ripened it fell to the concrete patio like heavy purple raindrops. The Italian immigrant could not take with him the little fishing boats that dotted the shoreline of their fishing villages. The language of my parents and grandparents has been lost through the process of assimilation, but some things will always remain. The memories of our lives and the impact others have contributed remain as anchors deeply embedded.

One summer day, I heard my wife say, "Take him fishing." Peter stood by anticipating a positive response from dear old dad. This was a Saturday in Brooklyn, not a fishing village in southern Italy. "Where in the world do you think, I can take him fishing," was my response. "Even if we find some fish, they probably already had breakfast! And we don't have any fishing gear. What are we supposed to do, jump in and grab the fish?" By this time, Peter (a very smart young boy) began to reflect in his countenance the possibility of other activities being suggested. That is, abandon all hope of going fishing and hang out with the neighborhood kids.

Suddenly, like Moses announcing the commandments of God, came the words, "Take him fishing!" There are times in our lives that we understand the real meaning of "Obedience," and this was one of those times. Obedience is often accompanied by a measure of fear, and it was evident to Peter that the fishing expedition had just begun.

We left the air-conditioned bus upon arrival at Sheepshead Bay, famous for sea food and fishing boats, as well as the piers that offered land based fisherman the opportunity to fish. As we walked along the piers we spied the bait and tackle shop, and purchased a dropline and some worms for bait. There were vendors stationed along the street and we asked one lady where the fish appear to be biting. Her answer was, "Everyone seems to think the end pier is the place to fish." In fact, there was a large crowd of fisherman on the pier and they were equipped with the latest of rods and reels; clearly, we were outgunned in this game of fishing.

We found a spot on the pier away from the crowd and began our quest. It was low-tide and the dropline barely made it into the water. We could see the hook and worm just below the water. I said to Peter, "This can't be too difficult son, let's get some fish! After staring, with anticipation at the float, for about an hour, Peter said to me, "Dad we aren't any good at this, let's go and get lunch." I answered by saying, "Son, you are right we are not good fishermen, but we know someone who is. Let's pray for a fish and maybe Jesus will give us one." Just after raising our heads from the short prayer, a man came up to us and said, "When you catch some fish you are going to need a place to put them." After he said this he pointed to the ladder leading down to the platform, used to get onboard and exit the boats as they are tied up to the pier, during low-tide. On the platform below there was a five-gallon pail complete with handle, and I went down to retrieve it. When I came back up from the staircase ladder the man was gone. I hadn't thought about this aspect of God's intervention into our fishing trip until some-time later. It is curious to think that the boats had probably left the pier for their day long trip to the fishing grounds, early in the morning hours while it was still nighttime, and while it was high tide! Surely, the pail could not have been there during high tide, it would have floated away or sunk; but there it was waiting for us to complete our needs. The man had disappeared as quickly as he had appeared.

Immediately after coming up from the platform the line in the water got taut and we could see a baby bluefish on the line. We watched as the snapper struggled against our formidable fishing gear and we hauled it in; we quickly baited the hook and sent the float back into the water. Pow! Another strike! We began to catch fish just as quickly as we could get the hook into the water. I realized that we didn't need to bait the hook, it appeared as if the fish were lining-up waiting for their turn to fulfill the prayer we made.

Fishing next to us were two teenage boys, and one asked me, "Mister, what are you using for bait?" I replied, "faith," and the other boy said, "O I don't believe that!" I replied, "Okay, no fish for you." But, the other boy said, "I believe it!" My response to him was, "Do you want a fish?" He said, "Yes," and I then told him to cast his line upon the water! I felt as confident as Jesus telling the apostles to cast out their net. The confidence came from the knowledge that Jesus was there with us. The young man had begun to catch fish as quickly as us. No one else was catching anything, and I began to wonder just when it would end? After all, we had only asked for one fish but now we were filling the bucket! At that moment, I had my answer, the fishing boat had appeared and was returning to the pier for the end of its expedition as well.

Peter and I returned home as conquering hero's fulfilling the hopes of awaiting dependents. We were marvelous to behold as we carried our catch into the Brooklyn village. Of course, my wife responded to our great catch by saying, "Get those fish out of here!" We laughed, and began to distribute the fish to our neighbors. We regaled, entertained and amused them, and they received the fish as if they were among the multitude fed by Jesus, so long ago. Decades later, I still have the dropline, complete with plastic float and miracle hook. Yes, the memories of our lives and the impact others have contributed remain as anchors deeply embedded.

RARE FIND

Diamonds pearls emeralds and jade
Can produce joyous sounds rippling with praise.
There's beauty and brilliance in nature's parade.
The rare find plays music sublime inside the seeker's domain.
He who listens to a child hears the voice of the heart.

Rainfalls passing lightning flashing,
clouds hang knowing their reign
Unknowing is man when his day began, he
and son would be seeking a fish.
Not only a fish was given but a faith anchor was delivered.
It permits remembrance of the day
Jesus and me and little Pete went to the Bay to fish.

Unknowing is man a rare find at his feet
Relenting to please the request of a child.
His wonderment has never ceased.
Prayer was added into the mix
Of baited hook plastic float and bucket of hope.
At once lined-up as if volunteers
Coming toward us in wave after wave
In awe at the thought of our Lord
Taking the time to fish with the hearts of those
Asking in prayer, saying,
"Lord, we're no good at this."

Genesis 1:26 Then God said, "Let us make man in our image, in our likeness, and let them rule over the fish of the sea and the birds of the air, over the livestock, over all the earth, and over all the creatures that move along the ground."

Mark 11:22 Have faith in God Jesus answered.

Lord We Are Going To Need More Than A Shovel

"Pete, we are going to need more than a shovel to dig our way out of this mess." "I see what you mean Gary, the car is buried, and not only that, it looks to be encased in ice. But you did offer me a ride home in the morning; the least I can do now, is to get a couple of shovels and ice choppers from the boiler room so we can start the dig." Three hours later and with the aid of a pot of coffee we finally, made-contact with the car. Still, having a ride home was much better than having to trudge through the still very high levels of snowdrifts, not to mention the always reliable rapid transit system had stopped working sometime during the night.

Well it is said, "God provides," and it looks like he has another chance to keep his streak alive! Finally, we were able, to get the car unlocked (the lock was frozen solid). Looking back on this episode in the life of "a day in the life of Brooklyn Alaskans" I'm glad this did not take place in my later years! There is much advantage to being young.

Once inside the car we begin to thaw, even though it is probably colder in the car than outside, no doubt a psychological milestone. Anticipation of the car being warm, in- just moments away, made the howling of the outside temperature (single digits) seem to be made lesser when all our work appears to be coming to fruition. "Okay," says Gary as he brings the car keys out from his pocket, "here we go!"

Well, you guessed it, as he turned the ignition key nothing happened. Not being a car mechanic, I could only guess that the battery was dead. After several tries at starting the car Gary finally said, "It's dead." It was then that I said we should pray and let God start the car. Gary laughed. After a minute, we simply asked God to start the car. I had convinced Gary that we had nothing to lose by praying and asking for God's intervention. After the short prayer, Gary placed the key into the ignition once again and with what sounded to be the roar of a lion the car started! It appears the singer Carrie Underwood knew what she was singing about when she sings, "Jesus take the wheel."

The next time I met my friend he would tell me he needed to buy a new battery for the car; it was completely dead. Seems to me there was a resurrection that took place with respect to the car's battery on that snow-filled day.

I'm reminded of the beatitudes, wherein Jesus spoke these words:

Matthew 5:3 "Blessed are the poor in spirit for theirs is the kingdom of heaven." *Another way of understanding this statement by our Lord can be expressed in this fashion: Blessed are you who know your need for God, the kingdom of heaven belongs to you. A simple prayer and a dark and dreary snow-filled night became for us a moment in time that can never be erased, by the mind's attempts to inject coincidence and luck into the intervention of God into our lives. The alternative to God's intervention was to remain in the predicament (until such time) as a tow truck/or mechanic with a new battery could be found; and most importantly, persuaded to make the necessary repair which would restore the vehicle to a reliable state of being. Having understanding, of the kingdom of heaven available for us in the here and now, and awaiting fulfillment in the hereafter is a paradoxical and somewhat difficult to understand situation. Having the kingdom available to us is a great advantage over the limitations presented to mankind. Still, where it is advantageous for us to call upon God who is always able to get the job done; we must also do so (call upon God) for the benefit of others who do not know of his desire to intervene in our behalf.*

DEEP TROUBLE

A mountain of snow ice and cold
Was left on the streets like a pile of old bones
Waiting for sun plows and shovels
To melt move and level
This very deep trouble.

The buses and trains did not move above ground
Sidewalks were filled with cries saying, "Shovel me now!"
Off limits to the people and plows, now.
Faith was the mover of snow and of car
The battery had died and the engine was cold
Only the young and the desperate were bold
To confront with the wind and the free-falling flakes
But even the heart that was fixed on the Lord
Had doubted, we could reap a reward.
The car started, was driven away
From the street filled with frozen display
Showing that faith can do all that's desired
No matter the troubles of wind frost or nature's advance
There's never a moment that says, "This
is too deep, for even a prayer."

Psalm 34:6 The poor man called and the Lord heard him; he saved him out of all his troubles.

Solo Flight

Because so much of our gained truth is life experience, a level of truth, belief, and trust in God, as well as in the promise of eternal life beginning when the body dies, may be directly confirmed proportionately to such life experience, by individuals whose experiential truth adds to the existing foundational faith, given by God at-the-moment of rebirth. Death or near-death experiences can also be a solidifying confirmation, not only directly but indirectly for those who have had similar experiences within the context of afterlife or near-death moments.

As such, in effort to support both biblical and modern-day witness presenting to us the existence of afterlife reality I'll relate a truthful experience. Just as the apostle Paul relates to us his being taken to the third heaven, unknowing, if he was in or out of the body. I also do not know if I was in or out of the body (only God knows). I found myself traveling among the stars and heavenly bodies, moving at what can only be described as incredible speed; the speed of thought.

Along the route there appeared large mathematical equations, that were instantly understood as easily as one would recognize the meaning in a traffic signal. While in route I was turned around. When I awakened, in my home and in my bed, and in the normalcy of corporeal life the disappointment felt was staggering, because of the quickly dissipating knowledge of the night's experience; dumb again. Again, I don't know if this was an experience prompted by the arrival of death or something that God wanted ingrained into my consciousness, but the reality of the event was most convincing. The accounts of afterlife experience enjoy numerous personal testimony. Just as numerous are those that relate a void of nothingness by those who have been pronounced dead by medical professionals, and others, have had horror stories that caused a complete turnaround within the manner in-which they had lived life. For the one whose experience is firsthand the foundation of existing faith finds exceptional renewal, and for the one hearing of another's experience, similar-to their own personal experience something positive is also added to faith. As for the one who had nothing to report, this also tells us something relative to the condition of the soul being saved or not.

SAND VISION

Each day the grain of sand by nature's wear diminished
Less and less until nothing, save the breath of the man.
Heavenly lights instantly discerned in spirit flight
Beginning of perceptions always present in the breath.
"Home" the insistent calling, direction known.
Across the universe the light of understanding flies
To impart direction in the breath of a newborn's cry.

Genesis 2:7 And the Lord God formed man from the dust of the ground and breathed into his nostrils the breath of life, and man became a living being.

About the author

I was born in Brooklyn New York, in 1946, and at the age of thirty-three was born again by the grace of God. I would like to clarify in the simplest way I can the definition of being born again. Many people who hear of this term immediately think it means one is attached to a religious brand of Christianity; as in, "He's a born again Christian." Nothing could be further from the truth. The receipt of a "new spirit" is a new way of thinking, because truth has been presented into the life of those so blessed. Prior to such receipt, life as God intended was hidden within the reality of being captured by the many traps and temptations of life. Value was given to endeavors that had no place upon the mantle of righteousness. Pursuit of worldly activities, no matter how harmful and depressing the aftereffects, were looked upon as just a temporary condition that rectified itself when next we attempted to break the bank at a casino, or when we went off into the pursuit of any number of harmful activities. The born-again experience lets us see the reality of both our present condition and the truth as it pertains to God. This presentation of truth is liberating!

I am also blessed to be husband, father and grandfather. Just recently we celebrated our marriage of forty-eight years. At the age of seventeen I enlisted in the US Navy (with parental permission), and served aboard the USS Cambria APA 36. This section of the Navy is called the "Gator Navy" better known as Amphibious Forces; it is also referred to as the "screwed gator" because many ships of the Amphibious forces during World War Two never made it back home. Although wanting to become a Navy Electrician ("E" division) I was "temporarily" placed into "B" division, (boiler room operations, aka, the fireroom). After this temporary assignment of three years, eight months and eighteen days I was separated from active duty, and at the completion of the six-year obligation, received an honorable discharge. It is from this initial exposure to marine power-plant operation that I ultimately became an operating (Stationary) engineer and am now retired from the City of New York.

Contained within this book are three poems dedicated to the events of September 11, 2001. At the time of the attack, I served as a civilian member of the NYPD, and had a firsthand view of the dedication of those sworn to protect and serve under this, a most trying time. It was my honor to serve (in a small way) with all who were called upon to protect from further harm, heal those who suffered from the attack, and unite under the common bond of love.

Having also worked within the New York City Health and Hospitals Corporation, and private hospital concerns, such exposure found deeper understanding of those who have dedicated their lives toward the betterment of others. It is now during retirement that I have found the best possible employment; being a grandfather! Thank God for his mercy in allowing me to reach this great height in life, and permitting me to recognize the responsibility that accompanies the title. Such responsibility is to spoil and otherwise cater to every request possible, from those who call me dad and grandpa.

PGIL2021USA